D0214596

CHILDREN'S KNOWLEDGE, BELIEFS AND FEELINGS ABOUT NATIONS AND NATIONAL GROUPS

Children's Knowledge, Beliefs and Feelings about Nations and National Groups

Martyn Barrett
in collaboration with Luciano Arcuri, Mark Bennett, Anna Emilia Berti, Anna Silvia Bombi, Luigi Castelli, Annamaria de Rosa, Arantza del Valle, Rauf Garagozov, Almudena Giménez de la Peña, Thea Kacharava, Giorgi Kipiani, Evanthia Lyons, Valentyna Pavlenko, Santiago Perera, Luixa Reizábal, Tatiana Riazanova, Fabio Sani, Jose Valencia and Ignasi Vila.

Psychology Press
Taylor & Francis Group
HOVE AND NEW YORK

First published 2007 by Psychology Press,
27 Church Road, Hove, East Sussex, BN3 2FA

Simultaneously published in the USA and Canada
by Psychology Press
270 Madison Avenue, New York, NY 10016

Psychology Press is an imprint of the Taylor & Francis Group, an informa business

Copyright © 2007 Psychology Press

Typeset in Times by RefineCatch Limited, Bungay, Suffolk
Printed and bound in Great Britain by
TJ International Ltd, Padstow, Cornwall
Cover design by Lisa Dynan

All rights reserved. No part of this book may be reprinted or reproduced or
utilized in any form or by any electronic, mechanical, or other means, now
known or hereafter invented, including photocopying and recording, or in
any information storage or retrieval system, without permission in writing
from the publishers.

The publishers makes no representation, express or implied, with regard to
the accuracy of the information contained in this book and cannot accept any
legal responsibility or liability for any errors or omission that may be made.

Every effort has been made to trace the copyright holders and obtain permission
to reproduce extracts from other sources.

This publication has been produced with paper manufactured to strict
environmental standards and with pulp derived from sustainable forests.

British Library Cataloguing in Publication Data
A catalogue record for this book is available from the British Library

Library of Congress Cataloging-in-Publication Data
Barrett, Martyn, D.
    Children's knowledge, beliefs, and feelings about nations and national groups /
Martyn Barrett.
        p. cm.
    Includes bibliographical references and indexes.
    ISBN 1-84169-301-4
1. Social perception in children.   2. Geographical perception in children.   I. Title.
BF723.S6B37   2006
304.2083—dc22   2006012142

ISBN13: 978-1-84169-301-9
ISBN10: 1-84169-301-4

For Adam and Alex,
two happy citizens of a globalized, postmodern world

Contents

Tables

Figures

About the author

Martyn Barrett studied at the Universities of Cambridge and Sussex, and is Professor of Psychology at the University of Surrey. He has worked extensively on the development of language in children and on the development of children's drawings. More recently he has been working on processes of national and ethnic enculturation in childhood and adolescence, the development of prejudice and stereotyping in children and adolescents, and acculturation processes in ethnic minority individuals. He is a Fellow of the British Psychological Society, Editor of the British Journal of Developmental Psychology, Academic Director of the Centre for Research on Nationalism, Ethnicity and Multiculturalism at the University of Surrey, and an Academician of the Learned Societies for the Social Sciences.

Preface

This book represents the culmination of a line of research that I first began over 15 years ago. In the late 1980s I was working on a number of other issues, primarily concerning children's language development. In the summer of 1989 I had a conversation with my two sons, Alex and Adam, who at that time were aged 5 and 8 years old. We were travelling to Italy for our family holiday, and to help pass the time on the journey, I asked them what they thought Italian people were like. Their responses were intriguing. The things they said to me suggested that they were generalizing to an entire national group on the basis of certain "prototypical exemplars" (who shall remain nameless here, as they are friends and fellow psychologists). We had a lengthy conversation about not only Italians but also Americans, Spanish people, etc. My curiosity was aroused. Consequently, when I returned from holiday, I ran a literature search. I found that developmental psychologists had not studied the development of children's conceptions of the people who live in other countries since the early 1970s. I did discover, however, that geographers were busy examining the development of children's understanding of the physical and social geographies of other countries, while political scientists were conducting some fascinating research which (in part) was exploring children's sense of pride in their own country. Stimulated by what I had read, I decided to start running some small-scale studies of my own in this area. I had some wonderful undergraduate students who helped me collect the data for these early studies, and I tentatively began to address some of the research questions that my sons' comments about Italian people had initially raised in my mind. From these small beginnings, a much larger programme of research slowly grew. By the mid-1990s, I realized that my years of working in the field of child language had passed, and that my research interests had radically shifted and lay in this new area instead.

There are many people who have contributed to this programme of research over the years, and I would like to acknowledge some of them here. Among all the colleagues I have worked with in this field, the most important has been Evanthia Lyons, who introduced me to many of the delights and perils of social-psychological theorizing. My debt to Evanthia is enormous, and I would like to express my very sincere thanks to her here. I also want to thank Xenia Chryssochoou, another wonderful instructor in social psychology. In addition, Eithne Buchanan-Barrow requires special mention. I have now been working with Eithne for many years, both in this field and in several others along the way—thank you for all your wonderful support and contributions over the years. Among the many undergraduate and postgraduate students who have worked with me in this area of research, I particularly want to thank Emma Alexander, Kelly Davey, Joanna Day, Alexandra Dixon, Nisha Karia, Stefanie Maehr, Athina Manouka, Jenny Maslin, Emily Morris, Andia Papadopoulou, Rachel Penny, Mona Sahlabadi, Hannah Trimby and Hannah Wilson. But an extra special thank you must go to Teresa Farroni, Louise Forrest, Janis Short, Kiren Vadher and Stephen Whennell, for your intellectual contributions and for significantly broadening my own thinking in this field.

The research reported in this book has been supported by three grants. The first of these was awarded by the Economic and Social Research Council to Evanthia Lyons and myself for a project entitled "English Children's Representations of European Geography" (Grant No. R000235753). Alison Bourchier and Caroline Purkhardt worked as the researchers on this project, and they were aided in the data collection by Mick Finlay, Julie Barnett and Barbel Pee. A big thank you to all of you.

The second grant was more substantial. This grant funded what has come to be called the CHOONGE project. The grant was awarded by the Commission of the European Communities (DGXII) to the Universities of Surrey, Dundee, Girona, Málaga, Padova and Roma "La Sapienza" for a project entitled "Children's Beliefs and Feelings about their Own and Other National Groups in Europe" (Human Capital and Mobility [Networks] Programme, Grant No. CHRX-CT94–0687). I coordinated the project with fantastic support and collaboration from all the individual team leaders on the project, Evanthia Lyons, Mark Bennett, Ignasi Vila, Almudena Giménez de la Peña, Luciano Arcuri and Annamaria de Rosa. Other key people who contributed to the conceptualization, design and execution of this project were Fabio Sani, Santiago Perera, Arantza del Valle, Anna Emilia Berti and Anna Silvia Bombi. Fabio Sani was employed at the University of Surrey as the coordinating research fellow for the project, and he had the monumental task of ensuring that the cross-national data were coded in a common format. For your Herculean labours, Fabio, an enormous thank you—I don't know what we would have done without you. In addition, all of the following individuals contributed to the empirical work for this project, and we are deeply grateful to them all: Luigi Castelli, Mara Cadinu, Sergio Olivares, Margarita Limon, Miguel Torregrosa, Pilar Monreal, Maria Victoria Trianes, Hannah Wilson, Katie Neale, Nicholas Messing, Sophie Whitehouse, Sian French, Sarah Scott, Dawn Taylor, Pilar Monreal, Monica Sanz, Monica Thomas, Elva Suárez, Lorena Belmonte, Eva Garcia-Claros, Santiago Rovira, Magdalena Morales, Maria Paz Dominguez, Monica Bedin, Antonella Cora, Lucia Rigante, Elena Pirro, Fiammetta Cambio, Riccardo Malafronte and Gabriele Alfano.

The third grant was awarded by INTAS (the International Association for the Promotion of Cooperation with Scientists from the New Independent States of the Former Soviet Union) to the Universities of Surrey, Dundee, Girona, Basque Country and Málaga, and to the Institute of Psychology of the Russian Academy of Sciences in Moscow, Kharkiv State University, the Institute of Psychology in Tbilisi, and the Azerbaijan Pedagogical Institute for Russian Language and Linguistics in Baku. This grant supported the NERID project, the full title of which was "The Development of National, Ethnolinguistic and Religious Identity in Children and Adolescents Living in the New Independent States of the Former Soviet Union" (Grant No. Open 1997, Project 1363). Once again, I was the project coordinator, and I was supported in this role by yet another superb group of team leaders, Mark Bennett, Ignasi Vila, Jose Valencia, Almudena Giménez de la Peña, Tatiana Riazanova, Valentyna Pavlenko, Giorgi Kipiani and Rauf Garagozov. Other key people who made significant contributions to this project were Evanthia Lyons, Xenia Chryssochoou, Eithne Buchanan-Barrow, Santiago Perera, Arantza del Valle, Luixa Reizábal, Thea Kacharava and Margarita Volovikova. In addition, all of the following individuals contributed to the empirical work for this project, and we are extremely grateful to all of them for their help and support: Pablo Fernández Berrocal, Jesus Canto Ortiz, Elena Sergienko, Sergei Grigoryev, Ludmila Grenkova-Dikevich, Natalia Gorodetchnaia, Olga Kuznetzova, Svetlana Tikhomirova, Margarita Mamaeva, Tatiana Pavliuchenkova, Igo Pavliuchenkov, Irina Kryazh, Olga Ivanova, Makvala Kharshiledze, Ketevan Kobaladze, Marima Gogava, Tamuna Grigolava, Nino Japharidze, Ketino Kobaladze, Thea Khabeishvili, Ketino Vashakidze, Nata Goderdzishvili, Nana Charkviani, Oleg Tevzadze and Rena Kadirova.

Because Chapters 5 and 6 of this book are based largely on the findings from the CHOONGE and NERID projects, these two chapters have been co-authored by all the individuals who made a substantive contribution to these two research projects and to the analyses and findings reported in these chapters. Because all of my co-authors inputted their ideas to the written content of these two chapters, they are consequently very much richer. My sincere thanks to all of you for your continuing contributions over the years, as well as for the personal friendships that have ensued from our collaborations together. Long may they continue.

A fourth research project in this area has also fed into some of the ideas presented in this book. This was a national research project in the UK that was set up and sponsored by the Developmental Psychology Section of the British Psychological Society. The project was entitled "Children's Views of Britain and Britishness in 2001", and it was undertaken in order to celebrate (in a practical way) the centenary of the British Psychological Society in 2001. Charles Crook was the Chair of the BPS Developmental Psychology Section at the time, and the project was his brainwave. He asked me to act as Chair of the Steering Group for the project, a task I was delighted to undertake. The other members of the Steering Group were Mark Bennett, Rupert Brown, Paul Ghuman, Karen Trew and Charles Crook. Once the project was under way, Eithne Buchanan-Barrow, Claire Byrne, Paul Webley and Adam Rutland also participated by recruiting students for the cause, and the following students subsequently assisted with the data collection for the project: Janet Jackson, Kate Arnold, Jenni Samson, Anni Ahmavaara, Marie Barkaway, Suzanne Miley, Una O'Dowd, Alexandra Dixon, Emma Alexander, Abigail Lear, Ayesha Shadat, Annie Lockyer, Clair Evans, Damien Randall and Emma Scott. A big thank you to all of you.

I would also like to thank three individuals who have read much of this book in manuscript form, and have provided me with a great deal of invaluable feedback on it: Peter Bryant, Kevin Durkin, and a third anonymous reader. Thank you for your incredibly helpful comments. Chapter 2 of this book is a substantial expansion of an earlier review chapter previously published by Barrett, Lyons and Bourchier (2006) in a book edited by Christopher Spencer and Mark Blades. I would like to express my sincere gratitude to Chris and Mark not only for their editorial feedback on that previous chapter but also for having drawn my attention to the wide range of research on children's geographical understanding which has been conducted in disciplines other than Psychology over the years. I would also like to thank Caroline Osborne who, on behalf of Psychology Press, commissioned this book in the first place, Lucy Kennedy, Lizzie Catford and Tara Stebnicky at Psychology Press, who have been immensely patient and understanding in awaiting the delivery of the final manuscript, and Kathryn Russel and Sue Ecob for all the work which they put into the production of the book.

Finally, I want to thank my wonderful family—my wife Annette, and my sons Adam and Alex—without whom the research in this book would not have been initiated. I thank you for your unstinting love, support, patience and tolerance while this book was in the process of being written.

Martyn Barrett
London, January 2006

CHAPTER ONE

On children, nations and national groups

During the course of their development, virtually all children, irrespective of the specific country or culture in which they live, learn that the country in which they live is not the only country that exists. Instead, they find out that there are many other countries in the world, and they usually acquire some factual knowledge about their own country and at least some of these other countries. In addition, children usually acquire various beliefs about other countries and the people who live in them. They also often display distinctive patterns of national preferences, prejudices and feelings, with their own nation and national group usually occupying a privileged position in their feelings, evaluations and judgements. This book describes our current understanding of how this body of knowledge, beliefs and feelings about nations and national groups develops through the course of childhood and early adolescence.

Much of the research that will be discussed in this book has been conducted by developmental and social psychologists. However, we will also be drawing on work that has been conducted by sociologists, anthropologists, educationalists, geographers and political scientists wherever this is relevant to the issues under discussion. Researchers in all of these disciplines have been drawn to the study of children's knowledge, beliefs and feelings about nations and national groups for a number of different reasons.

Developmental psychologists, for example, have investigated children's knowledge about nations and national groups because this knowledge differs in important respects from many other types of knowledge that have more traditionally been examined within the field of developmental psychology. Traditionally, cognitive-developmentalists have studied children's reasoning and thinking about the physical, psychological and biological worlds (e.g., Carey, 1985; P.L. Harris, 1989; Inagaki & Hatano, 2002; Perner, 1991; Siegal & Peterson, 1999; Spelke, 1991; Wellman & Gelman, 1998), children's information-processing capabilities and capacities (e.g., Case, 1985; Kail, 1990; Klahr & MacWhinney, 1998; Schneider & Bjorklund, 1998), and children's mastery of symbolic-representational systems such as language, drawing and mathematics (e.g., Bloom, 1998; P. Bryant & Bradley, 1985; Cox, 1992; Freeman, 1980; Gelman & Gallistel, 1978; Tomasello, 1992). By contrast, children's understanding of societal institutions, systems and structures has been relatively neglected by developmental psychologists over the years (see Barrett & Buchanan-Barrow, 2005, and Hatano & Takahashi, 2005, for discussions of this issue). This neglect is unfortunate, because children's thinking in societal domains differs in important respects from their thinking in non-societal domains.[1] For example, as far as their thinking about nations and national groups is concerned, such thinking is often accompanied by, or associated with, strong emotions. In other words, their thinking in this domain is often emotionally "hot". Furthermore, these emotions sometimes appear to be present prior to the child's acquisition of any factual knowledge or understanding. Hence, there is the possibility that children's emotions serve a significant motivational role in their knowledge acquisition in this area. In other words, children's knowledge, beliefs and feelings about nations and national groups provide developmental psychologists with an important opportunity to examine the relationship between cognitive and affective functioning in children and to investigate the development of emotionally "hot" cognition. As we shall see, the relationship between cognition and affect in this particular domain is complex and multifaceted.

In addition, some psychologists have been drawn to this field of research as a way of testing specific theories that have been proposed within their discipline. For example, several competing theories have been put forward to explain how preferences for, and prejudices against, social groups originate and develop through childhood (see, for example, Aboud, 1988; Aboud & Amato, 2001; Bandura, 1986, 1989; Bussey & Bandura, 1999; Nesdale, 1999, 2004; Ruble & Martin, 1998). To date, these theories have been tested primarily in relationship to children's gender and ethnic preferences and prejudices. However, these theories can also be tested using data drawn from the study of children's national preferences and prejudices. Similarly, a number of social-psychological theories have been put forward to explain the

---

[1] Throughout this book, the term "domain" is used in a non-technical sense simply to denote a particular conceptual area in which children acquire knowledge and construct beliefs. The term is not intended to convey any particular theoretical assumptions or connotations.

origins and contents of the stereotypes that people acquire as a consequence of belonging to, and identifying with, a particular social group. For example, two such theories are social identity theory (Tajfel, 1981; Tajfel & Turner, 1986) and self-categorization theory (Oakes, Haslam, & Turner, 1994; J.C. Turner, Hogg, Oakes, Reicher, & Wetherell, 1987). The predictions that are made by these theories can also be tested using data drawn from the study of children's national identifications and children's national stereotypes. As we shall see in the course of this book, the evidence that has been collected in this field is not always consistent with the predictions that are made by these various developmental and social-psychological theories.

However, there are also more practical reasons why social scientists in a number of different disciplines have been drawn to this field of enquiry. These practical reasons stem not so much from scientific curiosity but from the large-scale social changes that many countries are currently experiencing. The phenomenon of globalization means that many children who are growing up today (at least those who are growing up in more affluent societies) will live their future adult lives in a world that has shrunk dramatically. The advent of cheap and rapid international air travel, the invention of modern telecommunications and the Internet, the rise of globalized cultural industries, and the phenomenon of mass migration, have all created the potential for individuals to communicate and interact with people from other national groups on a scale that was unimaginable just 50 years ago. As a result, when they grow up, many of today's children will be living and working in a new kind of multicultural and transnational environment. At the same time, however, and despite the dramatic process of globalization (or perhaps, in some cases, because of it), the world remains riven by inter-nation discord, prejudice and hostility. Achieving a scientific understanding of how the emotional attachment to one's own nation develops, of how individuals come to view each other across national divides, and of how national prejudices and hostilities develop, is not only of scientific interest but also of considerable social importance.

Finally, in the case of some social scientists at least, their interests in this field stem from much more local, policy-related concerns. For example, in some countries such as the UK, Spain and Russia, greater political devolution and regional autonomy pose more specific challenges. These challenges concern the tension between maintaining national and state cohesion and loyalty while simultaneously accommodating demands for greater political and legislative powers at local and regional levels. At the same time, within the continent of Europe, the move towards a federal Europe is fiercely contested within many countries. Social policies, political and media campaigns, and even educational curricula within schools can all be used either to promote and facilitate further social change, or to prevent or inhibit further social change from taking place. However, for these policies, campaigns and curricula to be effective, they need to be grounded in appropriate evidence, particularly evidence about people's attitudes and behaviour in relationship to those social group memberships to which they feel strongly attached (such as their national and regional group memberships). Social scientists are in a position to provide that evidence.

In the case of children, of course, one of the principal influences on their judgements, affiliations and attitudes can be the school curriculum. Schools clearly have numerous educational objectives. In affluent societies, it is arguable that an important objective should be to equip children with the knowledge and skills that will enable them to operate effectively within the globalized world in which they now live. It is also arguable that a further goal should be to instil tolerance, concern, care and compassion for other people, and to minimize prejudice and hostility towards other people who belong to other national or ethnic groups. However, for educational programmes with these sorts of goals to be effective, we need to understand the relevant cognitive and affective developmental processes, so that the contents of these educational programmes can be optimally tailored to engage with children's emerging cognitive and affective competencies. In this way, the school curriculum could be used much more effectively to channel individual-acquisitional factors and processes towards socially desirable developmental outcomes. Hence the interest of some developmental psychologists and educationalists in this particular field of enquiry.

SOME INITIAL CONCEPTUAL DISTINCTIONS

Before we embark on our survey of the research that has been conducted in this field, it will be helpful to delineate the meanings of some of the terms we will be using throughout this book. In the English language, there are a number of different terms that can be used to refer to nations, and in informal conversations about nations, these terms are often used inconsistently. Three common terms which are frequently confused are "nation", "state" and "country". These terms are sometimes used by English speakers interchangeably to refer either to a community of people who are bound by a common history and shared culture, to a political entity that is ruled by a single government, or to a particular geographical territory delimited by internationally recognized borders.[2] Given this conceptual array and potential for conceptual confusion, it will be helpful to anchor our terminology at the outset.

---

[2] Adding to this terminological complexity, the word "state" is also used in the United States and some other countries not only to refer to a country as a whole (as in the state of Italy) but also to refer to a sub-unit of a country (as in the state of Texas). We are concerned here with the former use of the term, not the latter.

The term "nation" will be used in this book to refer to a named human community occupying a homeland and having a shared history, common myths of ancestry, a common mass public culture, and shared values, symbols, traditions, customs and practices. This definition is adapted from the work of A.D. Smith (1991, 1998, 2001, 2003, 2004), who emphasizes the origins of nations in ethnic communities, and the cultural-symbolic elements through which nations are represented, reproduced and interpreted by their members.[3] Smith stresses that this definition is intended to highlight the distinctive and characteristic features of nations, rather than their common denominators or necessary features. Notice that the emphasis of Smith's definition is on a community of people who are bound together by their sense of a common history and by a common culture. In this sense, nations are not unlike ethnic communities. Both nations and ethnic communities have collective names, myths of ancestry, historical memories, and shared traditions, customs and practices. However, Smith argues that nations are different from ethnic communities, in that nations occupy and live in their historic homeland, whereas ethnic communities are often only linked symbolically and affectively to a homeland. He also argues that ethnic communities, unlike nations, do not normally have a mass public culture, nor do they usually have a standardized and codified national history. We may add to Smith's list of differentiating characteristics the need for a nation (but not an ethnic community) to exhibit self-awareness as a nation (cf. W. Connor, 1994) and to have been politicized, particularly in its assertion of, or demands for the recognition of, its status as a nation (cf. Brass, 1991).

By contrast, the term "state" will be used in this book to refer to a sovereign political entity in which a government uses a set of institutions to exercise an administrative monopoly over a territory that has clearly demarcated borders, where the rule of that government is sanctioned by law, and where that government has the capacity to use coercion and violence in order to enforce its policies within that territory. This definition is adapted from the work of Giddens (1985), who views modern states as bordered power-containers. He emphasizes the fact that modern states are always defined by precisely specified borders, and that they lay claim to sovereign jurisdiction over all of the people, groups, organizations and institutions located within their borders. They also claim ultimate control over all matters that take place within their territory, including the maintenance of public order and the regulation of economic activity, and the threat of violence is used to back up

---

[3] There are two additional characteristics of a nation in Smith's definition: He argues that the members of a nation also share "a single economy" and have "common rights and duties" (A.D. Smith, 2001). These two elements have been omitted from the definition above as they have been vigorously contested by other scholars (see, for example, Guibernau, 2004a; W. Connor, 2004), and it is indeed arguable whether they are necessary elements in any formal definition of a nation.

these claims. Giddens argues that control is exercised through three characteristic features of the modern state: surveillance, which occurs through the collection and storage of information that is used to coordinate, administer and control the activities of people, groups, organizations and institutions within the state; bureaucratization, whereby specialized administrative officials are appointed who are specifically dedicated to the functioning of the state and to its apparatus of surveillance and control; and the development of police and military power, which is used to back up the demands of the state with the threat of violence. A further important feature of modern states, according to Giddens, is that they claim sovereignty; that is, each state asserts that it is the pre-eminent political authority within its own territory and has a right to self-governance, demands that this right be recognized by other states, and reserves the right to defend its territorial borders militarily against all external forces and threats from other states. Because the borders of states are demarcations of sovereignty, they have to be agreed by all of the states whose borders they are, and as such, states are necessarily embedded within a system of international relations.

According to these definitions of "nation" and "state", it follows that nations are *not* equivalent to states. For this reason, there are many stateless nations in the world (Guibernau, 1999; Keating, 2002; MacInnes & McCrone, 2001). The Palestinian and Kurdish people are two such nations. In each case, a group of people who are united by a common history, a common culture and a sense of their own common identity as a nation do not have their own state in which to live. Instead, Palestinian people are dispersed across the West Bank, the Gaza Strip, Israel, Jordan, Syria and Lebanon, while Kurdish people are dispersed across Iran, Iraq and Turkey. Neither of these two nations has its own state through which it can establish its own sovereign structure of governing institutions. Other stateless nations include Quebec (which lies within Canada), Catalonia (which lies within Spain and France, and is split in two by the border between these two states), the Basque Country (which lies within Spain), and both Scotland and Wales (both of which lie within the UK). Where a degree of political autonomy has been devolved to some of these stateless nations by the states in which they are located, such devolution of powers is nevertheless subject to the pre-eminent control of the superordinate state, and can be legally suspended or rescinded by that state. A further feature of stateless nations is that they are excluded from direct representation in international organizations such as the United Nations and the European Union, and they are therefore denied access to many of the resources and forms of power in the international arena to which states have access (Guibernau, 1999).

A corollary to the fact that there are many stateless nations is that there are many multination states in the world, that is, states that contain more than just a single nation within their territorial borders. Canada, Spain and the UK are three clear examples. Although English speakers some-times use the term "nation-state" as yet another synonym for "country" or "state", there are in fact very few true nation-states in the world, that is, states in which the borders of the state enclose just a single nation. W. Connor (1994; see also Tilly, 1990) estimates that only 10% of states are properly described as nation-states, the other 90% being multination states instead. Germany and Japan are two examples of nation-states, but Connor argues that it is erroneous to construe these two countries as the norm and to generalize from them to other states, as they are very much the exception.

A further feature of multination states is that they are often politically and culturally dominated by one of their constituent nations. This can convey the impression to outsiders (and indeed to many insiders) that they are a nation-state. For example, for several centuries, the UK has been dominated politically and economically by England. As a result, England, rather than either Scotland or Wales, has provided many of the most salient institutions, symbols, traditions, historical events and historical figures that are associated with the British state (Kumar, 2003). Analogously, the Spanish state has been dominated historically by the nation of Castile, rather than by either Catalonia or the Basque Country (Carr, 2001), with the Castilian nation furnishing many of the symbols and traditions that are associated with Spain (including both the capital city and the state language). It has also been argued that the USA is best viewed not as a nation-state but as a multination state that is politically and culturally dominated by its ethnically white, English-speaking, Christian nation, because the USA in fact incorporates several other nations such as the Navajo nation (Puri, 2004).

Although myths of origins, codified histories and shared values, symbols and traditions are most frequently discussed in connection with nations rather than states, it is important to note that states, including multination states, also usually have their own codified histories, their own myths of origin, and their own systems of shared values, symbols and traditions. Thus, not only nations but also states can be viewed as having distinctive cultures and histories with which individuals who live within those states may subject-ively identify. The terms "civic identity" and "civic nationalism" are some-times used to denote identity with and loyalty to the state rather than the nation (e.g., Ignatieff, 1993; Parekh, 2000), although W. Connor (1994, 2004) has argued that the term "patriotism" should be used here instead for the sake of conceptual clarity (in order to retain the term "nationalism" to denote identity with and loyalty to the nation, not the state).

The third term that we will be using throughout this book, in addition to "nation" and "state", is "country". This third term will be used in one of two ways. First, it will sometimes be employed relatively informally as a more generic term than either "nation" or "state". This is because it is sometimes appropriate to call both nations and states "countries", depending on the context (e.g., in the case of the UK, it is appropriate to call not only Britain but also Scotland a "country"). Second, "country" will also be used in this book when the emphasis is on physical-geographical territories and homelands rather than on historical-cultural communities or on political entities and institutions. A final pair of terms that will be used in this book are "national group" and "state group". These terms will be used to refer to the people who belong to a particular nation and to a particular state, respectively. This is because it is useful to differentiate between the collective entities denoted by the terms "nation" and "state" and the people who belong to those collective entities.

While it is helpful to make these various conceptual distinctions for analytic purposes, it ought to be noted that many adults (and indeed children) often do not draw such clear-cut conceptual distinctions themselves during the course of their everyday lives. In nation-states, because the nation and the state are coterminous, the conceptual distinction between nation and state is often blurred for those who live within these countries. Similarly, in multination states that are politically and culturally dominated by one of their constituent nations, because that dominant nation is typically the primary source of the codified state history and the symbols and traditions of the state, the members of that dominant nation also often confuse nation and state (because their own nation is so largely synonymous with the state). For example, this commonly occurs in Britain, Spain and the USA, where members of the dominant national groups frequently view the state as being synonymous with their own nation, rather than as a superordinate political construction. Research conducted in England, for instance, has revealed that many adults construe the terms "British" and "English" in a number of different ways. Sometimes these terms are construed as legal, state citizenship or nationality descriptors, sometimes they are construed as racial or ancestral descriptors, and sometimes they are construed as cultural or lifestyle descriptors (Condor, 1996; Jacobson, 1997). Furthermore, these different interpretations (some of which involve construing "British" as a national category rather than as a state category, and "English" as a state category rather than as a national category) can vary in their salience to different individuals depending on the particular ethnic, national and racialized group to which they themselves belong (Parekh, 2000). However, for the members of dominated nations within the same state (such as Scotland in the UK and Catalonia in Spain), such confusions between nation and state tend not to occur, with these individuals usually drawing a very clear distinction between their nation and their state (Guibernau, 2004b; McCrone, 2001). It is essential to keep these sorts of complexities and possible conceptual blurrings by individuals in mind when we consider the psychology of adults and children in relationship to states and nations.

THEORETICAL PERSPECTIVES ON THE NATURE OF NATIONS

Many theoretical perspectives on the historical origins and nature of nations have been offered over the course of the past 50 years, starting with the seminal work of Kedourie (1960) and Gellner (1964) and continuing right through to the present day (e.g., Guibernau, 2004b; McCrone, 2001; A.D. Smith, 2003). Helpful summaries of this very large literature are provided by A.D. Smith (2001) and Puri (2004). Limitations of space preclude a detailed coverage of what is currently a major field of scholarly activity across a number of different disciplines here. However, it will be helpful for the reader to be acquainted with some of the principal aspects of the most prominent theoretical positions, as an interpretative backdrop against which to understand children's acquisition of knowledge, beliefs and feelings about nations and national groups.

Both Kedourie (1960) and Gellner (1964, 1983) argued that nations and nationalism are very recent phenomena in world history. According to Kedourie, nationalism is an ideology that only emerged at the beginning of the 19th century, partly as a result of the French Revolution, and partly as the culmination of a number of other social and intellectual trends, associated with the Enlightenment, which were taking place within Europe at that time. Gellner also viewed the emergence of nations and nationalism as historically recent phenomena. However, he construed nationalism not so much as a doctrine or an ideology but as a necessary sociological product of the transition to modernity. A central feature of this transition, according to Gellner, was industrialization, which disrupted traditional agrarian culture. Earlier agrarian societies had consisted of numerous small local groups and cultures bound together by kinship relations and strong local traditions. These local groups lived within a state, but their everyday lives were relatively untouched by the state, which was typically run by small elites who maintained a significant distance from the larger population. Relatively few people were literate in such agrarian societies (usually only the aristocratic, administrative, military and religious elites were able to read and write). By contrast, industrial societies required a mobile workforce with a high degree of specialization, who frequently needed to communicate with strangers and to be literate. Gellner argued that the peasantry who moved to the cities in search of industrial employment were uprooted from their traditional cultures. To fill the cultural vacuum, more homogeneous and unified cultures were constructed based on the notion of national citizenship. In order to facilitate this cultural standardization, and to meet the need for a literate industrial workforce, mass public education systems were introduced by states, which helped to promulgate among their populations a new sense of cultural unity based on the nation. Thus, education was the principal means through which the shared culture of the nation was transmitted to individuals, replacing the traditional pre-literate folk cultures in the process. Gellner stressed that the nations that emerged from this process were artificial constructions developed from "cultural shreds and patches" (Gellner, 1983, p. 56), which were often arbitrary historical inventions, and that the nationalism which underlay the creation of these nations did not so much stimulate historical nations into self-consciousness as invent nations where they had not previously existed. Thus, Gellner claimed that both nations and nationalism are recent social phenomena that emerged primarily as a consequence of the transition to industrialized modernity.

Subsequent theorists have criticized Gellner's analysis for not taking sufficient notice of the diverse routes that different nations across the world have taken during the course of their emergence, especially the routes taken by nonindustrial societies (see especially A.D. Smith, 1998). However, many subsequent scholars have concurred with Kedourie's and Gellner's view that nations have only recently appeared in world history. Some authors, such as Giddens (1985) and Breuilly (1993), explain this recent emergence of nations by viewing them as the product of the modern centralized and professionalized state. For example, Breuilly postulates that the growth of a professionalized bureaucracy, capitalism and secularism created a split between the state and civil society. The "nation" emerged as a response to this split, being supported by sub-elites (such as middle-level bureaucrats, traders, professionals and intellectuals) as a way of bridging the gulf between state and society by representing them as a single unit in which the power of the state derived its political legitimacy from "the people". In contrast to Breuilly's and Giddens' overtly political perspectives on the emergence of nations, however, other authors, such as Anderson (1983) and Hobsbawm (1983, 1990), consider nations to be social constructions that are grounded in the cultural practices of modern societies. This latter approach is of particular relevance to the themes of the present book, and we will therefore examine this perspective a little more closely here.

According to Anderson (1983), nations are imagined political communities that are perceived as being both limited and sovereign by their own members. First, the nation is an imagined community because, even in the smallest nation, no member of that nation can ever know all the other members of the nation, can certainly never meet them all, and indeed will never even hear of them all. Yet despite this lack of personal knowledge and first-hand contact, the people who belong to an individual nation nevertheless imagine that there is a commonality that binds them all together within a single community. Second, nations are imagined by their members as limited communities, with boundaries beyond which there are other nations to which they themselves do not belong and which they do not wish to assimilate to their own nation. Third, nations are imagined as sovereign communities, with fundamental rights to freedom, autonomy and self-determination. Fourth, nations are imagined as social communities, because they are based on a sense of comradeship that provides such a strong sense of fraternity that their members are sometimes even willing to die for that community. Anderson attributes the willingness of individuals to die for their nation to the sense of immortality that such self-sacrifice confers, which is ratified through the rituals and ceremonies of commemoration that regularly take place at national cenotaphs and the tombs of Unknown Soldiers.

Anderson traces the historical origins of national consciousness to the emergence of print-communities based on a single vernacular language. He argues that the appearance of these communities was driven by a historically fortuitous interaction between the development of print technology and the development of capitalism. The co-occurrence of these two developments, precisely at a time when the elite use of Latin for religious purposes was in decline, led to the coalescence of standardized print-languages out of the multiplicity of local vernacular languages that were potentially available in any given location. This process was further consolidated by the adoption of these print-languages for state administration purposes. The wide communal sharing of such languages enabled new fields of popular communication and imagination to be opened up. Anderson draws attention to the fact that novels, in particular, portrayed imagined national communities in ways that emphasized their continuity with the historical past; through their vivid depictions of a communal past with which readers could readily identify, they effectively represented nations as cohesive sociological communities moving steadily through historical time. Newspapers also played a crucial role in the imagining of the nation, not only through the representations of the nation that they purveyed in their contents, but also through the practice of newspaper reading, a mass ritual performed on a daily basis by individuals in the full knowledge that large numbers of other people from the same imagined community also participate on a daily basis in exactly the same ritual. Thus, the origins of national consciousness are attributed by Anderson to the rise of print capitalism and to the effects of its products on large populations.

Like Anderson, Hobsbawm (1983, 1990) agrees with Gellner that nations are a recent historical phenomenon. However, Hobsbawm emphasizes the elements of deliberate artefact, invention and social engineering that were involved in the construction of nations during the course of the 19th century. He argues that the process of nation construction involved inventing a sense of continuity with a historical past, and that this was achieved through the invention of "national" traditions. These invented traditions were either novel creations or formalized adaptations of existing practices that were deliberately designed to sustain an illusion of historical continuity with the past, which, however, is largely factitious and artificial. Invented traditions are defined by Hobsbawm (1983) as sets of practices that are normally governed by rules and are of a ritual or symbolic nature, which seek to inculcate certain values and norms of behaviour through their repetition, with this act of repetition implying continuity with the past. Invented national traditions typically involve items such as flags, other emblems of the nation, costumes, anthems, other kinds of national music, national artistic styles, etc., and they may consist of either small-scale ritualistic practices or larger-scale formal ceremonies, festivals and national celebrations. Hobsbawm claims that much of the symbolic material that is used to represent the nation in these rituals has been artificially constructed and suitably tailored in order to meet nationalistic ends. Perhaps most important of all, history itself has been employed to meet these ends. Harnessed to the nationalist project, history does not consist of what is preserved in popular memory and can therefore be tapped through oral histories, but instead consists of what has been selected, written, pictured, popularized, institutionalized and codified into a nation's history. This standardized national history is then used to legitimate the political actions of the nation and to reinforce a sense of national cohesion. Hobsbawm's (1990) analysis reveals that the most fertile years for the invention of national traditions extended from 1830 to 1914, with this activity being especially pronounced from 1870 onwards.

Some of the issues discussed by Anderson and Hobsbawm have been analysed further by Billig (1995). He notes that, in the contemporary era, not only newspapers but also radio and television news reports continually refer to the nation, either by directly hailing the nation in headlines and editorials, by prioritizing fellow nationals in reports of natural or man-made disasters, by reporting the speeches of national politicians invoking the nation, by reporting the victories and defeats of national sporting teams, and by presenting weather forecasts and sporting results for their own nation only. He also observes that coins, banknotes, flags, patriotic colours, national anthems, military uniforms, national parades and celebrations, coronations, inaugurations, museums, monuments and sporting events have become routine objects, events and institutions in our daily lives, and they all serve to evoke the nation on a regular and routine basis. Commenting on this diversity of ways in which the nation is constantly being flagged in the course of our everyday lives, Billig draws attention to the fact that it is precisely because these reminders of the nation are so pervasive and have become such a familiar part of our everyday lives that they operate mindlessly rather than mindfully, and that in the very act of remembering the nation, we effectively forget it, because it has become so much a part of our regular habitual routines. He argues that this act of collective forgetting is neither fortuitous nor to do with absent-mindedness, but is a consequence of a particular ideological perspective that tends to construe nationalism as a dangerous and irrational phenomenon associated with other nations rather than with one's own nation.

In other words, Billig emphasizes that our everyday lives are saturated with characteristics, practices and rituals that are inherently linked to our own nation, but that this link has effectively become invisible to us through its very familiarity. Because the collective memory of the nation is thus pre-served but in the absence of conscious awareness by individuals, Billig draws on Bourdieu's (1990) concept of *habitus* to characterize the phenomenon. Habitus is the familiar everyday way in which we approach, think about and behave in the social world; our habitus is acquired and developed through the course of our experience and is internalized as a habitualized way of thinking and behaving. Habitus therefore represents an embodiment of our own per-sonal history that has been internalized as our second nature but which has been forgotten as history. In the same way, Billig argues, national practices and rituals have become so habitual and routine that they have come to embody the national past and yet are simultaneously forgotten. He uses the term "enhabitation" to denote the process of habit-formation; thus, as our thoughts, reactions and behaviours turn into routine habits, they become enhabited. In the case of the nation, the past of the nation is enhabited in the present through acts of forgetful remembrance, and the nation enhabits the present via its embodiment in the commonplace and banal routines and rituals of our lives. Thus, it is precisely because the nation is so thoroughly engrained within our everyday habits that it has such a deep impact and exerts such a potent hold over us.

All of the theoretical perspectives on the historical origins and nature of nations that we have been considering up to this point have been char-acterized as modernist theories, because they all emphasize that nations have only recently appeared in the course of world history and are a distinct-ive product of the conditions of modernity. Nations represent a qualitatively new form of community, polity and inter-state order compared with the forms that existed in previous eras. However, a very different approach to the nation is adopted by ethno-symbolist theorists such as A.D. Smith (1991, 1998, 2003; see also Armstrong, 1982; Hutchinson, 1994). Smith questions whether any of the modernist accounts can really account for the potency and the power of the nation as a focus for people's loyalties and affections. If nations are merely the products of arbitrary practices and traditions that were invented by nationalists in the 19th and early 20th centuries, and the sense of continuity with a historical past is entirely spurious (as Gellner, Hobsbawm and Anderson contend), then it is difficult to see why nations should command such extraordinary loyalty and commitment from their members. Smith himself argues that the reason why the invented traditions and the national histories created by nationalists are so readily adopted by the people is because they strike a chord with them; they are rooted in the collective myths, historical memories, symbols and traditions of the ethnic group to which they already belong. In their turn, the people then contribute further to the construction of the nation by embracing what is perceived to be an inspirational representation and narrative of the traditions, values and origins of their own ethnic group. The ethno-symbolists therefore view "the process of nation-formation as not so much one of construction, let alone deliberate 'invention', as of *reinterpretation* of pre-existing cultural motifs and of *reconstruction* of earlier ethnic ties and sentiments" (A.D. Smith, 2001, p. 83, italics in the original). Thus, according to Smith, it is precisely because nationalist discourse draws on elements of pre-existing ethnic culture that it can so readily mobilize an entire population, communicate a sense of collective purpose and belonging to that population, and sometimes inspire individuals to sacrifice themselves for the sake of the collective group.

Smith himself therefore traces the historical origins of nations to pre-modern ethnic communities. He analyses the processes through which these pre-modern communities were transformed into modern nations. He argues that there have been three different routes to nation formation (A.D. Smith, 1998, pp. 193–195). In one route, that of bureaucratic incorporation, the ruling elites of an existing state initially drew the middle classes into a politicized and territorialized "national" culture, and subsequently drew in the remainder of the working population to that culture. In these cases, the political bureaucratic state created the nation, and imposed a particular definition of the nation on the state, sometimes suppressing divergent definitions and cultures in the process. This route resulted in a "civic" conception of the nation based on a territorialized nationalism supplemented by ethnic and cultural elements. In the second route, that of vernacular mobilization, a demotic ethnic culture was actively transformed by intellectuals and professionals into a nation through the selective rediscovery and reappropriation of elements of the people's own ethnic culture, specifically for the purposes of forging a new national culture based on the vernacular language and indigenous history and culture. This second route resulted in an "ethnic" conception of the nation, based on an ethnic nationalism supplemented by territorialized and politicized elements. The third route, that of immigrant pluralism, was followed when nations were created out of several colonist-immigrant groups from a variety of different ethnic backgrounds who came together in a new geographical territory, where they forged a "pluralistic" conception of the new nation. Such nations acknowledged and accepted their internal ethnic diversity, with this diversity being allowed to flourish within an overarching legal and political framework.

In his analyses of nations and nationalism, Smith draws particular attention to the concept of the homeland and the role that this concept often plays in nationalist discourse (see especially A.D. Smith, 1991, 2003). He argues that the homeland is frequently construed in sacred terms in such discourse. Thus, the natural and man-made features of the homeland, such as its mountains, rivers, lakes, coastline, landscapes and cities, are revered and venerated. Furthermore, this national territory can never be just any stretch of geographical territory; instead, it has to be the historic land in which the ancestors and heroes of the nation lived and died, and where historic events of great national significance took place. The homeland is therefore a repository of rich and extensive collective memories and historical and cultural associations, and for this reason the homeland forms an integral component of the nation itself. Furthermore, because of the unique relationship that exists between the people who make up a national group and their homeland, the natural resources of that homeland are construed as being for the exclusive use of the national group. Thus, it is perceived as illegitimate for other national groups to invade the homeland and to appropriate and exploit any of these natural resources for themselves. Moreover, it is precisely because this sense of attachment to the homeland is so strong that the members of the nation may be willing to go to war and to sacrifice themselves in order to maintain national ownership of the homeland and its natural resources. Nations are therefore viewed by Smith not simply as large social collectivities bound together by a sense of shared history, common ancestry, and shared values, symbols, traditions, customs and practices; they are also bound together by an emotional attachment to a particular geographical territory, which itself functions as a material embodiment of the nation.

A number of the themes and issues identified by Gellner, Hobsbawm, Anderson, Billig and Smith will surface repeatedly through this book, as we examine in detail the development of children's knowledge, beliefs and feelings about nations and national groups. For example, one important issue that will appear repeatedly in several of the subsequent chapters is the role which school education plays in children's national enculturation, an issue originally highlighted by Gellner. Another issue is the role of the mass media in children's national enculturation. Anderson has drawn attention to the role of print media in transmitting a sense of the nation to individuals in earlier historical periods, but Billig has argued that not only novels and newspapers but also the broadcast media, especially television, play a crucial role in sustaining the nation in people's habitual routines today. In several chapters of this book, we will be looking at a range of evidence concerning the impact of mass media on children's representations of, and attitudes to, both nations and states. In addition, Hobsbawm, Anderson and Billig have all highlighted the role of traditions, rituals and practices in sustaining the nation in people's everyday lives. We will be examining how these various factors impact on the national enculturation of children, both in the family and at school. Finally, at the very core of our enquiry, we will be focusing on several issues that are directly related to the themes analysed by Smith in his writings on nations and nationalism. For example, we will be examining the development of children's understanding of, and attitudes to, their own nation's heritage, history, culture, emblems, traditions and homeland, as well as the development of children's understanding of, and attitudes to, the political institutions of the state. However, before we embark on our enquiry into the development of children, there is one final preliminary matter that needs to be discussed.

THE CONCEPT OF NATIONAL ENCULTURATION

In the preceding paragraph, the term "national enculturation" was used. It will probably be helpful to expand on this concept here, because this entire book is quintessentially all about the process of national enculturation. The term "national enculturation" will be used throughout this book in order to denote the extended developmental process through which children are gradually inducted into the heritage, history, representations, values, institutions, traditions, customs and practices of their own national and state group, and through which they acquire an emotional attachment to their own nation and state, to their national and state group, to the symbols of their own nation and state, and to their national homeland and state territory. Notice that the focus here is not only on the nation but also on the state. This is because children learn about, and frequently form attachments to, not only their nation but also their state. However, it would be stylistically awkward and cumbersome (although technically more accurate) to use the phrase "national and state enculturation" to denote this developmental process, and so the simpler term of "national enculturation" will be used instead. However, the reader should bear in mind the wider set of connotations intended by the use of this term.

As far as the word "enculturation" itself is concerned, this term is used here in preference to the alternative term, more commonly used in developmental psychology, namely "socialization". Within the disciplines of psychology and anthropology, "enculturation" is used to refer to the process through which an individual adapts to a culture by assimilating the representations, practices, customs and values that are required in order to function as a member of that culture (Reber, 1985; Rhum, 1997). By contrast, "socialization" is used by psychologists to refer to the process through which the child adapts to, and becomes integrated within, a society (rather than a culture) (Reber, 1985; Schaffer, 1996). The term "enculturation" is therefore preferred in the present context because it serves to emphasize one of the most important characteristics of a nation, namely that it is a culture, not merely a society. It also has the advantage of avoiding some of the older, outdated and problematic connotations associated with the term "socialization" (namely that the child is relatively passive in the process and is shaped primarily by external socialization influences from the environment; see Schaffer, 1996, for a lucid discussion of these associations to this term and some of the problems linked to these associations).

National enculturation is clearly an intricate and multifaceted process, and there are at least three different perspectives that can be adopted in order to explore its various aspects. One perspective involves a definitional approach. As we have seen, a nation can be defined as a named human community that occupies a particular homeland and that has a shared history, common myths of ancestry, a common mass public culture, and shared values, symbols, traditions, customs and practices; similarly, a state can be defined as a sovereign political entity in which a government uses a set of institutions to exercise an administrative monopoly over a territory that has clearly demarcated borders, where the rule of that government is sanctioned by law and this is backed up by the threat of violence. This definition of the term "nation" implies that the process of national enculturation entails the child learning about the particular national community to which he or she belongs, about its homeland, its shared history and myths of ancestry, its common mass public culture, and its shared values, symbols, traditions, customs and practices; it also implies that national enculturation involves the child learning how to participate in the shared traditions, customs and practices of his or her nation. In addition, the definition of the term "state" implies that national enculturation entails the child learning about the state to which he or she belongs, about its government, about the administrative apparatus through which that government controls the people, groups, organizations and institutions that fall within its borders, and about the role of the police and the military in backing up the demands of the government.

However, it is important to note that national enculturation is not only a process through which children are inducted into particular cognitive representations of their own nation and state and into particular cultural practices. It is also a process that generates a subjective sense of personal affiliation and belonging, and an emotional attachment to the history, culture and territory of the child's own nation and state, engendering in children a sense of who they are, influencing how they see themselves, and impacting on how they locate themselves within the wider world. In other words, national enculturation involves not only the child's cognitive and behavioural systems but also the child's affective and identity systems. For this reason, a simple definitional perspective is insufficient by itself: national enculturation must also be examined from a second perspective, the perspective of national identity. From this second perspective, national enculturation may be interpreted as the developmental process through which the child acquires a national identity, that is, a subjective sense of affiliation and a personal sense of belonging to a particular nation and state, as well as a sense of how they personally are positioned and situated in relationship to the world of nations and states.[4]

Considered as a psychological structure, the subjective sense of national identity has many different cognitive and affective aspects and components. These are discussed at length by A.D. Smith (1991, 2003) and by Barrett (2000, 2005a, b). Some of the more fundamental cognitive aspects include: knowing about the existence of the national or state group; knowing that the self is a de facto member of that group; knowing about the emblems that symbolically represent the nation or state in a concrete and perceptible form; and knowing about the geographical territory that comprises the national homeland or state territory (see Barrett, 2005b, and Barrett, Lyons, & Bourchier, 2006, for more detailed discussions of these various knowledge-based components). Thus, the acquisition of a subjective sense of national identity entails the child acquiring knowledge of the existence of the national or state group, acquiring knowledge that he or she is a member of that group, acquiring knowledge of national and state emblems, and acquiring knowledge of the national homeland or state territory.

In addition to such knowledge, however, a number of different beliefs can also form an integral part of the psychological sense of national identity. First, in the case of some nations, national identity involves an implicit belief in the common descent and kinship of the members of the national group, with the nation being construed as a large collection of individuals who are all interrelated, if only distantly, because they are all imagined as being descended from common ancestors who are thought of as the forefathers of the nation. W. Connor (1978), Horowitz (1985) and A.D. Smith (1991) have argued that this belief in common descent and kinship can be more or less pronounced in different national groups and at different points in historical time. For children who belong to such nations, part of the process of acquiring a sense of national identity will therefore entail acquiring this belief. Second, the members of national and state groups usually hold shared beliefs about the typical characteristics and traits of their own in-group, especially those characteristics and traits that distinguish and differentiate the in-group from other salient national and state out-groups. Consequently, acquiring a sense of national identity can entail the acquisition of these beliefs concerning the typical characteristics and traits of the in-group and of relevant comparison out-groups. Third, the sense of national identity can also involve beliefs about the self in relationship to the national or state in-group, particularly about how closely the self matches the characteristics

---

[4] Notice that the term "national identity" is used here to denote an individual's sense of belonging to, and relationship to, either the nation or the state (in those cases where these are two distinct entities); such usage is appropriate, given that individuals may subjectively identify with either the nation or the state.

and traits typically ascribed to that group. The term "authenticity" has been used by some authors (e.g., Gecas, 1991; Trew & Benson, 1996) to refer to this notion. Thus, if the group identity accurately reflects an individual's sense of self, the identity is construed as authentic, whereas if it does not reflect, or is inconsistent with, the self-concept, the identity is construed as inauthentic. Gecas argues that individuals tend to reject inauthentic identities in order to avoid feelings of self-estrangement. But for individuals for whom their nation or state provides an authentic identity, that identity can help to structure and facilitate their own personal sense of self by helping to locate and position the self within the larger world.

In addition to these various cognitive components of the psychological sense of national identity, there are many different affective aspects that can also be analytically distinguished. First, there is the level of importance that the individual attributes to his or her own national or state identity, the value that he or she places on being a member of the national or state group, his or her emotional attachment to the group, and the individual's emotional attachment to the national or state culture (see Barrett, 2000, 2005b, for more detailed discussions of these various aspects). Second, as A.D. Smith (1991, 2003) has cogently argued, the sense of national identity also involves an emotional attachment to the geographical territory of the homeland. Third, as has already been noted, there are subjective feelings of personal affiliation and belonging to the national or state group. These feelings of belonging may be related to the importance, value or authenticity that the individual attributes to the national or state identity, or to the sense of emotional attachment that the individual has to the culture or to the group. Feelings of belonging may also be related to the extent to which the individual is able to embed him- or herself within a network of other people who ascribe value and importance to the national or state identity, who reward the individual for holding that identity and enable the individual to obtain feelings of personal satisfaction from being a member of the group. The extent to which an individual is socially embedded in a group membership in this way has been termed identity "commitment" by some identity theorists (e.g., Burke & Reitzes, 1991; Stryker & Serpe, 1982). It is also possible that feelings of belonging are related to the extent to which the individual feels that he or she is a worthy, useful and valuable member of the national or state group, that is, to what has been called their "membership self-esteem" (Crocker & Luhtanen, 1990; Luhtanen & Crocker, 1992). Fourth, there are numerous social emotions that an individual can experience by virtue of his or her identification with a national or state group. These include emotions such as national pride, national shame, national embarrassment, national guilt, etc. These sorts of emotions may be elicited either by a generalized sense of the worthiness of the nation or state to which one belongs, by specific national or state emblems (e.g., by seeing the national flag, by hearing the national anthem, etc.) or by specific events either in the present or in the historical past (e.g., by the victory of a national sporting team, by witnessing hooligans from one's own nation rioting in the streets of a foreign city, by knowing about the complicity of one's own nation in war crimes in the past, etc.).

In short, there are numerous cognitive and affective components and aspects of the subjective sense of national identity. From this second perspective, then, national enculturation can be viewed as the extended developmental process through which children gradually acquire a sense of their own national identity, that is, this complex structure of knowledge, beliefs and feelings concerning their nation and state.

Three further important characteristics of the subjective sense of national identity should also be noted here. First, national identity is never defined solely in terms of its psychological cognitive and affective components. Instead, as Billig (1995) has argued, national identity is intimately and pervasively connected to everyday behaviours, routines and habits. In studying the process of national enculturation, therefore, we also need to examine children's developing mastery of, and participation in, the cultural traditions, customs and practices of their own nation and state, and investigate how aspects of children's national or state culture become embodied and enhabited in their daily routines and habits.

Second, as J.C. Turner et al. (1987, pp. 54–56) have noted, national identity is not a static psychological structure. Instead, it is a dynamic psychological structure that may or may not be mobilized according to particular situational and motivational contingencies. In other words, like most other social identities (such as gender identity, ethnic identity, etc.), national identity is not always salient to the individual concerned. Instead, its salience is context-dependent. Thus, national identity tends to enter conscious awareness only when the nation or state is explicitly evoked in a particular context (e.g., by a politician's speech, by a national flag, by a national victory in an international sporting competition, etc.) or when the prevailing context contains one or more salient comparison out-groups (e.g., when on holiday in another country). In studying children's national enculturation, therefore, it is also important to understand the types of contexts in which children's subjective sense of national identity becomes especially salient to them.

Third, national identity is just one of many different personal and social identities that any individual can hold. Other identities may be based on their personality, their interpersonal relationships and roles, their gender, their ethnicity, their religion, their social class, the region or city in which they live, etc. These various identities do not function in isolation from each other; instead, identities interact with each other in a variety of ways (Deaux, 1992; Rosenberg & Gara, 1985; Stryker, 1987). As a result, the specific set of values, symbols, traditions, customs and practices that are most closely associated with their national identity for different individuals may well vary, depending on the other identities held by those individuals and their own personal histories and life experiences. Hence, the precise set of meanings associated with, for example, being American by a male, middle-class, Muslim African-American living in New York City may well vary from those that are associated with being American by a female, working-class, Christian European-American living in the rural Midwest. In other words, it is unlikely that there will be a single invariant set of meanings that all indi-viduals who belong to a particular national or state group will attach to their membership of that group. Instead, different individuals are likely to select different aspects of what it means to be a member of the national or state group (from the full set of elements potentially available through the national or state culture), and to interpret those selected aspects in a variety of ways according to their own personal situations and circumstances. Hence, vari-ability across individuals may well be the norm, with different subsets of meanings, interpretations and construals being adopted and utilized by dif-ferent individuals in relationship to their membership of their national or state group. Thus, in investigating children's national enculturation, we also need to examine how their developing sense of their own national identity interacts with their other developing identities in helping them to locate, position and define themselves, and how that sense of national identity is personalized with respect to the specific life experiences of the individual child.

In addition to a definitional and an identity perspective, a third perspective that may be adopted to illuminate the process of national enculturation is based on an analysis of the influences and factors that might drive and channel the process. For example, on a priori grounds, it seems likely that children's national enculturation will be influenced, at least in part, by their developing information-processing capabilities, that is, by their developing cognitive capacities for attending to, interpreting and retaining information about nations and states. National enculturation is also likely to be influenced by children's interest in, and motivation for, attending to and processing information concerning nations and states. Motivational processes will also influence children's mastery of, and participation in, national or state prac-tices, rituals and traditions, depending on the extent to which these activities meet and fulfil their current interests and motivational needs. In addition to such endogenous psychological factors, it is likely that multiple exogenous influences stemming from cultural factors in children's environments will be involved in the process as well. As we have seen, theorists such as Gellner (1983), Anderson (1983), Hobsbawm (1983) and Billig (1995) have, between them, highlighted several such factors, including the schooling that children receive, the mass media to which they are exposed, and the everyday rituals, traditions and practices in which children are required to participate, all of which have been posited by one or more of these theorists to play a crucial role in fostering a sense of national identity and national belonging in individuals. We will be exploring the process of national enculturation from this third perspective at some considerable length through the course of this book, while in the final chapter we will be drawing some general conclusions based directly on empirical research with children, rather than on either historical or cultural analysis, concerning the role which both endogenous and exogenous factors play in children's national enculturation.

While these three perspectives on national enculturation yield a number of different lines of enquiry that can potentially be pursued in empirical research with children, it ought to be noted here that not all of these lines of enquiry have yet been taken up by researchers in this field. For example, to the best of our knowledge, no research has yet been conducted with children who belong to national groups that hold an implicit belief in the common descent and kinship of members of their group, in order to ascertain how this belief might be transmitted across generations. There is also very little research on the types of situations and contexts in which national identity becomes especially salient to children. There is also surprisingly little research on family practices in relationship to nations and states, and how children's participation in these practices impacts on their sense of national or state belonging. That said, there are numerous other aspects of the national enculturation process that have now been investigated in studies with children by researchers from a number of different social science disciplines. The following chapters of this book review the findings of this substantial body of existing research in detail.

THE STRUCTURE AND ORGANIZATION OF THIS BOOK

The remainder of this book is divided into six chapters. Chapters 2–6 provide a detailed survey of the empirical research that has been conducted into children's national enculturation. Chapter 2 begins the survey by reviewing those studies that have investigated children's knowledge and beliefs about countries construed as geographical territories, and children's feelings about the geographies of their own and other countries. The chapter opens by reviewing and evaluating a classic study in this field by Piaget and Weil (1951) and the subsequent line of research that Piaget's work and approach has inspired. It then moves on to review non-Piagetian studies that have investigated children's knowledge and beliefs about the geography of their own homeland, their emotional attachment to their homeland, and children's knowledge, beliefs and feelings about the geographies of foreign countries. As we will see, the studies in this area have revealed that an emotional attachment to the homeland is often present from 7 years of age onwards, even though children's factual knowledge of large-scale geographical territories is minimal at this early age. These studies have also revealed that there is substantial variability in the development of children's large-scale geographical knowledge, with this variability being systematically linked to children's gender, social class, nationality, ethnicity and geographical location within their own country. The evidence suggests that this variability results, at least in part, from children's differential levels of travel experience, from differences in the educational input that children receive, and from children's differential exposure to information about other countries through the mass media.

Chapter 3 reviews the research that has been conducted into children's understanding of, and attitudes to, the state. This chapter therefore explores the development of children's understanding of government, and of the political institutions and processes that governments use in order to administer states. As will be seen in the course of this chapter, there are significant developmental changes in children's political understanding between 9 and 12 years of age. For this reason, some prominent researchers in this area have argued that it is across this age range that children consolidate their understanding of the state as a political entity that exists within clearly demarcated territorial borders and is administered by a single government. In this chapter, we also review the research that has been conducted into children's and adolescents' attitudes to, and feelings about, the political institutions of the state. This body of research reveals, once again, that there is considerable variability in development. This variability is linked to a range of factors, including the availability of literacy resources in the family home, school curricular input, school practices, and levels of attention to the news in the mass media. Adolescents' attitudes to the state have also been found to vary as a function of the recent historical longevity of democracy in their own country, suggesting that the historical and political macro-context within which they develop can also impact (indirectly) on their national enculturation.

In Chapter 4, we review the research that has been conducted into children's knowledge, beliefs and feelings about nations and states when these are construed as historical and cultural communities. The chapter begins by examining the development of national and state pride in children. However, the major part of this chapter focuses on the role of the school in the national enculturation of children. As this chapter reveals, there is now a considerable body of evidence to substantiate the contention that the school plays a major role in children's national enculturation, partly through the provision of direct instruction about the child's own nation and state (especially about the history, geography, cultural heritage, emblems and symbolic imagery of that nation and state), partly through the ethnocentric biases that often characterize educational curricula and school textbooks, and partly through the adoption by schools of core aspects of the nation's civil culture within their own daily practices. The chapter concludes by reviewing studies that have been conducted into children's knowledge, understanding and utilization of national and state emblems (such as national flags, monuments, ceremonies and national historical figures and historical events, etc.). As we shall see, this evidence suggests that, once again, there is significant variability in children's knowledge and utilization of national and state emblems, which appear to be linked to school practices and teaching (and possibly to influences from the mass media and the family as well).

Chapter 5 reviews the research that has been conducted into the development of children's knowledge, beliefs and feelings about the people who belong to different national and state groups. This chapter begins by reviewing previous studies conducted into children's stereotypes of, and attitudes to, the people who belong to different national and state groups. A number of phenomena are examined here, including in-group favouritism, out-group denigration, and children's attitudes towards national and state groups that are the traditional enemies of their own nation or state. The chapter then goes on to present some of the findings that have emerged from two recent cross-national comparative research projects, the CHOONGE and NERID projects, which have been conducted by the collective authorship of this book. While individual aspects of the findings from these two projects have already been reported in a number of separate journal articles, we take advantage of the opportunity provided by the current book to present a more panoptic perspective on the findings that have emerged from these two projects. In Chapter 5, we report the findings that were obtained in these projects on the development of children's representations of, and attitudes to, national and state in-groups and out-groups. A major conclusion to emerge from these projects is that there is very considerable variability in the development of children's national and state attitudes as a function of the specific national and state context in which they live. Importantly, the findings show that children's national and state attitudes and feelings often reflect the set of prevailing political inter-group relations within which their own national or state group is "objectively" embedded. Thus, the evidence here substantiates the conclusion drawn in Chapter 3 that the historical and political macro-context in which children live can impact on their national enculturation. Chapter 5 concludes by reviewing the evidence on two further residual issues: the sources from which children obtain their information about other national and state groups (which, as we shall see, include print media, television, movies and school coursework), and children's beliefs about the factors that determine people's national and state group memberships.

Chapter 6 continues reporting findings from the CHOONGE and NERID projects, specifically those findings obtained in these two projects on the development of children's subjective identifications with their own nation and state. Again, one of the major findings to emerge from these projects is the variability that occurs in children's development. The data from these projects show that children's national and state identifications vary as a function of many different factors, including their country, their geographical location within their country, how the state category is interpreted within their local environments, their ethnicity, their use of language in the family home, and their language of schooling. Chapter 6 also reports analyses that were conducted on the CHOONGE and NERID data to examine whether children's attitudes to different national and state groups are related to the strength of their national and state identifications. The findings show that children's attitudes towards national and state out-groups are not usually related to their strength of identification with their own nation or state; however, the strength of children's national and state identifications is frequently related to how much they like their own national and state in-groups. Chapter 6 ends with a report of some further findings that have been obtained using two new measurement instruments, one for measuring the perceived status of the child's own national or state group, the other for measuring the strength of national and state (and ethnic) identification in children and adolescents. The findings here confirm the principal findings of the CHOONGE and NERID projects, namely that different groups of children living in different national and state contexts often exhibit very different patterns of identity development.

The final chapter of the book, Chapter 7, is qualitatively different from the five preceding chapters. It begins by summarizing some of the principal findings that have emerged through the course of the preceding chapters. These principal findings concern: the variability that clearly does occur in children's national enculturation; the role played in children's national enculturation by education, the mass media, significant others in the child's environment, travel experience and domain-general cognitive factors; the gender differences that sometimes appear in children's national enculturation; and the relationship between knowledge and affect in this developmental domain. Chapter 7 then examines and evaluates, against the empirical evidence reviewed in the preceding chapters, a number of different theoretical frameworks that might be used to interpret and explain children's development in this domain. All of the existing theoretical accounts are found to be inadequate for explaining the full range of phenomena documented in the main body of the book. These empirically inadequate theories include: Piagetian stage theory; more recent cognitive-developmental theory; social identity theory; self-categorization theory; and social identity development theory. Chapter 7 concludes by offering a new theoretical framework for explaining children's national enculturation, societal-social-cognitive-motivational theory (SSCMT).

Each chapter of this book ends with a bullet point summary. It is hoped that, while some of the material in this book may be complex, detailed and densely argued, these end-of-chapter summaries will ease the burden on the reader by extracting the most important points from each individual chapter.

SUMMARY

- Researchers in a number of social science disciplines have chosen to study children's knowledge, beliefs and feelings about nations and national groups for several different reasons:
  - the field provides an opportunity for examining the relationship between cognitive and affective functioning in children, and for investigating the development of emotionally "hot" cognition
  - the field provides an opportunity for testing theories of how preferences for, and prejudices against, social groups originate and develop through childhood and adolescence
  - it is judged socially important to understand how people's emotional attachments to their own nation are acquired and how national prejudices and hostilities develop
  - research in this field can be used to inform the design of social policies and political and media campaigns that are directed at social change
  - research in this field can be used to inform the design of educational programmes and curricula for use within schools.
- There is an important conceptual distinction between a nation and a state, despite the fact that this distinction is often blurred in everyday thinking and discourse:
  - a nation is a named human community occupying a homeland and having a shared history, common myths of ancestry, a common mass public culture, and shared values, symbols, traditions, customs and practices
  - a state is a sovereign political entity in which a government uses a set of institutions to exercise an administrative monopoly over a territory that has clearly demarcated borders, where the rule of that government is sanctioned by law, and where that government has the capacity to use coercion and violence in order to enforce its policies within that territory.
- It is therefore possible to distinguish between stateless nations, nation-states and multination states:
  - stateless nations are nations that do not have their own sovereign self-governing state in which to live
  - nation-states are states in which the borders of the state enclose just a single nation
  - multination states are states that contain more than one nation within their borders.

- As far as multination states are concerned:
  - it has been estimated that 90% of all countries in the modern world are multination states
  - multination states are often politically and culturally dominated by just one of their constituent nations, which can convey the (incorrect) impression that they are nation-states
  - states, including multination states, usually have their own codified histories, myths of origins, and shared values, symbols and traditions.
- Contemporary theories of nations and nationalism can be divided into modernist and ethno-symbolist theories:
  - modernist theories emphasize that nations have only recently appeared in the course of world history and are a distinctive product of the conditions of modernity
  - some modernist theories view the nation as a product of the modern centralized and professionalized state
  - other modernist theories view nations as social constructions that have emerged from the cultural practices of modern societies, and emphasize the "inventedness" and artificiality of nations
  - ethno-symbolist theories instead view nations as having emerged from pre-existing ethnic communities through the reinterpretation and reconstruction of existing ethnic symbols, ties and sentiments
  - together, these various theories have highlighted the school, the mass media, and the routine habits, rituals and traditions of everyday life as influences on the national enculturation of individuals.
- National enculturation is the key process on which this book will be focusing:
  - national enculturation is the extended developmental process through which children are gradually inducted into the heritage, history, representations, values, institutions, traditions, customs and practices of their own national and state group, and through which children acquire an emotional attachment to their own nation and state, to their national and state group, to the symbols of their own nation and state, and to their national homeland and state territory
  - national enculturation involves the child's acquisition of a subjective sense of national identity, which has numerous cognitive, affective and behavioural aspects and components
  - national enculturation is likely to be driven by the development of the child's information-processing capabilities and motivational system, as well as by various exogenous influences emanating from the school, the mass media, and the routine habits, rituals and traditions of everyday life.

- The remainder of this book falls into two parts:
  - ○ Chapters 2–6 provide a review of the empirical research that has been conducted into the various aspects of children's national enculturation
  - ○ Chapter 7 reviews and evaluates the existing theoretical frameworks that may be used to interpret and explain children's development in this domain, and offers a new theory, societal-social-cognitive-motivational theory (SSCMT) to explain children's national enculturation.

Children's knowledge, beliefs and feelings about countries construed as geographical territories

In this chapter, we begin our examination of the empirical research that has been conducted into children's national enculturation, by reviewing studies that have investigated the development of children's knowledge, beliefs and feelings about countries when these are construed as geographical territories. In this context, it is worth noting that over the course of the past century, the entire land surface of the world, apart from Antarctica, has been divided up into a set of identifiable countries, with the result that each country now occupies a particular geographical territory that is very precisely circumscribed and defined (Giddens, 1985; A.D. Smith, 1991). The particular geographical territory that comprises each country consists of a unique constellation of geological and ecological features, with countries differing from each other in terms of all sorts of characteristics, including their natural features (such as mountains, valleys, plains, rivers, lakes, coastlines, etc.), man-made features (such as cities, towns, villages, etc.), flora and fauna, and climate. During the course of their development, children acquire knowledge and beliefs about the geographical features that characterize not only their own country but also various other countries. In addition, children acquire distinctive patterns of feelings about the geographies of their own and other countries. In this chapter, we examine how such knowledge, beliefs and feelings develop.

The chapter is divided into three parts. The first part reviews and evaluates a classic study in this field, which was conducted by Piaget and Weil (1951). This study provides a useful starting point, not only because it raises a number of issues that have subsequently been investigated by other researchers, but also because the qualitative details of children's responses that Piaget and Weil report serve to illustrate various aspects of children's thinking in this domain. That said, as we shall see, Piaget and Weil's own conclusions about the nature of children's thinking about countries as geographical entities have been seriously undermined by the findings of subsequent research. However, later studies have supported one of the implications of Piaget and Weil's study, namely that some aspects of children's large-scale geographical understanding are related to their underlying domain-general cognitive competencies. The second part of the chapter then moves on to review the findings of more recent non-Piagetian studies that have investigated children's knowledge, beliefs and feelings about the geography of their own national homeland and state territory. Finally, the third part of the chapter reviews the findings of more recent studies that have investigated children's knowledge and beliefs about the geographies of foreign countries, as well as children's feelings about foreign countries in comparison to their feelings about their own national homeland.

THE PIAGETIAN PERSPECTIVE ON CHILDREN'S UNDERSTANDING OF, AND FEELINGS ABOUT, COUNTRIES

The study by Piaget and Weil

In this particular field of enquiry, as in so many other fields of developmental psychology, Jean Piaget (1928; Piaget & Weil, 1951) was the first researcher to conduct empirical research. His investigations ranged over a number of issues, including children's concepts of countries, their large-scale geographical knowledge, their feelings about both the homeland and other countries, and their understanding of people's national group memberships.

In his initial investigation, in which he interviewed Swiss children living in Geneva, Piaget (1928) found that the concept of country appeared to develop through three stages. In the first stage, a country was simply regarded as another geographical unit alongside towns and regions, and as being of a similar magnitude to these other units (e.g., Switzerland was conceived as existing alongside Geneva and Vaud,[5] and as being a similar size to them). In the second stage, children understood that towns and regions were inside the country, but they did not yet understand that they formed an integral part of that country; instead, towns and regions were conceptualized as pieces of land surrounded by the country (Switzerland, therefore, surrounds and

---

[5] Vaud is a canton (i.e., a constituent unit of the Swiss confederation) and a region of Switzerland that neighbours Geneva.

encloses Geneva and Vaud). During these first two stages, children failed to understand that a person could simultaneously be both Genevese and Swiss, as Geneva was not yet conceptualized as being included within Switzerland. In the third stage (which only began at about 9 or 10 years of age, according to Piaget), the children finally understood the correct relationship between towns, regions and countries, and acknowledged that an individual could be simultaneously both Genevese and Swiss. Piaget noted that the second stage was not always very clearly marked, and that children sometimes exhibited only vague and fluctuating ideas at this transitional stage.

Piaget and Weil (1951) revisited these initial ideas and explored them in greater depth. In this study, they assessed over 200 children aged between 4 and 15 years. Once again, these were all Swiss children living in Geneva. Piaget and Weil used both open-ended interviewing and drawings to investigate these children's understanding of countries. They found that the children's thinking exhibited four stages of development: an initial pre-stage of ignorance, followed by three proper developmental stages. The pre-stage occurred before 5 years of age. During this early period, the children knew that they lived in Geneva; that is, the children knew about their home town, what language was spoken there, and that it was a big city. However, they did not know what country they lived in, or what country Geneva was in. In other words, they did not yet appear to have any concept of country.

Piaget and Weil report that, following this initial pre-stage, the first proper developmental stage lasted from about 5 to 7–8 years of age. During this stage, the children knew that the name of their country was Switzerland, and they could answer that Geneva was in Switzerland when they were questioned verbally. However, when they tried to draw Geneva and Switzerland, they failed to show the correct spatial inclusion relationship between these two geographical units, and drew them as two separate circles side by side on the page instead. In addition, the children did not understand that they themselves were both Genevese and Swiss; instead, they would only say that they were one or the other, either Genevese or Swiss. For example, one child (aged 6;9, i.e., 6 years 9 months) responded as follows:

(What is Switzerland?) It's a country. (And Geneva?) A town. (Where is Geneva?) In Switzerland. [The child draws the two circles side by side, but the circle for Geneva is smaller.] I'm drawing the circle for Geneva smaller because Geneva is smaller. Switzerland is very big. (Quite right, but where is Geneva?) In Switzerland. (Are you Swiss?) Yes. (And are you Genevese?) Oh no! I'm Swiss now.

In addition, children at stage 1 sometimes expressed a preference for their own country, but sometimes they preferred other countries, apparently for idiosyncratic or subjective reasons. For example, one child (aged 5;9) said:

I like Italy. It's a nicer place than Switzerland. (Why?) I was there these holidays. They have the loveliest cakes, not like in Switzerland, where there are things inside that make you cry.

Piaget and Weil found that stage 2 lasted from about 7–8 to 10–11 years of age. They report that, during this stage, the children had a good grasp of the spatial inclusion relationship between Switzerland and Geneva (or Vaud), and were now able to express it not only through their verbal comments but also through their drawings. However, these children still did not understand the conceptual inclusion relationship between being both Swiss and Genevese (or Vaudois). For example, one child (aged 7;3) produced the following responses:

(What is Switzerland?) It's a country. (And Geneva?) It's a town. (Where is Geneva?) In Switzerland. [Drawing correct.] (What nationality are you?) I'm from Vaud. (Where is the canton of Vaud?) In Switzerland, not far away. [Drawing correct.] (Are you Swiss as well?) No. (How is that, since you've said that the canton of Vaud is in Switzerland?) You can't be two things at once, you have to choose; you can be a Vaudois like me, but not two things together.

At this second stage, the children invariably expressed a preference for their own home country over all other countries, based on their place of birth, their family loyalties, and their own sense of belonging. For example, one child (aged 8;3) said:

I like Switzerland because I was born there.

Another child (aged 8;9) said:

I like Switzerland because it's my own country. My mummy and daddy are Swiss, so I think Switzerland is a nice place.

Piaget and Weil report that stage 3 began at about 10–11 years of age. Children now understood not only the spatial inclusion relationship but also the conceptual inclusion relationship. For example, one child (aged 10;3) gave the following answers:

(What is your nationality?) I'm Swiss. (How is that?) Because my parents are Swiss. (Are you Genevese as well?) Naturally, because Geneva is in Switzerland. (And if I ask someone from Vaud if he is Swiss too?) Of course. The canton of Vaud is in Switzerland. People from Vaud are Swiss, just like us. Everyone living in Switzerland is Swiss and belongs to a canton too.

At this final stage, the children's attitudes to their own country were based on the collective abstract ideals of the national community. For example, one child (aged 11;2) said:

> I like Switzerland because it's a free country.

Another child (aged 11;5) said:

> I like Switzerland because it's the Red Cross country. In Switzerland, our neutrality makes us charitable.

According to Piaget and Weil, exactly the same three stages of development occurred in the children's understanding of foreign countries. During stage 1, up to 7–8 years of age, they exhibited a lack of both spatial knowledge and conceptual knowledge. Attitudes to other countries were subjective and idiosyncratic at this stage; for example, one child (aged 7;2) responded as follows:

> (Are there any differences between the different countries you know and the different people living there?) Oh yes. (Can you give me an instance?) Well, the Americans are stupid. If I ask them where the rue du Mont Blanc is, they can't tell me.

In stage 2, between 7–8 and 10–11 years of age, Piaget and Weil found that the children had mastered the spatial inclusion relationship between towns and countries, but still lacked the conceptual understanding. For example, one child (aged 9;11) gave the following answers:

> (Do you know any countries other than Switzerland?) Yes, Italy, France and England. (Do you know any town in France?) Yes, Paris and Lyons. [Draws their relationship to France correctly.] (And what are the people living in Paris?) French. (Are they Parisians too?) Oh no, you can't be two things at once.

Attitudes to foreign countries in stage 2 were based on stereotypes of the people who live in those countries, which had been picked up from the surrounding social environment. For example, one child (aged 8;2) made the following assertions:

> . . . the Germans are bad, they are always making war. The French are poor and everything is dirty there. Then I've heard of Russians too, they're not at all nice. (Do you have any personal knowledge of the French, Germans or Russians or have you read something about them?) No. (Then how do you know?) Everyone says so.

Finally, Piaget and Weil report that, in stage 3, from 10–11 years of age onwards, the children understood both the spatial and conceptual relationships between foreign towns and countries, and attitudes to foreign countries began to sound much more independent. For example, one child (aged 13;3) responded as follows (after mentioning a number of foreign countries):

> (Are there any differences between all those countries?) There is only a difference of size and position between all these countries. It's not the country that makes the difference, but the people. You find all types of people everywhere.

Thus, Piaget and Weil argued that children develop through three stages: in the first stage, children lack both spatial-geographical and conceptual understanding; in the second stage, from 7 years of age onwards, they master spatial-geographical inclusion relationships, but still do not understand more abstract conceptual inclusion relationships; in the third stage, from 10 years of age onwards, they finally master conceptual inclusion relationships as well. As far as affect is concerned, before 7 years of age, children do not necessarily exhibit any preference for their own home country, and instead exhibit idiosyncratic patterns of liking. At the second stage, they voice a clear preference for their own home country, based on an acceptance of ideas and traditions which are prevalent in their immediate environment. In the third stage, from 10 years of age onwards, children start to justify their preference for their own country by reference to the abstract collective ideals of their country.

The transitions in children's understanding which are proposed by Piaget and Weil to occur at the ages of 7 and 10 mean that their account is compatible with Piaget's broader stage-based theory of cognitive development, which postulates that children enter the concrete operational and formal operational periods at the ages of 7 and 10, respectively.[6] Similarly, the idiosyncratic and experientially-based attitudes to countries found before 7 years of age are characteristic of pre-operational thinking, while the ability to reason in terms of abstract collective ideals, found after the age of 10, is characteristic of formal operational thinking.

However, a significant problem with the report of the study given by Piaget and Weil is that they do not provide any quantitative data about

---

[6] We will examine this theory in detail later on in this book, in Chapter 7. In essence, it postulates that children's cognitive functioning in any particular conceptual domain is based on their domain-general cognitive capabilities (Piaget, 1950; Piaget & Inhelder, 1969). These underlying capabilities themselves develop through a sequence of four stages, namely the sensorimotor, the pre-operational, the concrete operational and the formal operational stages, with the transitions from one stage to the next occurring at approximately 2, 7 and 10 years of age. Thus, the theory proposes that the principal developmental changes that occur in any particular conceptual domain (such as geographical understanding of countries) must also take place at approximately 2, 7 and 10 years, as these changes are driven by the more profound changes that take place at these ages in children's underlying domain-general cognitive competencies.

exactly how many children at each age produced each type of response. Instead, they only provide a handful of selected illustrative examples of the different kinds of response. It is therefore unclear how many children did actually produce the responses which are said to be characteristic of each age. More recent research in fact suggests that Piaget and Weil's account ignores much of the variability which occurs in children's development in this domain, with the result that their account underestimates the real complexities of children's development. A more systematic study employing proper quantitative content analysis was conducted by Gustav Jahoda, and his findings contradict Piaget and Weil's account in several crucial respects.

Jahoda's critique of Piaget's account

In his study, Jahoda (1963a, 1964) interviewed 144 children aged between 6 and 11 years old. These children lived in the city of Glasgow in Scotland, which is one of the three countries making up Britain.[7] These children were interviewed about the spatial-geographical relationship which exists between Glasgow, Scotland and Britain. In addition to verbal questioning, Jahoda used a construction task in which a large rectangular board was used to represent Britain, two smaller boards were used to represent Scotland and England, and a brass disc was used to represent Glasgow. The children were asked to arrange these four items correctly in relationship to each other.

Jahoda found that four stages of geographical understanding were exhibited by the children. At the first stage, the children thought of Glasgow as a vague entity nearby which did not include their own location in geographical space. So when they were asked "Where is Glasgow?", they said things like "Beside the playground, in X street", and "It's up by the park there—you go round the corner" (both of these comments were made by 6-year-olds). These children also had no understanding of either Scotland or Britain. At the second stage, the children understood that Glasgow was the city in which they were located, but they still did not understand the concepts of Scotland or Britain, and showed no awareness that Glasgow was spatially located inside Scotland. For example, when asked where Scotland was, one 7-year-old child said "Scotland is a country outside Glasgow". At the third stage, the children understood that Glasgow was spatially located inside Scotland, but still did not understand that Scotland was a component part of Britain. For example, one 8-year-old child said "Scotland is a country. It's beside Wales and Ireland. Britain is mostly called Great Britain; it's sort of Scotland—another name for it." Finally, at the fourth stage, children understood that Glasgow was located inside Scotland, and that Scotland was a part of Britain.

---

[7] The other two countries are England and Wales. These three countries, together with the Province of Northern Ireland, make up the United Kingdom.

Contrary to Piaget and Weil's claims, Jahoda found that these four stages of development were not associated with particular ages. For example, among the 6- to 7-year-olds, there were some children who were at stage 1, others at stage 2, others at stage 3, and others at stage 4. Similarly, among the 10- to 11-year-olds, some children were at stage 2, others at stage 3, and others at stage 4. In other words, spatial-geographical understanding was not linked to age in a clear-cut manner. That said, however, the older children were more likely to be at a higher stage of development than the younger children. In addition, Jahoda found that middle-class children tended to be at higher stages of development than working-class children.

Jahoda also asked the children two specific questions about whether they were British and whether they were Scottish. The 6- to 9-year-olds sometimes (but not always) denied that they could be both. The most common explanation given by the children was the mutual exclusivity of the two categories: "You can't be two different things at once". By contrast, the 10- to 11-year-olds nearly always said that they were both Scottish and British.

Jahoda (1964) examined whether, despite the lack of a clear match between types of responses and age, all of the children could nevertheless still be classified into the developmental stage sequence postulated by Piaget and Weil. Remember that Piaget and Weil had proposed that less mature children do not exhibit either spatial understanding (e.g., that Scotland is included within Britain) or conceptual understanding (e.g., that a person can be both Scottish and British simultaneously); that intermediate level children exhibit spatial but not conceptual understanding; and that mature children exhibit both spatial and conceptual understanding. However, Jahoda found that a fourth pattern was sometimes exhibited by the children: almost a quarter of them understood the conceptual inclusion relationship between being Scottish and being British but did not yet understand the spatial inclusion relationship between Scotland and Britain. However, the Piagetian account implies that such a pattern should not be exhibited in practice, because spatial understanding should always be acquired before conceptual understanding. Jahoda's work therefore implies that Piaget and Weil's account of children's development is incorrect.

A more recent Piagetian account

Despite the fact that Jahoda's work shows that Piaget and Weil's own description of the development of children's large-scale geographical understanding is wrong, in more recent years several authors have argued in support of the broader Piagetian claim that children's geographical understanding is grounded in their domain-general cognitive capabilities. These authors suggest that there is a major discontinuity in the development of children's geographical knowledge at the age of 7, when they progress from the pre-operational to the concrete operational period.

For example, Piché (1977, 1981) assessed 5- to 8-year-old London children's geographical knowledge using verbal questioning, mapping exercises and geographic puzzles. The youngest children did not appear to construe individual geographical places as being linked together within a coherent spatial-geographical frame of reference. Instead, they viewed places as being the locations where things happen or where they themselves did particular things. As a consequence, active, affective and cognitive aspects of place appeared to be inter-mingled at this early age. The children subsequently learnt the names of some of these places, and could describe them in a more depersonalised manner, but still failed to link these places together within an integrated spatial-geographical framework. However, when the children entered the concrete operational period, they finally began to conceptualise the continuity of geographical space, and the children started to construct hierarchical relationships between locations such as home-London-England. That said, some of these children still had difficulties in grasping the idea that these relationships involved spatial inclusion, inventing solutions such as "London surrounds Buckingham Palace" and "England is linked with London". They also began to view the continuity of land in terms of the amount of time which is needed to travel from one place to another; for example, London is big because one can drive in it for a long time and still be in London, and Bournemouth is far away because it takes a long time to get there. Foreign countries now started to be imagined as real places which could be visited. Piché argues that the children's place representations only became properly integrated when they finally attained full concrete operational understanding at about 8 years of age.

The finding that children's geographical understanding is related to their domain-general cognitive development has also been obtained by other authors. For example, Daggs (1986; Downs, Liben, & Daggs, 1988) examined American children from school grades 1–3 (approximately 6–8 years old), testing their understanding of geographical hierarchical relationships and their abilities on Piagetian class inclusion and transitivity tasks. The children's geographical understanding was measured in two ways. First, they were questioned verbally about the geographical units in which they lived (including town, state and country) and about their understanding of the relationships between these units. For example, the children were asked "Are the people in (town X) in Pennsylvania?", "Can a person leave the United States and remain in Pennsylvania?", and "Would you explain that to me?". Second, the children were given a drawing task; they were shown a page containing a circle which was identified as a geographical unit, and the child was asked to draw another circle on the page which represented another kind of unit (e.g., "This circle shows Pennsylvania. Draw a circle to show (town X). Why did you put the circle showing (town X) there? Colour in Pennsylvania"). Class inclusion and transitivity were assessed using standard Piagetian tasks. Daggs found that performance on both of the geographical tasks was significantly correlated with performance on the class inclusion and the transitivity tasks: the better the child's performance on class inclusion and transitivity, the better the geographical understanding of the child.

Another recent study by Wilberg (2002), conducted with 4- to 7-year-old German children, produced similar findings. Wilberg administered a Piagetian test of class inclusion, and also asked the children a number of geographical questions. Effects associated with age were statistically controlled in this study. Wilberg found that the better the children's performance on the class inclusion task, the better their responses were to a number of geographical questions, including "Can you tell me in which country you live?", "Is X [name of town/city] in Germany or not in Germany?", and "If I draw a circle for Germany [interviewer draws a circle], where is your town/city? Could you please draw a circle for it?".

These studies by Piché (1977, 1981), Daggs (1986) and Wilberg (2002) therefore provide support for the broader Piagetian position that children's geographical understanding is related to their more general cognitive-developmental level. In other words, between 4 and 8 years of age, the development of children's thinking about large-scale geographical territories (particularly their thinking about nested geographical hierarchical relationships, such as those which exist between cities, regions and countries) does seem to be linked to the development of their underlying cognitive capacities, as the earlier work of Piaget and Weil (1951) had implied.

However, there are many other studies that have been conducted into the development of children's large-scale geographical knowledge that have not been based on Piaget's theoretical framework. In the remainder of this chapter, we examine these other non-Piagetian studies. We begin with those studies that have examined children's knowledge, beliefs and feelings about their own country, before looking at the studies that have examined children's knowledge, beliefs and feelings about foreign countries.

CHILDREN'S KNOWLEDGE, BELIEFS AND FEELINGS ABOUT THEIR OWN COUNTRY

Children's knowledge of their own country: The work of Gould

Gould (1973; Gould & White, 1986) examined children's knowledge of their home country using an approach based on the notion of mental maps. He tested Swedish children aged 7, 9, 11 and 13 years old. These children lived in central southern Sweden in the town of Jönköping, which is situated between the three major cities of Stockholm, Göteberg and Malmö. The children were asked to write down the names of all the villages, towns and cities in Sweden which they could think of, and they were given five minutes in which to complete the task. Gould then plotted the frequencies with which each place had been mentioned by the children on a map, and drew contours to link places that were mentioned with equal frequencies; these contours therefore represent an information surface. The information surfaces derived from the four age groups are shown in Figures 2.1 to 2.4.

At 7 years of age, the information surface was very low (see Figure 2.1). Around the town of Jönköping itself, there was a strong dome of local information, and there were three subsidiary peaks around Stockholm, Göteberg and Malmö. Elsewhere, the information surface was at zero level or just above it, with the exception of Kiruna in the north (where a miner's strike was receiving publicity on TV at the time that the data were being collected). By 9 years of age, the information surface had risen considerably (see Figure 2.2). The dome of local information was still present, and the peaks around the three major urban areas were also still evident. However, the information surface had begun to rise between Jönköping and the three cities, and a second hump of information had appeared to the north-east of Jönköping around the towns of Örebro (Ö on the map) and Linköping (L on the map). A corridor of information had also begun to appear from the local dome of information towards the long island of Öland; this island is a major holiday destination for families in southern Sweden. However, the children still knew very little about northern Sweden, with just a small information bump at Umeå, which is the northern capital. By the age of 11, the information surface for southern Sweden had risen still further. In addition, the children finally began to exhibit more knowledge about the north of the country, although they still had very little knowledge about central Sweden (see Figure 2.3). At 13 years of age, the process of filling in information between the peaks had continued still further (see Figure 2.4). However, Gould comments that it appeared as if a saturation level was now being reached.

This study therefore suggests that the developmental process begins with children acquiring information about their own local area and about the larger cities within the country. Subsequently, corridors of information seep out from these nodes to link them together. With this basic structure of nodes and links in place, the surface continues to rise as the filling-in process proceeds. Popular holiday destinations contribute to the process. In a similar study conducted with children living in Illinois in the US, Douglass (1969) found information peaks appearing over the larger states of the US, along with a corridor of information to Florida, the major holiday destination in the east of the country (similar to the information corridor which arose from Jönköping to the island of Öland). Gould reports that the amount of information which the children held about a region was related to the size of that

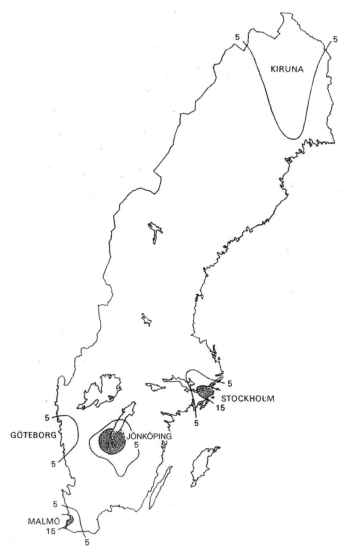

Figure 2.1. The information surface displayed by 7-year-old children living in Jönköping, Sweden (from Gould & White, 1986, p. 98; reprinted with permission from the authors).

region's population, and inversely related to its distance from Jönköping, with the principal exceptions consisting of popular holiday destinations and regions that receive coverage in the mass media.

In addition to examining their knowledge, Gould (1973) also examined the preferences of these Swedish children for different places within their own

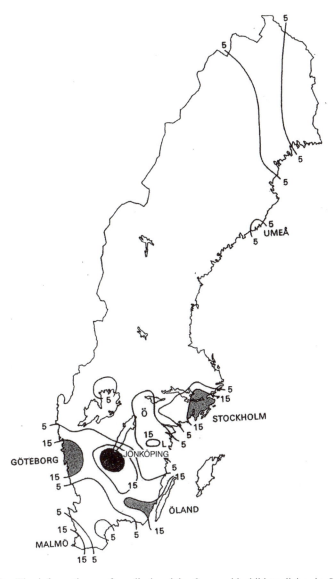

Figure 2.2. The information surface displayed by 9-year-old children living in Jönköping, Sweden (from Gould & White, 1986, p. 100; reprinted with permission from the authors).

country. The children worked directly on large maps showing the main regions, roads, towns and water bodies. The children were asked to mark on the map where they would most like to live, using numbers running from 1 to 70 to indicate their rank order of preference. The 7-year-olds were unable to

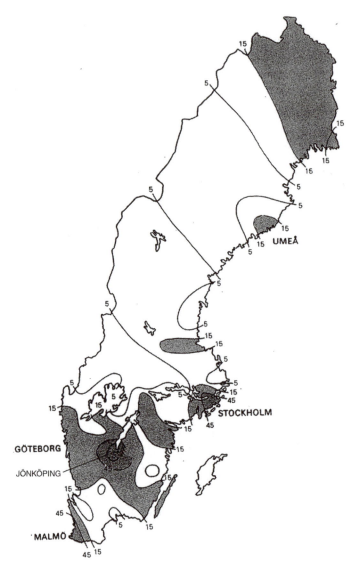

Figure 2.3. The information surface displayed by 11-year-old children living in Jönköping, Sweden (from Gould & White, 1986, p. 101; reprinted with permission from the authors).

perform the task. However, at 9 years of age, there was a strong local dome of desirability around Jönköping that stretched west to the city of Göteberg. Preferences declined in all directions from this ridge, but then rose once again to another lesser peak at the southern tip of Sweden around Malmö. The capital city, Stockholm, did not exhibit a peak but lay instead on a plateau of

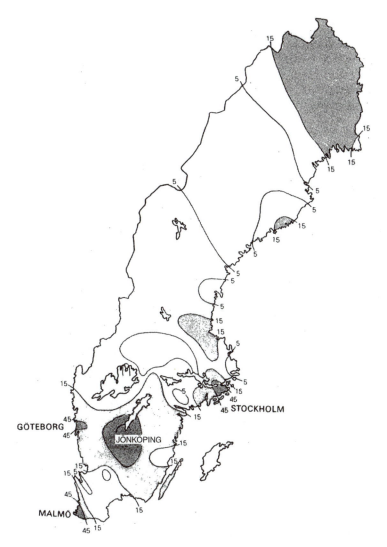

Figure 2.4.   The information surface displayed by 13-year-old children living in Jönköping, Sweden (from Gould & White, 1986, p. 102; reprinted with permission from the authors).

average values; the raw data revealed that this was because Stockholm had a split level of desirability, either very high or very low, and hence averaged out at the mean value. At 11 years of age, high preferences blanketed the whole of the south of Sweden, with a distinct north–south split. The Jönköping–Göteberg ridge had been joined by two other peaks, Halmstead to the south-west, and the island of Visby off the east coast; both of these are vacation areas. Stockholm continued to display its split image. However, at 13 years of age, Stockholm finally emerged as a major peak of desirability, joining the local area of Jönköping and the other two major cities of Göteberg and Malmö. The north of the country was still shunned by all the children. The preferences at 13 years were more discriminating than at earlier ages. Whereas the younger children generally blanketed the whole of the south with high scores, the 13-year-olds assigned their preferences with greater precision, with the major cities emerging much more clearly as peaks.

Gould (1973) reports that the children's information and preference scores were positively correlated with each other, but he also notes that there were exceptions (e.g., the children knew about Kiruna in the north, but shunned it completely in their preferences), and he observes that the relationship between cognition and affect in this domain is clearly complex. Gould's study provides a fascinating window onto how knowledge of, and preferences about, the child's own home country develop through the course of childhood into early adolescence.

Children's geographical knowledge of, and feelings about, their own country: Other studies

Gould's work implies that 7-year-olds generally have a low level of knowledge of their own country. However, 7-year-olds can often recognize their own country when shown a map or a satellite photograph of that country. McGee (1982) examined this issue with 6-, 8- and 10-year-old New Zealand children. He presented these children with a satellite colour photograph of New Zealand, and asked them what was shown in it. Over half of the 6-year-olds, all of the 8-year-olds except for one child, and all of the 10-year-olds correctly identified the photo as a picture of New Zealand. Notice that the task used by McGee was different from that used by Gould. Gould had asked his children to list the names of all the villages, towns and cities in Sweden that they could remember; in other words, this was a fairly demanding memory recall task. However, McGee showed his children a photograph and they merely had to name the place depicted in it; in other words, this was a much simpler recognition task. Recognition tasks are usually much easier for children than recall tasks (Flavell, Miller, & Miller, 2002; Kail, 1990). In interpreting the findings of such studies, it is vital to bear in mind the possible constraints that may have been applied to children's performance by the specific methods used; it is easy to underestimate levels of knowledge by using methods that make very high demands on children's cognitive systems.

That said, the work of both Gould (1973) and Piaget and Weil (1951) does clearly reveal that, while children are in the process of acquiring geographical knowledge about their own country, they also display distinctive patterns of affect towards this country and towards specific locations within it. A more recent study which has examined both the knowledge and the feelings which children have about their own homeland was conducted by Nugent (1994). He asked 10-, 12-, 14- and 16-year-old Irish children to write down their thoughts and feelings about Ireland. The written narratives produced by the children were then content-analysed. The descriptions of Ireland which were produced by the 10-, 12- and many 14-year-olds tended to focus on the man-made places, the physical geography, the ecology, and the flora and fauna of the country. For example, one of the 10-year-olds wrote:

I think Ireland is a beautiful place. Every summer the sun is shining in the sky. It is nice to live in Ireland and some mornings I wake up and hear the birds singing sweetly in the trees. Mostly I like the smell of fresh air. I think Ireland is the nicest place in the world. There are lots of other countries as well as Ireland but Ireland is full of beautiful towns and cities.

However, there was a quantitative and qualitative shift between 14 and 16 years of age, with the 16-year-olds producing much more abstract conceptualizations, and describing Ireland in terms of its history, traditions, culture and the Irish way of life. For example, one 16-year-old wrote:

Ireland is an island with its own traditions, culture, people and language. It is unique. We have a culture of our own and our own language which is unique in its descriptive qualities. Ireland is home to me and I am proud to be Irish. When I think of Ireland, I think of an island beside England and I think of its history of British occupation. At that stage, Irish people were made to feel inferior and ashamed of their culture and language. Present-day Ireland is a long way from the ideal Ireland where people live in harmony and share one culture.

As far as the children's emotional attachments to their country were concerned, Nugent reports that the 10-year-olds displayed unqualified, positive attachments to Ireland (as in the example above). Among the 12- and 14-year-olds, positive attachments were still apparent, but these children were more defensive towards their own country, often comparing it with other countries specifically in order to assert Ireland's superiority. At these ages, some of the children also expressed antagonism towards other countries. For example, one 14-year-old wrote:

I like Ireland because it is quieter than any other country, not like in other countries where people get shot every day, nearly.

The 16-year-olds instead tended to argue for the uniqueness rather than the superiority of Ireland's traditions and culture, as the following extract from a 16-year-old illustrates:

Ireland is a country with a culture of its own. It is a small country, but that does not matter, as long as it has its own characteristics that set it apart from other nations.

Nugent's study therefore implies that children's understanding of, and emotional attachments to, their own country change in a significant manner between 14 and 16 years of age.

A different approach was employed by Barrett and Davey (2001). They showed 5- to 10-year-old English children a set of photographs of typically English vs. non-English landscapes (as judged by English adults), and asked them to sort the photographs into the two sets.[8] They also assessed the children's emotional attachment to the various landscapes (by asking them "How would you feel about living in this place when you grow up?"), as well as their strength of national identification. The children's ability to sort the landscapes into English vs. non-English sets improved with age: the children's scores increased from 64% correct at 5–6 years, to 89% correct at 7–8 years, to 93% correct at 9–10 years. Attachment to the English landscapes also increased with age, while attachment to the non-English landscapes decreased with age. However, neither of the two attachment scores was correlated with the photograph differentiation scores when age was partialled out. As far as national identification was concerned, both the importance which the children ascribed to being English, and their degree of identification with being English (i.e., whether they felt very English, a little bit English, or not at all English), increased with age. The children's ability to differentiate between the two sets of photographs was correlated with both measures of national identification. However, neither measure of national identification was related to the emotional attachment scores. In other words, knowledge of the national homeland (as indexed by the photograph differentiation task) was related to the children's strength of national identification, but emotional attachment to the landscapes of the homeland was not.

The possibility of a link between children's knowledge of the geography of their own country and their strength of national identification was also examined by Barrett and Whennell (1998). They used a large battery of tasks to assess 5- to 11-year-old English children's geographical knowledge of the UK. Between them, the tasks assessed the children's knowledge of the four component parts of the UK (England, Scotland, Wales, and Northern Ireland), as well as their knowledge of the regions, cities, rivers, islands and seas surrounding the UK. The children's strength of identification with the nation

---

[8] The English landscapes included a picture of an English village located amongst green rolling hills, a picture of white cliffs on the south coast of England, etc., while the non-English landscapes included a picture of an Alpine village by a lake surrounded by snow-capped mountains, a picture of a tropical beach with palm trees, etc.

(i.e., with being English) and with the state (i.e., with being British) was also assessed. The children's knowledge of the UK increased as a function of age, with boys exhibiting higher levels of knowledge than girls. Correlations, with age partialled out, revealed that levels of geographical knowledge of the UK were positively correlated with both the degree of identification with being English and the degree of identification with being British (i.e., whether the child felt very, a little bit, or not at all English and British, respectively).

These last two studies are therefore consistent in revealing a relationship between the strength of national identification and levels of geographical knowledge of the homeland. However, the direction of the causality here remains ambiguous. It could be either that the acquisition of knowledge about the homeland strengthens children's national identifications, or that children who have strong national identifications are highly motivated to acquire information about their own country. That said, notice that this is the first time in this book that a relationship between the strength of national identification and some other aspect of children's national enculturation is being reported. Further examples of this kind of relationship will be reported in Chapters 4 and 6.

CHILDREN'S KNOWLEDGE, BELIEFS AND FEELINGS ABOUT FOREIGN COUNTRIES

Children's geographical knowledge of foreign countries: The work of Jahoda

We will now turn our attention to children's knowledge, beliefs and feelings about foreign countries. Once again, following the pioneering work of Piaget and Weil (1951), Jahoda (1962) was the first researcher to investigate children's knowledge of foreign countries. He used verbal interviewing to assess the knowledge of 6- to 11-year-old Scottish Glaswegian children. He began the interview by asking the children if they had heard of foreign countries, and if they had, they were asked to name them. Jahoda found that, round about the age of 8, the number of countries that could be named by the children increased substantially. Only 10% of the children aged less than 8 could name more than five countries, and 42% of these younger children could not name any foreign countries at all. However, among the 8- to 9-year-olds, 50% could name more than five countries, and only 10% could not name any foreign countries. Among the 10- to 11- year olds, the figures were 71% and 2%, respectively. The countries which were named most frequently by the children were, in order of decreasing frequency: France (named by 40% of the children), America (33%), Germany (32%), Africa (31%), India (28%), Australia (26%), Spain (26%) and Italy (25%).

Jahoda then asked the children to say which countries they liked best and which countries, if any, they disliked. The following pattern of development was found. At the age of 6–7 years, the children tended to like unusual and exotic countries (e.g., "It's nice and hot; you get coconuts there", 6-year-old) and countries in which relatives lived (e.g., "My auntie lives there", 7-year-old). Among these youngest children, 47% did not express any dislikes. However, among the 53% who did express a dislike, Germany was often identified, with past wars being used to justify this choice (e.g., "They fought against us", 6-year-old). Other occasional dislikes were based on minor concrete details which had been fortuitously acquired (e.g., "The butter is too salt", a 7-year-old's comment about New Zealand). At the age of 8–9 years, the children instead preferred familiar countries (such as holiday destinations) over unfamiliar countries. Stereotypical characteristics of these countries (e.g., sun, snow, skyscrapers, etc.) were used to justify these preferences. 32% of the 8- to 9-year-olds did not express any dislikes, but among those who did, the former enemy countries of Germany and Japan were once again singled out (e.g., "Because they bombed other countries", 9-year-old). Occasionally, other countries were disliked because of a misconception about their population (e.g., "Because of the head hunters", an 8-year-old's comment about Africa). At the age of 10–11 years, the children justified their preferences by reference to particular features of the country or of its people which they liked (e.g., "People are gay and friendly", 10-year-old; "I like all its mountains and the way there's a lot of snow", 11-year-old). 41% of these oldest children did not express any dislikes, but among those who did, Russia now topped the list of dislikes (the study was conducted during the Cold War era), with Germany also continuing to figure as a disliked country.

Jahoda also reports that there were social class differences in the children's knowledge and reasoning, with middle-class children tending to be more advanced in their thinking than working-class children. Notice that this finding echoes his finding of social class differences in his study of children's understanding of their own home country (Jahoda, 1963a): in that study too, the middle-class children were more advanced in their geographical understanding than the working-class children.

Children's geographical knowledge of foreign countries: The work of Wiegand

Wiegand (1991a) has also investigated children's knowledge about other countries. Two age groups of English children were assessed in this study, 7- to 8-year-olds and 10- to 11-year-olds. Both working-class and middle-class children were included, as were both ethnic majority (i.e., white English) and ethnic minority (Indian and Pakistani heritage) children. Wiegand asked these children to write down the names of all the foreign countries they knew, and to circle the places they had visited.

The younger children were generally only able to name about 5 or 6 countries. In addition to real countries, they sometimes also included "fantasy" places (e.g., Disneyland, Legoland, Never-never Land) and major cities (e.g., New York, Los Angeles and Paris) in their lists. These children tended to mention America, Africa, France, Spain, Russia, countries in the Indian subcontinent, China and Australia. Notice that these findings obtained with the younger children are broadly similar to Jahoda's (1962) findings. The older children were able to name 15 different countries on average, and some named more than 30 countries. In addition to the countries named by the younger children, the older children also named most Western European countries, and some of the larger countries of the Middle East. They also commonly paired America with Canada, Australia with New Zealand, and China with Japan. However, even these older children tended *not* to name many countries within the continent of Africa, Central or Eastern European countries, South East Asian countries, or Central or South American countries (with the exception of Brazil and Argentina, which were sometimes mentioned by the older boys, possibly because of the prominence of their national soccer teams).

Social class and ethnic group differences were apparent in the data. The middle-class children named twice as many countries as the working-class children. In addition, the children of Indian and Pakistani heritage exhibited more knowledge of the Indian subcontinent, Africa and the Middle East than the white English children; conversely, the white English children exhibited more knowledge of Western Europe than the children of Indian and Pakistani heritage. Wiegand subsequently interviewed the children in order to ascertain the extent and nature of their travel experience. He found that comparatively few of the children of Indian and Pakistani heritage had visited Western European countries, but that a third of them had visited India or Pakistan for a period of 6–12 weeks. As far as the white English children were concerned, only the middle-class children had visited other countries. More than 50% of these children had been to Spain and France, 16% had visited the USA, and some had been to Kenya and the Caribbean as well.

Wiegand (1995) subsequently conducted a further study, in which 4- to 11-year-old English children were asked to draw a map of the world. Wiegand found that France, Spain, America and Australia were prominent on the children's maps at all ages. However, there were few Central or South American countries (Brazil and Argentina again being the main exceptions), few Central and Eastern European countries, and few South East Asian countries. The countries which were included, and the omissions, were thus fairly similar to those which he had found using verbal methods in the previous study. As one might expect, the older children's maps were more accurate than the younger children's. The youngest children tended to produce maps which consisted of a set of enclosed shapes, mostly circular and of a similar size, placed randomly across the page, sometimes containing the names of individual countries (see Figure 2.5). With increasing age, the maps produced by the children became more accurate. From about 8–9 years, some individual countries were drawn using their distinctive shapes; the 8- to 9-year-olds also began to arrange at least some countries in their correct positions relative to each other (see Figure 2.6). The use of distinctive shapes and correct relative positions for countries became even more pervasive in the maps produced by the 10- to 11-year-olds, with some of the oldest children producing very accurate maps (see Figure 2.7).

Social group differences in children's knowledge of foreign countries

The study by Jahoda (1962) suggests that children's geographical knowledge of foreign countries varies according to both age and social class, while Wiegand's (1995) study suggests that such knowledge varies according to age, social class and ethnicity. Subsequent studies have confirmed that

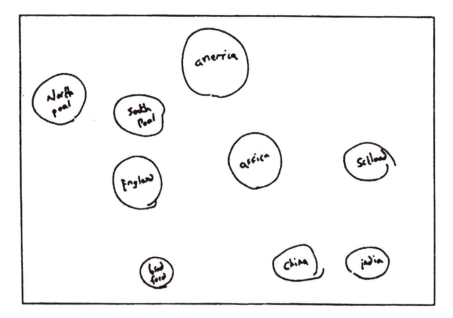

Figure 2.5   A freehand sketch map of the world drawn by a 6-year-old girl (from Wiegand, *International Research in Geographical and Environmental Education*, *4*, 1995, p. 22; reprinted with permission from Multilingual Matters).

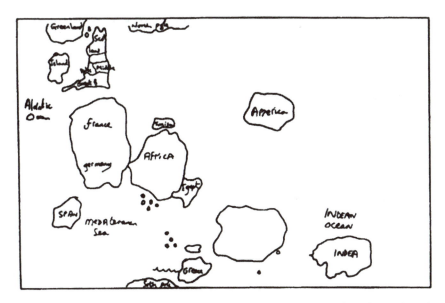

Figure 2.6   A freehand sketch map of the world drawn by a 8-year-old boy (from Wiegand, *International Research in Geographical and Environmental Education*, 4, 1995, p. 24; reprinted with permission from Multilingual Matters).

there are indeed differences in children's knowledge of foreign countries not only as a function of age, social class and ethnicity, but also as a function of gender, nationality, and children's geographical location within their own country.

For example, Barrett (1996) looked at 6-, 10- and 14-year-old English children's knowledge of European geography. When the children were asked for the name of the country in which they themselves lived, 83% of the 6-year-olds (and all of the 10- and 14-year-olds) answered this question correctly, with the majority of children referring to their country as "England", and just a small handful of children at each age calling it "Britain"; this pattern of response is also characteristic of English adults (Condor, 1996). The majority of the children at each age also knew that their own country was smaller than Europe (73%, 83% and 95%, respectively). However, unlike the two older groups of children, the 6-year-olds were typically unable to name *any* other European countries; by contrast, the 10-year-olds could name four to five other European countries on average, while the 14-year-olds could name six to seven. The countries mentioned tended to be Western European (i.e., France, Spain, Germany, etc.) rather than either Central or Eastern European countries. These findings were therefore broadly consistent with those of Jahoda and Wiegand. However, in addition to the differences associated with age, this study also found that, at all ages, boys tended to

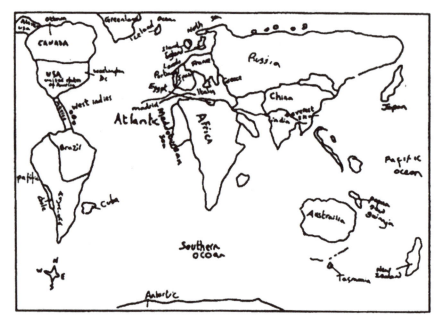

Figure 2.7 A freehand sketch map of the world drawn by a 9-year-old boy (from Wiegand, *International Research in Geographical and Environmental Education*, 4, 1995, p. 26; reprinted with permission from Multilingual Matters).

display higher levels of geographical knowledge than girls. For example, the boys could name significantly more European countries than the girls. The boys also provided significantly more correct answers than the girls to the question about whether their country was bigger or smaller than Europe.

Axia and Bremner (1992) instead examined 8- and 10-year-old Italian and English children's large-scale geographical knowledge by asking the children to draw maps of Europe. As one would anticipate, they found differences as a function of age: the 10-year-olds produced more detailed and more accurate maps than the 8-year-olds. However, in addition, Axia and Bremner found differences as a function of nationality: the Italian children produced more detailed and more accurate maps than the English children.

In interpreting the findings of this study (as well as the findings of Wiegand, 1995), it is important to bear in mind that map drawing is not an unproblematic method to use for assessing children's geographical knowledge. The production of a geographical map is a complex and demanding task for individuals of any age, but it is an especially difficult task for children. As a consequence, any group differences that are found (such as those between the 8-year-old and 10-year-old children) could be a result *either* of different levels of geographical knowledge *or* of different levels of drawing ability between the two groups of children. Drawing a map is a demanding task because it requires the child to plan the map in advance, to think about the constituent units of the map, and to plan very carefully the position, orientation and size of these units relative to one another before starting to draw. If all of these matters are not thought through in advance, then there is no guarantee that all of the constituent units will fit within the edges of the piece of paper on a suitable scale, and the map may end up being distorted as a consequence of the child trying to squeeze later elements onto an already overcrowded page. The child must also decide the sequence in which the constituent units of the map are to be drawn, and decide whether to draw the outline of the whole map first and fill in the details later, or whether to draw each major constituent unit in turn and to fill in its details before moving on to the outline of the next major unit. Finally, the drawing has to be physically executed; the production of a good map requires both good fine-motor skills and good perceptual monitoring skills. For all these reasons, a drawing of a map may easily underestimate or misrepresent a child's geographical knowledge.

Evidence that map drawing *does* underestimate children's geographical knowledge comes from McGee's (1982) study, mentioned earlier in this chapter. Recall that, in this study, 6-, 8- and 10-year-old New Zealand children were shown a satellite photograph of New Zealand, and asked to say what was shown in it. *Over half of the 6-year-olds*, all of the 8-year-olds except for one child, and all of the 10-year-olds, were able to name the country. In Wiegand's (1995) study, however, the maps which were drawn by the children did not usually start to exhibit *any* knowledge of the distinctive shapes of countries, including their own home country, until they were 8–9 years of age (see Figure 2.6). This discrepancy between the findings of these two studies is not surprising, given that map production is a much more difficult task than picture recognition.

Because of these considerations, and in order to control explicitly for the effects of different assessment methods, Barrett and Farroni (1996) conducted a study to compare English and Italian children's knowledge of the geography of Europe using a wide range of different methods. These methods included verbal interviewing, a physical arrangement task (in which children had to arrange pieces of cardboard representing countries into a map), an outline map interpretation task (which required the children to name the marked countries, and to place stickers representing mountains, rivers, lakes and towns onto the map), and a satellite photo interpretation task. This battery of tasks was administered to 7- to 11-year-old children in both England and Italy. It was found that, although there were indeed differences in levels of performance on the various tasks, all of the measures nevertheless correlated significantly with one another. In other words, those children who displayed higher levels of performance on one measure also displayed higher levels of performance on the other measures. The study also revealed pervasive differences in the children's geographical knowledge as a function of the children's age, nationality and gender: greater knowledge was exhibited by older children than by younger children, by Italian children than by English children (replicating the Axia & Bremner, 1992, finding), and by boys than by girls (consistent with the findings of Barrett, 1996).

These social group differences were, however, distributed differentially across the children's landmark, configurational and route knowledge. Landmark knowledge is knowledge that certain specific spatial-geographic locations exist; this includes knowledge of both man-made places (such as cities and countries) and natural features (such as mountains, seas, rivers and lakes). As we have seen, Gould's (1973) work suggests that rudimentary landmark knowledge probably constitutes children's earliest form of large-scale geographical knowledge, with later knowledge being structured around, and growing outwards from, these early initial landmarks. Configurational knowledge, by contrast, is knowledge of the spatial relationships that exist between different landmarks in terms of their direction and distance from each other (Golledge, Smith, Pellegrino, Doherty, & Marshall, 1985; Matthews, 1992). Finally, route knowledge is knowledge of the routes by which people can travel from one landmark to another, and how different routes interconnect at particular nodes (Allen, 1987; Matthews 1984). Barrett and Farroni (1996) found that the children's landmark knowledge of Europe varied according to their age and nationality but not their gender, their configurational knowledge of Europe varied according to their age, nationality and gender, while their route knowledge of Europe (e.g., of the route between Britain and Italy) varied according to their age and gender but not their nationality. (All these variations were in the directions noted at the end of the preceding paragraph.)

The existence of social group differences in children's large-scale geographical knowledge was confirmed in a subsequent study of 6- to 13-year-old English children conducted by Barrett, Lyons, Purkhardt, and Bourchier (1996; Bourchier, Barrett, Lyons, & Purkhardt, 1996), who also used a large battery of different assessment methods to measure the children's knowledge of European countries, cities, mountains, rivers, seas, etc. This study also found that older children displayed more knowledge than younger children, middle-class children displayed more knowledge than working-class children, and boys displayed more knowledge than girls. In addition, differences were found in children's knowledge according to their geographical location: children who lived in London exhibited higher levels of geographical knowledge than children who lived in a rural location on the borders of Surrey and Hampshire (in the south-east of England). The gender differences were, again, especially pronounced on measures tapping into the children's configurational knowledge, while the location (i.e., urban vs. rural) differences were most pronounced on the measures assessing the children's route knowledge. Measures of all three types of knowledge (landmark, configurational and route knowledge) were significantly correlated with the extent of the children's travel experience (differences associated with age were statistically controlled). A subsequent study by Rutland (1998), using very similar methods with 6- to 16-year-old English children, replicated the finding of a social class difference in geographical knowledge, and also found the same relationship between levels of geographical knowledge and the extent of children's travel experience.

Axia, Bremner, Deluca, and Andreasen (1998) conducted a more extensive study to compare the large-scale geographical knowledge of 8- and 10-year-old children living in northern Italy, southern Italy, England, Scotland, Spain and Switzerland. The children in all of these locations were asked to draw a map of Europe. This study also found that children living in different countries, and in different regions of the same country, exhibited different levels of geographical knowledge. For example, the northern Italian children included more European countries in their maps, and were more accurate in depicting both the location and shape of those countries, than children living in any other country. The northern Italian children also drew more detailed and more accurate maps than the southern Italian children. Interestingly, irrespective of location, the children's maps were often based around their own country, with the most accurately represented countries usually being those that were closest to the borders of their own country.

Finally, Jahoda and Woerdenbagch (1982) also found cross-national differences in levels of geographical knowledge among children. They gave 11- to 16-year-old Scottish and Dutch children the names of 12 countries: 4 Western European, 4 Eastern Bloc and 4 Commonwealth countries. The children were told that the countries belonged together in sets of four, and were asked to group them into their sets. They were also given various other tasks, including one in which they were asked if they had ever heard of "developing" or "Third World" countries, and to name some. On both tasks, the Dutch children exhibited higher levels of knowledge than the English children (although both groups of children generally exhibited very low levels of knowledge of supranational groupings such as the former EEC and Eastern Bloc).

The unambiguous message that emerges from this body of research (which has utilized a range of different research methods with a number of different populations both within and across countries) is that there are substantial and systematic differences in children's large-scale geographical knowledge as a function of their social group memberships. In particular, systematic differences in geographical knowledge of foreign countries have been found to occur not only as a function of children's age but also as a function of children's gender, social class, nationality, ethnicity and geographical location within their own country. The question that therefore arises is this: why do these differences occur?

Factors that influence geographical knowledge of foreign countries

A useful starting point for thinking about some of the factors that might impact on children's knowledge of foreign countries is a study conducted by Saarinen (1973). The participants in Saarinen's study were aged 16–18 years, and therefore a little older than the participants used in most of the other studies discussed in this book. Nevertheless, Saarinen's study serves to highlight several of the factors that are likely to influence children's acquisition of knowledge in this domain. Saarinen tested four groups of high school students, in the USA, Canada, Finland and Sierra Leone. These students were all given a blank piece of paper and asked to sketch a map of the world, labelling all of the places that they considered to be interesting or important.

Saarinen found that over half the names placed on the maps were those of countries. Continents and oceans were rarely named, except on the poorest maps. The only features of relatively small size that tended to be included were cities. There was a large preponderance of human over physical features drawn on the maps, with very few rivers, mountains, deserts, or lakes being included. A comparison of the maps drawn in the different countries enabled Saarinen to identify the factors influencing what was included in, and what was omitted from, the maps. The key factors were: (1) proximity, with countries closer to the student's own homeland being more likely to be included (consistent with the findings of Axia et al., 1998); (2) size, with larger countries being more likely to be included than smaller ones; (3) shape, with countries that have a distinctive shape (such as Italy's boot shape) being more likely to be included; (4) island vs. being landlocked, with islands being more likely to be included than landlocked countries; (5) peripherality, with places or islands that mark the furthest edge of a country or continent (such as Newfoundland or the Cape of Good Hope) being more likely to be included than less peripheral places; (6) presence within current affairs, with places which were being featured in the news media within a country at the time being more likely to be included (consistent with the findings of Gould, 1973); and (7) cultural links, with countries that have cultural relationships with the homeland (e.g., other Commonwealth countries in the case of the Canadian students) being more likely to be included.

Of course, an individual in Saarinen's study might have omitted a place because he or she had simply decided that it was not sufficiently interesting or important on a global scale to be included in the map. However, Saarinen's analysis is consistent with findings that have emerged from other studies using different methods (although, once again, these are studies that have been conducted with older students). For example, Gould and White (1986) examined American university students' knowledge of the USA, by asking them to write place names on a provided outline map. They found that levels of knowledge were affected by the distance of a place from the students' own location (with greater knowledge about nearby American states and cities), the size of a city or American state (with greater knowledge of the more populous cities and larger states), peripheral location (with greater knowledge of peripheral states such as California, Florida and Maine), distinctive shape (with greater knowledge of American states, such as Texas, which have a clearly recognizable shape), and travel field (with greater knowledge of places to which the individual had travelled). Fryman and Wallace (1985) also tested American university students, looking at these individuals' ability to recognize the names of 168 countries presented to them in a list. It was found that the recognizability of countries was related directly to their size: larger countries were more likely to be recognized than smaller ones. In addition, the students were asked to estimate the relative sizes of those countries that they did recognize. Fryman and Wallace found that the students' judgements were influenced by whether a country had cultural relations with the USA, and whether it was currently receiving coverage in the American mass media.

Notice that the various factors identified by these studies fall into two main categories. First, some of the factors (e.g., size, shape and peripherality) appear to be related to the potential memorability of a geographical place after it has been viewed on a map. Thus, countries (and American states) that are very large, that have a distinctive shape on a map (such as Italy), and that serve to end-anchor the furthest edges of a continent, are more perceptually salient on a map, and are therefore more likely to be remembered than countries (or American states) that do not exhibit these features. Second, some of the factors (e.g., distance, media coverage and cultural relations) appear to be related to an individual's likelihood of having been exposed to information about a foreign country (or American state). So, an individual is more likely to have been exposed to information about geographically proximal places (via personal travel to those places), countries that regularly appear in the mass media, and countries with which the individual's own country has cultural relationships of one kind or another. In other words, it seems probable that these factors exert their effects either via their impact on the memorability of map information, or via their impact on the exposure of an individual to information about a particular country.

Unfortunately, these kinds of studies have so far only been conducted with students in their late teens; comparable studies with children have not yet been conducted. In particular, there is a paucity of developmental-psychological research into the memorability of map information for children so far as maps of countries, continents and the world are concerned. However, research that has been conducted with children suggests that personal exposure to information about other countries is, indeed, one of the key factors that impacts on levels of geographical knowledge in children. Such exposure, in the case of children, typically occurs through one of three main routes: personal travel experience, educational input at school and the mass media (especially television).

The impact of travel experience, schooling and the mass media on children's knowledge of the geographies of other countries

It is certainly intuitively plausible that children's geographical knowledge about foreign countries is at least partially derived from their personal experiences of travelling to those countries, either on family holidays, school trips, or foreign exchange visits. This idea was examined by Moss and Blades (1994). They tested 8- and 11-year-old British children living in Britain, and 8- and 11-year-old British children living in Germany on British army bases. The latter group of children had not only lived in but had also visited more European countries than the former group. However, contrary to expectations, when the children's geographical knowledge of European countries was examined, it was found that the latter group of children did *not* in fact possess more knowledge than the former group overall. Similarly, Barrett (1996), Barrett and Farroni (1996) and Barrett et al. (1997) all failed to find any relationship between geographical knowledge of foreign countries and children's travel experience.

However, as noted already, Barrett et al. (1996; Bourchier et al., 1996) did find a relationship between travel experience and geographical knowledge of other countries. This study revealed that levels of landmark, configurational and route knowledge were all positively correlated with levels of travel experience (with age partialled out) in a group of 6- to 13-year-old English children. In addition, Barrett et al. found that the younger children, working-class children and rural children had travelled less than the older children, middle-class children and urban children. This suggests that the differences which were present in the children's geographical knowledge of foreign countries as a function of age, social class and location may well have been due to the more extensive travel experience of the older, middle-class and urban children. In another independent study, Rutland (1998) also found social class differences in both travel experience and geographical knowledge, as well as significant correlations between the two variables.

These findings are reminiscent of those of Weigand (1991a). Remember that he found differences in geographical knowledge as a function of children's ethnicity, as well as differences in the patterns of the children's travel experience that seemed to parallel those in their geographical knowledge. In another study, Wiegand (1991b) examined the travel experiences of 9- to 11-year-old English children much more directly. In this study, children who had travelled to India or Spain were given a word-association test, and their responses were compared to those of children who had not travelled to these countries. Not surprisingly, he found that, for both countries, children who had visited the country concerned provided much more accurate and diverse descriptions than children who had not visited it; the latter children instead gave more stereotyped and inaccurate details. For example, those who had not visited India tended to say that it was a place which was hot and dry, where people ate rice and curry, and lived in huts among herds of elephants. By contrast, those who had visited the country mentioned bazaars, mosques, wells, decorated trucks, taxis, motorcycles, sleeping under the stars, jewellery, beggars, thieves, bare feet, dogs, insects and snakes (rather than elephants). All of the children who had been there also produced positive evaluative responses (e.g., "nice", "exciting", "good", etc.). Wiegand followed these findings up by interviewing those children who had visited other countries, encouraging them to reflect on similarities and differences between those foreign places and their own country. He found that the children who had travelled were able to name accurately the countries and resorts that they had visited, and could provide detailed information about the routes taken, including ferry crossings and airports, and could relate these to an atlas map. These children also had a good understanding of scale and distance, and weather was a particularly salient feature of the foreign countries that had been visited. These travelled children viewed stereotypes of the countries that had been visited very cautiously, evaluating them against their own personal experience. Some of the children also appeared to have generalized their sceptical attitude to stereotypes of other countries that they themselves had not visited.

Turning to the effects of education on children's geographical knowledge, Axia et al. (1998) found that 10-year-old children who had received formal instruction at school about European geography produced more accurate and detailed maps of Europe than 10-year-old children who had not received such instruction. This finding applied irrespective of the children's nationality. Notice that this finding suggests that cross-national differences in children's levels of geographical knowledge may be, at least in part, a consequence of the different educational curricula and practices which are used in different countries. For example, the studies by Axia and Bremner (1992), Barrett and Farroni (1996) and Axia et al. (1998) all consistently revealed that English children typically have lower levels of large-scale geographical knowledge than northern Italian children. In the 1990s, when these studies were executed, England and Italy operated very different school curricula. In Italy, the National Curriculum for Elementary Schools (Laeng, 1985) required all 10-

to 11-year-old Italian children to be taught about all of the countries in Europe and about their geographical, political, economic and social relationships with one other. By contrast, in England, the National Curriculum in Geography (Department of Education and Science, 1991) only required English children to know, by the age of 11, the names of four European countries beyond the British Isles (i.e., France, Germany, Spain and Italy). The fact that the English children in these studies had lower levels of geographical knowledge than their Italian peers is therefore not surprising (and it is perhaps much more surprising that the southern Italian children did not display higher levels of knowledge than the English children in the study by Axia et al., 1998).

However, in schools, geographical knowledge is not only acquired from teacher instruction but also from other incidental sources. Stillwell and Spencer (1973) examined 9-year-old English children's acquisition of information about other countries from classroom posters, maps and wall charts. They began by assessing the children's knowledge about India, Germany, Russia and the USA. They then mounted displays about these countries on the walls of the children's classrooms for a period of one week, and after this period they retested the children. They found that the children had acquired information about all four countries from the displays, even though they had not received any formal instruction about them from their teacher. It is noteworthy that Italian children may well have more non-curricular information about other countries available to them in their classrooms than English children. For example, Barrett and Farroni (1996) observed in the course of conducting their study that Italian school classrooms were much more likely to have a map of Europe on permanent display than English classrooms. A similar observation has been made by Axia (personal communication). Hence, the cross-national differences in geographical knowledge which have been found in children may stem not only from differences in the school curricula in different countries but also from differences in the general availability of information about other countries in children's everyday environments.

In addition to travel experience and schooling, the mass media (especially television, but also books, magazines and comics) can also provide children with information about other countries. One interesting study which has demonstrated the influence of the mass media on children's representations of other countries has been reported by Holloway and Valentine (2000). They asked 13-year-old children in Britain and New Zealand (over 1,000 children in total) to email each other with descriptions of what they thought the other country and its people were like.

The British children all placed New Zealand in the southern hemisphere, many located it in relationship to Australia, and some noted that it consisted of two main islands. Many of them also displayed stereotypical ideas about what it means to be "in the south" (hot, potentially beautiful, but also potentially dangerous as nature there is wild and untamed). There was widespread agreement among the British children that New Zealand is populated by large numbers of sheep. The majority of British children thought that New Zealanders looked like British people but with a better suntan (an inference they appeared to have drawn from their belief that it was hot and sunny in New Zealand). New Zealand was also sometimes regarded as an offshoot of Australia, and considerable numbers of British children thought that the native population were Aborigines rather than Maoris. Many also thought that New Zealanders wore hats with corks dangling from them.

The New Zealand children, in their turn, located Britain in the northern hemisphere, many positioning it in relationship to mainland Europe. Some thought it was made up of two principal islands, while others thought it was attached to a continental landmass. Many of the children thought it was cold and wet (although some thought that cold and wet winters were accompanied by hot and sunny summers). Some New Zealand children held romantic notions of the British countryside (green hills, stone walls, thatched cottages, etc.), a view of urban housing as being old and quaint (old terraced houses, cobblestone streets, etc.), but many of them also talked about British cities as being big, exciting and ultra-modern places. British people were often described as having pale skins (an inference apparently drawn from beliefs about the climate). In general, Britons were thought to live in a more exciting, albeit colder and wetter, urban environment than New Zealanders.

Holloway and Valentine discovered that both groups of children had derived many of their images of the other country from movies, television programmes (particularly soap operas), and adverts. For example, in their descriptions of Britain, the New Zealand children often referred to "Coronation Street" (a British soap opera, which was watched by many of the children's mothers):

> The houses are old and of an older style than seen in New Zealand. They often have two storeys and no front or back gardens like Coronation Street.

> I assume your house is like the ones off Coronation Street as these are the only British houses I have seen.

By contrast, the British children had not seen many TV programmes or movies about New Zealand itself. Instead, they drew on images of Australia which are available in Britain through soap operas such as "Neighbours" and "Home and Away", movies such as "Crocodile Dundee", and adverts for Foster's Lager:

> We think you probably dress like Crocodile Dundee in Bermuda shorts and a hat with corks dangling.

In addition, some of the children appeared to have constructed their images of the other country on the basis of information that had been acquired during trips to the local supermarket:

> I know for a fact that New Zealand is hotter than England. I think one of your main industries would be farming e.g., sheep farming because when I buy lamb in the shop it says "a New Zealand lamb".

There is, in fact, large-scale export of lamb from New Zealand to Britain, and New Zealand lamb products are usually on prominent display in British supermarkets. Holloway and Valentine suggest that globalized trade seems to have had the rather interesting side effect of providing the current generation of children (at least those who live in the more affluent economies) with a greater volume of information about other countries than would have been available to children in earlier generations.

Hence, there is good evidence that children learn about other countries from travel experience, school and the mass media. Notice that these sources of information are all likely to vary as a function of numerous factors, including children's age, social class, nationality, ethnicity and locality. Thus, older children typically have acquired more travel experience than younger children, affluent middle-class children tend to have more opportunities to travel to other countries than working-class children, ethnic majority and ethnic minority children often visit different countries abroad, and children living in different localities may also have different levels of travel experience. Children's schooling also varies according to age, nationality and locality, and possibly ethnicity and social class as well (e.g., in countries with diversified school systems). The television programmes and adverts that children watch, and the books, magazines and comics that they read, also vary according to age, gender and nationality, and possibly ethnicity as well. Thus, it is almost certainly because children's travel experience, schooling and exposure to the mass media (their three primary sources of information about other countries) vary as a function of all these various factors that children's knowledge about other countries also varies according to the same set of factors.

Gender differences in children's geographical knowledge of other countries

The one social group difference that has been found to occur in children's geographical knowledge that is perhaps somewhat harder to explain is the gender difference between boys and girls: boys often display higher levels of large-scale geographical knowledge than girls (Barrett, 1996; Barrett & Farroni, 1996; Barrett et al., 1996; Barrett & Whennell, 1998). Some of the variance here may be attributable to the different mass media sources to which boys and girls attend. For example, boys probably watch international sporting fixtures on television to a much greater extent than girls, because of their higher level of interest in sport (Beal, 1994), and indeed Wiegand (1991a) speculates that one possible reason why the English boys in his study included Argentina and Brazil in their lists of foreign countries more frequently than girls could be because these two countries have prominent national soccer teams.

However, other factors may be operating here as well. As we have seen, the various studies in this field have actually examined all sorts of different kinds of knowledge that an individual can have about a foreign country. Studies have varied in terms of whether they have examined children's landmark knowledge, configurational knowledge, route knowledge, knowledge of climates, knowledge of flora and fauna, knowledge of typical landscapes and cityscapes, knowledge of the lifestyles that people lead in other countries, etc. These are all very different types of knowledge. It is noteworthy that the superior knowledge of boys has been documented to date primarily in relationship to children's configurational knowledge (Barrett & Farroni, 1996; Barrett, et al., 1996).

Given the fact that it is children's configurational knowledge that tends to show this effect, it is possible that, in addition to the impact of the mass media, motivational and/or cognitive factors could also be contributing to the production of this gender difference. Motivationally, it could be the case that girls are just as capable as boys in cognitively constructing integrated spatial-configurational representations of other countries, but are simply less inclined to do so, because their primary interests lie elsewhere, in other types of knowledge about foreign countries (e.g., in the people, the flora and fauna, and the lifestyles that people lead in other countries). However, a cognitive explanation is also possible. As we have seen, children's earliest large-scale geographical knowledge probably consists of rudimentary landmark knowledge (Gould, 1973), and such knowledge is presumably acquired on an item-by-item basis; thus, on one occasion a child might learn of the existence of France, on another occasion he or she might learn of the existence of Italy, etc. If this is the case, then such learning is probably heavily dependent on the availability of information in children's environments, and so there is no reason to expect gender differences as far as the acquisition of landmark knowledge is concerned (other than those that stem from the different information sources to which boys and girls attend). However, the construction of spatial-configurational representations probably requires additional cognitive skills over and above those required to acquire landmark knowledge. For example, on one occasion the child might learn about the spatial relationship between Spain and France, and on another occasion the child might learn about the spatial relationship between France and Germany. However, the child then has to integrate the two items of information cognitively, to construct a single representation of the three-way relationship between Spain,

France and Germany. It is possible that boys have an advantage over girls in their facility for linking up and integrating separate spatial-relational items into more general representations. Such an interpretation would be consistent with the findings of research into gender differences in children's spatial cognition (e.g., Bettis, 1974; J.M. Connor, Schackman, & Serbin, 1978; J.M. Connor & Serbin, 1977; L.J. Harris, 1981; Matthews, 1987; see Matthews, 1992, for a detailed review), which indicates that such differences are especially prevalent in tasks that involve both spatial orientation and spatial visualization. Thus, the gender differences that occur in children's large-scale configurational knowledge could be due to the fact that boys have an advantage in the cognitive construction of integrated spatial-configurational representations.

Children's feelings about foreign countries

We have been noting throughout this chapter that children do not only acquire knowledge about other countries; they also acquire attitudes towards and feelings about those countries. These attitudes and feelings have been assessed by different investigators in various ways, including open-ended interviewing, free associations, paired comparisons, card sorts and rating scales. Piaget and Weil (1951) used interviewing, and they found idiosyncratic likes and dislikes about foreign countries being expressed by Swiss children up until 7–8 years of age; at 7–8, an affective preference for Switzerland over all other countries emerged. Jahoda (1962) also used interviewing to investigate Scottish children's feelings about other countries, and found that children younger than 8 years felt positively about countries which were unusual and exotic, but otherwise tended to express random likes and dislikes based on haphazardly acquired items of information about particular countries; after the age of 8, the children preferred familiar to unfamiliar countries, basing their attitudes on either stereotypical images of the distinctive physical features of countries or stereotypes of the people who live in those countries. Wiegand (1991b) instead used a free association task; he found that when children had visited either India or Spain, they produced positive evaluative responses to those countries.

In his study, Jahoda also found that the Scottish children he interviewed tended to exhibit negative feelings towards Germany at all ages, and used past wars to justify these feelings. This finding, that children typically view traditional enemy countries more negatively than other countries, was also obtained by Johnson (1966, 1973), who assessed 8- to 10-year-old English children's feelings about other countries using a rating scale. This consisted of a stick labelled *"like very much indeed"* at one end, and *"dislike very much indeed"* at the other end; the children had to place dolls with the names of the countries hanging around their necks at the position on the scale which showed how they felt about that country. Johnson found that, overall, the children felt negatively about Germany, Japan and Russia. Examining the idea that these negative attitudes might stem from their reading habits, he discovered that those children who regularly read war comics held the most negative attitudes towards the 'enemy' countries of Germany, Japan and Italy, and the most positive attitudes towards the Allied countries of England, America, Australia and France.

Johnson, Middleton, and Tajfel (1970) used the same rating scale to assess the feelings of English 7-, 9- and 11-year-olds towards a number of countries. They found that the children tended to rate their home country, England, more positively than other countries, with this preference for England becoming more pronounced with age. Jaspers, van de Geer, Tajfel, and Johnson (1972) instead measured 7- to 11-year-old Dutch children's feelings towards different countries using a method of paired comparisons. They too found that the children preferred their own home country over all other countries, with this preference becoming more pronounced with age. However, Middleton, Tajfel, and Johnson (1970) re-examined the data from the Johnson et al. (1970) study, inspecting the data for each individual child. They discovered that, although the mean scores for each age group suggested that the children preferred their own country to all other countries, in fact only 22% of the 7-year-olds, 44% of the 9-year-olds, and 56% of the 11-year-olds had actually rated England higher than all other countries. Thus, while mean scores may suggest that children always prefer their own home country from 7 years of age onwards, this general trend may actually mask considerable individual variability, with many children preferring at least one other country to their own.

The relationship between children's knowledge of, and feelings about, foreign countries

Because children acquire both factual knowledge and feelings about foreign countries at the same time, there is the possibility that the two are related. For example, having positive feelings about a country might motivate the child to learn more about that country, whereas having negative feelings about a country might predispose the child to avoid information about it. Another possibility is that the reverse causality applies: a child might feel more positively about some countries as a direct consequence of knowing a lot about them (and the findings of Wiegand, 1991b, do imply that this might be the case).

Early research by Tajfel (1966) suggested that while children usually have at least some knowledge about countries towards which they feel positively, they often have little or no factual knowledge about countries towards which they feel negatively. In their study with 9-year-old English children, Stillwell and Spencer (1973) assessed the children's feelings towards the four targeted foreign countries. In an initial session (before the children had been exposed to information about these countries via posters and wall charts), it was found that the children had the most factual knowledge about countries towards which they felt positively, less knowledge about countries which were regarded neutrally, and the least knowledge about the countries they disliked. Stillwell and Spencer then exposed the children to the information via the posters and wall charts. After one week, the children's feelings towards the target countries were assessed again, and it was found that, in general, the acquisition of knowledge had led to more positive feelings. However, there was a notable exception. In the case of one of the target countries, India, exposure to information about that country had actually had the opposite effect, with the children's feelings shifting from positive (prior to information exposure) to negative (after exposure). Stillwell and Spencer speculate that this might have occurred because the information provided emphasized the differences between India and Britain. This particular finding implies that the relationship between knowledge and affect might actually be rather complex, and could vary depending on the child's own country and the specific foreign country involved.

Johnson et al. (1970) also explored the relationship between geographical knowledge and feelings in their sample of 7-, 9- and 11-year-old English children. Like Stillwell and Spencer, they used a test of factual knowledge and an affect rating scale, but they obtained different results. Instead of a linear relationship between knowledge and affect, they found a curvilinear relationship. The children had the highest levels of knowledge about the countries they liked, the lowest levels of knowledge about the countries about which they felt neutrally, and an intermediate level of knowledge about the countries they disliked.

More recently, Giménez, Belmonte, Garcia-Claros, Suarez, and Barrett (1997) also investigated this issue with 6- to 15-year-old Spanish children. They did not find any relationship between the children's affect for and geographical knowledge about countries. However, when these Spanish data were amalgamated with additional data collected from British and Italian 6- to 15-year-olds, Barrett et al. (1997) found, in the sample as a whole, small but statistically significant linear, not curvilinear, relationships between the children's factual geographical knowledge about Spain, Britain and Italy and their feelings towards these three countries, with the correlations ranging in magnitude from 0.12 to 0.17. That said, there were no significant relationships between the children's knowledge and feelings about either France or Germany.[9]

Because of these discrepancies in the findings of the different studies, this

---

[9] These data were collected as part of the CHOONGE project, which will be described in greater detail in Chapter 5 of this book.

issue was investigated in greater detail by Bourchier, Barrett, and Lyons (2002), who tested 6- to 13-year-old English children. Whereas previous studies had either measured differences in mean levels of knowledge about liked vs. neutral vs. disliked countries (e.g., Johnson et al., 1970; Stillwell & Spencer, 1973) or used simple bivariate analysis (e.g., Barrett et al., 1997), Bourchier et al. used multiple regression. The children's geographical knowledge of five different target countries (France, Germany, Ireland, Italy and Spain) was measured, as was the children's affect towards these countries. In addition, the children's travel experience to each country was assessed. Multiple regressions were run to examine, for each individual target country: (1) whether the demographic variables of social class (middle-class vs. working-class), age, gender and locality (urban vs. rural) predicted the children's levels of travel experience to that country; (2) whether travel experience to that country predicted, independently of the demographic variables, the children's affect for that country; and (3) whether affect for a country, independently of the demographic variables and levels of travel experience, was related to the children's geographical knowledge of that country. The results of these analyses are shown in Figures 2.8 to 2.12.

The children's travel experience was sometimes, although not always, predicted by age and social class, with older children and middle-class children typically having higher levels of travel experience than younger children and working-class children, respectively. In addition, in the case of three of the target countries, travel experience predicted affect: children who had visited France (see Figure 2.8), Ireland (see Figure 2.10) and Spain (see Figure 2.12) exhibited more positive affect for these countries than children who had not visited them (NB the negative β weights shown in the path diagrams between travel experience and affect are due to the direction of scoring of the affect variable). This relationship between travel and affect did not apply in the case of either Germany (see Figure 2.9) or Italy (see Figure 2.11), however.

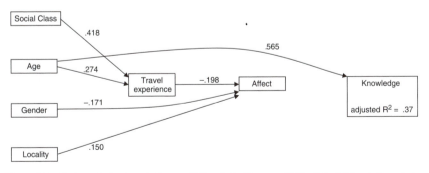

Figure 2.8   Path analysis of variables predicting 6- to 13-year-old English children's knowledge of France (Reprinted from Bourchier et al., 2002, p. 86, *Journal of Environmental Psychology*). Copyright © 2002. Reproduced with permission of Elsevier.

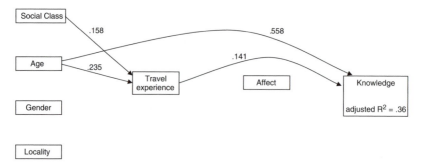

Figure 2.9   Path analysis of variables predicting 6- to 13-year-old English children's knowledge of Germany (Reprinted from Bourchier et al., 2002, p. 87, *Journal of Environmental Psychology*). Copyright © 2002. Reproduced with permission of Elsevier.

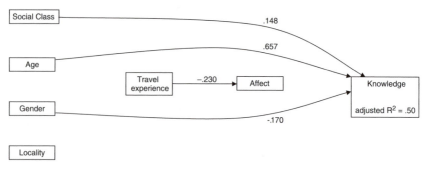

Figure 2.10   Path analysis of variables predicting 6- to 13-year-old English children's knowledge of Ireland (Reprinted from Bourchier et al., 2002, p. 88, *Journal of Environmental Psychology*). Copyright © 2002. Reproduced with permission of Elsevier.

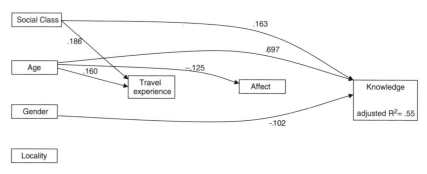

Figure 2.11   Path analysis of variables predicting 6- to 13-year-old English children's knowledge of Italy (Reprinted from Bourchier et al., 2002, p. 89, *Journal of Environmental Psychology*). Copyright © 2002. Reproduced with permission of Elsevier.

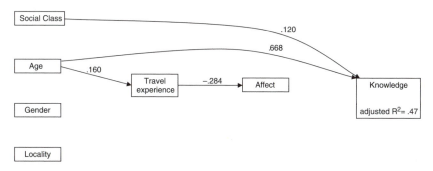

Figure 2.12   Path analysis of variables predicting 6- to 13-year-old English children's knowledge of Spain (Reprinted from Bourchier et al., 2002, p. 90, *Journal of Environmental Psychology*). Copyright © 2002. Reproduced with permission of Elsevier.

Notice that, in all five sets of analyses, there was no relationship at all between the children's affect for a particular country and their geographical knowledge of that country. Thus, even though there were sometimes significant bivariate correlations between knowledge and affect for some target countries, these correlations vanished once the covariance of the two variables with travel experience and demographics had been taken into account statistically. In addition, travel experience only predicted geographical knowledge in the case of Germany; for the other four target countries, there was no relationship at all between travel experience and knowledge. In interpreting this finding, it is important to note that the type of knowledge which was assessed in this study was primarily landmark and configurational knowledge. It is possible that, had other types of geographical knowledge been assessed (e.g., knowledge of landscapes, flora and fauna, or climate), travel experience might have predicted the children's levels of knowledge.

It can be seen from Figures 2.8 to 2.12 that the overall patterns of relationships between the different variables varied according to the particular target country concerned. In the case of France (Figure 2.8), only age predicted knowledge; in the case of Germany (Figure 2.9), both age and travel experience predicted knowledge; in the case of Ireland (Figure 2.10) and Italy (Figure 2.11), age, social class and gender all predicted knowledge (with middle-class children and boys having greater knowledge than working-class children and girls, respectively); while in the case of Spain (Figure 2.12), only age and social class predicted knowledge (with middle-class children having greater knowledge than working-class children). These findings caution against drawing any oversimplistic conclusions about the determinants of children's geographical knowledge of other countries, as different influences may well be operating for different foreign countries. Furthermore, the sheer variability in the patterns of relationships suggest that it could be the case that, had other target countries been used, a relationship between affect and knowledge might have been found for at least some of these other countries.

However, if such relationships between knowledge and affect do sometimes exist, it needs to be borne in mind that this relationship may not always be positive: recall that Stillwell and Spencer (1973) found that an increase in knowledge about India actually had the effect of making children feel more *negative* about this particular country. The overall conclusion to be drawn from these various studies, therefore, is that the patterns of relationships between variables in this domain are complex and can vary considerably, depending on the specific target country concerned. We certainly cannot naïvely assume that simply exposing children to greater levels of information about other countries through either personal travel experience, schooling or the mass media will always increase children's levels of positive affect towards other countries. Further research is clearly required to unpack the full pattern of complex interrelationships that apply to children's development in this area.

SUMMARY

The conclusions which can be drawn from the body of research that has been reviewed in this chapter are as follows.

- As far as Piagetian research is concerned:
  - the early claim made by Piaget and Weil (1951), that children's understanding of, and attitudes to, countries develop through a sequence of stages, has not been supported by subsequent research
  - however, some aspects of children's large-scale geographical understanding (e.g., their understanding of nested hierarchical spatial-geographical relationships, such as those between cities and countries) are related to their domain-general cognitive capabilities between 4 and 8 years of age.
- As far as children's geographical knowledge of, and attitudes to, their own country are concerned:
  - such knowledge starts to develop from about 5 or 6 years of age onwards
  - this knowledge probably begins with children first learning about their own local area and the larger cities within the country, with later knowledge being structured around, and growing outwards from, these initial landmarks
  - the amount of information that children acquire about a location in their own country is related to the size of that location's population, and inversely related to its distance from the child's own location,

with the principal exceptions consisting of holiday destinations and locations that receive coverage in the mass media.
- however, even as early as 6 years of age, some children are already able to recognize the shape of their own country from a map or satellite photograph, even though they may not yet be able to depict that shape accurately in a map themselves
- a positive correlation has been found to exist between children's knowledge of the geography of their home country and the strength of their national identification
- there may be a shift in how adolescents spontaneously think and feel about their own country around 15 years of age, away from thinking about it primarily in terms of its man-made places, natural physical geography, and flora and fauna, towards thinking about it in terms of its history, culture, traditions and way of life.

- As far as children's geographical knowledge of, and attitudes to, foreign countries are concerned:
  - such knowledge begins to develop at a slightly later age than knowledge of the home country, with a significant increase in knowledge of foreign countries occurring at around 8 years of age
  - there are widespread differences in knowledge of the geographies of other countries as a function of children's gender, social class, nationality, ethnicity, and geographical location within their own country
  - children acquire information about other countries from travelling to other countries, from formal teaching at school, from incidental sources such as posters and wall charts, and from the mass media
  - children's preferences for other countries can be rather haphazard and idiosyncratic before about 7 years of age, although an exception occurs in the case of traditional enemy countries, which are often disliked from an earlier age
  - from 7 years of age onwards, children usually exhibit a preference for their own country over all other countries, with this preference strengthening still further through middle childhood
  - however, certain other countries may still be very positively liked, and may even be preferred to their own country, by individual children
  - children sometimes exhibit more positive affect towards countries they have visited
  - however, there does not appear to be any consistent relationship between the way that children feel about a particular country and the amount of factual knowledge they acquire about that country.

CHAPTER THREE

Children's knowledge, beliefs and feelings about the state construed as a political entity

In Chapter 1, we saw that a state can be defined as a sovereign political entity in which a government uses a set of institutions to exercise an administrative monopoly over a territory that has clearly demarcated borders, where the rule of that government is sanctioned by law, and where that government has the capacity to use coercion and violence in order to enforce its policies within that territory. In this chapter, we will focus on the development of children's understanding of, and attitudes towards, the government of states, state territorial borders, state administration, law, and the role of the police and the military in the running of states.

A large volume of research has been conducted since the late 1950s into the development of children's political understanding (e.g., Amadeo, Torney-Purta, Lehmann, Husfeldt, & Nikolova, 2002; Berti, 1994, 2005; Berti & Andriolo, 2001; Berti & Benesso, 1998; Berti & Ugolini, 1998; Berti & Vanni, 2000; Bynner & Ashford, 1994; Connell, 1971; Dennis, Lindberg, & McCrone, 1972; Dennis, Lindberg, McCrone, & Stiefbold, 1968; Easton & Dennis, 1965, 1969; Easton & Hess, 1961, 1962; Emler & Frazer, 1999; Flanagan & Tucker, 1999; Greenstein, 1960, 1961, 1965; Hahn, 1998; Haste & Torney-Purta, 1992; Hess, 1963; Hess & Easton, 1960, 1962; Hess & Torney, 1967; Jennings & Niemi, 1968; Moore, Lare, & Wagner, 1985; Nie, Junn, & Stehlik-Barry, 1996; Niemi, 1974; Niemi & Junn, 1998; Niemi & Kent, 1974; Torney, Oppenheim, & Farner, 1975; Torney-Purta, 2002; Torney-Purta, Lehmann, Oswald, & Schulz, 2001; Torney-Purta, Schwille, & Amadeo, 1999; Weissberg, 1974; Youniss, McLellan, & Yates, 1997). Some of this research is somewhat tangential to the principal concerns of the current book, as it relates either to children's knowledge of specific social issues and debates within their own countries or local communities, or to children's own personal patterns of civic engagement and participation. That said, however, some of this research has examined the development of children's understanding of, and attitudes to, the state, and it is the findings that have been obtained on these issues which are of interest to us here.

This chapter is divided into three parts. The first part reviews the studies that have been conducted into the development of children's understanding of the state and its machinery of government and administration. The second part reviews a number of studies that have found variability in children's and adolescents' understanding of, and attitudes to, the state. As we shall see, there is significant variability in the development of children's political understanding and attitudes, both across countries and within individual countries. The third part of this chapter reviews studies that have directly examined the effects of school textbooks and school curricula on children's understanding of the state.

CHILDREN'S UNDERSTANDING OF THE STATE

The findings of early studies

One of the earliest studies to examine the development of children's political understanding was conducted by Hess and Easton. This study, which was reported in detail by Hess and Torney (1967) and Easton and Dennis (1969), examined over 17,000 American children living in eight cities located across the USA. The children were drawn from school grades 2 through to 8, and were aged approximately 7 to 13. Initial interviews and pretests were conducted with roughly 5000 children, and on the basis of the findings obtained, a questionnaire was then constructed and administered to over 12,000 children during 1961 and 1962. Many different issues were addressed in this study, but here we will focus on the findings that were obtained in relationship to children's understanding of the state.

The study revealed that there was a shift with age in children's understanding of how the USA is governed, away from a focus on the personal figure of the American President, towards the recognition that government is based on a set of more impersonal institutions (such as Congress) and processes (such as elections and voting). For example, one of the questions contained in the questionnaire asked the children to choose two pictures that "show best what the government is"; the pictures available to choose from included representations of George Washington, Uncle Sam, voting, the Supreme Court, Capitol, Congress, the USA flag, a policeman, the Statue of Liberty, and the President (Kennedy). Pictures of the President and of George Washington were chosen by 46% and 39% of the second-graders, respectively, while Congress and voting were chosen by less than 10% of these youngest children. By contrast, 45% and 50% of the eighth-graders chose Congress and voting, respectively. The children were also asked the question "Who makes the laws?". Among the second-graders, 76% chose the President and only 5% chose Congress. However, among the eighth-graders, only 5% chose the President and 85% chose Congress.

Thus, at younger ages, the children's conceptualization of how the USA is governed appeared to be strongly linked to the personal figure of the President, but by 12 or 13 years of age, the children's conceptualizations appeared to focus much more on political institutions and processes instead. The study also revealed that the younger children typically viewed the President in highly positive terms. For example, the youngest children expressed a strong emotional attachment to, and a strong sense of trust in, the President. However, this positive view declined with increasing age (Easton & Dennis, 1969; Hess & Easton, 1960; Hess & Torney, 1967). For example, support for the statement "The President is about the best person in the world" declined from 52% among second-graders to only 10% among eighth-graders, while support for the statement "The President would always want to help me if I needed it" declined from 67% to 27% across this age range. It is relevant to note here that, in another early study of American children drawn from school grades 4 through to 8 (i.e., aged approximately 9 to 13), Greenstein (1960, 1961, 1965) also found that American children tended to view the US President as a highly benevolent figure. For example, one of the questions in Greenstein's questionnaire was "What kinds of things do you think the President does?". Despite the fact that this question only asked for factual information, many of the children nevertheless expressed positive evaluative comments about the President, for example "The president is doing a very good job of making people be safe" (fourth-grader), "I think that he has the right to stop bad things before they start" (fifth-grader), and "The president gives us freedom" (eighth-grader). However, just as in the case of the Hess and Easton study, Greenstein found that the frequency of positive evaluations of the President in the children's answers declined with age.

A further issue examined by Hess and Easton concerned the children's understanding of the range of personnel who work for the government. To examine this issue, the children were asked the question "Here are some people. Which ones work for the government?". The children were then shown six successive pictures of a policeman, a soldier, a judge, a postman, a teacher and a milkman (the milkman is non-governmental, the policeman and teacher are employed by local government, the soldier and postman are employed by the US government, and the judge is of ambiguous status). The children were asked in connection with each picture individually "Does the . . . [job title] work for the government?", and they were required to make a forced-choice *yes/no* response (notice that the chance level of the child saying *"yes"* is therefore 50%). It was found that, at second grade, a clear majority of the children stated that the policeman and the judge worked for the government, with 86% of the children responding *"yes"* in both cases; 68% of the second-graders stated that the soldier worked for the government; but only 57% of the second-graders stated that the postman worked for the government. The figure for the teacher was 48%, which is not significantly different from chance. In the case of the milkman, 71% of the second-graders stated correctly that he did *not* work for the government. By eighth grade, a clear majority of the children stated that the policeman (81%), the soldier (98%), the judge (94%) and the postman (93%) worked for the government, and that the milkman did not work for the government (92%). However, only 59% of the eighth-graders stated that the teacher worked for the government. Easton and Dennis (1969) comment that the lower figures for the policeman and teacher may be due to the greater salience of US government over local government (an effect also found by Greenstein, 1965). Easton and Dennis argue that, overall, these findings reveal that, between second and eighth grade, children increasingly refine their capacity to differentiate the governmental sector from the non-governmental, with their awareness of how the government runs the USA progressively expanding.

Subsequent studies conducted with children living in countries other than the USA confirmed Hess and Easton's finding that a major shift in children's understanding of the state does indeed usually occur between roughly 9 and 12 years of age. For example, Dennis et al. (1968, 1972) conducted a survey in which data were collected from children living in England, Germany, Italy and America. In all four countries, Dennis et al. found that the main change in children's understanding of government, away from a personalized to an institutionalized concept of government, occurred between approximately 8–10 and 11–13 years of age. For example, the English children were asked, in one question, to choose from among a number of symbols and institutions of government the one that "tells best what our government is". At 8–10 years of age, the British Prime Minister was the single most frequent choice. However, at 11–13 years of age, hardly any children chose the Prime Minister; instead, the two most frequent choices at this age were Parliament and the House of Commons, and the frequency with which these two items were chosen increased still further at 14–17 years of age. In another question, the English children were asked to choose from a list the item that "has most to do with making the laws in this country". The Queen was far and away the most frequent choice among the 8- to 10-year-olds. However, Parliament and the Cabinet were chosen most frequently by the 11- to 13-year-olds, and the frequencies with which these two items were selected increased still further among the 14- to 17-year-olds. Parallel findings were obtained in Germany, Italy and America. These findings fit closely with those obtained in Hess and Easton's study.

Moore et al. (1985) examined the development of political understanding in children younger than those studied by either Hess and Easton or Dennis et al. They interviewed American children from kindergarten through to grade 4 (i.e., from 5 to 9 years of age, approximately). This study was also distinctive in that it was longitudinal rather than cross-sectional, with the same children being re-interviewed once per year across a five year period (the interviews took place from 1974 to 1978). Moore et al. found that the youngest children frequently confused the political and non-political spheres. For example, the kindergartners' most frequent responses to the questions "Who is the boss of our country?" and "Who does the most to run the country?" were *"don't know"*, God and Jesus. However, the frequency of references to the President in response to these two questions increased across each successive year and, by second grade, the President was the most frequent response. By fourth grade, 86% of the children perceived the President to be the boss of the country, and 79% believed that he did the most to run the country. Moore et al. also found that responses to the question "Who makes the laws?" showed a similar developmental trend. In order of decreasing frequency, the kindergartners said either *"don't know"*, the police, God or Jesus, and the President. In first, second and third grades, references to the President were the most frequent response, increasing in frequency across each successive year. However, in fourth grade, references to the President started to decrease, and references to the government, and to the President plus other people, started to increase in frequency. The children were also asked by Moore et al. "What does the President do when he goes to work?". The responses of one particular child to this question across successive years provides a clear illustration of how children's understanding develops across this age range:

KINDERGARTEN: I don't know.
FIRST GRADE: Sometimes makes speeches and works in his office.
SECOND GRADE: Makes speeches and does laws.
THIRD GRADE: He signs bills and all that; he signs laws.
FOURTH GRADE: He signs bills, goes to meetings in Congress, signs laws.

Notice that the findings that Moore et al. obtained when the children were aged 7–8 years onwards are consistent with those obtained from children of similar ages by Hess and Easton and by Dennis et al.

Moore et al. also examined the children's understanding of the range of personnel who work for the government. To do this, they employed a similar method to the one used by Hess and Easton, by asking the children to answer, in reference to a set of different jobs, the question "Does a . . . [job title] work for the government?". Moore et al. found that, at kindergarten age, the majority of the children said that a judge and a policeman worked for the government (76% and 67% of the children, respectively). However, the children's judgements of whether a soldier, teacher and mailman worked for the government were not significantly different from chance (49%, 46% and 45%, respectively), while 65% of the kindergartners correctly stated that a milkman did *not* work for the government. By fourth grade, the majority of children stated that a judge, policeman, soldier, teacher and mailman all worked for the government (97%, 96%, 87%, 71% and 90%, respectively). However, the majority of children in fourth grade also stated, incorrectly, that a milkman, gas station man and TV news person worked for the government (59%, 78% and 78%, respectively). Thus, the children's responses suggested that, at kindergarten age, they initially underestimated the range of people who worked for the government, but that, over subsequent years, they progressively broadened this range until, in fourth grade, they were overestimating the range of people who worked for the government. Because Hess and Easton only included a single non-governmental role in their earlier study (a milkman), it is not possible to compare the findings from the two studies on fourth-grade children's failure to distinguish properly between the state and private sectors. That said, however, Moore et al.'s findings, along with those of Hess and Easton, do suggest that children's awareness of the pervasiveness of governmental control of many different aspects of state functioning grows considerably across the course of middle childhood, while Moore et al.'s findings further suggest that children do not understand the distinction between the state and private sectors before 10 years of age at the very earliest.

Children's understanding of the state: The work of Connell

Another early study, which provided much more detailed qualitative information about the development of children's understanding of how the state is governed and administered, was conducted by Connell (1971). The data for this study were collected in 1968 in Sydney, Australia. Open-ended interviews were conducted with 119 children aged between 5 and 16 years old. The children were interviewed about a wide range of topics, and were allowed the opportunity to elaborate their thoughts on each topic. They were also cross-examined in detail on many of the specific points that they brought up.

Analysis of the interview transcripts revealed that virtually all of the 5- to 6-year-olds had heard of the Queen, and just over half of them had also heard of the Australian Prime Minister. However, in their interviews, these youngest children tended to make ad hoc and inconsistent statements about these figures based on scraps of information that were unrelated to each other, and frequently confused the political and non-political worlds, mixing up, for example, the worlds of politics and fairy tales. By 7–8 years of age, virtually all of the children were aware of the Australian Prime Minister, and half the children at this age were also aware of the American President. Up until 9 years of age, however, the children showed considerable confusion in relationship to these various political figures. Many children confused the titles of the positions, referring, for example, to the *"Prime Minister of America"* and the *"President of Australia"*. Below the age of 9, the children also failed to distinguish between different levels of government, or between ceremonial positions (such as the Queen's) and positions of real political power. As one child expressed it, ". . . all those people are the same". In other words, below the age of 9, the children showed little knowledge of political structure or of the power hierarchy of the state, and all of these political figures were seen as being equally responsible for ruling, for making people happy, and for making good laws (thus, these Australian children, like the younger American children in the Hess & Easton and Greenstein studies, tended to assume the benevolence of political leaders). Hence, although the 7- to 9-year-olds appeared to have identified a "political" sphere of activity related to state government, there was little internal differentiation within this general sphere.

Connell reports that the first internal differentiation of the political sphere seemed to involve the Queen. Initially, some of the children started to talk about the Queen as being the "boss" of the Australian Prime Minister, thus beginning to place these actors in a vertical power structure. In addition, from about the age of 9 onwards, many of the children seemed to acquire the conceptual distinction between reigning and ruling, with the Queen coming to be distinguished by the ceremonial activities of reigning (for example, wearing jewels and a crown, holding balls, living in a castle, etc.) rather than ruling. At the same time, the children started to allocate figures such as the Australian Prime Minister and the American President with parallel tasks that were associated with ruling but in their own different countries. Over the next year or so, the children showed an increasing awareness of other political figures (such as other ministers, who were incorporated into an expanding power hierarchy beneath the Prime Minister), of the political parties, party leaders and the Leader of the Opposition, and of laws and taxes. As these concrete details accumulated, the children began to perceive multiple relationships between the various political actors, but the precise details of the political hierarchies that were being constructed by the children tended to be somewhat idiosyncratic and varied from child to child. By about 11 years of age, some children also began to recognize that the USA has a different political system from Australia (e.g., by acknowledging that the American President has a different role from the Australian Prime Minister). By the age of 12, most of the children had a firm idea that different political roles had different tasks associated with them. By this age, they were also beginning to take consistent positions on some political issues, and to express political preferences. Connell argues that, from 9 to 12 years of age, the children were elaborating their basic understanding that political power is institutionalized (rather than personal) and that there is a permanent apparatus of power that governs the state; in other words, Connell effectively argues that it is between the ages of 9 and 12 that the concept of the state is acquired by the child. Finally, during the teenage years, Connell found that the children began to link their own personal preferences together to form coherent sets of opinions, sometimes going on to construct much more abstract and holistic interpretations and systems of values in the form of a personal ideology.

Thus, all of the studies we have looked at so far are consistent in revealing that that there is a fundamental shift in the way in which children think about government from about the age of 9 onwards, when their conceptions begin to alter from a personalized to a more institutionalized view of government, and they acknowledge the pervasiveness of the government's control of state functioning. In addition, Connell's study suggests that between 9 and 12 years of age, children gradually acquire the understanding that there is an institutional apparatus and hierarchy of power that is responsible for governing the state.

Children's understanding of the state: The work of Berti

In more recent years, Berti has conducted a sequence of studies that have focused much more directly on children's understanding of the political apparatus and bureaucratic administration of the state. All of Berti's studies were conducted with Italian children, and used open-ended questions followed by detailed cross-examination in order to pursue specific issues that the children mentioned in their answers.

In her initial study, Berti (1994) examined 8-year-old children's understanding of political terms and concepts that were taken for granted, rather than explained, in the textbooks these children were using at school. The children were first asked the question "What is a state?" (the Italian word *"stato"* was used in the question, which carries similar connotations to both *"state"* and *"country"* in English). The most frequent response was *"don't know"* (54%), followed by *"a large territory"* (28%) and *"a group of people"* (8%). Only 10% of the children referred to any political bodies. However, even though they could not define the term very well, all of the children could give the names of some states when they were asked to do so (cf. the findings of Jahoda, 1962, Wiegand, 1991a, and Barrett, 1996, reviewed in Chapter 2, on children's abilities to name other countries). The children were then asked how these states had been formed (a topic that had already been studied in school). Forty-one per cent of the children mentioned wars or the joining together of villages; *"don't know"* was the next most frequent answer (34%), followed by references to building dwellings (15%). When they were asked what a government is, and what the word *"govern"* means, 44% of the children appeared to think of governing as consisting of giving commands (usually by a king) in order to obtain personal services for oneself and for one's family. The other 56% of the children referred not only to these personal functions but also to public functions such as issuing laws and leading the army.

In a second study, Berti (1994) examined 7- to 13-year-old children's understanding of a piece of text taken from a third-grade history textbook about how the Egyptian kingdom had been founded. After reading the text to each child, questions were asked about how the Egyptian villages had been united into a large kingdom, and what, if anything, had changed in the lives of the people after this union had taken place. Up to 10 years of age, the children tended to mention spatial or physical links, for example saying that union involved either the inhabitants moving their homes in order to live closer together, or the building of roads, houses and bridges to join the different villages together, or the building of walls around the kingdom. Some 8- to 10-year-olds also talked about greater friendship and collaboration between the people, and about having laws and/or a chief. However, from 10 years of age onwards, many of the children started to produce much more overtly political explanations, describing the process of union as involving the imposition of laws and political authority on all the inhabitants. Some of the older children also talked about the government collecting taxes from the people.

In a third study, Berti (1994) asked 8- to 13-year-old children questions about a hypothetical scenario of four small kingdoms that were united into one large kingdom. She found that the 8- to 10-year-olds tended to talk about the process either as involving just spatial or physical links between the four kingdoms (with no reference being made to any political relations), or as involving spatial or physical links but under a single chief (who then governs by giving direct orders to the people personally). It was only from about 10 years of age onwards that the children started to talk about a political order, with some authorities at the top of the hierarchy and others below.

In a fourth study, Berti (1994) asked 8- to 13-year-old children questions about a range of current political events, including the reunification of Germany, Iraq's annexation of Kuwait, and European union, while in a fifth study she examined 8- to 13-year-old children's understanding of the break-up of Yugoslavia. Similar results to those of the first three studies were obtained. In other words, up to about the age of 10, most of the children tended to give answers which suggested that they did not yet understand the concept of a hierarchical political organization. These younger children instead tended to view the processes of union and secession in spatial or physical terms, although they did sometimes also mention new laws and a new chief after union or secession had taken place. By contrast, it was only from about 10 years of age onwards that the children started to talk about power hierarchies, independent governments (thus beginning to show signs of understanding the concept of state sovereignty), intermediate authorities, and the assent of the population (obtained either peacefully or through war). Berti (1994) concludes from this line of research that the shift previously identified by Connell (1971) as taking place between the ages of 9 and 12, when children first acquire an understanding of the political apparatus of the state, does indeed take place round about 10 years of age in Italian children.

Berti and Benesso (1998) subsequently examined 5-, 8- and 11-year-old Italian children's comprehension of seven specific words: *"kingdom"*, *"king"*, *"border"*, *"tax"*, *"soldier"*, *"capital city"* and *"policeman"*. Semi-structured interviews were used once again. Berti found that the 5-year-olds could say nothing about some of the words (such as *"border"*, *"capital"* and *"kingdom"*), and could only define other words (such as *"king"*, *"soldier"* and *"policeman"*) using characteristic features (e.g., the types of clothes worn, or the individuals' observable behaviours) rather than their defining features (i.e., the roles which they fulfil). The 8-year-olds had a grasp of more concepts than the 5-year-olds, but they too tended to use characteristic rather than defining features, and had a limited understanding of the relationship between the seven concepts and the concept of the state. Even when a few of the 8-year-olds spontaneously talked about the state, they merely described it as a group of important people who organized certain services and paid the soldiers and policemen for the jobs that they did. By contrast, most of the 11-year-olds were aware of the defining characteristics of all of the key concepts except *"capital city"* (in the sense of this being the seat of government— the 11-year-olds instead tended to define it simply as a large and important city). Thus, the 11-year-olds understood the notion of a state territory with borders that have been fixed through historical events, in which a population lives, which is ruled by a single government financed by taxes and which uses some of those taxes in order to employ soldiers and policemen to regulate, control and protect the population.

In her next two studies, Berti homed in on children's understanding of more specific aspects of the state. Berti and Ugolini (1998) examined children's (and university students') understanding of the law and the judicial system.[10] The participants in this study were aged 6, 8, 10, 13 and 20 years old. These individuals were asked questions about judges, public prosecutors, lawyers, witnesses and juries, including who employed and paid them for their services, followed by questions about what the law is, and how a law originates. All of the children, apart from a very few of the youngest ones, knew the term "law" and defined it as a rule or something that must be obeyed. The 6- and

---

[10] Children's understanding of the legal system, particularly from the perspective of their possible roles within that system as either witnesses or victims, has been the subject of a great deal of research; see Ceci, Markle, & Chae (2005) for a detailed review. Here, we focus more on children's understanding of the links between the legal system and the state.

8-year-olds, however, either did not know who makes the laws, or thought that they were made by local figures such as the mayor, the police or a judge (these Italian children therefore differed from the 6- to 8-year-old American and Australian children examined in previous studies who, as we have seen, instead believed that laws are made by the President, the Prime Minister or the Queen). By comparison, the majority of 10- and 13-year-olds stated that laws were made by the state, the President or the government, while the university students instead tended to say that laws were made by Parliament. As far as knowledge of the various legal roles was concerned, only judges and witnesses were familiar to a significant number of the younger children. Lawyers were only really understood from the age of 10 onwards, juries from the age of 13 onwards, and public prosecutors were only understood by a significant number of the university students. It is noteworthy that the shift in understanding that the state employs and pays judges for their services co-occurred with the shift in understanding that the state is the source of laws, with both shifts taking place between 8 and 10 years of age.

In a final study, Berti and Vanni (2000) explored 7-, 9-, 11- and 13-year-old children's understanding of war. The children were asked a series of open-ended questions about why wars start, who decides to start them, how these people make them start, who decides how a war has to be fought, how long a war can last, how it is stopped, and who decides to stop it. The children were also asked if the people who actually do the fighting decide to do so themselves, and if not, who sends them to fight. The majority of the 7-year-olds attributed all decisions about starting, continuing and ending wars to individual fighters (who were described variously as either *"men"*, *"bad people"*, or *"grown-ups"*), although a minority of the 7-year-olds gave mixed answers, attributing decisions not only to individual fighters but also to political authorities such as the President, the government or the state. These youngest children either could not give a reason for why wars start, or they said they started because of hatred, envy or revenge. They thought that wars stopped either when the fighters were dead, or when they were tired and did not want to fight any more. Very few of these children mentioned leaders commanding the fighters. From the age of 9, however, the majority of the children said that wars were clashes between states, in which decisions about starting and ending the fighting were made by political authorities, and the fighting was performed by an army in which decisions are made by the military leaders, who are subject to the control of the political authorities. The cause of war mentioned most often by the 9-year-olds was greed for something specific that the other state had. Interestingly, both the 7- and the 9-year-olds said that fights between families and between soccer fans could also be classified as wars. At 11 and 13 years of age, the majority of children mentioned the desire for the political, economic and/or cultural domination of one state by another as the principal cause of war, and these older children denied that the fighting that happens between groups which do not have any political organization (such as families or soccer fans) can be construed as war. Thus, a gradual shift in understanding appeared to take place between 7 and 11 years of age, with the 9-year-olds being at a transitional stage in their understanding of the nature of war as a conflict between states. These findings are therefore in accordance with the findings from Berti's previous studies, that it is at around 10 years of age that Italian children seem to consolidate their understanding of the power hierarchy and political apparatus through which the state regulates activities within its sphere of influence. This conclusion clearly fits well with the findings of the previous studies we have examined in this chapter, especially those of Connell (1971).

VARIABILITY IN CHILDREN'S UNDERSTANDING OF, AND ATTITUDES TO, GOVERNMENT

Cross-national variability in children's understanding of, and attitudes to, government

The studies we have been examining so far provide a general picture of how children's understanding of the state develops. However, these same studies have also revealed that there are cross-national differences in the development of children's understanding of, and attitudes towards, government. For example, Dennis et al. (1968, 1972) explicitly compared the development of children who were growing up in England, Germany, Italy and America. As we have seen, children in all four countries exhibited the same shift from a personalized to an institutionalized conception of how states are governed between approximately 8–10 and 11–13 years of age. However, some notable cross-national differences in the children's conceptions of government were also found. For example, the children were asked to indicate their level of agreement with the statement "People can't get along without government". Among the youngest children (i.e., the 8- to 10-year-olds) in England, America, Germany and Italy, the proportions who believed that government was *not* necessary for people to get along were 49%, 26%, 7% and 4%, respectively; the corresponding proportions of the oldest children (i.e., the 14- to 17-year-olds) in the four countries were 40%, 8%, 6% and 1%. Thus, the English children, in particular, showed a very different profile on this question from the other three groups of children. The perceived benevolence of government also varied across the four countries. For example, the children were asked to rate how frequently "The government wants to help me". The proportion of the youngest children whose responses fell into the two most positive categories (*always* and *almost always*) in America, Italy, Germany and England were 51%, 42%, 28% and 32%, respectively; the corresponding proportions of the oldest children whose responses fell into these two most positive categories were 41%, 21%, 11% and 9%. The children were also asked to rate their level of agreement with the statement "Usually government does people more harm than good". Dennis et al. do not report the figures for the younger children, but the proportions of the oldest children (14- to 17-year-olds) who agreed with this statement in America, Italy, Germany and England were 3%, 12%, 60% and 29%, respectively. Finally, the children were asked to rate how frequently "The government makes mistakes". Among the youngest children, the proportion of children in America, Italy, Germany and England whose responses fell into the three most negative categories (*almost always, usually* and *often*) were 12%, 13%, 23% and 25%, respectively; among the oldest children, the corresponding proportions in the four countries were 11%, 24%, 37% and 51%, respectively. Thus, there is clear evidence here of cross-national variability in the extent to which children perceive government to be benevolent and trustworthy. The children in England and Germany, in particular, appeared to hold government in much lower regard than the children in America and Italy.

In recent years, much more extensive evidence about the cross-national variability that can occur in children's understanding of, and attitudes to, government has been found in the IEA Civic Education Study (Amadeo et al., 2002; Torney-Purta et al., 1999, 2001).[11] As part of this study, a survey was conducted in 1999 with nationally representative data being collected from over 90,000 children aged 14 years, living in 28 different countries (Torney-Purta et al., 2001). The survey assessed these children's levels of civic knowledge, their understanding of democratic principles and processes, their understanding of citizenship, their attitudes towards democratic institutions, and their future intentions to engage in civic-related activities such as voting. The data collected on the children's civic knowledge, and on their attitudes towards government institutions, are pertinent to the discussion here.

Civic knowledge was assessed using a set of 38 questions, 25 of which assessed civic knowledge per se, and 13 of which assessed skills at interpreting political and civic information. The knowledge questions did not assess the children's knowledge of the specific political institutions that characterized their own country, but instead assessed their knowledge of the general principles that underlie the government of states. For example, one of the questions was: "Which of the following is most likely to cause a government to be called non-democratic?: A. People are prevented from criticizing the government. B. The political parties criticize each other. C. People must pay very high taxes. D. Every citizen has the right to a job." Another question was:

"Which of the following is an accurate statement about laws?: A. Laws forbid or require certain actions. B. Laws are made by the police. C. Laws are valid only if all citizens have voted to accept them. D. Laws prevent criticism of the government." The survey revealed that the children's civic knowledge varied significantly across countries. Children living in 10 countries (including Poland, Greece, the USA, Italy and the Czech Republic) had scores significantly higher than the overall international mean; children living in 10 other countries (including Australia, Germany, Russia and England) had scores not significantly different from the international mean; and children living in 8 countries (including Portugal, Belgium, Estonia and Romania) had scores significantly lower than the international mean. Notice that both the high performing group and the low performing group included not only long-standing democratic countries but also newly democratic countries that had undergone significant political changes during the preceding decade, that is, within the lifetime of the children who were tested. Thus, the longevity of democratic traditions within the child's own country did not seem to be a major influence on the children's levels of civic knowledge.

The IEA study also examined the children's levels of trust in government. Qualitative case studies conducted in 24 different countries prior to the survey had suggested that, in some countries at least, adolescents had relatively low levels of trust in government institutions (Torney-Purta et al., 1999). In the survey, the 14-year-olds were asked explicitly "How much of the time can you trust each of the following institutions? The national government. The local council or government of town or city. Courts. The police. Political parties. National parliament." For each institution, the response scale was *"never"*, *"only some of the time"*, *"most of the time"*, and *"always"*. The survey revealed that courts and the police were the most trusted institutions; national parliament, local council or government, and national government, were trusted to an intermediate extent; political parties were trusted the least. Overall, the levels of trust expressed were moderately high. For example, across all countries, both national parliament and national government were *"always"* trusted by about 10% of the children and trusted *"most of the time"* by about 40% of the children. However, once again, there were cross-national differences. Children living in 8 countries (including Denmark, Australia, Greece and the USA) had levels of trust in government-related institutions significantly higher than the overall international mean; children living in 12 countries (including England, Germany and Italy) had scores not significantly different from the international mean; and children living in 8 countries (including the Czech Republic, Bulgaria, Estonia and Russia) had scores significantly lower than the international mean. This time, there was a relationship with the longevity of continuous democracy in the child's own country: all of the countries in which the 14-year-olds had levels of trust in government-related institutions significantly below the international mean had experienced less than 40 years of continuous democracy. By comparison, nearly all of the countries in which the 14-year-olds had levels of trust above the international mean had experienced more than 40 years of continuous democracy.

Finally, of relevance here, the IEA study asked the children "What responsibilities should the government have?". The children were asked this question in relation to a number of different societal and economic affairs, including the provision of basic health care, the provision of free basic education, ensuring employment for all, the control of pollution, guaranteeing peace and order within the country, providing an adequate standard of living for the unemployed and for old people, keeping prices under control, etc. In general, a large majority of the 14-year-olds thought that most of these matters should be the government's responsibility, although the children were more likely to say that government should have responsibility for societal matters than for economic matters. However, there were, once again, cross-national differences in the children's responses. For example, the idea that government should be responsible for societal matters was most strongly endorsed (significantly above the international mean) by the 14-year-olds in England, Greece and Poland, and least strongly endorsed (significantly below the international mean) by the 14-year-olds in Germany and Denmark. Similarly, the notion that government should be responsible for economic matters was most strongly endorsed (significantly above the international mean) by the 14-year-olds in Bulgaria and Russia, and least strongly endorsed (significantly below the international mean) by the 14-year-olds in Belgium, Denmark, Germany, Hong Kong and the USA. It is notable that children who lived in countries that had been run by a socialist regime in the recent past and had a low GNP per capita (e.g., Bulgaria and Russia) tended to believe that the government should be responsible for economic matters, while children who lived in countries with strong free-market traditions and a high GNP per capita (e.g., Western European countries and the USA) tended to believe that the government should *not* be responsible for economic matters.

In a subsequent survey conducted in 2000, the IEA study collected additional data on the same issues from a further 50,000 16- to 18-year-olds who had remained in secondary education in 16 different countries (Amadeo et al., 2002). The questionnaire used in this additional wave of data collection was largely the same as that used with the 14-year-olds, but with some new items included that were appropriate for these older students. Perhaps not surprisingly, it was found that these older students had higher levels of civic knowledge than the 14-year-olds in all of the countries that participated in the second wave of data collection. However, levels of trust in government and public institutions were lower than those displayed by the 14-year-olds in two thirds of the countries involved. These older students were also more likely than the 14-year-olds to believe that government should be responsible for societal and economic matters. Again, there were cross-national differences in the data. For example, levels of civic knowledge differed across the 16 countries, and these cross-national differences in civic knowledge were different from those exhibited by the 14-year-olds (this was possibly due to the fact that the second wave of data collection used a different sampling strategy, with the respondents consisting only of individuals who had remained at school beyond the age of 16). In contrast, the cross-national differences in levels of trust in government-related institutions were similar to those displayed by the 14-year-olds: the 16- to 18-year-olds in countries that had longstanding democratic traditions (e.g., Denmark and Switzerland) displayed the highest levels of trust, while those in countries to which democratic traditions had only recently been introduced (e.g., Latvia, Poland and Slovenia) displayed the lowest levels of trust. The cross-national differences in the 16- to 18-year-olds' judgements about the responsibilities of government were also similar to the cross-national differences exhibited by 14-year-olds: the 16- to 18-year-olds who lived in countries that had been run by a socialist regime in the recent past and had a low GNP per capita (e.g., Russia and Poland) gave the strongest endorsements of the view that government should be responsible for economic matters.

The findings of the IEA study are therefore consistent with, but extend very considerably, the findings of earlier studies which had indicated that there are cross-national differences in the development of children's knowledge of, and attitudes to, the state and government. The IEA study further suggests that, in some cases (such as children's levels of trust in government-related institutions, and children's attitudes to the responsibilities of government), these cross-national differences are linked to the recent political circumstances of the specific states within which the children live.

Variability within countries in children's understanding of, and attitudes to, government, and the factors linked to this variability

However, there is not only variability in the development of children's understanding of, and attitudes to, government across countries; the research also reveals that there is considerable variability within individual countries. Furthermore, this within-country variability has been found to be systematically linked to a wide range of factors.

This conclusion emerges very clearly from Hess and Torney's (1967) report. They adopted a socialization framework to guide their analysis of the data from the Hess and Easton eight-city study. They hypothesized that American children are inducted into political understanding, attitudes and participation by a number of socialization agents, the most important of which are the school, the family, peer group organizations and religious organizations. They further hypothesized that social class and IQ mediate the impact of these socialization agents on the child. This framework therefore led them to examine the variability that existed within their data, to ascertain whether this variability was linked to these various factors.

They found that the children's understanding of both government and the law did indeed vary as a function of both social class and IQ: middle-class children and higher IQ children displayed more advanced understandings than working-class and lower IQ children, respectively. Hess and Torney's analyses also revealed that the school was one of the most important agents of these children's political socialization. As part of the study, the children's teachers completed an adapted version of the same questionnaire as the children. It was found that, by eighth grade, the children's attitudes to government and to a range of political institutions were often approximating to those of their own teachers (although, as one might expect, teachers tended to express greater levels of cynicism about the political system in general). As far as family effects are concerned, examination of the responses of siblings within the dataset suggested that the family was primarily responsible only for transmitting preferences for a particular political party to the child. This effect aside, the main role of the family appeared to be to support the school in the transmission of political knowledge to the child. Similarly, the main impact of religious affiliation appeared to be on political party affiliation and candidate preference (the data were collected shortly after President Kennedy's election, in which his Catholic faith had been a salient factor). Finally, participation in peer group organizations (such as the YMCA, Scouts, and school-sponsored bands and sporting clubs) was found to be linked to a greater interest in political affairs and to an enhanced perception that government is responsive to citizen influence. Overall, however, social class, IQ and the school appeared to be the principal factors that were systematically linked to the variability in these American children's understanding of, and attitudes to, government and the state.

Moore et al. (1985) also examined the variability in the data they collected from their sample of American children, in order to see if it was associated with any specific factors. They found evidence that, at all ages from kindergarten through to fourth grade, the boys were more knowledgeable about government and the state than the girls. In addition, there were significant relationships between the children's levels of political knowledge and their academic ability (as assessed by their teachers), but there were relatively few differences in the children's political knowledge as a function of their ethnicity. Finally, Moore et al. found that the children's political knowledge was related to the frequency with which they viewed the news on television. The differences in political knowledge between regular television news watchers and those who never watched the news on television was most pronounced in the fourth grade, the oldest age at which this group of children was interviewed.

During the course of the interviews he conducted with 5- to 16-year-old Australian children, Connell (1971) found that the children often spontaneously mentioned the sources from which they thought they had picked up their information about the state. Television was the source that was cited the most frequently by the children, followed by the family and then the school. The children were regular television viewers, and frequently watched the news (much more so than the children in Moore et al.'s study); this was because the news was broadcast in the middle of the children's viewing hours, between 6.00 and 7.30 pm each day. Of the 119 children in Connell's sample, 108 said they watched the news and could give corroborating details that they had done so; indeed, many said that they watched the news three or four times a week, and some children said they watched it every day. Television was the principal source the children cited for their knowledge of the Prime Minister, the American President and the Leader of the Opposition. The school was another salient information source cited by the children (and indeed, infant-school and primary-school teachers in Australia are instructed to teach young children about the Queen, the flag, the national anthem, the British Commonwealth, and national history). As far as the family is concerned, the children's comments suggested that their parents were mainly responsible for commentaries on, and interpretations of, the information that had already been picked up from television and the school, via conversations in which the children and their parents talked over the events or issues concerned. Connell also found that parents were cited by the children as the primary source of their opinions on, and preferences for, particular political parties (consistent with the findings of Hess & Torney, 1967).

Despite this attention to information sources, Connell's own interpretation of his findings differs from Hess and Torney's interpretation of their findings. He argues that the children in his study were *not* simply being inducted by these various socialization agents into reproducing prevailing adult ideas. Instead, he argues that the children were actively constructing their own understandings, by selectively appropriating the material made available to them by these different information sources, and using this material to build quite personal and sometimes idiosyncratic structures of belief in order to explain the political phenomena and events that they encountered, drawing on their own general cognitive capacities and skills in order to do so. Connell's description of how children construct their political understanding in fact draws heavily on Piagetian cognitive-developmental theory, and Connell employs the developmental stages postulated by Piaget (see Chapter 2, foot-note 6) in order to explain the distinctive characteristics of the children's thinking at any given age, and to locate the major discontinuities that occurred in the development of their political thinking. He further argues that it was the developmental changes that were occurring in the children's underlying cognitive capacities that were responsible for the developmental changes in their political thinking and understanding, rather than environmental influences per se. Moore et al. (1985) also interpret their findings from a similar Piagetian perspective. However, it is noteworthy that neither study included any Piagetian measures of the children's domain-general cognitive capacities. As a consequence, neither study provides any direct empirical evidence to support the view that the development of political understanding is driven by changes in children's underlying domain-general cognitive competencies (rather than by input received from socialization agents such as television and the school).

The 1999 IEA study (Torney-Purta et al., 2001) also examined the factors linked to the variability in the civic knowledge scores achieved by their sample of 90,000 14-year-olds. The study revealed that the single most important factor related to the children's levels of civic knowledge was "expected years of further education": the longer the children anticipated remaining within the educational system, the higher their levels of civic knowledge. This relationship did not only apply across the sample as a whole, but also within each of the 28 countries individually. "Expected years of further education" is, of course, a measure of the future educational aspirations of each child, which in turn is likely to be linked to a child's IQ, academic abilities and social class. The next most important factor was found to be "home literacy resources", that is, the number of books present in the child's home (which was used in the IEA study as an indirect index of the children's social background): the higher the number of books, the higher the children's levels of civic knowledge. This link between civic knowledge and home literacy resources was found within the sample as a whole and within 27 of the 28 countries individually. The third most important factor was "open classroom climate", that is, the extent to which the children believed that they were encouraged to speak openly in class, and could investigate issues and explore their opinions and those of their peers: children who perceived that they had an open climate for discussion in their classrooms displayed higher civic knowledge scores. This factor was found in the sample as a whole and within 22 of the 28 countries individually. Other less important, but still statistically significant, factors in the sample as a whole were: the frequency of watching news on television (which also applied individually within 16 of the 28 countries); gender, with boys having slightly higher civic knowledge scores than girls overall (in 11 of the 28 countries); and participation in a school council or parliament (which applied within 10 of the 28 countries individually). The data collected from the 16- to 18-year-olds in the IEA study (Amadeo et al., 2002) largely replicated these findings, but revealed that, in addition, parental educational level, the size of the family, the frequency of reading news in the newspaper and political interest were also systematically linked to levels of civic knowledge in these older individuals.

Many of these same factors have also been identified in a number of other studies. For example, both the earlier 1971 IEA study (Torney et al., 1975) and Niemi and Junn (1998) found socioeconomic status to be a key predictor of children's levels of civic knowledge, with children from higher socio-economic backgrounds typically displaying higher levels of civic knowledge. The impact of education on children's levels of political and civic knowledge, as well as their levels of political engagement and participation, has also now been confirmed in a wide range of research (see, for example, Bynner & Ashford, 1994; Emler & Frazer, 1999; Fiske, Lau, & Smith, 1990; Krosnick & Milburn, 1990; Nie et al., 1996). As far as media influences are concerned, there is now clear evidence from a number of different studies that there is a relationship between levels of political knowledge and the extent to which children attend to news reports on the television and in newspapers (Chaffee, Ward, & Tipton, 1970; Hahn, 1998; Linnenbrink & Anderman, 1995). Hess and Torney's (1967) early finding of a link between children's political atti-tudes and their participation in peer group organizations has also been con-firmed by subsequent studies: participation in peer group organizations and extra-curricular activities are now known to be strongly associated with higher levels of civic responsibility and political engagement and action (Otto, 1975; Verba, Schlozman, & Brady, 1995; Youniss et al., 1997). And the relationship that Hess and Torney found between the political party preferences of parents and those of their children has also been confirmed by subsequent research (e.g., Jennings & Niemi, 1968; Niemi & Jennings, 1991).

To summarize, then, there are many different factors related to the vari-ability that occurs within countries in the development of children's under-standing of, and attitudes to, government and the state. Although the 1999 IEA study has shown that all factors do not invariably apply within all countries, some of the key factors commonly related to within-country variability would appear to be the socioeconomic status of the child's family; education and school practices; the child's own intellectual or academic ability; the child's levels of attention to the news in the mass media; the child's participation in peer group organizations and extra-curricular activities; and, more variably, the child's gender, with a tendency for boys to display higher levels of political knowledge than girls.

THE ROLE OF THE SCHOOL IN FOSTERING CHILDREN'S UNDERSTANDING OF THE STATE

It is noteworthy that many studies have identified the school as an important agent of children's enculturation in this domain, with education being sys-tematically related not only to children's levels of political knowledge and expertise but also to their levels of civic engagement and participation (Bynner & Ashford, 1994; Emler & Frazer, 1999; Fiske et al., 1990; Hess & Torney, 1967; Krosnick & Milburn, 1990; Nie et al., 1996; Torney-Purta et al., 2001). The specific role that the school can play in fostering children's understanding of the state has been investigated in a sequence of further studies conducted by Berti (1994; Berti & Andriolo, 2001; Berti & Benesso, 1998; see also Berti, 2005). In these studies, Berti examined whether the particular textbooks that children use at school, and the contents of the curriculum to which children are exposed at school can impact on children's knowledge and understanding of the state.

In the first of these studies (reported in Berti, 1994), she examined two groups of 8-year-old Italian children. These groups had used different history textbooks at school. One of the textbooks contained a high number of political terms, while the other textbook contained a low number of political terms. Both groups of children had already studied their own respective textbook during the course of the preceding school year. Berti interviewed the children about what a state is, how states are formed, what a government is, and what the term "govern" means. She found that the two groups of children produced significantly different patterns of responses. Specifically, the children who had used the book containing the high number of political terms produced significantly fewer *"don't know"* responses when they were questioned about states, and produced significantly more details of government tasks (such as the issuing of laws and commanding the army), than the group of children who had used the book containing the low number of political terms.

In a subsequent intervention study, Berti and Benesso (1998) first assessed 9-year-old Italian children's concepts of state, region, province, border and capital city. An educational programme on the concept of a state was then administered to these children over a 2-month period. Two weeks after the end of this programme, the children were reassessed, and significant improvements in their understanding were found. While these findings are suggestive, the lack of an appropriate control group makes interpretation problematic. However, this omission was rectified in Berti's third study (Berti & Andriolo, 2001). Here, 8-year-old Italian children's understanding of the state, government and law was assessed prior to the implementation of an educational curriculum on these topics. The curriculum was then administered over an 11-week period. The children were subsequently reassessed twice, 1 month and 10 months after the end of the curriculum. This time, a control group of children who had not been exposed to this curriculum was also assessed at the same three points in time. At the pre-test, the majority of the children in both the experimental and the control groups did not have a clear understanding of the state, government or the law. At the post-test and at the delayed post-test, the children in the experimental group displayed significantly better understanding than the children in the control group. In particular, they displayed better knowledge of political offices (such as the President and Prime Minister) and of the fact that the capital city was the seat of government; these children also had a much better understanding that schools, the police and judges are financed by the state using revenue raised through taxation. Improvements in the children's understanding of the law were more uneven and variable. At the delayed post-test, the experimental group displayed very few significant regressions, and retention of what had been taught appeared to be stable. By contrast, the control group showed very few changes from pre-test to immediate post-test through to delayed post-test, and this group in fact showed very little progress in mastering any of the political concepts during the period of the study.

Based on this sequence of studies, Berti (2005; Berti & Andriolo, 2001) argues that the explicit and systematic teaching of political information is one of the principal factors responsible for driving the development of children's understanding of how states are governed, organized and administered. Because of the lack of any real developmental progress by the control group in the third study across a time period of more than a year (and at an age when Connell, 1971, had proposed children are first beginning to understand the structure of the state), Berti concludes that children's development at this age is influenced to a much greater extent by the educational input they received at school than by their underlying domain-general cognitive development.

Notice that Berti's research suggests that some of the cross-national differences that have been found to exist in the development of children's understanding of government and the state (by, for example, the IEA study) may be, at least in part, a consequence of the different educational curricula and textbooks used in different countries in order to teach children about political and civic issues. Berti's research also demonstrates, much more directly, that within-country differences (such as those within Italy) are likely to arise when different textbooks and curricula are employed by different schools in that country in order to teach children about political issues.

SUMMARY

The following conclusions emerge from the body of research which has been examined in this chapter.

- As far as the development of children's understanding of the state is concerned:
  - between 7 and 13 years of age, children shift from a personalized to an institutionalized conceptualization of how a state is governed
  - initially, their thinking about government focuses on the personal

figure of the President, Prime Minister or Queen, but by early adolescence their thinking focuses on political institutions (such as Congress or Parliament) and processes (such as voting) instead

- at 7 or 8 years of age, children usually hold very positive attitudes towards the personal figure of the President or Prime Minister who, at this early age, is frequently perceived as a benevolent figure
- however, children's trust in political figures declines significantly with increasing age
- children's awareness of the pervasiveness of governmental control of many different aspects of state functioning grows through the course of middle childhood, although children do not appear to have a proper understanding of the distinction between the state and private sectors before 10 years of age at the very earliest
- children gradually acquire the understanding that there is a power hierarchy and political apparatus through which the state regulates activities within its sphere of influence between 9 and 12 years of age
- between 9 and 12 years of age, children begin to understand that states consist of geographical territories with borders that have been fixed through historical events, in which particular populations live, ruled by a single government
- it is also between 9 and 12 years of age that children begin to understand the independent sovereignty of states and state governments, and that the population of a state is regulated through laws made either by the government or by the political institutions of the state
- children also begin to understand, between 9 and 12 years of age, that the governments of states raise taxes from their populations, and that some of these taxes are then used by these governments to pay soldiers, policemen, judges, etc., in order to regulate, control and protect the people who live within their borders.
- There is substantial variability across countries in the development of children's and adolescents' understanding of, and attitudes to, government and the state:
  - there are differences in the extent to which government is perceived to be trustworthy and benevolent, with levels of trust in government tending to be higher in countries that have longstanding democratic traditions, and lower in countries to which democratic traditions have only recently been introduced
  - adolescents' judgements about the responsibilities of government also vary across countries, with adolescents who live in countries that have been run by a socialist regime in the recent past and that have a low GNP per capita usually giving the strongest endorsement of the view that governments should be responsible for economic matters

- adolescents' levels of civic knowledge also display considerable variation across countries, although these variations have not been linked to any particular societal factors.
- There is also substantial variability within individual countries in children's knowledge of, and attitudes to, government and the state:
  - this variability is linked to a number of factors, including social class, intellectual or academic ability, education, levels of attention to the news in the mass media, and participation in peer group organizations
  - there are also sometimes gender differences within particular countries, with a tendency for boys to display more political knowledge than girls.
- As far as educational effects are concerned:
  - the contents of both school textbooks and the school curriculum can influence children's understanding of how states are governed and administered
  - some of the variability that occurs in the development of children's political understanding may be due to the different educational curricula and textbooks used at school to teach children about the state.

Children's knowledge, beliefs and feelings about nations and states construed as historical and cultural communities

As we saw in Chapter 1, a nation can be defined as a named human community occupying a homeland and having a shared history, common myths of ancestry, a common mass public culture, and shared values, symbols, traditions, customs and practices. However, it was also noted in Chapter 1 that, although myths of origins, codified histories and shared values, symbols and traditions are most frequently discussed in relationship to nations rather than states, states also have their own codified histories, their own myths of origins, and their own systems of shared values, symbols and traditions (which, in the case of a multination state, can be markedly different from those of some of its constituent nations). As a result, not only nations but also states have distinctive cultures and histories with which individuals may subjectively identify. Consequently, children's national enculturation can entail the acquisition of knowledge about, and identification with, not only the history and culture of their own nation, but also the history, values, symbols and traditions of the state in which they live.

In this chapter, we explore several different aspects of the national enculturation process. In particular, we examine how children acquire a sense of pride in their own nation and/or state, how they acquire narratives about the historical origins of their nation and state, how they appropriate the core collective values for which their own nation or state stands, and how they learn about and utilize the emblems and symbols that represent their nation and state. The chapter is subdivided into three parts. In the first part, we review the studies that have been conducted into children's pride in their own country. In the second part, we review, at some length, the role of the school in the national enculturation of children. Here, we focus in particular on how the school provides children with explicit instruction about their own nation and state, how educational curricula and textbooks often exhibit ethnocentric biases that can channel children towards more positive representations of their own nation and state than of other nations and states, and how the adoption by schools of aspects of their own nation's civil culture within their daily practices can help to transmit national values and practices to children. In the third part of the chapter, we review the studies that have investigated children's knowledge, understanding and utilization of national and state emblems and symbols.

CHILDREN'S PRIDE IN THEIR OWN COUNTRY

It is clear from numerous studies that, during the course of their development, children often acquire a strong sense of pride in their own country. Children's levels of pride have been examined in several of the studies into children's understanding of government and the state that we looked at in the previous chapter, in particular the studies conducted by Hess and Easton (Hess & Torney, 1967), Dennis et al. (1972), Moore et al. (1985), Torney-Purta et al. (2001) and Amadeo et al. (2002).

Some of these studies suggest that a strong sense of pride can already be present in children at 7 years of age. For example, in Hess and Easton's eight-city study, second- to eighth-grade American children were asked to indicate their level of agreement with the statements "America is the best country in the world" and "The American flag is the best flag in the world" (Hess & Torney, 1976). It was found that nearly 95% of the children agreed with these two statements; furthermore, there were only minimal differences in responses to these two questions as a function of age, social class, IQ, religious affiliation and gender. In other words, in this study, very little individual variability was found in the children's responses, and even the youngest 7-year-old children displayed very strong pride. For example, one second-grade boy, when asked in an interview whether he would rather be American or English, responded:

> Well, I wouldn't like to be an Englishman because I wouldn't like to talk their way, and I'd rather be an American because they have better toys, because they have better things, better stores, and better beds and blankets, and they have better play guns, and better boots, and mittens and coats, and better schools and teachers.

These types of responses occurred in the youngest children even though, at this early age, their knowledge and understanding of the state and of its geographical territory were still extremely rudimentary. Such strongly patriotic responses are, of course, very similar to those discovered by some of the studies we looked at in Chapter 2, for example, the studies by Johnson et al. (1970), Jaspers et al. (1972) and Nugent (1994). All of these studies are consistent with one another in suggesting the early emergence and subsequent endurance of a strong sense of pride in their own country among children.

Hess and Easton also asked the children in their study the question "What makes you most proud to be American?". They found that, with increasing age, there were changes in the children's responses to this question (Hess & Torney, 1967). Younger children tended to select concrete or material aspects of their country such as *"our President"* and *"beautiful parks and highways"*, while older children instead tended to select collective abstract ideals such as *"freedom"* and the *"right to vote"*. In other words, there was a shift in children's answers with increasing age from the concrete to the more abstract. Because this question was administered as part of a longer questionnaire that focused explicitly on the children's political understanding, the context in which the question was asked may have cued these overtly political answers from the children. However, notice that this shift is very similar to the shift that occurred in the children's thinking about government across these same ages (see Chapter 3), as well as to the shift found by Piaget and Weil (1951) when they asked children (in a non-political context) why they liked their own country (see Chapter 2).

Moore et al. (1985) also asked the American children who participated in their longitudinal study the question "Is America the best country in the world?". This question was not asked when the children were in kindergarten, but it was asked each year as the children passed through grades 1 to 4. They found a different pattern of results from Hess and Easton. In grade 1, only 48% of the children said *"yes"* in response to this question, with 33% of the children saying *"no"*. By grade 4, only 30% of the children said *"yes"*, while 40% said *"no"*. The remaining children at each grade tended to say *"don't know"*, with just a few children giving qualified answers instead. Thus, levels of pride (as assessed by this question) were much more variable in this study and tended to decline as the children got older. Moore et al. comment that, by grade 4, some of the children were showing an awareness of the relativity of values when judging different countries. For example, one fourth-grade child said "It depends on your point of view. There are lots of problems and crime everywhere"; another fourth-grader said "A country shouldn't be judged because each country has different customs, culture, and its own way of living". Moore at al. suggest that the children's increasing exposure to other countries and cultures through television had probably reinforced their own positive first-hand experiences of other countries, which they had obtained through foreign travel, and that television documentaries on crime, delinquency and drugs in the USA, reinforced by parental comments, had possibly contributed to the decline with age in the children's levels of pride in their own country.

As part of their study of children's political socialization, Dennis et al. (1972) also examined both English and American children's levels of pride. They found significant cross-national differences. For example, when the English children were asked to indicate their level of agreement with the statement "Britain is the best country in the world", 48% of the 8- to 10-year-olds, 42% of the 11- to 13-year-olds, and 48% of the 14- to 17-year-olds agreed with this statement; in other words, there was variability among the English children in their responses. In the American sample, by contrast, 64% of the youngest children agreed with the corresponding statement about America, while 76% of the oldest children agreed with it. While these figures were higher than those for the English children, they are nevertheless lower than those reported for American children by Hess and Torney (1967) and suggest, much like the findings of Moore et al. (1985), that there is in fact rather more variability in American children's levels of pride than Hess and Torney's early findings had implied (it is, of course, possible that such pride among American children declined after 1961–2, when the data for the eight-city study were collected). Dennis et al. also asked the children "What are the things about this country that you are most proud of?" Among the English children, only 20% of the 8- to 10-year-olds, 22% of the 11- to 13-year-olds, and 33% of the 14- to 17-year-olds referred to political institutions and social legislation in their answers. By comparison, among the American children, 48% of the youngest group, 61% of the middle group, and 64% of the oldest group referred to political institutions and social legislation. The English children instead placed greater emphasis in their responses on their quality of life, the history of their country, and the contributions that their country had made to the arts. Dennis et al.'s study therefore suggests that there is considerable variability in the types of issues that make children feel proud, as well as in their levels of pride, depending on the particular country in which they live.

The existence of differences across countries in children's levels of pride was confirmed by the 1999 IEA Civic Education Study (Torney-Purta et al., 2001). Four items were used in this study to measure the children's pride in their country (notice that these questions were different from those used in the previous studies): "The flag of this country is important to me", "I have great love for this country", "This country should be proud of what it has achieved", and "I would prefer to live permanently in another country". The response options were *"strongly agree"*, *"agree"*, *"disagree"* and *"strongly disagree"* (with responses to the final statement being reverse scored). The scores on these four items scaled reliably. Overall, the study found that the children had highly positive feelings for their own country: 83% of the children chose the two most positive responses to these various questions. However, there were significant differences between the scores across countries. Children in 9 countries (including Greece, Cyprus, Chile and Poland) exhibited scores significantly higher than the international mean; children in 9 countries (including Australia, Bulgaria, Russia, Slovenia and the USA) exhibited scores not significantly different from the international mean; and children in 10 countries (including England, Germany, Switzerland, Estonia, Sweden and Belgium) exhibited scores significantly lower than the international mean. However, the mean score of even the lowest scoring group of children (in Belgium) was still on the positive side of the scale. Thus, the large majority of the children did indeed express positive attitudes towards their own country. There were also gender differences in 10 of the 28 countries: in 9 of these (which included England, Germany, Italy and Russia, but not the USA), boys exhibited higher levels of pride than girls.

These findings were largely replicated in the second wave of the IEA study, in which data were collected from 16- to 18-year-olds who had remained in secondary education in 16 countries (Amadeo et al., 2002). Overall, about 80% of these participants also chose the two most positive responses to the four questions. Children in five countries (including Chile, Cyprus and Poland) exhibited scores significantly higher than the international mean (Greece did not participate in this part of the study); children in two countries (Russia and Slovenia) exhibited scores that did not differ from the international mean (Australia, Bulgaria and the USA did not participate in this second part of the study); and children in seven countries (including Switzerland, Estonia and Sweden) exhibited scores significantly lower than the international mean (England, Germany and Belgium did not participate in this second part of the study). Notice that, where data were collected from both 14-year-olds and 16- to 18-year-olds in a particular country, the relative international positioning of that country was similar at both ages. However, statistical comparison between the 14-year-olds and the 16- to 18-year-olds revealed that the older children tended to be less positive than the younger children towards their own country overall. That said, the large majority of 16- to 18-year-olds did still have positive attitudes towards their own country. Gender differences among the older children were found in only two countries (the Czech Republic and Slovenia); in both cases, boys had higher scores than girls.

Thus, it is clear that there are indeed differences in children's levels of pride across different countries. Although the studies by Moore et al. (1985) and Dennis et al. (1972) suggest that children do not always regard their own country as the best country in the world, there are nevertheless a number of other studies (e.g., Hess & Torney, 1967; Johnson et al., 1970; Jaspers et al., 1972; cf. also Piaget & Weil, 1951) that converge in their findings that children's pride in their own country can emerge at an early age, certainly by 7 years. The IEA study also shows that, despite the differences that occur in levels of pride from country to country, teenagers also often feel very positively about their own country. In addition, the IEA study has revealed that there are sometimes gender differences within some countries, the trend being for boys to exhibit higher levels of pride than girls.

THE ROLE OF THE SCHOOL IN THE NATIONAL ENCULTURATION OF CHILDREN

As we noted in Chapter 1, there are almost certainly multiple exogenous influences on children's national enculturation. These influences are likely to include family practices, the mass media, the school curriculum and school practices. Of these various influences, the school has been identified by many commentators as one of the most important influences on the national enculturation of children, precisely because schools are often employed by the state precisely in order to inculcate children with a detailed knowledge, understanding and appreciation of their own state and nation. For example, numerous scholars have noted that, when new states have just been formed and national leaders are striving to consolidate a diverse and heterogeneous population into a new inclusive national culture, the state educational system is often used explicitly and strategically as a means to try to achieve national-cultural integration, cohesion and pride. This has occurred routinely in the postcolonial world, in South Asia (Chitnis, 1992; Shukla, 1992), Africa (Ishumi, 1992; Young, 2001), Latin America and the Caribbean (Albornoz, 1992). However, it should not be assumed that educational systems are used in this way only by states that have just emerged from a period of colonial rule. State educational systems have also been used strategically for nation-building purposes in many other countries as well, both in the past and in the present, for example, in England (Grosvenor, 1999; Kumar, 2003), France (Weber, 1979), Turkey (Berkes, 1964; Kushner, 1977), Japan (Yoshino, 2001) and the USA (Meyer, Tyack, Nagel, & Gordon, 1979). And indeed, a wide swathe of educational research has shown that, in practice, the educational systems of virtually all countries are used to induct children into the representations of the nation that are culturally dominant within those countries (Anyon, 1979; Apple, 1993; Crawford, 2000; Kozma, 1992; Nieto, 1996; Schiffauer, Baumann, Kastoryano, & Vertovec, 2004; Schleicher, 1992; cf. also Gellner, 1983, and A.D. Smith, 1991, 1998).

There appear to be three main ways in which schools impact on children's national enculturation: through the provision to those children of direct and explicit instruction about their own state and nation; through the ethnocentric biases that often characterize both educational curricula and school textbooks; and through the adoption by schools of particular aspects of their nation's civil culture within their own daily practices. In the following sections, we will examine each of these issues in turn. In the process, we will see how, during the course of their school education, children are exposed not only to culturally dominant historical narratives about how their own state and nation originated, but also to the core collective values for which their own nation or state stands, and to information and practices that are likely to bolster children's sense of pride in their own country.

The provision by the school of direct instruction about the child's own state and nation

To begin with, it needs to be noted that schools expose children to an extensive range of explicit instruction about the history, cultural heritage, emblems and symbolic imagery of their own state and nation. This instruction is routinely provided when children study the school subjects of language, literature, history, geography and civic/citizenship education. In language and literature, for example, the school curriculum almost always focuses heavily on the study of the national language and the literature written in that language, rather than on the languages and literatures of other nations. Similarly, history and geography curricula typically place much greater emphasis on the history and geography of the child's own state or nation than on the histories and geographies of other states and nations. And in the course of civic/citizenship education classes, children receive explicit instruction about key aspects of the political and civic systems of their own state rather than those of other states. This is not to say that children do not learn about the languages, literatures, histories, geographies and political and civic systems of some other countries while they are at school; instead, it is simply to note that the language, literature, history, geography and political/civic system of their own country routinely receive far greater prominence and more detailed coverage within the school curriculum. As a consequence, by the time they leave school, children have typically been exposed to a very wide range of information about the distinctive history, cultural heritage, values, emblems and imagery associated with their own state and nation.

However, direct instruction may exert its effects not only through exposing children to a greater quantity of information about their own country than about other countries, but also through exposing them to particular types of information about their own nation or state that are distinctive and specific to that nation or state. This point emerges very clearly from a recent study by Schiffauer and Sunier (2004). They analysed a sample of the history textbooks used in secondary schools in England, France, the Netherlands and Germany, focusing in particular on the different ways in which the child's own nation was represented in those textbooks.

They found that, in England, children were presented with a model of their own nation in which the internal plurality, heterogeneity and multi-cultural composition of the nation were stressed. Immigration was represented as a longstanding historical phenomenon, and language was viewed as the foundation of the constituent people's own cultures and identities. The problems that can arise within a multicultural society were depicted as being solved by respecting other peoples' cultures and by adopting reasonable, fair and pragmatic courses of action for the sake of the greater common good.

In French history textbooks, by contrast, the French nation was instead depicted as emerging from a series of revolutionary reconstructions that had enabled the nation to continually adapt itself to new historical circumstances. French history was viewed as a battle between, on the one hand, progressive, enlightened, civilized and rational forces and, on the other hand, the unenlightened forces of reaction. Although rationality and enlightenment were presented as not being restricted to a single people or nation, France was presented as having played a fundamental role in the global advancement of enlightenment, with the French Revolution having established republican principles and providing a model of rationality for the whole of mankind. Much greater consideration was given to general world history than in the textbooks used in the other three countries, and there was an expectation that French children should master criteria that would enable them to make judgements about the rationality or irrationality of social and cultural developments.

In the case of the Netherlands, yet another model of the child's own nation prevailed in the history textbooks examined by Schiffauer and Sunier, with the emphasis instead being placed on how the Dutch nation developed historically through a process of gradual evolution to a peaceful society in which all citizens are equal although not uniform. Dutch history was presented as having occurred, not through successive waves of immigration, nor as a battle between the forces of progress and reaction, but through ordinary people participating in and contributing to the national community even though they might have held different opinions. The Dutch nation was therefore presented as a collection of individuals who might have different backgrounds, lifestyles and opinions but who are able to live peacefully together through negotiation and democratic participation. Although the English and Dutch models of the nation were similar in emphasizing how the common good had been reached by respecting cultural differences, there was greater emphasis in the Dutch textbooks on the commonality and mutual obligations of the members of the national group, and less emphasis on internal diversity, than in England.

Finally, in the case of Germany, Schiffauer and Sunier found that the history textbooks adopted a defensive model of the German nation-state.[12] The underlying message was that, while modern Germany has been an economic success, the nation must bear collective responsibility for the atrocities of the Nazi era. Consequently, German citizens always need to be alert to

---

[12] Recall from Chapter 1 that, unlike the other three countries, Germany is an example of a nation-state rather than a multination state.

totalitarian tendencies, and must defend the centre ground of the common good, as well as democracy itself, against all forms of extremism. In other words, democracy was represented as a fragile condition, which members of the nation had to defend. The modern German state itself was presented as a direct answer to the crimes of the Nazi period, and as offering a second chance for the German people. Hence, what the modern German nation stands for was presented within German textbooks in the essentially negative terms of "never again".[13]

Thus, the history textbooks in these four countries appeared to be providing children with four very different models of what their own nation stands for and represents. In commenting on Schiffauer and Sunier's study, Mannitz (2004b) argues that these models of the national culture contained in the textbooks can be viewed as totalizing images of what schoolchildren are expected to pick up in the course of their education. Thus, the textbooks reveal which aspects of the national culture and history have been chosen to be passed on to the children of the nation by the educational system and, by omission, which aspects have been excluded from the national collective's self-representations. Mannitz further argues that these different models of the nation were not only propagated by the children's teachers during formal lessons, but were also implicit within the everyday practices and patterns of discourse that were used more widely within the schools.

We will explore the issue of school practices in a moment. For now, it should be noted that it does not necessarily follow that, just because these are the representations of the nation that are to be found within textbooks and the curriculum, children themselves will necessarily internalize and appropriate these particular representations for themselves. In fact, the evidence available from other studies actually suggests that children often exhibit considerable diversity in their responses to the material about their own nation that they are taught at school. Wertsch (1998), in particular, has shown that there are several different ways in which individuals can respond to historical narratives about their own nation. Individuals may simply fail to learn those narratives in the first place; or they may learn them and appropriate them for themselves; or they may learn them but nevertheless resist them; or they may learn them but reject them and believe in alternative narratives instead. In support of this conclusion, Wertsch draws on the evidence yielded by a number of studies in which children's (and adults') knowledge of their own nation has been examined, which have shown that individuals can respond in a

---

[13] Schiffauer and Sunier's analysis of how the modern German nation is represented in school textbooks is consistent with other analyses of contemporary German national identity (see, for example, Knischewski, 1996, Merkl, 1992 and Rossteutscher, 1997). For analyses by other scholars of the self-representations of the English, French and Dutch, see C.G.A. Bryant (2003), Jenkins and Copsey (1996), Kumar (2003), Lunn (1996), Schama (1987), Van Ginkel (2004) and Weber (1979).

variety of different ways to culturally dominant historical narratives about their own nation.

For example, in one series of studies, Beck and colleagues examined how information about the American Revolutionary period is learnt by American fifth- and eighth-grade schoolchildren (Beck & McKeown, 1994; Beck, McKeown, & Gromoll, 1989; Beck, McKeown, Sinatra, & Loxterman, 1991). They found that this information is sometimes *not* mastered by these children, despite its extensive coverage in their history textbooks and in teacher instruction. Tracking individual children longitudinally, they found that some of the children they studied began with skeletal information that became more detailed through fifth grade and was maintained through into eighth grade; other children began with incomplete knowledge that gradually improved through fifth grade but then regressed by eighth grade; while other children never had any accurate information and never mastered the taught information, even through eighth grade. Many of this final group of children simply never acquired an understanding of the narrative events of this historical period and how these were interrelated, and these children instead exhibited a highly fragmented pattern of understanding with little overall coherence.

By contrast, Wills (1994) found that children do sometimes master the dominant historical narratives of their own nation. He investigated the educational presentation and uptake of information about American history in three classes of eighth-grade American schoolchildren. Examining the history textbooks that were being used by these children in their classrooms, Wills found that there were several biases and stereotypes in the presentation of information about Native Americans. In particular, these books tended to privilege representations of Native Americans as nomadic, buffalo-hunting, Plains Indians; the representations of other Native Americans, who had lived in houses, farmed, and had a sense of ownership of the land prior to the arrival of Europeans, were instead marginalized in these books. Wills found that, while the teachers themselves acknowledged the presence of farming Indians, they too marginalized these groups in their own teaching. And these biases (which effectively serve to justify the acquisition of land and the removal of Native Americans from that land by the early European settlers) did indeed appear to have impacted on the children's understanding of the historical origins of their own country. This was especially marked in the children's own narrative constructions and moral justifications of the European conquest of North America, in which they too marginalized the role and experiences of racial and ethnic minorities, and instead adopted a Eurocentric perspective and narrative.

Wertsch and O'Connor (1994) found that a third type of outcome can sometimes occur when individuals appropriate a narrative of the origins of their own country. They conducted a study with college students who ranged in age from 18 to 21 years. These students were asked to spend 30 minutes writing an essay describing the origins of the United States. There was a high level of agreement among the participants about the key episodes and the central narrative of how their country originated (which revolved around a "quest for freedom" theme). As in Wills' study, some individuals had clearly mastered and appropriated this dominant narrative. However, other individuals, although they had mastered and were able to relate this narrative, distanced themselves from it, either through direct commentary or through sarcasm. For example, one individual wrote as a commentary on events which they had related: "It's sadly ironic that the Pilgrims left England so they could be free but when they got here, they inflicted their views on the Indians. It's unfortunate, and unfair, that that happened." Other individuals used sarcasm, for example: "Along their journey to freedom, however, there were a few minor difficulties. The first problem they encountered was that the land WAS inhabited after all ["was" underlined and capitalized in the original]. But seeing as how these natives were clearly far too primitive to match the battling skills of our pilgrims, these pilgrims sat down to a nice meal of turkey and cranberries with the natives, and then killed them." Wertsch (1998) argues that, although these individuals were invoking the same basic national narrative as the other participants, they were resisting it "from within". They had difficulties with this hegemonic narrative, and tried to resist the constraints it imposed on their understanding. However, they were unable to step outside this narrative framework to provide an account of the origins of their country from a completely different perspective (e.g., that of Native Americans).

However, in some cases, individuals do in fact adopt alternative narratives of the history of their own nation to those that have been officially taught to them at school. In a fascinating study that explored the beliefs adult Estonians hold about the history of their nation, Tulviste and Wertsch (1994) found that, despite the fact that these individuals had all been exposed to an official Soviet history of their nation at school, all of them drew a very clear distinction between this official history and a parallel unofficial history. The official Soviet history (according to which Estonia had voluntarily become a part of the USSR in 1940) had been learnt at school from textbooks and curricula, the contents of which had been stringently controlled by the centralized state Ministry of Education. This official history had also been reinforced through the Soviet media and through Soviet rituals such as the celebrations of the Day of Revolution. The unofficial history (according to which Estonia had been coerced into joining the USSR, with only a small minority of Estonians wanting their country to join the Soviet Union) had instead been acquired from conversations with family members and friends, from information picked up via foreign radio and television broadcasts, and from clandestine publications. Importantly, all of these individuals drew a very strong distinction between knowing the official national history and believing in it, and they all gave credence only to the unofficial history. Being educated under a totalitarian regime obviously represents a special set of circumstances. That said, however, this Estonian study shows very clearly that it cannot be assumed that, just because a particular version of the history of a nation has been taught at school, individuals will necessarily believe in that history, especially if it conflicts with information they receive from other sources.

Thus, it is important to bear in mind that the culturally dominant narratives about their own nation or state to which children are exposed at school are sometimes learnt and appropriated by those children, but sometimes they are not learnt, sometimes they are learnt but resisted, and sometimes they are learnt but rejected. Wertsch (1998) himself argues that national narratives are important cultural tools that mediate individuals' ways of thinking about their nation. They empower and facilitate particular ways of thinking, but they simultaneously constrain and limit the individual by precluding alternative possible ways of thinking. Although children are expected to master and appropriate the privileged narratives during the course of their schooling, these narratives can nevertheless be either resisted or rejected by individual children. Wertsch's line of thinking is important to remind us that children do not always internalize and appropriate for themselves those representations of the nation or state to which they have been exposed at school; they may instead acquire alternative representations from other salient sources of information (which can include the family, the peer group and the mass media).

Ethnocentric biases in educational curricula and school textbooks

A second way in which schools may play a role in children's national enculturation is via the ethnocentric biases that are often present in the educational curriculum and the school textbooks children use. We have already seen one example of ethnocentrism in the study by Wills (1994). He found that both the textbook the children were using, and the instruction provided by their teachers, were biased by a Eurocentric point of view, which privileged one particular way of representing Native Americans (one that is especially convenient for the dominant national narrative) while marginalizing other representations of Native Americans (especially those that create problems for that dominant narrative). "Ethnocentrism", within the educational context, has been defined as occurring when a particular group attributes to itself a more central position than any other group, values positively its own achievements and characteristics, and interprets out-groups' achievements and characteristics only through the in-group's mode of thinking (Preiswerk & Perrot, 1978). In the light of this definition, the way in which Native

Americans were represented by both the textbook and the teachers in Wills' study was clearly ethnocentric, attributing a more central position to the European settlers than to the Native Americans, placing a higher value on these settlers' activities and westward expansion than on the Native Americans' pre-existing ways of life, and presenting the out-group of Native Americans in a manner that is particularly convenient for a Eurocentric narrative of the historical origins of the United States.

A serious problem faced by educators is that ethnocentrism can arise very easily within educational curricula and textbooks. This is because the contents of those curricula and textbooks have to be, by necessity, highly selective. From the enormous body of available knowledge that could potentially be taught to children, for purely practical reasons educators have no choice but to extract, simplify and condense particular parts of this body of knowledge in order to construct the school curriculum. In practice, what is included within, and what is excluded from, educational curricula and school textbooks is often a reflection of the history, geography and civic culture of the state or nation as these are viewed by dominant groups rather than by subordinate or minority groups. In addition, the particular way in which even the included "facts" are presented to children is often value-laden and driven by the culturally dominant ideological perspective. As a result, conflicting views and interpretations held by less powerful groups and by subordinate nations within the state can easily be either ignored or marginalized within the school curriculum and/or textbooks. The end result is an educational curriculum that is ethnocentrically biased.

Educational research has revealed that this kind of ethnocentric bias of school curricula and textbooks is widespread and pervasive. For example, it has been found to occur within the USA (Anyon, 1979; Apple, 1993; Loewen, 1996; Nieto, 1996; Wills, 1994), England (Coulby, 1995; Doyle, 2002; Maw, 1991a, b; Winter, 1997), Germany (Kallis, 1999), Austria (Szabolcsi, 1992), Italy (Kallis, 1999), Greece (Kallis, 1999), Latvia (Silova, 1996), Russia (Lisovskaya & Karpov, 1999), China (Kwang, 1985) and Japan (C. Smith, 1994). The literature on this topic is far too large for us to review it all here. Instead, we will just consider two further specific examples. Whereas the Wills (1994) study concentrated on an ethnocentric bias in how the child's own country is represented, the two examples considered here both concern how *other* countries are represented. As we shall see, even when the child is being taught about other countries, there can be implicit biases present in the teaching material that still serve to convey an underlying message about the child's own state or nation. The first example of ethnocentric bias comes from an analysis of a geography textbook, while the second comes from an analysis of history textbooks.

The geography example is taken from Winter (1997). She analyses passages from a textbook entitled *"Key Geography: Connections"* (Waugh & Bushell,

1992), which was written to support English children's secondary education and follows the state-prescribed national curriculum in Geography (Department of Education and Science, 1991). The analysed passages are entitled *"Kenya—what is the Maasai way of life?"* (Waugh & Bushell, 1992, 78–79). Winter shows how an ethnocentric view underlies the presentation of information about Kenya. First, Kenya is described in the book as an *"economically developing country"*, which is explained as meaning that it *"has less capital (money) and fewer services compared with a 'developed' country like the UK"*. Thus, Kenya is immediately presented as exhibiting two deficits when compared with the UK (which is, of course, the child's own country). The book further states that *"although there are many different 'ethnic' groups living in the country, there is little tension between them"*. This sentence appears to be based on the assumption that, because there are multiple ethnic groups, tension is to be expected; the absence of such tension is therefore worth commenting on. Winter raises the question of whether this assumption might be implicitly based on a view of African peoples as savage and warring, and hence in need of European governance. Descriptions bearing negative connotations are also given of Maasai housing (*"tiny passages"*, *"huts barely reach the height of an adult Maasai"*, *"the inside is dark and full of smoke from the fire"*, *"apart from an opening the size of a brick, there are no windows or chimneys"*) and Maasai cultural practices (they use *"sticks"* to clean their teeth, and *"animal fat and vegetable fat to clean themselves"*, and they drink *"milk mixed with blood of cows"*). In her analysis, Winter also notes what is excluded from the description of the Maasai in the book: there are no references to modernization, to the changes taking place in Maasai housing, to the introduction of schools and community health care projects, to the historical exploitation of Kenya and the Maasai by European settlers, and, perhaps most seriously of all, to the views of the Maasai people themselves concerning their own culture and material circumstances. Thus, what is included and what is excluded is driven entirely by a Eurocentric perspective. Furthermore, the very way in which the included information is presented implies that Kenya is deficient vis-à-vis the child's own country. In learning about other people and places, then, the child is simultaneously being taught about the superiority of his or her own country.

The second example comes from Maw's (1991b) analysis of textbooks used to teach secondary level history in England. She focuses specifically on how Russia and the USSR are presented within these textbooks. Maw identifies three different ways in which ethnocentric bias can arise: through the exclusion of information from the text, through direct expression in the text, and through indirect expression. As an illustration of exclusion, she cites a sentence used by Snellgrove (1981, p. 188) to describe the battle of Stalingrad in World War II: *"German troops fought savagely because they feared falling into Russian hands"*. Maw comments that no explanation is given of why the

Germans feared the Russians, and no explanation is given of whether their fear was justified; instead, an unspecified dread of the Russians is invoked that plays to a particular stereotype of Russian people. The most common stereotypes of Russian people which occur throughout the various texts that Maw analyses are that Russians are superstitious, drunkards, gullible and backward. The term *"superstitious"* is used as a direct expression in the texts of several of the books, for example, "Superstitious Russians whispered among themselves that the tragedy was a bad omen for the reign of Nicholas II" (Pimlott, 1985: 5) and "Nothing was left which a superstitious people might worship" (Snellgrove, 1981: 111). Drunkenness as an attribute of Russian people is also repeatedly expressed directly, as in "One great problem remained; the ordinary Russian worker. Heavy drinking and high absence rates had long caused difficulties" (Aylett, 1987a, p. 12). The suggestion of both drunkenness and gullibility occur together in the following extract: "At the same time, the government carried out a big propaganda campaign against the Church. It said that the Holy Communion service helped to encourage drunkenness. And a newspaper even reported an interview with two airmen who said that God definitely did not exist. How did they know? They had flown up into the skies but had not seen him" (Aylett, 1987a, p. 17). The attribute of backwardness is also explicitly stated in many of the textbooks that were examined, as in the following examples: "Big and backward. That was Russia at the start of this century [i.e., the 20th century] . . . The backwardness of Russia showed in the people's lives. Only one in four had any schooling. Four out of five were poor farmers" (O'Callaghan, 1987, p. 60); "They still used wooden ploughs pulled by horses. There were no tractors" (Aylett, 1987b, p. 4); "They still used old farming methods, working by hand on their plots" (Culpin, 1986, p. 33); and "It was a backward land with few cities . . . Many harvests were still cut by hand with a sickle and threshed by hand with a flail" (Culpin, 1986, p. 71). Maw notes that these explicit passages about Russian backwardness also express an indirect message. Because no contextualization of these descriptions is provided within the books themselves, students are most likely to draw on their knowledge of their own country, that is, contemporary Britain, as the comparison, which is, of course, completely inappropriate. Students are told nothing about the extent to which Britain and other countries also used these "backward" methods of farming at the start of the 20th century (in fact, tractors only started to be used in farming from about 1910 onwards), or about the extent to which these methods are still used in many other parts of the world. These texts therefore invite students to overexaggerate the differences between Russia and the child's own country, and to place Russia at a position on a scale of modernization which is well below that of their own country. Thus, even without any explicit reference to Britain within these texts, Britain is being indirectly invoked and, by a process of comparison, found to be superior.

Lest it be thought that these two examples are extreme cases that have been selected for ease of demonstration, the reader is referred to the wide range of educational research that has now been conducted into ethnocentric bias, which has demonstrated that educational materials in many different countries, including the USA, Germany, Italy, Russia, China and Japan, frequently exhibit this type of bias (see, for example, Apple, 1993; Coulby, 1995; Doyle, 2002; Kallis, 1999; Kwang, 1985; Lisovskaya & Karpov, 1999; Loewen, 1996; Nieto, 1996; Silova, 1996; C. Smith, 1994; Szabolcsi, 1992). Once again, we need to be cautious about claiming that, merely because these biases are present within textbooks and the school curriculum, children will necessarily internalize them, or that, if they do, they will all internalize these biases in exactly the same way. That said, however, the very pervasiveness of these kinds of ethnocentric bias has alerted many educators to their potential impact on the representations that children may internalize during the course of their schooling and, as Winter (1997) and Maw (1991b) both note, there have been increased efforts in recent years to try to develop teaching materials that do not display this level of ethnocentric bias.

The school's adoption of aspects of the nation's civil culture within its own daily practices

The third way in which schools can be involved in children's national enculturation is by their adoption of particular aspects of the nation's civil culture within their own daily school practices, which children themselves then appropriate and internalize. As we saw in Chapter 1, Billig (1995), in particular, has drawn attention to the way in which commonplace objects, events and rituals continually serve to flag the nation within people's everyday lives, thereby creating an environment in which the nation is embodied within, and enhabits, many of their daily routines and practices. Schools within some countries in fact adopt very overt and explicit practices involving the state or nation. For example, in the case of the USA, on a daily basis, schoolchildren stand in front of the American flag and recite the words *"I pledge allegiance to the Flag of the United States of America, and to the Republic for which it stands: one Nation under God, indivisible, with Liberty and Justice for all"*. This pledge of allegiance was first introduced to the USA in 1892 (with slight changes of wording having taken place in 1923, 1924 and 1954). Although children may recite these words in a ritualistic fashion, with very little thought for their actual meaning, this practice nevertheless represents a daily celebration of their own country in American children's lives. Schools in other countries may not celebrate the state or nation in such an overt manner on such a regular daily basis, but other school practices, such as displaying pictures of national historical figures, national or state monuments and national landscapes in classrooms and in corridors, the singing of patriotic songs and/or hymns, and school trips to national or state museums, may be just as effective in flagging the nation or state to schoolchildren and in reinforcing their sense of attachment to it.

Very little concrete research has been conducted into the effects of these kinds of school practices on children's sense of national and state belonging or on the way in which children themselves think about and understand their own state or nation. Indeed, there is only one significant study that has explored these issues in any real depth: this is the cross-national investigation reported in Schiffauer et al. (2004), of which Schiffauer and Sunier's (2004) analysis of English, French, Dutch and German history textbooks forms one part. This study examined the relationship between national civil culture, school practices and children's own patterns of discourse and the argumentative strategies they used. Four multi-ethnic secondary schools located in London, Paris, Rotterdam and Berlin participated in the study, and the investigation focused, in particular, on the practices that were adopted within the four schools to handle issues concerning ethnic difference and diversity, as well as the relationship between these school practices and the dominant civil culture within the four nations.

Schiffauer and Sunier (2004) began the study by analysing the history textbooks used in the four schools. As we have seen already, they identified a different model of the nation in each of the four nations. Baumann and Sunier (2004), Mannitz and Schiffauer (2004), Sunier (2004a, b) and Mannitz (2004a, b) argue that these different models of the nation were not only present within the textbooks themselves, but were also embedded in the everyday practices of the schools.

In the case of the English school, for example, the textbooks were found to represent the nation as a mosaic of ethnic communities, with the internal plurality, heterogeneity and multicultural composition of the nation being emphasized, and respect for other peoples' cultures being depicted as one of the key ways in which societal problems could be solved. In accordance with this model, special consideration was given to the ethnic and cultural diversity of the school in all of its everyday practices. For example, in school corridors, posters, signs and leaflets were displayed in many different languages; ethnic foods and religious diets were catered for at mealtimes; at initial enrolment, children were classified by ethnic group and mother tongue; special attempts were made to involve the parents of minority children with the school; and the curriculum was explicitly based on a multicultural and anti-racist perspective (Mannitz & Schiffauer, 2004). Over and above these standard practices, the teachers themselves showed great sensitivity to labelling, stereotyping and name-calling; they were very concerned to ensure that cultural background did not result in any disadvantage for the minority children; and some teachers even argued for additional culture-specific strategies to accommodate the special needs of minority pupils. The children themselves constantly flagged their own ethnicities within the school. For example, the children engaged in frequent language-switching, both within and outside the classroom (Sunier, 2004a). They also commonly supported their own arguments about issues by ethnicizing those issues and then trying to mobilize their fellow ethnic pupils to support them (Sunier, 2004b).

In the case of the French school, however, the textbooks were found to present the French nation as the embodiment of republican principles and as a model of rationality based on liberty, equality and fraternity, which themselves were depicted as progressive and enlightened values. And the principles of liberty, equality and fraternity were indeed applied rigorously within the school itself: liberty was interpreted as freedom from the particular ethnic, religious and social class backgrounds from which the children came; equality was construed as equality of opportunity; and fraternity as a requirement for civility among all those who entered the school. Thus, the principle of liberty required the children to abandon all religious, linguistic and other markers of their ethnic backgrounds when they entered the school, while the principle of equality required the children to suspend all cultural differences while they were within school.[14] Thus, on enrolment, the children's ethnicity was not even recorded, and the teachers did not know, and indeed did not wish to know, the ethnic background and origins of the children (Mannitz & Schiffauer, 2004). No language other than French was spoken within the school (Sunier, 2004a) and, in argumentation and discourse, both teachers and children alike viewed the ethnic card as taboo and a deviation from the French republican project (Sunier, 2004b).

In school textbooks in the Netherlands, the nation was instead found to be depicted as a collection of individuals who have different backgrounds, lifestyles and opinions but who live peacefully together through negotiation and democratic participation in the national community; thus, ethnicity was viewed in much the same way as any other subcultural grouping within the nation. Once again, this model of the nation was implemented within the school via its everyday practices. For example, the ethnicity of children was not recorded on enrolment (Mannitz & Schiffauer, 2004). The children also tended to speak Dutch rather than their minority language in the school. Although minority language use in the school was not banned, it was generally discouraged by the teachers, on the grounds that it prevented full participation and interaction between the pupils in the overarching school community and could potentially lead to segregation and non-participation (Sunier, 2004a). There were no brochures or signs written in any minority languages, and if

[14] These same principles were, of course, famously invoked to support the Government-imposed ban in 2004 on the wearing of the *hijab* (the headscarf worn by Muslim girls and women) in all French schools: the ban was justified on the grounds that it emancipated the Muslim girls from their parents' demands that they adopt their family's religious practices.

parents had difficulties with the Dutch language, it was their own responsibility to get an interpreter. Sunier (2004b) argues that teachers implicitly followed the national model when handling class discussions. The teacher's role was to keep the discussion going. The expectation was that all children should participate actively in the discussion; everyone should give their own opinion; everyone should pay attention to and respect everyone else's opinions; there should be shared responsibility for the outcome; and if a common opinion did not emerge, there should nevertheless be a respectful appreciation of the different opinions expressed. Sunier comments that not only the teachers but also the pupils accepted these general principles and adhered to them.

Finally, in Germany, the model of the nation-state that was found to be presented in textbooks is that democracy is fragile and needs to be protected against all forms of extremism, with democratic participation being both a virtue and a duty, and protection of the democratic order being a civic imperative that must be internalized by the responsible citizen. Sunier (2004b) compares the class discussions that took place in the German school with those that occurred in the Dutch school. He notes that the discussion styles were very different: in the German school, the teacher adopted a central role in steering the discussion, with the conversation going from teacher to pupil and back again. The teacher operated as an expert who reminded and corrected pupils of the proper answer, and strongly guided the discussion towards a predetermined outcome, which was a rational and responsible judgement compatible with the common good. Crucially, however, pupils were encouraged to self-reflect on their own opinions and to generate conscience-based statements. As far as ethnic minority children were concerned, because being German is construed by many German people as an ethnic category determined by descent, a boundary is commonly perceived to exist between being a German and an *Ausländer* (foreigner). Consequently, language itself is irrelevant to these two statuses. And indeed, within the school, there was no specific language policy, and no clear regulations or rules about the use of minority languages in the school (although mastering the German language was widely recognized by both teachers and children as essential for an individual to participate effectively in German society). As a result, minority languages were used by the children both within and outside the classroom (Sunier, 2004a).

In commenting on these findings, both Baumann (2004) and Mannitz and Schiffauer (2004) draw on Billig's (1995) work to argue that the national histories depicted within textbooks reveal images of the nation that become deeply engrained within children through their everyday habits of discourse and practice. Mannitz (2004b) further argues that the school functions as the crucial institution through which these representations of the nation are transmitted to children; in other words, it is the school that mediates between the dominant civil culture of the nation on the one hand and the behaviour, identifications and discourse of its children on the other hand. She postulates that, through these various school practices, the children in all four national settings did not simply master the prevailing civil conventions of their own nation but also internalized them, and came to use them within their own discourse, argumentation and practices. Thus, the children in these four countries were nationally encultured by their schools in ways that were specifically either English, French, Dutch or German.

In evaluating this argument, it is important to bear in mind two points. First, this study was conducted in just one school in each of the four countries. This raises the possibility that there may have been school-specific effects in the findings. In fact, this is highly likely, given that the four schools were all multi-ethnic schools located in major cities. It would be interesting to examine children who are attending ethnically more homogeneous schools located outside major urban centres in order to ascertain whether similar patterns of thinking and arguing emerge in these other types of schools within the same nation as well. Second, the data that these authors use to support their argument are drawn primarily from qualitative analyses of selected extracts of discourse produced by the children in each of the four schools studied. However, we do not know how representative these selected extracts of discourse were even of those four schools; that is, how pervasive these ways of talking and arguing actually were within these schools. As we have seen already, Wertsch's (1998) work suggests that there may well be rather more individual variability in children's appropriation of a particular model of the nation than this body of work suggests. Systematic sampling supplemented by quantitative content analysis, accompanied by a greater sensitivity to the possible variability between children, is really required in order to establish the generality of the patterns described by Schiffauer et al. (2004).

In fact, individual variability among ethnic minority children, in particular, is highly likely, given what we know from research into the acculturation of ethnic minority children (see, for example, Ali, 2003; Anwar, 1998; Bernal & Knight, 1993; Bernal, Knight, Garza, Ocampo, & Cota, 1990; Ghuman, 1999, 2003; Hutnik, 1986, 1991; Hutnik & Barrett, 2003; Phinney, 1990; Phinney & Devich-Navarro, 1997; Phoenix, 1995; Portes & Rumbaut, 2001). These studies have revealed that minority children can exhibit considerable variability both in their levels of identification with the nation in which they live and in their attitudes towards, and adoption of, the majority cultural practices of that nation. For example, ethnic minority children sometimes identify with the majority culture but sometimes they do not; and they sometimes adopt but sometimes reject the dominant cultural practices of the nation. Furthermore, identification and cultural practices are not always related to one another (Hutnik, 1991; Hutnik & Barrett, 2003). Ethnic minority children's adoption or rejection of the majority culture is influenced by a number of factors, including the prevailing socio-political situation, social policies and institutionalized arrangements relating to issues of cultural difference and diversity, and perceived levels of racial prejudice and discrimination (Ghuman, 2003). Furthermore, this body of research has revealed that minority children often adopt different cultural practices in different life domains, especially in private (i.e., within the home) vs. public (i.e., outside the home) domains, with minority practices sometimes being preferred within private domains but majority national practices or bicultural practices being preferred in public domains (Anwar, 1998; Ghuman, 2003). Thus, there is considerable variability among ethnic minority children in their attitudes to, and appropriation of, the dominant national culture in which they live. Given the considerable amount of within-nation variability that we know occurs in other aspects of the national enculturation process more generally, it would not be at all surprising if future research were to reveal that ethnic majority children also exhibit substantial variability in their appropriation of dominant national cultural practices.

Conclusions on the role of the school in children's national enculturation

It is clear from the existing research that has been conducted into this issue that the school is a very important influence on children's national enculturation. Indeed, it is for this very reason that schools are often used strategically by states for precisely this purpose. Schools can impact on children's national enculturation through the direct teaching they provide about the state and the nation, through the ethnocentric biases that school textbooks and educational curricula often contain, and through the everyday practices of the school that often embody aspects of the dominant civil culture of the nation. However, much more research is required to establish how children themselves actually respond to these various influences from the school. There has also been insufficient attention by previous researchers to the individual variability that almost certainly occurs in children's appropriation of the national cultural representations and practices to which they are exposed at school.

CHILDREN'S KNOWLEDGE AND UTILIZATION OF NATIONAL AND STATE EMBLEMS

During the course of their development, children also acquire a personal sense of familiarity with, and an emotional attachment to, the emblems used to represent their own state and nation (i.e., emblems such as flags, anthems, ceremonials, buildings, monuments, etc.). Theorists such as Anderson (1983), A.D. Smith (1991, 1998) and Billig (1995) have attributed considerable importance to the role of national emblems in mediating and sustaining people's awareness of, and feelings towards, their own national group (see also Boswell & Evans, 1999), because they provide concrete representations of the national group, which in itself is only an imagined, rather than a personally experienced, community. Thus, national emblems provide perceptible salient entities with which group members can identify in the course of their everyday lives, with these emblems functioning to objectify and concretize something (i.e., the nation) that is, in fact, a highly abstract cultural and historical construction. These emblems also serve to differentiate the individual's own nation or state from other nations and states. National historical emblems (that is, the people, places and artefacts associated with the history of the nation, which are embedded within the historical narratives of the nation's past) have been hypothesized to be especially important in this regard, due to the fact that they are claimed to embody the national group's collective memories, and serve as a reminder to group members of what they share, their common cultural heritage and history, differentiating them from other groups, and providing them with a sense of cohesion and group belonging that might otherwise be lacking (Devine-Wright & Lyons, 1997; Lyons, 1996; A.D. Smith, 1991, 1998; Tanaka, 1994; Wertsch, 1994, 1998). In this section, we will examine the research that has been conducted into children's knowledge, understanding and utilization of these national and state emblems.

Children's knowledge and understanding of national and state emblems

One of the earliest studies in this area was conducted by Weinstein (1957). He interviewed American 5- to 12-year-old children about their understanding of the American flag. On the basis of the children's answers to a set of 22 questions, Weinstein identified the following developmental progression. The lowest level of understanding, displayed by many of the 5-year-olds, entailed recognizing the flag only in terms of its physical characteristics, including its colours and stars, and knowing that it is linked to singing and celebrations, but not knowing anything about any other countries' flags. By 6 years of age, the children knew that different countries had different flags, and by 7 years of age, they thought the function of flags was to indicate which country owns something (such as a ship or a building). Over the next year or so, children's knowledge of the number of countries, and of the assets that belong to them, expanded considerably. However, Weinstein found that it was not until approximately 8 years of age that children finally began to understand the symbolism associated with the flag, that is, that the flag can be used to honour and celebrate their country. From about 9 years, Weinstein found that the children started to talk about their country not just as a geographical territory but also as a group of people who share common purposes and a common allegiance; the flag was now clearly recognized as a conventional symbol that stands for the whole country and its population who share broad common goals. From about 10 years of age, the children began to understand that the flag stands for loyalty to a more abstract set of principles and goals than to any particular government as such. Finally, at about 11–12 years, there was an increased knowledge of the rituals associated with the flag, and an understanding of the full implications of convention. For example, one older child said: "Well, I don't think the government could change the flag like that [i.e., to green and white with a red apple in the middle] unless all of the people agreed to it. If they did, it would be a true American flag because it stood for the American people". Thus, across this age range, there was a gradual shift away from a conceptualization of the flag in terms of its physical characteristics and functional utility (e.g., to show which country owns a particular piece of land, building, ship, etc.) to an understanding of flags as conventionally agreed emblems representing nations and states containing people who share common allegiances and goals, which can be used for the symbolic function of signifying loyalty to that nation or state. The main transition appeared to occur at around 9 years of age. Notice that this is the same age at which children also begin to understand the nature and structure of the state as a political entity (see Chapter 3).

In a subsequent study, Jahoda (1963b) examined 6- to 11-year-old Scottish children's knowledge of a much wider range of national and state emblems, including songs, flags, costumes, landscapes, buildings and famous historical people. He played the songs to the children and showed them pictures of the other emblems, and asked the children whether they recognized them, what they knew about them, to which country the emblems belonged, and to pick out the emblems that belonged to Scotland. The 6- to 7-year-olds displayed moderately good knowledge of Scottish national emblems, which they could pick out with about 60% accuracy; the 8- to 9-year-olds identified the Scottish emblems with about 80% accuracy; while the 10- to 11-year-olds could pick these emblems out with about 90% accuracy (these oldest children could also identify many other countries' emblems).

Moore et al. (1985) also tested the American children who participated in their longitudinal study for their knowledge of American emblems. Each year, they gave the children a set of pictures to identify. As far as the American flag was concerned, 99% of the children in kindergarten could pick this out from a set of four flags. These children were therefore significantly more advanced in their ability to recognize the flag of their own country than Jahoda's Scottish children: only 58% of Jahoda's 6- to 7-year olds could identify the British flag as being the flag of either Scotland or Britain, and it was not until the Scottish children were 10–11 years old that they showed similar levels of performance to Moore et al.'s kindergartners (Jahoda does not report any data concerning the children's ability to identify the St Andrew's

Cross, i.e., the Scottish flag). All of the 5-year-old American children in Weinstein's (1957) study also appeared to be able to recognize the American flag. The American children's advantage here is possibly a consequence of their having to recite the pledge of allegiance to the American flag on a daily basis. Hence, this may well be an example of how a regular school practice impacts on one small but highly significant aspect of children's knowledge in this domain. In this context, it is pertinent to note that Connell (1971) also found that all of his Australian children, at the age of 5, already knew about both the Queen and the Australian flag; Connell notes that these children all received explicit teaching at school about these two emblems. These various findings are consistent with the suggestion that teaching and school practices can be important influences on children's knowledge of national and state emblems.

Moore et al. also assessed their children's ability to recognize six pictures of George Washington, Abraham Lincoln, the Statue of Liberty, the Liberty Bell, the White House and the Capitol building. From first grade onwards, the children were also asked two additional questions, "What is the Star Spangled Banner?" and "What do we celebrate on July 4th?". In kindergarten, 35% of the children did not know any of the six pictorial emblems; this figure dropped to 18% in first grade and to 5% in second grade. In fourth grade, 21% of the children responded correctly to all eight questions, and 46% of the children responded correctly to seven of the eight questions. Thus, at about 9 years of age, two thirds of these American children recognized all or virtually all of these emblems. These figures appear to be roughly comparable to those obtained by Jahoda (1963b) with his 8- to 9-year-old Scottish children. Thus, the American children's advantage was restricted to their recognition of the American flag alone. Moore et al. also found that the boys tended to know more of the emblems than the girls.

In a more recent study, Barrett et al. (1997) examined 6- to 15-year-old British, Spanish and Italian children's ability to recognize the flags, currencies, monuments, landscapes, foods and ceremonies of Britain, France, Germany, Spain and Italy.[15] In the case of the children living in Britain and Spain, knowledge of both national (i.e., English, Scottish or Catalan, as appropriate) and state (i.e., British and Spanish) emblems was examined. Not surprisingly, there was an increase in the children's knowledge with age. The study also found that the children tended to exhibit more knowledge of their own state's and nation's emblems than of other states' and nations' emblems. However, there were some exceptions here. For example, the Italian children recognized the Eiffel Tower as a French emblem more frequently than they recognized the Tower of Pisa as an Italian emblem. In other words, emblems of the

---

[15] These data were collected as part of the CHOONGE project, which will be described in greater detail in Chapter 5.

child's own country are not always better known than those of other countries. There were also differences between the British, Spanish and Italian children's knowledge of the emblems associated with their own state and nation. However, these differences varied depending on the particular type of emblem involved. For example, the Italian children had a better knowledge of the Italian flag and currency than the British and Spanish children had of their own state flags and currencies. However, famous ceremonials associated with the child's own state or nation (e.g., the Changing of the Guards, bullfights, and the Sienese Palio) were better known by the British and Spanish children than by the Italian children. This was probably due to the fact that Italian ceremonials are not so emblematic of Italy as British and Spanish ones are of Britain and Spain, respectively.

In another recent study, Helwig and Prencipe (1999) returned to the issue originally investigated by Weinstein (1957), examining 6-, 8- and 10-year-old Canadian children's understanding of flags, as well as their understanding of the act of flag-burning. The children were interviewed about their understanding of flags as symbols. They were also read a series of stories about different flag-burning incidents, in which the person's intention in burning the flag and the location of the incident were systematically manipulated, and the children were asked questions about these various incidents. Helwig and Prencipe found that the children at all ages, including the 6-year-olds, viewed flags as social conventions that could be altered by consensus or shared agreement. These Canadian children therefore exhibited a more advanced understanding than that shown by Weinstein's American children. However, the older children were more likely to recognize flag-burning as a symbolic expression of disrespect. Although younger children were just as likely to recognize that flag-burning was offensive, they focused more on the loss of the flag's functional utility rather than on the symbolic transgression and the wilful disrespect to the country that flag-burning entails, which was instead emphasized by the older children. Hence, the younger children actually viewed the burning of a map of a country as a more serious offence than the burning of its flag, unlike the older children. Also, older children showed an awareness of possible contextual influences, whereas the younger children did not. For example, the older children were more likely to acknowledge that if a country was "unfair" (whether it be Canada or elsewhere), then it might be more acceptable to burn that country's flag.

Thus, these studies show that children already know some national and state emblems by 5–6 years of age. However, their knowledge and understanding of such emblems continues to develop through subsequent years. Children's understanding of flags, in particular, shifts from a functional to a symbolic conceptualization across the course of middle childhood. Emblems of the child's own nation and state are usually, although not always, better known than those of other nations and states. However, there are cross-national differences in children's knowledge of such emblems, which are likely to be a consequence either of the different school practices and teaching that take place in different countries, or of the fact that particular kinds of emblems are more emblematic of some states and nations than of others.

Children's utilization of national and state emblems

A second interrelated set of issues concerns children's utilization, rather than their knowledge, of national and state emblems. Given the key role that theorists have attributed to national emblems in sustaining people's awareness of national and state groups, it is of particular interest to know which emblems children themselves use spontaneously when thinking about their own nation and state. Furthermore, given the potential power of these emblems for mobilizing national and civic sentiment among populations, it is also important to understand the ontogenesis of the emotional responses that can be elicited by these emblems, and of the factors responsible for the emergence of these emotions. It is also of interest to know how children themselves use and interpret such emblems within specific contexts (e.g., international sporting occasions, when visiting other countries, etc.). However, relatively little developmental research has been conducted into these various issues.

One very early study was conducted by E.L. Horowitz (1940). He showed 6- to 15-year-old American children a page containing pictures of 24 flags, and asked them to pick out *"the best looking flag"*. When the child had made his or her choice, that flag was covered up and the child was asked to choose the next best looking one. This procedure was repeated until five choices had been made. Many of the youngest children picked out the American flag among their choice of five, as did *all* of the older children. However, the younger children often chose the flags of other nations *before* they selected the American flag. The rank order position of the American flag increased significantly as a function of the children's age, and the American flag was *always* chosen first by the oldest group of children. When the older children were asked about why they had chosen the American flag as the best looking flag, they usually acknowledged that it was because it was the flag of their own country. The younger children, when questioned, usually said that they had chosen a particular flag *"because I like it"*. Hess and Easton, in their eight-city study, also found that the American flag was a highly salient emblem for American children. When they asked the children to choose from a large set of pictures depicting different emblems of America *"the best pictures to represent America"*, the American flag and the Statue of Liberty were the two emblems most frequently chosen by the children at all ages (Hess & Torney, 1967).

Moodie (1980) conducted a study with white South African children. These children were aged between 6 and 13 years, and half of them attended an Afrikaans-language school, while the other half attended an English-language school. The data were collected in the late 1970s. The children were asked to draw *"the people of my country"*. They were then interviewed about their country, and shown photographs of everyday scenes and emblems of South Africa and asked to describe these. Both the drawings and the verbal responses about *"the people of my country"* showed the same shift with age, from an initial focus on family and friends at younger ages to a focus on extrafamilial groups (especially racialized and language groups) at older ages. Across this age range, there were also significant increases both in the number of positive mentions of the children's own language group, and in the number of negative mentions of the other language group; attitudes towards black people in both groups of children did not show any significant changes with age.[16] Not unexpectedly, the children's ability to identify the state emblems increased significantly with age, and the two groups did not differ in this respect. However, they did differ in terms of their affective responses to these emblems. From 8 years of age onwards, the Afrikaans-speaking children were more likely to express positive affect towards the South African flag than the English-speaking children and were more likely to prefer the South African flag to other flags. Furthermore, when the children were asked what the best thing about their country was, 37.5% of the Afrikaans-speaking children mentioned the flag or the anthem. However, only 3.6% of the English-speaking children mentioned either of these two emblems; they instead produced significantly more references to the flora, fauna and geographical features of South Africa. Moodie notes that for the English-speaking children, loyalty to the country meant an affection for the land, whereas for the Afrikaans-speaking children it meant civic pride in the state. In other words, within the same country, the affective connotations of, and emotional responses to, state emblems appeared to vary significantly as a function of the language group to which the children belonged.

In addition to this variability within countries, Cutts Dougherty, Eisenhart, and Webley (1992) have shown that there can also be significant variability across countries in the types of national and state emblems used by children. They interviewed English and Argentine schoolboys who were aged 7, 10, 12 and 17 years old about their territorial images and their concepts of war; the boys were also asked about the Falklands/Malvinas conflict, which had taken place 2 years previously (in which Britain and Argentina had gone to war over ownership of the islands). The English and Argentine boys produced

---

[16] Children's intergroup attitudes will be discussed at length in Chapter 5. Where we will see that there is considerable variability in the development of such altitudes.

very similar descriptions of war, and the age-related differences in their descriptions were not dissimilar to those found by Berti and Vanni (2000); thus, the younger children tended to refer to concrete actions (e.g., *"war is fighting, lots of bombs"*) while the older children, particularly the 12- and 17-year-olds, produced more (negative) evaluations of war and explicit references to politicians. However, differences between the English and Argentine boys began to appear when they were asked the question "Why do you think your country would go to war?". In both countries, defence of the country was the most frequent response, but the English and Argentine boys differed over which specific aspect of the country would be defended through war: 64% of the Argentine boys referred to territorial sovereignty, with only 15% mentioning people, and 8% mentioning political principles; by comparison, only 28% of the English boys mentioned territorial sovereignty, 31% mentioned defence of the people, and 21% mentioned political principles. In reference to the Falklands/Malvinas, similar differences arose. Here, the Argentine boys, from as early as 7 years of age, invoked national territory, with material possession and ownership of this territory representing a major aspect of being Argentine; at all four ages, these boys were persistent in their belief that their country would go to war over territorial issues. The English boys, however, gave far greater emphasis to the Queen, the people and the political principles that hold their country together than they did to territorial integrity: younger children talked about defending the Queen and the English people, while older children talked about upholding the people's rights and the defence of democracy and freedom. Cutts Dougherty et al. argue that these differential responses reflected the different types of symbolic content which the boys had acquired to represent their own country, with the Argentine boys using geographical territory as a core emblem, and the English boys using the Queen, the people and political principles as their core emblems instead.

Forrest and Barrett (2001) focused more specifically on children's use of *historical* emblems to represent the nation. They asked a group of 11- to 15-year-old English children to name two people, two places and two events from history that they thought were *"very English"*; they also assessed the children's strength of identification with being English. In general, and irrespective of age and gender, the children tended to cite *Henry VIII, Buckingham Palace* and the *Battle of Hastings* with relatively high frequency. However, there were other differences in the children's responses as a function of age and gender. For example, the older children cited *Winston Churchill* and *William Shakespeare* more frequently than the younger children, whereas the younger children cited *Queen Elizabeth I* more frequently than the older children. These differences appeared to be a consequence of recent educational input that the children had received in their history and literature lessons at school. In addition, the boys cited *Wembley* (the location of the national soccer stadium) as a historical place, and *England Winning the Soccer World Cup in 1966* as a historical event, more frequently than the girls; by comparison, the younger girls cited *Princess Diana* (a figure who had received major news and media coverage within these children's own lifetimes) as a historical figure more frequently. These gender differences are explicable in terms of boys' greater interest in sport (Beal, 1994; Lever, 1978; Zill, 1986), and children's heightened attention to same-gender role models in the mass media (Durkin, 1985; Eckes & Trautner, 2000; Gunter & McAleer, 1997; Luecke-Aleksa, Anderson, Collins, & Schmitt, 1995; Ruble & Martin, 1998). In addition, the boys exhibited higher levels of national identification than the girls. Forrest and Barrett also examined whether those children who had a strong sense of identification with being English produced different national historical emblems from those who had a weaker sense of national identification; however, there were no significant differences here.

In another study, Maehr and Barrett (2005) examined 12- to 18-year-old German children's production of national emblems; they also assessed these children's strength of identification with being German. The children were first asked to list as many German national emblems as they could; they were then asked to list the people, places and events that they associated with Germany. Boys and girls of all ages tended to cite the *national flag*, the *Federal eagle*, *Hitler* and the *Fall of the Berlin Wall* to the same extent. However, the younger children were more likely to cite the *Brandenburg Gate* than the older children, while the older children were instead more likely to cite the *swastika*, *World War I* and *World War II* than the younger children. These age differences appeared to be due to educational input: whereas the younger children had only studied Germany in the Middle Ages in their school history lessons so far, the older children had studied the two World Wars. Gender differences were also exhibited: the boys were more likely to cite the *swastika*, *Berlin*, *World War I* and *World War II* than the girls, whereas the girls were more likely to cite the *Brandenburg Gate* than the boys. The boys also exhibited significantly stronger national identifications than the girls. A striking feature was the high overall frequency with which both *Hitler* and *World War II* were spontaneously mentioned by the children irrespective of age and gender: by 62.6% and 44.4% of the children overall, respectively. By comparison, the national flag was only mentioned spontaneously by 40.2% of the children. Notice that these figures are consistent both with the prominence that the Nazi period receives in contemporary representations of the German nation (Knischewski, 1996; Rossteutscher, 1997; Schiffauer & Sunier, 2004) and with the low level of regard displayed by many German adults towards the national flag (Merkl, 1992). There were also significant associations between the strength of national identification and the national emblems produced by the children; those with a high level of national identification were more likely to mention the *swastika*, *Berlin*, *World War I* and *World War II*, whereas those with a low level of identification were more likely to mention the *Brandenburg Gate* and the *Berlin bear*.

Finally, Trimby and Barrett (2005) examined the production of national emblems by 6- to 11-year-old Welsh children, and also measured the children's strength of identification with being Welsh. The children were successively asked to name *"some things"*, *"some famous people"* and *"some places which you can go to and visit"* which they thought were *"very, very Welsh"*. The most frequently produced responses were *Cardiff* (the capital city of Wales), the *Welsh Red Dragon*, the *Welsh flag*, the *Welsh language*, and *Ryan Giggs* (a famous Welsh soccer player). Not surprisingly, the older children produced more emblems than the younger children. In addition, the boys produced significantly more emblems than the girls. However, the boys did not exhibit stronger national identifications than the girls. In addition, there were statistically significant associations between the strength of identification with being Welsh and the particular national emblems produced by the children: those with stronger national identifications were more likely to mention the *daffodil* (a Welsh national emblem), *rugby* and *Ryan Giggs* than those with weaker national identifications. Furthermore, those children who had stronger national identifications produced significantly more national emblems than those with weaker identifications. Thus, the strength of national identification did appear to be related to national emblematic knowledge. The direction of the causality here is ambiguous however: it could be the case that having a strong sense of national identification motivates a child to acquire more knowledge about national emblems; or that when a child has a large store of knowledge about national emblems, this generates a stronger sense of national identification in that child; or it could be that both variables are a consequence of other factors, such as family discourse and practices, with some families attributing greater importance to the nation than others, with the consequence that children from such families develop both a stronger sense of national identification and a greater knowledge of national emblems.

Thus, there is considerable variability in children's utilization of national and state emblems. In different countries, children may adopt different types of emblems as the core emblems of their own state or nation, while within an individual country, children may utilize different emblems for representing their state or nation as a function of their language group (and presumably their ethnic group as well, although concrete evidence is lacking on this particular issue), their gender, their age and their strength of national identification. Furthermore, the existing evidence suggests that children's knowledge and utilization of national and state emblems is probably influenced by educational input and possibly by the mass media and the family as well. Notice, however, that there has been very little research into children's emotional responses and affective attachment to national and state emblems, or into children's use and interpretation of such emblems within specific social contexts.

SUMMARY

The following general conclusions emerge from the research reviewed in this chapter.

- As far as children's pride in their own country is concerned:
    - such pride is often present at 7 years of age, and persists through into late adolescence
    - although children do not always regard their own country as the best country in the world, children and adolescents in all countries do generally hold positive attitudes towards their own country
    - however, there is considerable variability not only across different countries but also within individual countries in children's levels of pride
    - there are sometimes gender differences in children's levels of pride in their own country, with boys tending to exhibit higher levels than girls.
- It is clear that the school is an important agent of children's national enculturation for a number of reasons:
    - the school routinely provides a considerable amount of explicit teaching about the child's own state and nation, and children therefore acquire knowledge about the history, cultural heritage, emblems and values of their own nation and state directly from this source
    - within different nations, children can be exposed, via the school curriculum and school textbooks, to very different models of the values for which their own nation stands, and as a consequence, children may acquire through their schooling a model of the nation that is specific to their own nation
    - however, children do not always learn the culturally dominant narratives about the historical origins of their own state and nation to which they are exposed at school
    - furthermore, even when these narratives are learnt, they may nevertheless be either resisted or rejected by some children
    - school curricula and textbooks frequently contain ethnocentric biases, in which children's own country is presented in a positive or flattering light, with the result that children's representations of their own country may be positively skewed through their appropriation of these biased representations
    - the everyday practices of schools frequently embody aspects of the

dominant civil culture of the nation in which they are located, and through their participation in these school practices, children may master and internalize the prevailing civil conventions of their own nation.

- As far as children's knowledge and utilization of national and state emblems is concerned:
  - most children already know some national and state emblems by 5–6 years of age, and this knowledge continues to develop through subsequent years
  - children's understanding of flags, in particular, changes significantly across the course of middle childhood, from a functional to a symbolic conceptualization
  - boys sometimes display better knowledge of national and state emblems than girls
  - however, there is significant variation across different countries in children's knowledge of national and state emblems, which may be a consequence either of the different school practices and teaching that take place in different countries, or of the fact that certain types of emblems are more emblematic of some countries than of others
  - variability across countries also exists in children's utilization of, and affect for, national and state emblems, with children in different countries sometimes adopting different kinds of emblems as the core emblems for their own nation or state
  - there is also significant variability within individual countries in children's utilization of, and affect for, national and state emblems as a function of their language group (and probably also their ethnicity), their gender, and their age
  - children's knowledge and utilization of national and state emblems appear to be influenced by educational input and possibly by the mass media and the family as well.

CHAPTER FIVE

Children's knowledge, beliefs and feelings about the people who belong to different national and state groups

Martyn Barrett, Luciano Arcuri, Mark Bennett, Anna Emilia Berti, Anna Silvia Bombi, Luigi Castelli, Annamaria de Rosa, Arantza del Valle, Rauf Garagozov, Almudena Giménez de la Peña, Thea Kacharava, Giorgi Kipiani, Evanthia Lyons, Valentyna Pavlenko, Santiago Perera, Luixa Reizábal, Tatiana Riazanova, Fabio Sani, Jose Valencia and Ignasi Vila

In the previous chapters, we have examined the development of children's knowledge, beliefs and feelings about the geographical territories of countries, the development of children's understanding of and attitudes to the state as a political entity, and the development of children's knowledge, beliefs and feelings about nations and states when these are viewed as historical and cultural communities. In this chapter, we shift our focus once again, to look at the development of children's representations of, and attitudes to, the people who belong to different national and state groups.

This chapter is subdivided into five parts. In the first and second parts, we review the findings of previous studies that have been conducted into children's representations of, and attitudes to, the people who belong to different national and state groups. We examine, in particular, the phenomena of in-group favouritism and out-group denigration, and children's attitudes to national and state groups that are the traditional enemies of their own nation or state. The third part of this chapter then presents some findings on these issues that have emerged from two recent cross-national comparative research projects, the CHOONGE and NERID projects, which have been conducted by the collective authorship of this book. In the fourth part of the chapter, we examine the sources of children's knowledge and beliefs about the people who live in other countries. In the final part of the chapter, we review studies that have investigated children's beliefs about the factors which determine people's national and state group memberships. We begin by looking at three early studies.

EARLY STUDIES INTO CHILDREN'S REPRESENTATIONS OF, AND ATTITUDES TO, THE PEOPLE WHO LIVE IN DIFFERENT COUNTRIES

The initial work of Piaget and Weil

The earliest study to examine children's conceptions of the people who live in different countries was that conducted by Piaget and Weil (1951). As we saw in Chapter 2, on the basis of interviews they conducted with 4- to 15-year-old Swiss Genevan children, Piaget and Weil postulated that children's large-scale geographical knowledge develops through a sequence of four stages, an initial pre-stage of ignorance (up to about 5 years of age), followed by three proper developmental stages. In this same study, Piaget and Weil also examined the children's representations of the people who live in different countries. On the basis of their findings, they proposed that children's thinking about such people develops through the same sequence of stages as their geographical thinking.

During the first proper developmental stage (between approximately 5- to 7–8 years of age), children start to learn about the existence of groups such as Swiss people, French people, Italian people, etc. However, Piaget and Weil argue that children's patterns of preferences and attitudes at this early age are idiosyncratic, and are often based on transient personal experiences. Instead, they propose that it is only during the second stage (i.e., between 7–8 and 10–11 years of age) that children's views converge with those that are commonly expressed in their social environment, with their own views towards particular groups becoming either positive, neutral or negative depending on the specific stereotypes that prevail in the child's social milieu. For example, one child (aged 9;6) who they interviewed responded as follows:

> (Have you heard of such people as foreigners?) Yes, the French, the Americans, the Russians, the English ... (Quite right. Are there differences between all these people?) Oh yes, they don't speak the same language. (And what else?) I don't know. (What do you think of the French, for instance? Do you like them or not? Try and tell me as much as possible.) The French are not very serious, they don't worry about anything, an' it's dirty there. (And what do you think of the Americans?) They're ever so rich and clever. They've discovered the atom bomb. (And what do you think of the Russians?) They're bad, they're always wanting to make war. (And what's your opinion of the English?) I don't know ... they're nice ... (Now look, how did you come to know all you've told me?) I don't know ... I've heard it ... that's what people say.

Another child (aged 8;2) responded as follows:

> (Have you heard of foreigners?) Yes, there are Germans and French. (Are there any differences between these foreigners?) Yes, the Germans are bad, they are always making war. The French are poor and everything is dirty there. Then I've heard of Russians too, they're not at all nice. (Do you have any personal knowledge of the French, Germans or Russians or have you read something about them?) No. (Then how do you know?) Everyone says so.

Piaget and Weil argue that, in addition to acquiring these socially shared stereotypes, children at this intermediate stage begin to exhibit a systematic preference for the people who belong to their own group. In other words, Piaget and Weil propose that the phenomenon of in-group favouritism first appears during this stage.

In the final stage of development (from about 10–11 years onwards), Piaget and Weil argue that children become much more independent of their social environment in making their judgements and evaluations. For example, one child (aged 13;9) responded as follows (after he had mentioned a large number of foreign countries):

> (Are there any differences between all those people?) Yes, they're not all of the same race and don't have the same language. And you don't find the same faces everywhere, the same types, the same morals and the same religion. (But do all these differences have any effect on the people?) Oh yes, they don't all have the same mentality. Each people has its own special background.

Another child (aged 13;3) responded in the following way:

> (Are there any differences between all those countries?) There is only a difference of size and position between all these countries. It's not the country that makes the difference, but the people. You find all types of people everywhere.

An interesting idea pursued by Piaget and Weil in their paper concerns the child's understanding of the reciprocity of the foreigner, that is, the child's understanding that foreigners feel exactly the same emotional attachments to their own countries as the child experiences towards his or her own country. Piaget and Weil report that, before the age of about 7–8 years, the children simply believed that foreigners were people who belonged to other countries, whereas Swiss people could never be foreigners, even when they were in another country. The children were also asked the hypothetical question "If you were born without any nationality and you were allowed to choose what nationality you liked, which would you choose?". Up to 7–8 years of age, the children said that they would choose to be Swiss; in addition, they said that a French or English child in exactly the same situation would also choose to be

Swiss, rather than their own nationality. In the second stage, between 7–8 and 10–11 years of age, the children began to show some understanding of the relativity of the concept of a foreigner, but this understanding was still somewhat confused and inconsistent, with the children sometimes saying that a foreigner in Switzerland was simultaneously both a foreigner and Swiss, whereas a Swiss person in France was simultaneously both a foreigner but still Swiss. At this intermediate stage, the children also began to acknowledge that, if given the choice, a foreign child would choose his or her own nationality and country; however, at the same time, they asserted that these foreign children would be making the wrong choice, because Switzerland and being Swiss were always the best choices to make. Piaget and Weil claim that it was only in the final stage of development, after 10–11 years of age, that the children finally began to acknowledge both the relativity of the concept of a foreigner, recognizing that the meaning of this concept depended on the perspective of the individual using it, and the relativity of people's judgements about which is the best country and nationality. Subsequent researchers have not pursued these ideas. However, it would be interesting to ascertain the extent to which this developmental process occurs in other populations, and indeed whether the developmental process is as systematic as Piaget and Weil's description implies (cf. Jahoda's 1963a, 1964 studies, which undermined Piaget and Weil's stage-based description of the development of children's geographical knowledge about countries; see Chapter 2 for details).

Jahoda's work on children's attitudes to the people who live in other countries

Jahoda (1962) also collected data about children's attitudes towards the people who live in other countries. The participants in his study were Scottish Glaswegian children aged between 6 and 11 years old. Although the primary focus of this study was children's geographical knowledge of other countries (see Chapter 2), Jahoda found that many of the children spontaneously offered him comments about the people who lived in foreign countries.

In contradistinction to Piaget and Weil, Jahoda found that even the youngest children in his study sometimes expressed a strong dislike of German people, with the war being cited as the reason for this dislike. For example, one 6-year-old justified this feeling with the comment "They fought against us"; another 7-year-old said "Because they fight with the British". This dislike of Germans was also present among the older children. For example, one 9-year-old child said: "Hitler was bad, so I don't like Germans. He used to come here and take wee children back and stab them and put them into camps and there is still a lot of British people kept in those camps". However, in addition, the 8- to 9-year-olds sometimes expressed a dislike of Japanese people as well, also for reasons relating to the war. So, for example, one 9-year-old child said that they disliked Japanese people "Because they bombed other countries", while another 9-year-old said it was because "They started war with us". In addition, the 8- to 9-year-olds occasionally mentioned particular incidents or situations as a reason for their dislike of a particular group of foreign people. For example, one 9-year-old said that they disliked Czechoslovakian people because "They were pushing about when they played Rangers" (Rangers being a local football team). As far as the 10- to 11-year-olds were concerned, Russians topped their list of disliked people (the study was conducted during the Cold War era). Comments such as the following were used to justify their dislike of Russians: "The way they're behaving. (Please explain.) They think they're going to start another world war" (10-year-old); "They're not like, say, Americans—they're awful into themselves. If they get anything of importance they get big ideas. In years to come they might start a war" (11-year-old).

As far as the children's likes, rather than their dislikes, were concerned, the youngest children (6- to 7-year-olds) tended to produce idiosyncratic judgements and evaluations based either on the appeal of unusual or exotic features, or on isolated pieces of information that the children had fortuitously acquired. However, both the 8- to 9-year-olds and the 10- to 11-year-olds used the perceived similarity of a foreign group to themselves to justify liking that group; for example, one 11-year-old said that they liked Australian people because "Their people are a bit similar to us. They speak the same language, although they have a different accent". In addition to perceived similarity, the 10- to 11-year-olds sometimes referred to the positive characteristics of a group to justify their positive feelings towards that group. Examples included "People are gay and friendly" (a 10-year-old's comment about French people), and "Most of them have a good sense of humour— you never see them with dour faces" (an 11-year-old's comment about American people).

Jahoda's study therefore suggests that, contrary to Piaget and Weil's claims, children as young as 6 years of age may already hold negative stereotypes of some foreign groups, but that at this early age, and consistent with Piaget and Weil's claims, they may not yet hold any positive stereotypes. However, a limitation of the studies conducted by Piaget and Weil and by Jahoda is that they both only involved interviewing children from a single group living in one particular location (i.e., Swiss children living in Geneva, and Scottish children living in Glasgow, respectively). Furthermore, both studies used semi-structured interviewing to collect their data. By contrast, a much more ambitious study, using a structured interview schedule, was conducted by Lambert and Klineberg (1967). The findings of their study challenge the generality of the findings reported by Piaget and Weil and by Jahoda in several important respects.

Lambert and Klineberg's cross-national study

Lambert and Klineberg (1967) collected their data from 3300 children living in 11 different parts of the world. Children from three age groups were sampled in each location. Altogether, they interviewed 100 each of 6-year-olds, 10-year-olds and 14-year-olds living in the USA, South Africa (Bantu children only), Brazil, English Canada, French Canada, France, Germany, Israel, Japan, Lebanon and Turkey. All of these children were questioned individually about their own national or state in-group, and about a number of out-groups, using a set of standardized questions.

Two very general open-ended questions were used to question the children about their own in-group. These questions were "What are the . . . [child's own group] like?" followed by "Tell me what else you know about them?" Lambert and Klineberg found that the descriptions the children produced in response to these two questions contained three different types of statements: factual descriptive statements (e.g., about the group's physical appearance, clothing, language spoken, etc.), evaluative statements (e.g., *good, bad, aggressive, peaceful, hardworking, lazy*, etc.), and similarity statements (e.g., *they are like us, they dress as we do*, etc.).

The children in all countries at all ages, including the 6-year-olds, produced factual descriptive statements about their own in-group. However, children from some countries (such as South Africa and Brazil) used these kinds of statements much more frequently than children from other countries (e.g., Turkey).

Evaluative statements about the child's own group tended to be produced less frequently than factual descriptive statements overall. Many of the evaluative statements that the children produced were positive. However, there were some exceptions. For example, the Japanese children tended to say that Japanese people were *poor, intelligent* and *bad* (the data were collected in 1959), while the Bantu children tended to use just factual and similarity statements instead. In other words, not all children produced descriptions of their own group that were positively biased towards that group (although many were).

Similarity statements about the child's own group (e.g., *they are like us, they dress as we do*, etc.) were only produced by the children in some countries (for example, they were not produced by either American or Canadian children). Notice that, when these sorts of statements are used, they suggest that these particular children are not including themselves as full members of their own group. Lambert and Klineberg report that similarity statements characterized not only the responses of some 6-year-olds (as might be expected, if such young children are not yet aware of their own national and state group memberships), but the responses of some 10- and 14-year-olds as well. For example, the Lebanese and Bantu children produced similarity statements at all ages. Lambert and Klineberg suggest that these responses, at such an advanced age, may reflect social divisions within these children's countries, with ethnic, religious or linguistic group differences making it difficult for these children to identify with the superordinate state group. Hence, there may be variability both within individual countries and across different countries in the ways in which children think about, and identify with, national and state groups, with children's patterns of thinking and identification possibly depending on the specific internal structure of their state and their own position within that structure. We will return to this idea later on in this chapter, and in Chapter 6 (where we consider children's patterns of national and state identification).

As one would expect, age-related changes in the contents of the descriptions produced by the children of their own in-group were also found. Overall, with increasing age, there was a decrease in the frequency of references to physical features, and an increase in the frequency of references to personality traits, habits and political beliefs. However, once again, there were exceptions to these general trends. For example, the Bantu and Japanese children (which, interestingly, are both non-white groups) continued to make frequent references to the physical features of their own groups even at 14 years of age.

The children's descriptions of foreign groups were also elicited using two open-ended questions. The initial question was of the form "In what way are the . . . [name of target group] like you/not like you/similar to you/different from you?", and this initial question was followed by "Tell me what else you know about them". Lambert and Klineberg found that the 6-year-olds responded less frequently than the other two age groups to these questions. That said, however, and contrary to the claims of Piaget and Weil (1951), the 6-year-olds were not without some stereotypical knowledge of a number of different out-groups. The information that the 6-year-olds produced tended to consist primarily of factual descriptive statements, mainly referring to these groups' typical physical features, clothing, language, and habits. The 6-year-olds produced relatively few evaluative statements other than *good* and *bad*. However, with increasing age, there was an increase in the number of evaluative terms used, the more frequent ones being *good, bad, intelligent, aggressive, poor, wealthy* and *peaceful*. The older children also produced more descriptions than the 6-year-olds of the personality traits, habits, political and religious beliefs of the target group in question, as well as more statements about their material possessions. In other words, stereotypes of at least some foreign groups do seem to be acquired by 6 years of age, but through the course of middle childhood and early adolescence, children's knowledge of, and beliefs about, the people who live in other countries expands considerably. Interestingly, there was a high level of agreement in the contents of the children's stereotypes of particular foreign out-groups, irrespective of the particular country in which the children themselves lived.

Lambert and Klineberg also examined the children's feelings towards foreign out-groups. They did this by asking each child, after he or she had described a particular group, the single question "Do you like them?". For each child, a ratio score was then calculated of the number of foreign groups liked divided by the total number of foreign groups that the child was able to describe. Although this method of assessing the children's feelings is quite limited, some interesting results were obtained. It was found that, overall, the children became more positive towards foreign people between 6 and 10 years of age, but that the 14-year-olds were roughly similar to the 10-year-olds in their mean levels of liking.

However, within this general pattern, there were significant differences across countries. First, there were differences in the children's overall levels of liking. For example, the Japanese and Turkish children at all three ages were the least positive towards foreign groups, whereas the American children were the most positive. Second, there were differences in the specific developmental patterns displayed. For example, among the Canadian (both groups) and Japanese children, the 10-year-olds were the most positive towards foreign groups, with the 14-year-olds being similar to the 6-year-olds (i.e., less positive than the 10-year-olds). However, the American and French children showed a linear increase in their levels of liking from 6 to 10 to 14 years of age. By comparison, the Bantu children showed no changes at all in their levels of liking of foreign outgroups as a function of age.

Lambert and Klineberg also examined the relationship that existed between the children's conceptions of foreign groups and their feelings towards those groups. They found the following pattern. Those children who liked a particular foreign group tended to be well informed about that group, and were able to produce a high number of factual descriptive statements about it (e.g., about their appearance, ways of life and habits, etc.); furthermore, these children tended to use relatively few evaluative statements (e.g., *good, nice,* etc.) about the group. In contrast, those children who disliked a particular foreign group tended to produce relatively few factual descriptive statements about that group, and instead produced large numbers of (negative) evaluative statements. This trend was most pronounced among the 10-year-olds.

In addition, Lambert and Klineberg found that the children's perceptions of how similar they thought the various out-groups were to their own in-group also changed with age. The overall degree of perceived similarity increased significantly between 6 and 10 years of age, but levelled out between 10 and 14 years of age. In other words, the 6-year-olds viewed foreign groups as being different from their own group more frequently than either of the two older age groups. Perceived similarity was not always related to how the children felt about out-groups. In other words, the children did not always show positivity towards out-groups that were seen as similar to their own, and negativity towards those that were seen as dissimilar. In fact, at 6 years of age, there was as much positivity expressed towards dissimilar groups as similar groups. However, by 10 years of age, a discrepancy had started to appear, and by 14 years of age, it was clear that less positivity was indeed being expressed towards groups that were viewed as dissimilar to the child's own group.

Lambert and Klineberg's study is important for revealing that, contrary to the claims of Piaget and Weil (1951), children as young as 6 years of age do already hold stereotypes of a number of different out-groups, with some of these stereotypes being negative (as Jahoda, 1962, had found) and some being positive. This study is also important for revealing that there is considerable variability in children's development in this domain, with different developmental patterns being exhibited by children who grow up in different countries. Furthermore, in some groups of children (e.g., the Bantu children), there were no changes in the levels of liking of foreign out-groups between 6 and 14 years of age. As we shall see later on in this book, the finding of variability in development has important theoretical implications, particularly for Aboud's (1988; Aboud & Amato, 2001) cognitive-developmental explanation of the development of children's intergroup attitudes. Another important finding from a theoretical perspective is that children do not always describe their own in-group in positive terms. This finding, too, has important theoretical implications, this time for attempts to apply Tajfel's (1978; Tajfel & Turner, 1986) social identity theory to the development of children's judgements and evaluations of national and state groups. We will return to these theoretical issues in Chapter 7.

MORE RECENT STUDIES INTO CHILDREN'S REPRESENTATIONS OF, AND ATTITUDES TO, THE PEOPLE WHO LIVE IN DIFFERENT COUNTRIES

The development of the contents of children's stereotypes of national and state groups

Children's stereotypes of the people who belong to different national and state groups have also been examined in several more recent studies. Some of these studies have continued to employ open-ended interviewing. For example, Hengst (1997) interviewed 8- to 13-year-old English and German children, as well as 8- to 13-year-old Turkish children living in Germany and in Turkey. Curiously, and contrary to Lambert and Klineberg's findings, Hengst reports that the German children he interviewed could not think of anything much to say in answer to a question that enquired about the characteristics of typical German people, with the children mostly saying that their fellow nationals were quite nice, or emphasizing that there are both good and bad people in their own country as in every other country. However, this may have occurred because these children actually held negative views of Germans and because the interviewers themselves were German; Hengst reports that, in response to another question, the children did say that Germans are unpopular abroad, referring to recent attacks on foreigners in Germany, the activities of neo-Nazis, and stating that it was Germans who started the two World Wars (cf. Merkl, 1990; Rossteutscher, 1997; Schiffauer & Sunier, 2004). If these children did indeed hold a negative view of their own in-group, then they may have been reluctant to express their view about what is "typically German", especially to an adult German interviewer. By contrast, Hengst found that both the English and the Turkish children did indeed hold stereo-types of the people who belong to their own group, and willingly discussed these in the interviews. However, Hengst does not provide any information about how the children's stereotype content developed or changed with age.

Howard and Gill (2001) also examined the stereotypes of Australian people held by 11- to 12-year-old Australian children. In this study, the chil-dren engaged in group discussions about what it means to be Australian. Howard and Gill report that the children knew what stereotypes were, with one group taking great pleasure in describing the stereotype of an Australian male while at the same time openly acknowledging that most people do not actually conform to this stereotype. For example, one conversation went as follows:

INTERVIEWER: What's a typical Australian like then?
MARK (AGED 12): I reckon it's like a guy who's got a check shirt that's all dirty.
SHARON (AGED 12): G'day mate.
MARK: All jeans, you know, the VB in one hand.
SHARON: Overalls.
ROBERT (AGED 11): And an Akubra hat.
SHARON: With the corks hanging down.
MARK: Yeah.
INTERVIEWER: OK. So why is that a stereotype?
SHARON: Because most people aren't like that.

However, because of the limited age range of this study, Howard and Gill's findings merely attest to the fact that 11- to 12-year-old Australian children do indeed hold stereotypes of Australian people while simultaneously recog-nizing that most people do not conform to this stereotype; their findings do not inform us about how the children's views developed or changed with age.

A much more substantial study was conducted by Byram, Esarte-Sarries, and Taylor (1991). They examined 10- and 14-year-old English children, using open-ended qualitative interviews supplemented with a few quantita-tive measures. The study focused primarily on the children's perceptions of, and attitudes to, French people, and whether these perceptions and attitudes were related to the learning of the French language (which also involves learning about French people and French culture) at school; however, the children's perceptions of, and attitudes to, German and American people were also examined for comparative purposes. Consistent with the findings of Lambert and Klineberg, the older children tended to use more personality and psychological attributes to describe all three groups of foreign peoples than the younger children. As far as the effects of school teaching were concerned, the older children's self-reports in the qualitative interviews suggested that curricular input had indeed influenced their representations of French people as well as their knowledge about France (the younger children had not yet studied French at school). Evaluations of French, German and American people were also readily made by the children during the course of the interviews, often in terms of how friendly or nice these people were. For the quantitative measures, the children were given 12 pairs of evaluative terms (such as *good/bad, strong/weak*, etc.) and had to indicate on a 7-point scale that ran between the two terms within each pair where the target people fell on that dimension. Averaging the scores across the 12 dimensions, it was found that the children made the most positive evaluations of Americans and the least positive evaluations of Germans, with the French being midway between the two. The children's evaluations of Germans became more positive with age, while their evaluations of French and American people did not change with age. Girls were more positive than boys to all three out-groups. Evaluations of all three groups bore no relationship to whether or not the children had visited France, the total length of their visits to France, the total length of their visits to other countries, or their personal contact with French people. The qualitative interviews also suggested that the children's evaluative attitudes to French people more generally were also not related to the school teaching they had received.

In another study, Barrett and Short (1992) examined 5- to 10-year-old English children's stereotypes of four foreign out-groups, using a structured interview schedule to examine the characteristics these children ascribed to French, German, Spanish and Italian people. For analysis purposes, the children were divided into two age groups, 5- to 7-year-olds and 8- to 10-year-olds. Consistent with Lambert and Klinberg's findings, this study also found that even the youngest children had acquired some stereotypical traits for these groups. In addition, similar stereotypes of each individual target group were held by many of the children. Table 5.1 lists the attributes which were ascribed to each out-group by at least 50% of the children in each age group.

Notice that among the 5- to 7-year-olds, there were no consensual beliefs about the characteristics of either German or Italian people. However, these younger children did already hold consensual stereotypes of French and Spanish people. Furthermore, the characteristics attributed to these two

Table 5.1

Attributes ascribed by 5- to 10-year-old English children to French, German, Spanish and Italian people; the attributes which are shown here are those which were ascribed to each national group by 50% or more of the children within each of the two age groups (from Barrett & Short, 1992, p. 354)

Age group	National group			
	French	German	Spanish	Italian
5- to 7-year-olds	brown/suntan hardworking		brown/suntan tall thin happy	
8- to 10-year-olds	brown/suntan strong speak French clean peaceful clever hardworking	white tall speak German happy aggressive hardworking	brown/suntan brown hair dark eyes strong speak Spanish happy clean peaceful	brown/suntan strong speak Italian smart clothes poor eat spaghetti/ pasta happy peaceful

groups were already distinctive, with French people being viewed as hardworking, and Spanish people being viewed as happy. In the case of the 8- to 10-year-olds, they exhibited consensual stereotypes of all four groups. The clusters of attributes continued to be distinctive for each group. One principal attribute that distinguished between the four groups was the language spoken. However, in addition, Germans were uniquely characterized as being white and aggressive, while Italians were differentiated by the characteristics of having smart clothes, being poor, and eating spaghetti and pasta. French and Spanish people were not only differentiated from each other by the language spoken; French people were also seen as hardworking, whereas Spanish people were seen as happy. Notice that this last differentiation is the same as that present among the younger group of children, suggesting that there was some developmental continuity in the contents of the children's stereotypes.

In addition to eliciting these stereotypes, Barrett and Short examined the amount of variability that the children perceived to exist within the four populations around these stereotypes. They did this by asking the children, after they had produced their descriptions of each group, whether they thought *all, most* or *just some* of the people in that group were like that. There was a significant shift with age from *most* to *just some* responses in relationship to all four groups, suggesting that the perceived variability of all foreign out-groups may increase across middle childhood.

This finding was supported in a subsequent study by Barrett, Wilson, and Lyons (1999, 2003). All of the studies we have looked at so far in this chapter used interviewing in order to collect their data. However, while interviewing can be very revealing, there are significant problems associated with this method when working with children (cf. Ceci & Bruck, 1998; Lamb & Brown, 2006; Lamb, Sternberg, Orbach, Hershkowitz, & Epslin, 1999). First, the specific wording used in a question can easily cue particular types of answers from children. A second problem is that children's responses in interviews are often biased by social desirability effects, and children can withhold answers that they think are unacceptable to adults (as may have been the case in Hengst's study). Third, answering an open-ended question, in particular, is cognitively very demanding for young children. They have to comprehend the vocabulary and the syntax of the question, make an inference about what the interviewer wants to know through asking that question, use that information to access information in memory, retrieve that information from memory, and then encode that information in a verbal response. Errors can occur at any stage in this process. Hence, interviewing can easily underestimate children's knowledge, beliefs and patterns of reasoning (although see Lamb et al., 1999, for strategies that may be used to enhance the accuracy of children's responses to open-ended questions).

For these reasons, Barrett et al. (1999, 2003) used a trait attribution task rather than interviewing in order to examine children's stereotypes. They gave 5- to 11-year-old English children a set of cards, each of which had the name of an individual trait written on it (e.g., *clean, dirty, happy, sad, clever, stupid*, etc.). The children were asked to put into a box, which was labelled with the name of a target group, all of the words that they thought could be used to describe the people who belonged to that group; the children were explicitly instructed to discard a word if they thought that it could not be used to describe those people. The children's trait attributions to three different target groups were examined: English, American and German people. English was used as a target group because it was the children's own in-group; American and German were used as target out-groups because previous work had revealed that American people tend to be the most positively evaluated foreign out-group for English children, while German people tend to be the most negatively evaluated foreign outgroup for them (Barrett, Day, & Morris, 1990; Wilson, Barrett, & Lyons, 1995; cf. also Byram et al., 1991).

For the purposes of analysis, the children were divided into three age groups, a Young group (mean age 6.9 years), a Middle group (mean age 8.9 years) and an Old group (mean age 10.6 years). The findings obtained are summarized in Figures 5.1 and 5.2. These figures show the results of correspondence analyses of the data; they include all of the traits that were attributed to the target groups by at least 20% of the children in any one age group. In these figures, the geometric distance of a particular trait from a

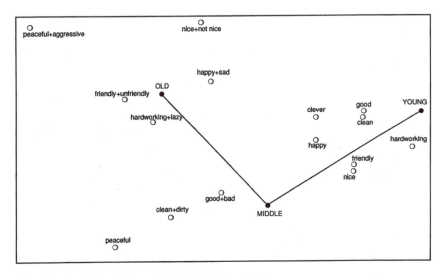

Dimension 1: $\chi^2(16) = 54.63$, $p<.0001$, % of inertia = 68.52
Dimension 2: $\chi^2(14) = 24.91$, $p<.05$, % of inertia = 31.48

Figure 5.1. Trait attributions to the English in-group by the three age groups (from Barrett, Wilson & Lyons, 2003, p. 207; reproduced with permission from the *British Journal of Developmental Psychology*, © The British Psychological Society).

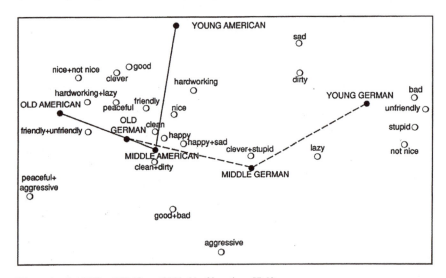

Dimension 1: $\chi^2(28) = 360.83$, $p<.0001$, % of inertia = 57.49
Dimension 1: $\chi^2(26) = 113.53$, $p<.0001$, % of inertia = 18.67

Figure 5.2. Trait attributions to the American and German out-groups by the three age groups (from Barrett, Wilson & Lyons, 2003, p. 208; reproduced with permission from the *British Journal of Developmental Psychology*, © The British Psychological Society).

particular age group shows how likely it was that this trait had been attributed to a particular target group by the children in that age group: the smaller the distance, the greater the likelihood.

Figure 5.1 shows that the three age groups attributed different sets of traits to the English in-group. The cluster of univalent positive traits that are situated close to the Young group (e.g., *good, clean, hardworking*, etc.) shows that the youngest children were most likely to attribute only univalent positive traits to English people. The Middle group of children were also quite likely to attribute some of these univalent positive traits to English people (e.g., *happy, nice* and *friendly*), but they were also likely to make some multivalent attributions (i.e., both *good* and *bad*, and both *clean* and *dirty*) to English people as well. The multivalent response categories clustered around the Old group show that the oldest children tended to make more multivalent attributions than either of the other two age groups.

Figure 5.2 shows that the Young group were more likely than the other two age groups to attribute only univalent negative traits to German people (*bad, unfriendly, stupid* and *not nice*) and to attribute only univalent positive traits to American people (e.g., *good* and *hardworking*). Some of the Middle group's attributions to Germans were still fairly negative (e.g., *lazy*), but multivalent attributions to Germans (e.g., both *clever* and *stupid*) were more likely to be made by this age group than by the Young group. The Middle group's attributions to Americans and the Old group's attributions to Germans were quite similar, consisting of a mixture of positive univalent attributions and multivalent attributions. Finally, the Old group were more likely than the other two groups to make multivalent attributions to Americans.

These two figures therefore reveal that, across this age range, the children shifted from making univalent attributions (either positive or negative) to the three target groups, to making multivalent attributions to these groups instead. This conclusion was supported in a further analysis of the data. Deriving a quantitative measure of perceived variability from the attributed traits, Barrett et al. (1999) found that there was a significant increase in the amount of perceived variability attributed to all three target groups with age. This particular finding is therefore consistent both with Barrett and Short's (1992) finding (obtained using direct questioning) that the perceived variability of groups increases across middle childhood, and with Howard and Gill's (2001) finding (obtained using group discussions) that 11- to 12-year-old children acknowledge that most people do not actually conform to the stereotype of their own in-group. In addition, Barrett et al. (1999) found that there was no significant difference between the amount of variability attributed to the in-group and to the two out-groups, at any age. In other words, there was no evidence of either an out-group homogeneity effect (i.e., the out-groups were not perceived as being more homogeneous than the in-group), or an in-group homogeneity effect (i.e., the in-group was not perceived as being more homogeneous than either of the two out-groups).

Barrett et al. asked the children to attribute these traits to English people (i.e., to their own national in-group) under three different experimental conditions: the traits were attributed either to just English people on their own, or while the child was simultaneously attributing traits to either German or American people. It was found that the children attributed exactly the same characteristics (and the same degree of variability) to English people irrespective of the specific comparative context that prevailed while they were making their attributions. It had been expected that the manipulation of the comparative frame of reference would influence the children's attributions of traits. For example, English children typically view German people as being aggressive and Americans as being friendly (Wilson et al., 1995); hence, it had been expected that, when they were describing English people alongside German people, they would be more likely to describe them as being peaceful, but when describing them alongside American people, they would be less likely to describe them as being friendly. However, no such effects occurred in these 5- to 11-year-old children. It is well established that national stereotype content is adjusted in this way as a function of the prevailing comparative context by university students (Haslam, Oakes, Turner, & McGarty, 1995; Hopkins, Regan, & Abell, 1997). It has also been found that young children vary the contents of their gender stereotypes depending on the specific comparative frame of reference that prevails while they are making trait attributions to boys and to girls (Sani & Bennett, 2001; Sani, Bennett, Mullally, & McPherson, 2003). However, the children in the study by Barrett et al. did not alter the contents of their national in-group stereotype in this manner. Hence, phenomena that occur with one kind of stereotype (e.g., gender stereotypes) at a particular age do not necessarily occur with other kinds of stereotypes (e.g., national stereotypes) at the same age.

To summarize: the studies by Barrett and Short (1992) and Barrett et al. (1999, 2003) confirm that, contrary to the claims of Piaget and Weil (1951), but consistent with the findings of Lambert and Klineberg (1967), 5- to 6-year-old children do indeed hold stereotypes of some national and state groups. Furthermore, these stereotypes already have distinctive contents according to the particular groups that they represent. With increasing age, children come to produce more detailed descriptions of the distinctive characteristics that are exhibited by the members of a larger number of different national and state groups. In addition, the perceived variability of such groups increases across the course of middle childhood, and by 10 to 12 years of age, children readily acknowledge that there is a great deal of variability within these groups. Stereotypes of national and state groups tend to be consensually shared with other children, both within countries (Barrett & Short, 1992) and across countries (Lambert & Klineberg, 1967), but the contents of children's national in-group stereotypes are not affected by the comparative context in which they are elicited (Barrett et al., 2003).

Methods that have been used to examine children's feelings towards national and state groups

Children's feelings towards national and state groups have been assessed in different studies in a variety of ways. As we have seen, the early studies examined how much children liked or disliked particular groups using interviewing. In these interviews, children were asked either open-ended questions (Jahoda, 1962; Piaget & Weil, 1951) or *yes–no* questions (e.g., "Do you like them?", used by Lambert & Klineberg, 1967), with the responses to these questions then being used either qualitatively (Piaget & Weil, 1951) or quantitatively (Lambert & Klineberg, 1967) to draw conclusions about how much those children like different target groups.

Barrett and Short (1992) also employed interviewing, but utilized several different methods in order to assess the children's feelings towards the targeted out-groups, and they then examined whether the results from these different methods converged with one another. One method they used involved asking a pair of linked questions, "Do you like . . . [target] people?" followed by "Do you like/dislike them a little or a lot?"; the children's responses were then scored on a 5-point scale (*like a lot, like a little, neutral, dislike a little*, and *dislike a lot*; notice that this scale allows more differentiated responses than the single question used by Lambert & Klineberg, 1967). In addition, they asked the children questions containing evaluative terms such as "Do you think . . . [target] people are nice or not nice or what?" and "Do you think . . . [target] people are bad or good or what?". Finally, they administered a simple sorting task. The children were given cards with the names of the target groups written on them, and they were asked to place the groups in the order in which they liked them. Barrett and Short found that, in practice, the findings yielded by all these various methods tended to converge.

Other studies have used trait attribution tasks rather than interviewing (e.g., Barrett et al., 1999, 2003). As we have seen, these tasks require children to attribute positive and negative traits to target groups (usually by putting cards that have the names of those traits written on them into boxes representing the target groups). The numbers of positive and negative traits attributed to each group can then be analysed directly, and an overall positivity score can also be computed for each group based on the numbers of positive vs. negative traits that have been attributed to that group. Byram et al. (1991) used a variant of this method, by employing 7-point rating scales between pairs of positive and negative traits (such as *good/bad, strong/weak*, etc.), asking children to rate the target group on the dimension formed by each pair of traits, and then calculating a mean positivity–negativity evaluation score for that group across all pairs of traits.

Another method that has been used in some studies (e.g., Verkuyten, 2001) is based on the notion of social distance. Here, the child is asked a question such as "What would you think about having X friends" (where X is the name of a particular national group), or "How would you feel about having X friends?". The child's response can then be measured on a rating scale running from *very happy* to *very sad* (which can be administered to young children using a set of "smiley" faces).

Finally, some studies (e.g., Jaspers et al., 1972; Tajfel, Jahoda, Nemeth, Campbell, & Johnson, 1970; Tajfel, Jahoda, Nemeth, Rim, & Johnson, 1972) have asked children to rate photographs of individual people on a scale running from *like very much* to *dislike very much*; at another point in time, the children are asked to classify these photographs according to whether they show a member of the child's own in-group or a member of an out-group. The two tasks are administered in a counterbalanced order. Mean liking ratings for the photographs that have been assigned to the in-group and to the out-group are then calculated. A variant of the photograph task involves comparing children's affect ratings of photographs of individual people when they are unlabelled (again, on a scale running from *like very much* to *dislike very much*) with their affect ratings of the same photographs on the same scale when they have been labelled with the name of a particular national or state group (Rutland, 1999).

The phenomenon of in-group favouritism

Studies using these methods have generally found that, irrespective of the particular method used, children frequently display a systematic bias towards members of their own in-group. This in-group bias is often already present at 5–6 years of age and appears to persist until at least 12 years of age. Furthermore, this bias has been found to occur among children living in many different countries.

For example, Barrett et al. (1999, 2003) examined the trait attributions made by their group of 5- to 11-year-old English children to English, German and American people. They found that the children made the most positive attributions to English people, and the least positive attributions to German people, at all ages. However, with increasing age, attributions to English people did become less positive, while attributions to both American and German people became more positive. The net result was therefore an overall reduction in the extent of in-group bias across this age range, although the bias was still present even among the oldest children in this sample. In addition, Barrett and Short (1992) found clear evidence of in-group favouritism among the group of 5- to 10-year-old English children who they interviewed.

They asked these children to sort the names of five target groups (English, French, German, Spanish and Italian) into the order in which they liked the people from these different groups. They found that, at all ages, English was the most liked group, French was the second most liked group, Spanish the third, and Italian the fourth, with Germans consistently being the least liked group among these children, at all ages. Byram et al. (1991) also found that 10- and 14-year-old English children's trait attributions to English people were more positive than their trait attributions to American, French and German people.

Tajfel et al. (1970, 1972; see also Jaspers et al., 1972) obtained a similar finding using the photograph-based method with 6- to 12-year-old children living in six different countries: England, the Netherlands, Austria, Belgium, Italy and Israel. They found that, in all of these countries, the children were more likely to assign the photographs of the people who they liked the most to their own in-group. This occurred at all ages (although this in-group bias did become less pronounced with age in all groups except the Belgian children). Verkuyten (2001) also found in-group favouritism among 10- to 12-year-old Dutch children, using the social distance measure. He found that the children were significantly more positive towards in-group Dutch peers than they were to out-group German, American and Turkish peers.

However, although in-group bias has frequently been found to be present in children at 5–6 years of age, some exceptions have been reported in the literature. For example, Piaget and Weil (1951) report that, in their study of Swiss children, in-group favouritism did not appear until the children were 7–8 years of age; before that age, the children's patterns of likes and dislikes were based on more transient and idiosyncratic personal experiences. Similarly, Tajfel et al. (1970, 1972), using the photograph-based method, found that although in-group bias was present in 6- to 12-year-old English, Dutch, Austrian, Belgian, Italian and Israeli children, it was absent in similarly aged Scottish children (in the late 1960s), who expressed significantly higher levels of liking of English people than Scottish people. And Rutland (1999), using his photograph-based method, found that English children only exhibited in-group favouritism from 10 years of age onwards. This last finding, however, may have been due to the fact that the state category *British* was used in this study rather than the national category *English* (relatively few English children and adults spontaneously use the term *British* to denote their own in-group; Barrett, 1996; Condor, 1996) and to the fact that the children were asked to make judgements of individual people rather than state groups per se. Some caution therefore needs to be exercised in making claims concerning the prevalence of in-group favouritism, as different findings have been obtained depending on the particular measure used, the particular group of children under study, and whether the national or the state category is used as the in-group category.

The phenomenon of out-group denigration

Although in-group favouritism is a common phenomenon, this does not mean that national and state out-groups are denigrated. Indeed, several studies have found that most out-groups are positively liked and evaluated by children at all ages, but just to a lesser extent than the child's own in-group. Indeed, actual out-group denigration (where children display negative affect or make predominantly negative trait attributions to an out-group) appears to be a comparatively rare phenomenon. For example, Lambert and Klineberg (1967) found that many of the children they tested held very positive feelings towards most out-groups; American, French, German, English-Canadian, French-Canadian and Bantu children, in particular, were found to like a large number of out-groups. Similarly, Barrett and Short (1992) and Barrett et al. (1999, 2003) both examined English children's attitudes towards Germans, the out-group towards which English children are typically the least positive. The former study found that the most frequently occurring answers to questions about whether German people were *good* and *nice* were affirmative rather than negative, while the latter study found that the children attributed more positive than negative traits to German people overall.

On the other hand, Lambert and Klineberg (1967) did find that Japanese and Turkish children, in particular, disliked a comparatively large number of different out-groups (the Japanese children disliked, in particular, Russian, Indian and African people, while the Turkish children disliked, in particular, Russian, Chinese and African people). In addition, Jahoda (1962) found that children may hold negative attitudes towards one particular type of out-group, namely out-groups that children perceive to be either the historical or the current enemies of their own in-group. As we saw earlier, Jahoda found very negative views being expressed by many of his 6- to 12-year-old Scottish children about German, Japanese and Russian people, with the children making frequent references either to past wars or to the possibility of a future war in order to justify their attitudes.

Buchanan-Barrow, Bayraktar, Papadopoulou, Short, Lyons, and Barrett (1999) explored this issue in greater detail, examining whether groups that are the traditional enemies of the child's own in-group are indeed evaluated less positively than other out-groups by children. They used both trait attributions and affect ratings on a *like-dislike* scale to explore this issue, and looked at: 5- to 10-year-old English children's views of French, Spanish, Italian and German (the "enemy" group) people; 5- to 10-year-old Turkish children's views of English, German, Italian and Greek (the "enemy" group) people; and 5- to 10-year-old Greek children's views of English, German, Italian and Turkish (the "enemy" group) people. They found that, among all three groups of children, the traditional enemy out-group received fewer positive trait attributions and less positive affect than all the other comparison out-groups. This effect was most pronounced among the younger children. With increasing age, both trait attributions and affect ratings to all the out-groups gradually became more positive, although the enemy out-group was always the least positively evaluated and the least liked group at all ages. There were also differences across countries; in particular, the Turkish children were significantly more positive about Greeks than either the English children were about Germans or the Greek children were about Turks.

In another study, Povrzanović (1997) examined the attitudes of 11- to 14-year-old Croatian and Bosnian children living in the former Yugoslavia in the 1990s. Many of these children had experienced actual armed conflict within their own lifetimes at first hand. Povrzanović asked the children to write their life stories, and the only suggestion that was made to them was that their essays should cover not only the past and present but also the future. They were not told to write about the war, nations or enemies. However, many of the children's essays consisted almost exclusively of accounts of their experiences of war and exile. Furthermore, an extremely negative attitude towards Serbs was widely shared among these children (including both those with first-hand experience and those with only a mediated experience of the war). The negative accounts of Serbs in the children's essays ranged from relativizing comments (in which individual and collective guilt were distinguished) through to the generalization of a negative image that included contempt, disdain, insults and fear, through to statements of outright hatred. Povrzanović argues that the experience of war had accelerated these children's national awareness by making national boundaries emotionally salient to them. She cites anecdotal evidence suggesting that national awareness and negative attitudes towards Serbs were evident even among very young children. For example, she cites one 3-year-old who said "This is my Croatian homeland!", another 3-year-old who invited Povrzanović to engage in the role of "Serb" by throwing objects at her from a balcony, and a 5-year-old who produced a drawing of a Chetnik (i.e., a Serb who fought against Croatia in the name of a Greater Serbia) as the devil. There is certainly very clear evidence from Povrzanović's work that extremely strong out-group denigration can occur among children who have first-hand experience of war.

Developmental changes in children's attitudes towards national and state groups: A summary of the evidence reviewed so far

From the studies we have examined so far, the following general picture emerges. Children develop a range of differentiated attitudes towards national and state groups. Their own national or state group is often the most positively evaluated group, and groups that are either the historical or current enemies of their own nation or state are often the least positively evaluated. In-group favouritism, although not universal, does commonly exist throughout middle childhood. However, in-group favouritism usually becomes less pronounced across the course of middle childhood, as children's attitudes towards out-groups gradually become more positive; after 10 years of age, this general increase in positive regard for other groups often levels out.

But although this is the general pattern found to occur in many children, there are exceptions. For example, recall that Lambert and Klineberg (1967) found that, unlike the other groups of children they interviewed, the South African Bantu children showed no significant changes in their feelings towards foreign out-groups between 6 and 14 years of age. In addition, Lambert and Klineberg found that different developmental patterns were sometimes displayed by children who were growing up in different countries, with some groups of children displaying an increase in positive regard for out-groups, and others displaying a reduction in positive regard for out-groups, between 10 and 14 years of age. Hence, the evidence actually suggests that there may be considerable variability in children's development as a function of the specific national or state context in which they grow up.

However, as we have seen already, Lambert and Klineberg only used general open-ended questions to elicit children's descriptions of foreign groups; they did not use a controlled trait attribution task (which eases the task demands on young children considerably compared with open-ended interviewing). In addition, they used a relatively weak measure of the children's affect for foreign groups, only asking the children, after they had described a particular group, the single question "Do you like them?". As a result, Lambert and Klineberg's findings, while undoubtedly important and suggestive, are not as methodologically well-grounded as they might be. However, two further cross-national comparative studies have been conducted in more recent years, in which both a trait attribution task and a more discriminating affect measure have been used. These two studies are the CHOONGE and NERID projects, which were conducted by Barrett, Lyons, Bennett, Vila, Giménez, Arcuri, and de Rosa (1997) and by Barrett, Bennett, Vila, Valencia, Giménez, Riazanova, Pavlenko, Kipiani, and Karakozov (2001), respectively.

THE *CHOONGE* AND *NERID* PROJECTS

Background information about the projects

CHOONGE and NERID are acronyms for the full titles of these two projects, which were *"Children's Beliefs and Feelings about Their Own and Other National Groups in Europe"* and *"The Development of National, Ethnolinguistic and Religious Identity in Children and Adolescents Living in the New Independent States of the Former Soviet Union"*, respectively. Some of the findings from the two projects have been reported so far in the following publications: Bennett, Lyons, Sani, and Barrett (1998); Vila, del Valle, Perera, Monreal, and Barrett (1998); Giménez, Canto, Fernandez, and Barrett (1999, 2003); de Rosa and Bombi (1999); Barrett (2000, 2001); Karakozov and Kadirova (2001); Kipiani (2001); Pavlenko, Kryazh, Ivanova, and Barrett (2001); Volovikova, Riazanova, and Grenkova-Dikevitch (2001); Volovikova and Kuznetzova (2001); Riazanova, Sergienko, Grenkova-Dikevitch, Gorodetschnaia, and Barrett (2001); Castelli, Cadinu, and Barrett (2002); Barrett, Lyons, and del Valle (2004); Bennett, Barrett, Karakozov, Kipiani, Lyons, Pavlenko, and Riazanova (2004); and Reizábal, Valencia, and Barrett (2004). However, in these previous publications, only individual aspects of the datasets have been analysed and reported, in isolation from each other. Here we provide a more detailed report of the overall patterns of the findings obtained in these two projects.

Across the two projects, data were collected from over 4000 children and adolescents, aged 6, 9, 12 and 15 years old, living in 10 different national contexts: England, Scotland, Catalonia, the Basque Country, southern Spain, Italy, Russia, Ukraine, Georgia and Azerbaijan (see Figure 5.3 for the locations of these various places). The projects together had the overall aim of identifying the cross-national constancies and differences that can occur in the development of children's beliefs and feelings about their own and other national and state groups, and the constancies and differences that can occur in the development of children's patterns of national and state identification. In other words, the aim was to document what remains constant in children's development despite variations in national context, and what can vary in children's development as a function of their national context. In order to address this general aim, the various countries and locations were chosen for participation in the research because each provides a distinct and arguably unique national context for children's development in this domain, with each location being characterized by very different political circumstances and patterns of intergroup relations.

In the case of Scotland and England, these two countries are both constituent parts of Great Britain (the third constituent country being Wales, with Great Britain and Northern Ireland together making up the United Kingdom). However, the respective situations of Scotland and England within Great Britain are very different. England has dominated Britain both politically and economically for several centuries and, as a result, the concept of Britishness has acquired strong Anglocentric connotations. Consequently, Scottish people tend to draw a very clear distinction between their Scottish national identity and their British state identity. By contrast, many English people are far less clear about the difference between their English and their British identity, and indeed often confuse the two. Scottish national identity itself has been heavily influenced through its struggle against English

Figure 5.3. The national contexts in which data were collected in the CHOONGE and NERID projects.

domination and, within Scotland, there is a prominent national-separatist political movement challenging Scotland's subordination to English political control. As part of a political devolution process, a Scottish parliament was finally established in Edinburgh in 1999. In the CHOONGE project, data were collected from children in London (the capital of both England and Britain) and in Dundee (a provincial city in Scotland).

By contrast, the modern state of Spain is divided up into 17 autonomous regions. Catalonia, the Basque Country and Andalusia (where the CHOONGE and NERID data were collected) are three of these autonomous regions. The inhabitants of Andalusia speak Spanish and perceive no incompatibility between being Spanish and Andalusian. However, a large proportion of the populations of Catalonia and the Basque Country are bilingual, speaking not only Spanish but also Catalan or Euskara (Basque), respectively. Because of their distinctive linguistic and cultural heritages, many people living in Catalonia and the Basque Country perceive their regions to be very different from other parts of the Spanish state. However, this perception is not homogeneous for a number of reasons, one of the most important being that many people have now migrated to Catalonia and the Basque Country from other regions of Spain. Under Franco's regime, there was considerable persecution and repression of Catalan and Basque institutions and of the use of the Catalan and Euskara languages. When Franco died, Catalonia and the Basque Country achieved a certain level of political autonomy. However, the right to self-determination, one of the most important principles for many of the people who live within these two regions, has not been granted by the Spanish state government. Thus many Catalan and Basque individuals are concerned with the defence of their regions' distinctive cultural and linguistic identities against the dominance of Spanish culture and language. The data in the CHOONGE and NERID projects were collected in the provincial cities of Girona (in Catalonia), San Sebastian and Pamplona (both in the Basque Country) and Malaga (in Andalusia in southern Spain).

In Italy, the overwhelming majority of the population speaks Italian, although there are also small German, French and other linguistic minorities living mainly in the north of the country. Over the past few decades, Italy has been at the centre of the movement towards European political and economic integration. A separatist political movement in northern Italy, the Lega Lombarda, which subsequently expanded into the Lega Nord, came to prominence in the 1980s and early 1990s, and by the mid-1990s (when the data for the CHOONGE project were collected) the Lega had obtained more than 20% of the vote in northern regions of the country. In 2001, the powers and responsibilities of regional government within Italy were enhanced, while those of central government were reduced. In the CHOONGE project, data were collected from children living in Rome (the capital city, located in central Italy) and Vicenza (a northern provincial city in Veneto, where the Lega Nord has strong local support).

Within the New Independent States of the former Soviet Union, national identities have been in a state of rapid transition since the disintegration of the Soviet Union in 1991. Russia itself is the former imperial power, and Soviet patriotism was based to a large extent on traditional Russian nationalism. When the Soviet Union disintegrated, the multinational state of the Russian Federation was formed, in which ethnic Russians make up approximately 82% of the population. However, many ethnic Russians also live in the former Soviet republics: 22% of the population of Ukraine, 6% of the population of Georgia, and 2% of the population of Azerbaijan are ethnic Russians. Furthermore, although Ukraine is now an independent state, for many Russian people, the historical origins of the Russian nation lie in Kieven Rus, and as a consequence Ukraine is still conceptualized by many Russians as a "Russian land". In Chechnya, a southern Muslim region of Russia, a separatist guerrilla conflict has been occurring for several years, and during the period in which the NERID project was being conducted there were terrorist bombs in Moscow, which were widely believed to be the work of Chechen separatists. The Russian data for the NERID project were collected in Moscow (the capital city, situated in Central European Russia) and in Smolensk (a provincial city situated in Western European Russia).

Ukraine itself has experienced Russian political and cultural domination since the latter part of the 18th century, when its territory was first absorbed into the Russian Empire. Following the collapse of Tsarist Russia in 1917, the country experienced a brief period of independence until 1920, but it was subsequent reconquered by the Soviets. Ukraine was one of the first republics to declare independence from the Soviet Union in 1991. Ukrainian is an East Slavonic language related to Russian. Under Stalin, there was considerable repression of individuals who promoted the use of the Ukrainian language, but people's identification with Ukrainian cultural and linguistic heritage is entrenched, and Ukrainian identity is now being reconstructed, particularly in the more western regions of Ukraine, to distinguish it from the older russocentric view. In the NERID project, data were collected in Kharkov (the second largest city situated in north-east Ukraine), from children attending Ukrainian language schools and from children attending Russian language schools.

Georgia was absorbed into the Russian Empire early in the 19th century. Like Ukraine, it also experienced a brief period of independence after the Russian revolution, before being forcibly incorporated into the USSR in 1921. Georgia also achieved independence when the Soviet Union disintegrated in 1991; 70% of the population are Georgian, and there are large minorities of Armenians (8% of the population), Russians (6%), Azeris (5%), Ossetians (3%) and Abkhazians (2%) living within its borders. There is considerable ethnic instability, with inter-ethnic wars having occurred in both Abkhazia and South Ossetia during the 1990s, with both regions breaking away from Georgian political control to be administered by separatist regimes. Partly due to Russian involvement in Abkhazia, Russian-Georgian relations are strained. Armenians are not an underprivileged group within Georgia, and open controversy between Armenians and Georgians is generally avoided. Three sets of data were collected in Georgia in the NERID project, all in Tbilisi (the capital city): from Georgian children attending Georgian language schools, from Georgian children attending Russian language schools, and from Armenian children attending Russian language schools.

Azerbaijan differs from Russia, Ukraine and Georgia in that the majority of its population is Muslim. Azerbaijan also experienced a brief period of independence from Russia after the Russian revolution, only to be absorbed into the Soviet Union in 1920. It also regained its independence after the collapse of the USSR in 1991. Azerbaijan has not yet resolved a conflict with neighbouring Armenia over the area of Nagorno-Karabakh (inhabited by ethnic Armenians), and as a result of this conflict, large numbers of ethnic Azeris have fled from Armenia to Azerbaijan (and Azerbaijani Armenians to Armenia), with the result that there are now large numbers of refugees and internally displaced persons living within the country. The Azeri language is a Turkic language related to Turkish, and Azeris are less russified than most other former Soviet Turkic groups. In the NERID project, two sets of data were collected in Baku (the capital of Azerbaijan): from children attending Azeri language schools, and from children attending Russian language schools.

Table 5.2
The numbers of children who were interviewed in the CHOONGE and NERID projects

Location of children	6 years	9 years	12 years	15 years	Total
England (London)[a]	59	60	62	59	**240**
Scotland (Dundee)[a]	49	51	60	60	**220**
Catalonia (Girona)[a]	115	128	132	120	**495**
Basque Country (San Sebastian and Pamplona)[b]	63	63	62	58	**246**
Southern Spain (Malaga)[a]	60	60	66	60	**246**
Italy (Vicenza)[a]	60	60	60	60	**240**
Italy (Rome)[a]	60	59	60	60	**239**
Russia (Smolensk)[c]	60	60	60	61	**241**
Russia (Moscow)[c]	60	62	60	60	**242**
Ukraine (Ukrainian language schools, Kharkov)[c]	60	60	60	60	**240**
Ukraine (Russian language schools, Kharkov)[c]	60	60	60	60	**240**
Georgia (Georgian language schools, Tbilisi)[c]	67	72	70	72	**281**
Georgia (Georgians in Russian language schools, Tbilisi)[c]	59	66	74	66	**265**
Georgia (Armenians in Russian language schools, Tbilisi)[c]	60	72	68	66	**266**
Azerbaijan (Azeri language schools, Baku)[c]	60	62	73	74	**269**
Azerbaijan (Russian language schools, Baku)[c]	60	60	61	60	**241**
Total	**1012**	**1055**	**1088**	**1056**	**4211**

Notes
[a] Data collected 1995–1996.
[b] Data collected 1997–1998.
[c] Data collected 1999–2000.

The total sample across the CHOONGE and NERID projects consisted of 4211 children, aged 6, 9, 12 and 15 years old. Details of the sample, broken down by age and location, are shown in Table 5.2. The dates when the data were collected in each location are also given in the footnotes to this table. In all locations, the children were recruited from state schools rather than private schools, and both middle-class and working-class children were included in the samples by recruiting them from appropriate schools. Approximately equal numbers of boys and girls were recruited at each age. The samples only included children who were of British, Spanish, Italian, Russian, Ukrainian, Georgian and Azerbaijani nationality (as appropriate) and who had been resident in the relevant country since birth (ignoring holiday visits to other countries). As already noted, in Ukraine, Georgia and Azerbaijan, data were collected both from children who attended schools that used the local national language for educational purposes and from children who attended Russian language schools; in addition, in Georgia, data were collected from both ethnic Georgian and ethnic Armenian children who attended the Russian language schools. Otherwise, within these general constraints, the children in all locations were sampled randomly.

These children were all interviewed individually, using a large battery of questions and tasks. The methods used included open-ended questioning, fixed-alternative questioning, selection tasks, rank ordering tasks and trait attribution tasks. All questions and tasks were initially prepared in English, and then translated into local languages using appropriate backtranslation procedures to ensure the linguistic equivalence of the materials in the different languages. The questions and tasks were designed to measure a large number of variables. These included:

- the children's self-categorizations at a variety of levels (e.g., as Gironean, Catalan, Spanish and European)
- the strength of the children's identification with these various self-categorizations
- the children's beliefs about the typical characteristics and traits of their own national and state in-groups
- the children's beliefs about the typical characteristics and traits of various national and state out-groups
- the children's feelings about these various in-groups and out-groups
- the children's language status, travel experience and family regional origins.

In addition, the CHOONGE project, but not the NERID project, used tasks to assess:

- the children's factual knowledge of European geography

- the children's factual knowledge of national emblems.

However, the NERID project, but not the CHOONGE project, measured:

- the perceived status of the national in-group.

Of specific interest to us here, in the context of the present chapter, are the children's trait attributions to national and state in-groups and out-groups, and their feelings about these in-groups and out-groups. The children's trait attributions and feelings were measured in both the CHOONGE and NERID projects with exactly the same tasks, but using different target groups according to the children's location. The target groups themselves were chosen on the basis of pilot work, which had shown that these were salient out-groups for the children who were being interviewed in any given location.

The trait attribution task and the questions used to measure affect

In the trait attribution task, the children were given a set of 12 cards on which were written 6 positive and 6 negative adjectives: *clean, dirty, friendly, unfriendly, clever, stupid, hardworking, lazy, happy, sad, honest* and *dishonest*. The cards were presented to the children in a random order, and the instructions were as follows:

> Here are some cards with words on them that describe people. So, we can say that some people are (word on first card in pile). And some people are (word on second card). And some people are (word on third card). Right? Now, what I want you to do is to go through all these words one by one, and I want you to sort out those words which you think can be used to describe X people (where X was the name of the target national group). Can you do that for me? Sort out the words which you think describe X people.

The children were allowed to select as many or as few of the cards as they wished, and if there was any doubt about the child's reading ability, the cards were read out to the child by the interviewer. From this task, two scores were derived: the total number of positive traits and the total number of negative traits that the child assigned to the target group in the question. The task was administered separately in relationship to the child's own in-group(s) and in relationship to a number of specified out-groups that were administered in a random order. For the Western European children, the target groups always included British, Spanish, Italian, French and German people; for the children living in the New Independent States (NIS) of the former Soviet Union, the target groups always included Russian, Ukrainian, Georgian, Azeri, English, German and American people.

In order to measure the child's affect towards each group, immediately after the child had finished the trait attribution task for a particular group, he or she was asked "Now I just want to ask you one more thing about X people. Do you like or dislike X people?" If the child expressed either liking or disliking, a follow-up question was asked: "How much? Do you like/dislike them a lot or a little?". From these two questions, a single score was then obtained which ranged between 1 and 5, where 1 = *dislike a lot*, 2 = *dislike a little*, 3 = *neither like nor dislike*, 4 = *like a little*, 5 = *like a lot*.

The findings of the trait attribution task

The results of the trait attribution task are shown in Tables 5.3 and 5.4. These tables show the mean numbers of positive and negative traits attributed to each target group by each subgroup of children. These scores could range from 0 to 6. Table 5.3 presents the data for the Western European samples, and Table 5.4 for the NIS samples.

First, notice that in these two tables, in almost all pairs of cells (i.e., the cells representing the positive and the negative traits attributed to a particular group by a particular subgroup of children), the children attributed more positive than negative traits to the target group in question. Furthermore, in many cases, these differences were statistically significant (pairs of cells showing a statistically significant difference are printed in bold in the two tables). In other words, there was little evidence of widespread out-group denigration (that is, a preponderance of negative over positive attributions) among any of the children.

Second, however, the data shown in these two tables also suggest that a "traditional enemy" factor may have been operating in the case of some groups of children. For example, Table 5.3 shows that the English and Scottish children's positive attributions to German people were not *significantly* higher than their negative attributions to German people, at all ages, with the German out-group being unique among the out-groups in this respect. The attributions made by the Russian and Ukrainian children to Georgian and Azeri people showed a similar although slightly less consistent trend, as did the attributions made by the Azeri children attending Azeri language schools to both Russian and Ukrainian people. Notice also that the only four pairs of cells in the two tables in which the children actually made *significantly more negative than positive* attributions to a particular target group were: the attributions made by the Smolensk 9-year-olds to German people; the attributions made by the Ukrainian 9-year-olds attending Ukrainian language schools to German people; and the attributions made by the Azeri 9- and 12-year-olds attending Azeri language schools to Russian people.

Third, notice that, at 6 years of age, the Scottish children only attributed significantly more positive than negative traits to Scottish people, and the Azeri children who were attending Azeri language schools only attributed significantly more positive than negative traits to Azeri people. Hence, in these two specific cases, at the age of 6, there was a different pattern associated with the in-group vs. the out-groups. This finding is consistent with Nesdale's (1999, 2004) social identity development theory (SIDT), which proposes that, at an early age, young children tend to focus on and attend to in-groups rather than out-groups (we will examine SIDT in greater detail later on in this book, in Chapter 7). However, it should also be noted that this differentiation between in-groups vs. out-groups was not exhibited by the 6-year-old children living in any of the other locations, all of whom attributed significantly more positive than negative traits to at least one out-group as well as to the in-group. Interestingly, these positively biased (i.e., non-random) attributions to selected out-groups were made even by some 6-year-olds who had previously professed not to know anything about the particular target out-group in question. In other words, some 6-year-old children were willing to express an evaluative attitude towards certain groups even though they had said that they did not have any knowledge about them. This finding is consistent with a conclusion that Tajfel (1966) drew many years ago, namely that young children sometimes acquire and express evaluative and affective responses towards particular nations and national groups before they possess any factual information about them.

Fourth, Tables 5.3 and 5.4 show that the children's trait attributions to the in-group changed with age in different ways in different locations. To begin with the attribution of *positive* traits to the *in-group* many different developmental patterns were exhibited here. For example, some children showed an increase with age in the number of positive traits attributed to the in-group (e.g., the Scottish children's positive attributions to both British and Scottish people increased between 6 and 9 years of age), some children showed a decrease (e.g., the positive attributions made by both groups of Italian children to Italian people decreased across a wider age range), some children showed an initial increase followed by a decrease (e.g., the Russian Smolensk children's positive attributions to Russian people), and some showed no changes at all with age (e.g., the positive attributions made by Ukrainian children in Ukrainian language schools to Ukrainian people).

The attribution of *negative* traits to the *in-group* also exhibited a variety of developmental patterns. For example, some children showed an increase in the number of negative attributions to the in-group with age (e.g., the negative attributions made by both groups of Russian children to Russian people), some showed a decrease (e.g., the Scottish children's negative attributions to Scottish people), and some showed no changes at all with age (e.g., the negative attributions made by both groups of Ukrainian children to Ukrainian people).

Table 5.3

Mean numbers of positive (+) and negative (−) traits attributed to the target groups by each subgroup of children in the Western European samples

Location of children	Age	British people +	British people −	Spanish people +	Spanish people −	Italian people +	Italian people −	French people +	French people −	German people +	German people −	English people +	English people −	Scottish people +	Scottish people −	Catalan people +	Catalan people −	Basque people +	Basque people −
England (London)	6	2.85	1.39	1.80^a	1.92^a	2.22^a	1.52	2.24^{ab}	1.76	1.66	1.97	3.85	0.85^a	2.75	1.03				
	9	3.30	1.38	2.82^b	1.23^{ab}	2.70^{ab}	1.33	2.68^{ab}	1.25	2.00	1.95	4.17	0.97^a	3.30	0.70				
	12	3.74	2.16	3.08^b	0.97^b	3.39^b	0.95	3.18^a	1.32	2.42	1.95	3.95	2.00^b	3.56	1.11				
	15	3.25	1.71	2.63^{ab}	0.90^b	3.07^{ab}	0.78	2.12^b	1.47	2.03	1.76	3.42	1.32^{ab}	3.10	0.85				
		*		*		*		*				*							
Scotland (Dundee)	6	1.51^a	1.22	0.71^a	0.45	0.35^a	0.35	0.65^a	0.45	0.45^a	0.35^a	0.71^a	0.41	1.92^a	1.02^a				
	9	3.69^b	0.86	1.37^{ab}	0.49	1.25^{ab}	0.31	1.51^{ab}	0.59	1.14^{ab}	0.82^{ab}	2.25^b	0.84	3.82^b	0.69^{ab}				
	12	3.02^b	0.77	2.00^b	0.83	2.03^b	0.53	2.57^c	0.40	1.93^b	1.32^b	2.73^b	0.95	3.73^b	0.63^{ab}				
	15	2.77^b	0.65	2.03^b	1.00	2.17^b	0.47	2.03^{bc}	0.85	1.60^b	1.12^b	2.23^b	0.92	3.45^b	0.45^b				
		*		*		*		*		*		*		*					
Catalonia (Girona)	6	1.65^a	0.71	4.44^a	1.67^a	3.89^a	2.07^a	4.28^a	1.80^a	4.04^a	2.03^a					4.96^a	1.17^a		
	9	3.53^b	1.36^{ab}	4.22^b	1.13^b	3.20^b	1.46^b	3.38^b	1.49^{ab}	2.95^b	1.58^{ab}					4.79^{ab}	0.80^{ab}		
	12	3.50^b	0.95^b	3.84^b	1.36^{ab}	3.31^{ab}	0.84^c	3.33^b	1.02^b	2.73^b	1.15^b					4.30^c	0.81^{ab}		
	15	2.98^b	0.94^b	3.08^c	1.29^{ab}	2.39^c	1.22^{bc}	2.31^c	1.42^{ab}	2.47^b	1.32^b					4.36^{bc}	0.46^b		
		*		*		*		*		*						*			
Basque Country (San Sebastian and Pamplona)	6	2.75	0.71	2.60	1.02	1.90	1.13^a	2.06	1.32	2.02	1.02							3.57	0.44
	9	2.57	0.95	3.11	0.97	2.00	1.14^a	2.08	1.33	1.86	1.25							3.46	0.33
	12	2.66	0.90	2.52	1.26	2.31	1.05^a	2.21	1.31	2.03	1.18							3.68	0.24
	15	2.17	0.64	2.14	1.14	2.24	0.48^b	1.78	1.14	1.90	0.84							3.47	0.26
						*													

Southern Spain (Malaga)	6	2.48^{a}	1.50	4.57^{a}	0.75	2.17^{a}	1.67	2.73^{a}	1.42	1.70^{a}	1.57
	9	3.97^{b}	1.78	5.48^{b}	0.45	3.87^{b}	1.80	4.12^{b}	1.57	3.72^{b}	1.72
	12	3.80^{b}	2.02	5.45^{b}	0.59	3.58^{b}	2.21	3.94^{b}	1.79	3.20^{b}	2.24
	15	2.77^{a}	1.43	3.75^{b}	0.93	2.03^{a}	2.10	2.03^{a}	1.88	2.08^{a}	1.48
		*		*		*		*		*	
Italy (Vicenza)	6	4.83^{a}	1.48	4.92^{a}	1.37^{ab}	5.75^{a}	0.95^{a}	4.75^{a}	1.73^{a}	4.62^{a}	1.90^{a}
	9	5.02^{a}	1.28	4.77^{ab}	1.55^{a}	5.22^{b}	1.88^{b}	4.73^{a}	1.25^{ab}	4.27^{ab}	2.13^{a}
	12	4.80^{a}	0.80	4.10^{bc}	1.12^{ab}	4.57^{c}	1.58^{b}	4.67^{ab}	0.78^{b}	3.93^{ab}	1.52^{ab}
	15	3.67^{b}	1.05	3.67^{c}	0.73^{b}	4.10^{b}	1.83^{b}	3.87^{b}	0.83^{b}	3.73^{b}	0.88^{b}
		*		*		*		*		*	
Italy (Rome)	6	4.10^{a}	1.93^{a}	4.08	2.12^{a}	4.93^{a}	1.38^{a}	3.98^{a}	1.80^{a}	3.93	1.95^{ab}
	9	4.93^{b}	1.27^{b}	4.66	1.61^{ab}	4.42^{ab}	2.27^{b}	4.71^{ab}	1.54^{ab}	4.19	2.17^{a}
	12	5.12^{b}	0.87^{b}	4.67	1.13^{bc}	4.40^{ab}	1.98^{ab}	4.85^{b}	1.17^{ab}	3.67	1.75^{ab}
	15	4.02^{a}	1.23^{b}	4.18	0.83^{c}	3.88^{b}	1.88^{ab}	4.10^{ab}	0.87^{b}	3.57	1.35^{b}
		*		*		*		*		*	

Notes

Where there is a statistically significant difference between the number of positive and negative traits attributed to a particular national or state group by a particular subgroup of children, those two figures are both shown in bold. Where there is a statistically significant effect of age on the number of either positive or negative traits attributed to a group, an asterisk appears beneath the relevant column of four figures, and the specific location of the significant differences within the column of four figures is shown using superscript letters, with mean scores which do not differ significantly from one another sharing the same superscript letter.

Data analysed using paired-samples *t*-tests, ANOVAs and Tukey's HSD post hoc tests.

Table 5.4

Mean numbers of positive (+) and negative (−) traits attributed to the target groups by each subgroup of children in the NIS samples (see Table 5.3 for an explanation of the use of bold type, asterisks and superscripts; where an asterisk appears in parentheses, the age effect could not be located by the post hoc tests)

Location of children	Age	Russian people		Ukrainian people		Georgian people		Azeri people		English people		German people		American people		Armenian people	
		+	−	+	−	+	−	+	−	+	−	+	−	+	−	+	−
Russia (Smolensk)	6	**4.10^{a}**	**0.35^{a}**	2.67	**1.65^{a}**	2.33	1.88	2.30	1.77	3.00	**1.42^{a}**	**2.22^{a}**	**1.98^{ab}**	2.75	**1.63^{a}**		
	9	**5.05^{b}**	**0.48^{a}**	3.00	**1.58^{a}**	2.57	1.77	2.20	2.17	3.36	**1.03^{ab}**	**1.37^{a}**	**2.72^{a}**	3.37	**1.03^{ab}**		
	12	**4.30^{a}**	**0.63^{ab}**	3.47	**0.72^{b}**	2.13	1.52	2.15	1.63	3.80	**0.50^{b}**	**2.73^{b}**	**1.23^{bc}**	3.23	**0.83^{b}**		
	15	**4.03^{a}**	**1.00^{b}**	3.18	**0.70^{b}**	2.16	1.61	1.70	1.85	3.58	**0.82^{ab}**	**2.72^{b}**	**1.02^{c}**	3.07	**1.08^{ab}**		
		*	*		*						*		*		*		
Russia (Moscow)	6	**5.52^{a}**	**0.46^{a}**	**3.45^{a}**	**2.35^{a}**	3.23	2.58	3.41	2.66	**4.03^{a}**	**1.97^{a}**	**3.38^{a}**	**2.62^{a}**	**4.18^{a}**	**2.07^{a}**		
	9	**5.66^{a}**	**0.58^{a}**	**4.68^{b}**	**1.50^{ab}**	3.55	2.69	3.81	2.52	**5.40^{b}**	**0.74^{b}**	**3.97^{b}**	**2.31^{a}**	**5.55^{b}**	**0.63^{b}**		
	12	**4.90^{b}**	**1.13^{b}**	**4.97^{b}**	**1.07^{b}**	3.85	2.15	3.23	2.83	**5.32^{b}**	**0.72^{b}**	**4.08^{b}**	**1.92^{ab}**	**4.62^{b}**	**1.38^{ab}**		
	15	**4.75^{b}**	**1.33^{b}**	**4.40^{b}**	**1.70^{ab}**	3.63	2.37	3.30	2.70	**4.80^{b}**	**1.20^{b}**	**4.88^{b}**	**1.13^{b}**	**3.90^{a}**	**2.12^{a}**		
		*	*	*	*					*	*	*	*	*	*		
Ukraine (Ukrainian language schools, Kharkov)	6	3.77	1.02	4.15	0.68	2.26	2.05	**2.62^{a}**	1.33	3.40	**1.00^{a}**	**2.03^{ab}**	**2.08^{ab}**	3.34	1.07		
	9	3.19	0.81	3.81	0.46	1.67	1.75	**2.06^{ab}**	1.32	3.54	**0.54^{ab}**	**1.15^{a}**	**2.51^{a}**	3.09	1.05		
	12	3.10	0.47	3.52	0.35	1.68	1.64	**2.05^{ab}**	1.11	3.43	**0.38^{b}**	**2.10^{ab}**	**1.50^{bc}**	3.10	0.71		
	15	3.17	0.88	3.53	0.66	1.39	1.73	**1.43^{b}**	1.61	3.38	**0.30^{b}**	**2.52^{b}**	**0.80^{c}**	2.80	1.02		
								*			*	*	*				
Ukraine (Russian language schools, Kharkov)	6	**3.47^{ab}**	**0.33^{a}**	**3.80^{ab}**	0.40	**1.33^{a}**	**1.07^{a}**	**1.73^{a}**	**0.61^{a}**	**2.82^{a}**	0.55	**1.63^{a}**	**1.34^{a}**	**2.55^{a}**	0.64		
	9	**4.18^{a}**	**1.02^{b}**	**4.33^{a}**	0.85	**2.55^{b}**	**2.21^{b}**	**2.82^{b}**	**2.07^{b}**	**4.42^{b}**	0.64	**2.16^{ab}**	**2.69^{b}**	**4.08^{b}**	0.88		
	12	**3.34^{ab}**	**0.92^{ab}**	**3.75^{ab}**	0.78	**2.22^{ab}**	**1.49^{ab}**	**2.11^{ab}**	**1.84^{bc}**	**4.03^{bc}**	0.34	**2.39^{ab}**	**1.58^{a}**	**3.76^{ab}**	0.81		
	15	**3.19^{b}**	**0.76^{ab}**	**3.54^{b}**	0.69	**1.90^{ab}**	**1.33^{a}**	**1.94^{ab}**	**1.27^{ab}**	**3.37^{ac}**	0.44	**2.70^{b}**	**0.93^{a}**	**3.05^{ac}**	0.91		
		*	*	*		*	*	*	*	*		*	*	*			

Group																
Georgia (Georgian language schools, Tbilisi)	6	3.57	2.15ᵃ	4.67	1.14ᵃ	5.73ᵃ	0.47ᵃ	3.36	2.60ᵃ	5.04	0.65	4.98	1.12	5.26	0.74	
	9	4.45	1.47ᵃᵇ	4.96	1.02ᵃᵇ	5.78ᵃ	0.50ᵃ	3.30	2.47ᵃᵇ	4.79	1.02	4.71	1.14	5.18	0.82	
	12	4.24	1.29ᵇ	4.59	1.04ᵃᵇ	5.70ᵃ	0.57ᵃ	3.57	1.89ᵃᵇ	5.24	0.62	4.55	1.14	4.88	0.85	
	15	3.91	1.22ᵇ	4.74	0.41ᵇ	5.24ᵇ	1.08ᵇ	3.44	1.71ᵇ	4.72	0.46	4.33	0.74	4.56	0.70	
			*		*	*	*		*				*	(*)		
Georgia (Georgians in Russian language schools, Tbilisi)	6	5.00ᵃ	0.54ᵃ	4.00	1.44ᵃ	4.86	0.74	3.44	2.00	5.19	0.48	3.64	1.94ᵃ	4.72	1.07	
	9	5.43ᵃ	0.38ᵃ	4.52	0.93ᵃᵇ	5.24	0.61	3.84	1.62	5.14	0.32	4.00	1.61ᵃᵇ	5.13	0.41	
	12	4.87ᵃᵇ	0.78ᵃᵇ	4.96	0.65ᵇ	5.26	0.47	3.38	1.57	5.33	0.22	3.98	1.45ᵃᵇ	5.07	0.60	
	15	4.34ᵇ	1.13ᵇ	4.47	0.41ᵇ	4.95	0.78	3.86	1.30	4.86	0.53	4.15	0.95ᵇ	4.33	0.88	
		*	*		*								*	(*)	*	
Georgia (Armenians in Russian language schools, Tbilisi)	6	4.78ᵃ	0.80ᵃ	4.39	1.39	4.50	1.12	3.65	1.97	4.53	1.22ᵃ	3.58	2.06ᵃ	4.33ᵃ	1.40ᵃ	5.21ᵃ / 0.36
	9	5.46ᵇ	0.34ᵇ	4.64	1.00	4.76	0.93	3.48	1.90	5.35	0.37ᵇ	3.46	2.09ᵃ	5.47ᵇ	0.31ᵇ	5.68ᵇ / 0.24
	12	4.87ᵃᵇ	0.54ᵃᵇ	4.65	0.69	4.63	0.74	3.53	1.33	5.02	0.45ᵇ	3.91	1.48ᵃᵇ	4.77ᵃᵇ	0.59ᵇ	5.43ᵃᵇ / 0.32
	15	4.52ᵃ	0.92ᵃ	4.31	0.64	4.97	0.58	3.33	1.43	5.02	0.34ᵇ	4.36	0.87ᵇ	4.44ᵃ	0.69ᵇ	5.44ᵃᵇ / 0.38
		*	*							*		*	*	*	*	*
Azerbaijan (Azeri language schools, Baku)	6	1.22	1.77ᵃᵇ	0.67	0.52	1.13	0.78	4.10ᵃᵇ	0.62	0.97ᵃ	0.68	0.68ᵃ	0.78ᵃ	1.07ᵃ	0.67ᵃ	
	9	1.15	2.34ᵃ	1.15	0.69	1.44	0.90	4.65ᵃ	0.34	2.18ᵇ	0.53	0.94ᵃ	1.44ᵇ	2.13ᵃᵇ	0.56ᵃᵇ	
	12	1.18	2.29ᵃᵇ	1.08	0.71	1.42	0.70	4.21ᵃᵇ	0.71	2.70ᵇ	0.26	1.37ᵃᵇ	0.79ᵃᵇ	2.88ᵇ	0.27ᵃᵇ	
	15	1.16	1.46ᵇ	1.23	0.36	1.73	0.47	3.58ᵇ	0.71	2.11ᵇ	0.24	1.74ᵇ	0.55ᵃ	2.30ᵇ	0.19ᵇ	
			*					*		*	(*)	*	*	*	*	
Azerbaijan (Russian language schools, Baku)	6	2.00	1.05	0.98	0.23	1.10ᵃ	0.37ᵃᵇ	3.53ᵃᵇ	0.47ᵃᵇ	1.57ᵃ	0.18	0.92ᵃ	0.50ᵃᵇ	1.63ᵃ	0.38	
	9	1.88	1.07	0.97	0.60	0.88ᵃ	0.77ᵃ	3.92ᵃ	0.30ᵃ	2.40ᵃᵇ	0.30	0.70ᵃ	1.02ᵇ	2.27ᵃᵇ	0.37	
	12	1.79	1.15	1.44	0.33	2.23ᵇ	0.43ᵇ	2.95ᵇᶜ	0.85ᵇᶜ	2.77ᵇ	0.26	1.44ᵃ	1.03ᵇ	2.74ᵇ	0.44	
	15	2.00	0.83	1.17	0.38	2.20ᵇ	0.28ᵇ	2.73ᶜ	1.18ᶜ	2.47ᵃᵇ	0.28	2.60ᵇ	0.38ᵃ	2.52ᵃᵇ	0.37	
			*			*	*	*	*	*		*	*	*		

Notes

Data analysed using paired-samples *t*-tests, ANOVAs and Tukey's HSD post hoc tests.

The picture that arises in the case of trait attributions to out-groups is equally varied. As far as the attribution of *positive* traits to *out-groups* is concerned, in some cases there were increases with age (e.g., the Scottish children's positive attributions to Spanish, Italian, French, German and English people), in some cases there were decreases with age (e.g., the Italian Vicenza children's positive attributions to British, Spanish, French and German people), in some cases there were initial increases followed by decreases (e.g., the southern Spanish children's positive attributions to British, Italian, French and German people), and in some cases there were no changes at all with age (e.g., the positive attributions made by the Georgian children in Georgian language schools to Russian, Ukrainian, Azeri, English and German people). Several groups of children showed different developmental patterns in relationship to different out-groups (e.g., the Russian Moscow children showed an increase with age in the number of positive attributions to Ukrainian, English and German people, but an increase followed by a decrease in relationship to American people, accompanied by no changes in positive attributions to Georgian and Azeri people). There was also one case where different patterns were shown in relationship to NIS and non-NIS out-groups (namely the Azeri children in Azeri language schools, who showed no age-related changes in their positive attributions to Russian, Ukrainian and Georgian people, but an increase with age in their positive attributions to English, German and American people).

Finally, the attribution of *negative* traits to *out-groups* also showed a varied set of developmental patterns, including no changes with age (e.g., the Basque children's attribution of negative traits to British, French and German people), increases with age (e.g., the negative attributions made by the Georgian children in Russian language schools to Russian people), decreases with age (e.g., the Russian Moscow children's negative attributions to English and German people), and patterns where there was a significant increase followed by a decrease (e.g., the negative attributions made by the Azeri children in Azeri language schools to Germans).

The sheer variety of developmental patterns here is bewilderingly diverse. However, it is extremely important to emphasize and to acknowledge the existence of this diversity. This is because some of the theories that have been put forward over the years in order to explain the development of children's intergroup attitudes have explicitly postulated that a similar pattern of development is exhibited universally by children. For example, Aboud's (1988; Aboud & Amato, 2001; Doyle & Aboud, 1995; Doyle, Beaudet, & Aboud, 1988) theory of the development of prejudice has postulated that children's intergroup attitudes are based on, and driven by, their current cognitive capabilities; as these cognitive capabilities develop in a universal manner, it is postulated that children's intergroup attitudes also change in a similar manner as a direct consequence. However, the sheer variety of developmental patterns exhibited in the development of national attitudes poses a serious problem for this cognitive-developmental theory. We will return to this theory in Chapter 7, where we will also consider alternative theories that are arguably much better placed to explain this developmental diversity.

The data that appear in Tables 5.3 and 5.4 are shown in a different format in Tables 5.5 and 5.6. Here, the various target groups have been rank ordered in terms of the mean number of *positive* adjectives attributed to them by each subgroup of children, and in terms of the mean number of *negative* adjectives attributed to them by each subgroup of children. Looking first at the rankings in terms of the number of positive attributions, Table 5.5 shows that in the cases of the children living in England, Scotland, Catalonia, the Basque Country and southern Spain, the highest number of positive attributions were always made to the in-group (although notice that these attributions were not always *significantly* higher than those made to all of the out-groups). The Italian children showed a slightly different pattern, but even here there was only one group of children out of the eight (namely the 12-year-old Rome children) who attributed *significantly* fewer positive traits to Italian people than to an outgroup. Table 5.6 reveals that in the NIS samples, a similar pattern prevailed in all groups and at all ages, and here there was not a single subgroup of children who attributed *significantly* fewer positive traits to their own in-group.

As far as the ranking in terms of the number of negative attributions is concerned, there is a rather more mixed picture, as the in-group did not always receive the fewest number of negative attributions. Notable examples here are the Italian children (where the older children actually attributed the highest number of negative traits to their own in-group) and, to a lesser extent, the Azeri children (where the oldest groups also attributed a comparatively high number of negative traits to their own in-group).

The "traditional enemy" effect also shows its presence in these two tables. In the Western European samples (Table 5.5), German people commonly received a relatively low number of positive attributions by all groups of children (although notice that the trend to make a relatively high number of negative attributions to German people was less marked). It is arguably inappropriate to regard this as always being a literal "enemy" effect, though, given that the Italian children also displayed this pattern in relationship to German people (Italy having been, historically, an ally of Germany). In other words, there are probably factors other than either historical or current conflictual relations with the child's own country that can lead to this effect; indeed, it seems plausible that prevailing representations of, and beliefs about, a country's activities and actions in the past (irrespective of the actual relationship between the child's own country and that other country) may also sometimes play a role here. In the NIS samples (Table 5.6), the Russian and Ukrainian children (all groups) displayed an "enemy" effect in relationship to

Table 5.5

The target groups ranked in terms of the mean number of positive and negative traits attributed to each target group by each subgroup of children in the Western European samples

Location of children	Age	Positive traits	Negative traits
England (London)	6	English^a British^b Scottish^{bc} French^{bcd} Italian^{bcd} Spanish^{cd} German^d*	German^a Spanish^a French^a Italian^{ab} British^{ab} Scottish^b English^b*
	9	English^a British^b Scottish^b Spanish^b Italian^b French^{bc} German^c*	German^a British^{ab} Italian^{ab} French^{bc} Spanish^{bc} English^{bc} Scottish^c*
	12	English^a British^a Scottish^a Italian^a French^{ab} Spanish^b German^b*	British^a English^b German^a French^{ab} Scottish^b Spanish^b Italian^b*
	15	English^a British^{ab} Scottish^{ab} Italian^{ab} Spanish^{bc} French^c German^c*	German^a British^a French^a English^b Spanish^b Scottish^b Italian^b*
Scotland (Dundee)	6	Scottish^a British^{ab} English^{bcd} Spanish^{bcd} French^{bcd} German^{cd} Italian^d*	British^a Scottish^{ab} French^b Spanish^{ab} English^b German^b Italian^b*
	9	Scottish^a British^a English^b French^{bc} Spanish^{bc} Italian^c German^c*	British English German Scottish French Spanish Italian
	12	Scottish^a British^b English^b French^{bcd} Italian^{cd} Spanish^{cd} German^d*	German^a English^{ab} Spanish^{ab} British^{ab} Scottish^{ab} Italian^b French^b*
	15	Scottish^a British^b English^b Italian^{bc} French^{bc} Spanish^{bc} German^c*	German^a Spanish^{ab} English^{ab} French^{abc} British^{abc} Italian^{bc} Scottish^c*
Catalonia (Girona)	6	Catalan^a Spanish^b British^b French^b German^b Italian^b*	Italian^a German^a French^a Spanish^a British^a Catalan^b*
	9	Catalan^a Spanish^b British^c French^{cd} Italian^{cd} German^d*	German^a French^{ab} Italian^{ab} British^{ab} Spanish^b Catalan^c*
	12	Catalan^a Spanish^b British^{bc} French^{bc} Italian^c German^d*	Spanish^a German^{ab} French^{ab} British^{ab} Italian^b Catalan^b*
	15	Catalan^a Spanish^b British^b German^c Italian^c French^c*	French^a German^a Spanish^{ab} Italian^{ab} British^b Catalan^c*
Basque Country (San Sebastian and Pamplona)	6	Basque^a British^b Spanish^{bc} French^{bc} German^{bc} Italian^c*	French^a Italian^{ab} Spanish^{abc} German^{abc} British^{bc} Basque^c*
	9	Basque^a Spanish^a British^{ab} French^{bc} Italian^{bc} German^c*	French^a German^a Italian^a Spanish^{ab} British^{ab} Basque^b*
	12	Basque^a British^b Spanish^{bc} Italian^{bc} French^{bc} German^c*	French^a Spanish^{ab} German^{ab} Italian^a British^{ab} Basque^b*
	15	Basque^a Italian^b British^b Spanish^b German^b French^b*	French^a Spanish^a German^{ab} British^{ab} Italian^b Basque^c*
Southern Spain (Malaga)	6	Spanish^a French^b British^b Italian^{bc} German^c*	Italian^a German^{ab} British^{ab} French^{ab} Spanish^b*
	9	Spanish^a French^b British^b Italian^b German^b*	Italian^a British^b German^a French^a Spanish^{ba}*
	12	Spanish^a French^b British^{bc} Italian^{bc} German^c*	German^a Italian^a British^a French^a Spanish^b*
	15	Spanish^a British^b German^c French^c Italian^c*	Italian^a French^{ab} German^{abc} British^{bc} Spanish^c*

Italy (Vicenza)	6	Italian[a] Spanish[b] British[b] French[b] German[b]*	German[a] French[ab] British[ab] Spanish[ab] Italian[b]*
	9	Italian[a] British[ab] Spanish[ab] French[ab] German[b]*	German[a] Italian[ab] Spanish[ab] British[b] French[b]*
	12	British[a] French[ab] Italian[abc] Spanish[bc] German[c]*	Italian[a] German[a] Spanish[ab] British[b] French[b]*
	15	Italian French British Spanish German	Italian[a] British[b] German[b] French[b] Spanish[b]*
Italy (Rome)	6	Italian[a] British[b] Spanish[b] French[b] German[b]*	Spanish German British French Italian
	9	British French Spanish Italian German	Italian[a] German[a] Spanish[ab] French[ab] British[b]*
	12	British[a] French[ab] Spanish[ab] Italian[b] German[c]*	Italian[a] German[ab] French[bc] Spanish[c] British[c]*
	15	Spanish French British Italian German	Italian[a] German[ab] British[b] French[b] Spanish[b]*

Notes

An asterisk indicates a statistically significant difference in the number of either positive or negative traits attributed to the target groups by a particular subgroup of children, and the specific location of the significant differences is shown using superscript letters, with groups which did not receive significantly different numbers of traits sharing the same superscript letter.

Data analysed using ANOVAs and Bonferroni-corrected post hoc paired-samples *t*-tests.

Table 5.6

The target groups ranked in terms of the mean number of positive and negative traits attributed to each target group by each subgroup of children in the NIS samples (see Table 5.5 for an explanation of the use of asterisks and superscripts)

Location of children	Age	Positive traits	Negative traits
Russia (Smolensk)	6	Russian^a English^b American^b Ukrainian^b Georgian^b Azeri^b German^b*	German^a Georgian^a Azeri^a Ukrainian^a American^a English^a Russian^{ba}*
	9	Russian^a American^b English^{bc} Ukrainian^{bcd} Georgian^{cd} Azeri^{de} German^c*	German^a Azeri^{ab} Georgian^b Ukrainian^{bc} American^{cd} English^{cd} Russian^d*
	12	Russian^a English^{ab} Ukrainian^{bc} American^{bc} German^{cd} Azeri^{cd} Georgian^d*	Azeri^a Georgian^a German^{ab} Ukrainian^{bc} Russian^{bc} English^c*
	15	Russian^a English^{ab} Ukrainian^{bc} American^{bc} German^{cd} Georgian^{de} Azeri^{ce}*	Azeri^a Georgian^{ab} American^{bc} German^c Russian^c English^c Ukrainian^c*
Russia (Moscow)	6	Russian^a American^b English^{bc} Ukrainian^{bc} Azeri^{bc} German^{bc} Georgian^c*	Azeri^a German^a Georgian^a Ukrainian^a American^a English^a Russian^b*
	9	Russian^a American^a English^{ab} Ukrainian^b German^b Azeri^c Georgian^c*	Georgian^a Azeri^a German^a Ukrainian^b English^{bc} American^c Russian^c*
	12	English^a Ukrainian^{ab} Russian^{ab} American^{bc} German^{bcd} Georgian^{cd} Azeri^d*	Azeri^a Georgian^b German^{bc} American^{bc} Russian^{cd} Ukrainian^{cd} English^d*
	15	German^a English^a Russian^a Ukrainian^{ab} American^{bc} Georgian^c Azeri^c*	Azeri^a Georgian^{ab} American^{ab} Ukrainian^{bc} Russian^{cd} English^{cd} German^d*
Ukraine (Ukrainian language schools, Kharkov)	6	Ukrainian^a Russian^a English^{ab} American^{ab} Azeri^{bc} Georgian^c German^c*	German^a Georgian^a Azeri^{ab} American^b Russian^b English^b Ukrainian^b*
	9	Ukrainian^a English^{ab} Russian^a American^{ab} Azeri^{bc} Georgian^{cd} German^{d}*	German^a Georgian^b Azeri^c American^{bcd} Russian^{cd} English^{cd} Ukrainian^d*
	12	Ukrainian^a English^a Russian^a American^a German^a Azeri^b Georgian^b*	Georgian^a German^a Azeri^a American^{bc} Russian^c English^c Ukrainian^c*
	15	Ukrainian^a English^a Russian^{ab} American^{ab} German^{ab} Azeri^c Georgian^c*	Georgian^a Azeri^a American^{ab} Russian^b German^{bc} Ukrainian^{bc} English^c*
Ukraine (Russian language schools, Kharkov)	6	Ukrainian^{ab} Russian^{ab} English^{ab} American^b Azeri^c German^c Georgian^c*	German^a Georgian^{ab} American^{ab} Azeri^{bc} English^{bc} Ukrainian^c Russian^c*
	9	English^a Ukrainian^a Russian^a American^a Azeri^c Georgian^c German^c*	German^a Georgian^a Azeri^a Russian^b American^b Ukrainian^b English^b*
	12	English^a American^a Ukrainian^a Russian^{ab} German^{bc} Georgian^c Azeri^c*	Azeri^a German^{ab} Georgian^{abc} Russian^{bc} American^a Ukrainian^{ab} English^{d}*
	15	Ukrainian^a English^a Russian^a American^a German^{ab} Azeri^b Georgian^b*	Georgian^a Azeri^a German^a American^a Russian^{ab} Ukrainian^{ab} English^b*
Georgia (Georgian language schools, Tbilisi)	6	Georgian^a American^{ab} English^{ab} German^{ab} Ukrainian^{ab} Russian^b Azeri^{b}*	Azeri Russian Ukrainian German American English Georgian
	9	Georgian^a American^b Ukrainian^b English^b German^b Russian^b Azeri^c*	Azeri^a Russian^b German^b Ukrainian^{bc} American^{bc} Georgian^c*
	12	Georgian^a English^{ab} American^{bc} Ukrainian^{bc} German^c Russian^c Azeri^{d}*	Azeri^a Russian^{ab} German^{ab} Ukrainian^{bc} American^c English^{bc} Georgian^c*
	15	Georgian^a Ukrainian^{ab} English^{ab} American^{abc} German^{bc} Russian^{cd} Azeri^{d}*	Azeri^a Russian^{ab} Georgian^b German^b American^{bc} English^{bc} Ukrainian^c*

Group	n		
Georgia (Georgians in Russian language schools, Tbilisi)	6	English Russian Georgian American Ukrainian German Azeri	Azeri German Ukrainian American Georgian Russian English
	9	Russian^a Georgian^a English^a American^a Ukrainian^a German^{ab} Azeri^b*	Azeri^a German^a Ukrainian^{ab} Georgian^b American^b Russian^b English^b*
	12	English^a Georgian^a American^a Ukrainian^{ab} Russian^{ab} German^b Azeri^c*	Azeri^a German^a Russian^b Ukrainian^{bc} American^{bc} Georgian^{bc} English^c*
	15	Georgian^a English^a Ukrainian^a Russian^{ab} American^{ab} German^{ab} Azeri^b*	Azeri^a Russian^a German^{ab} American^{ab} Georgian^{ab} English^b Ukrainian^b*
Georgia (Armenians in Russian language schools, Tbilisi)	6	Armenian Russian English Georgian Ukrainian American Azeri German	German^a Azeri^a American^{ab} Ukrainian^{ab} English^{ab} Georgian^{ab} Russian^{ab} Armenian^b*
	9	Armenian^a American^{ab} Russian^{ab} English^{ab} Georgian^b Ukrainian^{bc} Azeri^c German^c*	German^a Azeri^{ab} Ukrainian^{abc} Georgian^{bc} English^c Russian^c American^c Armenian^c*
	12	Armenian^a English^{ab} Russian^b American^b Ukrainian^{bc} Georgian^{bc} German^{bc} Azeri^c*	German^a Azeri^{ab} Georgian^{bc} Ukrainian^{bc} American^c Russian^c English^c Armenian^c*
	15	Armenian^a English^{ab} Georgian^{abc} Russian^{bc} American^{bc} German^c Ukrainian^c Azeri^d*	Azeri^a Russian^{ab} German^{abc} American^{abcd} Ukrainian^{abcd} Georgian^{bcd} Armenian^{cd} English^d*
Azerbaijan (Azeri language schools, Baku)	6	Azeri^a Russian^b Georgian^b American^b English^b German^b Ukrainian^b*	Russian^a Georgian^b German^b English^b American^b Azeri^b Ukrainian^b*
	9	Azeri^a English^b American^b Georgian^{bc} Russian^{bc} Ukrainian^c German^c*	Russian^a German^b Georgian^b Ukrainian^c American^c English^c Azeri^c*
	12	Azeri^a American^b English^b Georgian^c German^c Russian^c Ukrainian^c*	Russian^a German^b Ukrainian^{bc} Azeri^{bc} Georgian^c American^c English^c*
	15	Azeri^a American^b English^b Georgian^{bc} German^{bc} Ukrainian^c Russian^c*	Russian^a Azeri^b German^c Georgian^{bc} Ukrainian^{bc} English^c American^c*
Azerbaijan (Russian language schools, Baku)	6	Azeri^a Russian^b American^{bc} English^{bc} Georgian^c Ukrainian^c German^c*	Russian^a German^{ab} Azeri^{ab} American^b Georgian^b Ukrainian^b English^b*
	9	Azeri^a English^b American^b Russian^b Ukrainian^c Georgian^c German^c*	Russian^a German^{ab} Georgian^{abc} Ukrainian^{abc} American^{bc} Azeri^c English^c*
	12	Azeri^a English^a American^a Georgian^{ab} Russian^{ab} Ukrainian^{bc} German^c*	Russian^a German^{abc} Azeri^{abc} American^{bcd} Georgian^{cd} Ukrainian^{cd} English^d*
	15	Azeri^a German^{ab} American^{ab} English^{ab} Georgian^{ab} Russian^b Ukrainian^c*	Azeri^a Russian^{ab} Ukrainian^{bc} German^{bc} American^c Georgian^c English^c*

Notes

Data analysed using ANOVAs and Bonferroni-corrected post hoc paired-samples *t*-tests.

Georgian, Azeri and German people, although there are some interesting exceptions (e.g., notice the 15-year-old Russian Moscow children's attributions to German people). The Georgian children in Georgian language schools showed the effect in relationship to Azeri and Russian people, whereas the Georgian and Armenian children in Russian language schools tended to show the effect in relationship to Azeri and German people instead. Finally, the Azeri children tended to attribute a relatively high number of negative traits to Russian people, at all ages, but showed a somewhat less consistent pattern in their positive attributions.

A further question that can be addressed using the results of the trait attribution task is whether or not children's attitudes to the in-group are related to their attitudes to out-groups. One possibility is that in-group and out-group attitudes are directly related to each other, with children who are more positive to their own in-group also being more positive towards out-groups (i.e., some children are just generally more positive towards all national and state groups than others, irrespective of whether they are in-groups or out-groups). A second possibility is that in-group and out-group attitudes are *inversely* related to each other, with children who are more positive towards their own in-group being more negative towards out-groups. A third possibility is that in-group and out-group attitudes are independent of each other.

This question can be addressed by subtracting the number of negative traits that each child attributed to a particular target group from the number of positive traits that that child attributed to that group. The resulting score is a measure of the child's overall level of positivity towards that particular group. These positivity scores can then be factor analysed in order to ascertain whether (and how) the children's attitudes to the different groups are related to one another. The results of such factor analyses are presented in Tables 5.7 and 5.8.

The findings for the Western European samples are shown in Table 5.7. Intriguingly, the factor structures exhibited by the English and Scottish children differed from each other, as did those exhibited by the Catalan and Basque children. In the case of the English children, there was a simple disjunction between attitudes to all of the out-groups, which loaded onto one factor, and attitudes to the two in-groups, which loaded onto a second factor. In the case of the Scottish children, however, attitudes to the two in-groups (British and Scottish) formed one factor, attitudes to three of the out-groups formed a second factor, while the children's attitudes to German and English people (both traditionally perceived as "enemy" nations by Scottish people) loaded onto a third factor. The Catalan children exhibited a similar factor structure to the English children, with their attitudes to the four out-groups loading onto a different factor from their attitudes to the two in-groups (Spanish and Catalan). In the case of the Basque children, however, attitudes

Table 5.7
The results of the factor analyses of the overall positivity of the trait attributions to the target groups by each subgroup of children in the Western European samples, together with the factor loadings, eigenvalue and percentage of variance explained for each factor

Location of children	Factor 1	Factor 2	Factor 3
England (London)	Italian .73	English .88	
	Spanish .67	British .75	
	French .66		
	German .65		
	Scottish .52		
Eigenvalue	2.19	1.56	
% variance explained	31.21%	22.31%	
Scotland (Dundee)	British .88	French .88	German .88
	Scottish .83	Italian .76	English .70
		Spanish .44	
Eigenvalue	1.66	1.64	1.34
% variance explained	23.70%	23.43%	19.12%
Catalonia (Girona)	French .75	Spanish .82	
	Italian .70	Catalan .78	
	German .68		
	British .59		
Eigenvalue	1.88	1.35	
% variance explained	31.47%	22.57%	
Basque Country (San Sebastian and Pamplona)	German .79	Basque .97	
	French .77		
	Italian .76		
	Spanish .69		
	British .63		
Eigenvalue	2.65	1.05	
% variance explained	44.16%	17.56%	
Southern Spain (Malaga)	French .72	Spanish .97	
	German .71		
	British .70		
	Italian .67		
Eigenvalue	1.95	1.03	
% variance explained	39.07%	20.63%	
Italy (Vicenza)	German .78	Italian .96	
	French .77		
	British .76		
	Spanish .61		
Eigenvalue	2.15	1.09	
% variance explained	42.99%	21.85%	
Italy (Rome)	British .78	Italian .97	
	French .77		
	Spanish .71		
	German .63		
Eigenvalue	2.10	1.05	
% variance explained	42.02%	20.98%	

Notes
Data analysed using principal components analysis with Varimax rotation.

Table 5.8
The results of the factor analyses of the overall positivity of the trait attributions to the target groups by each subgroup of children in the NIS samples, together with the factor loadings, eigenvalue and percentage of variance explained for each factor

Location of children	Factor 1	Factor 2	Factor 3
Russia (Smolensk)	Azeri .75	Russian .90	
	Ukrainian .72		
	English .72		
	Georgian .71		
	American .67		
	German .59		
Eigenvalue	2.92	1.08	
% variance explained	41.65%	15.38%	
Russia (Moscow)	Azeri .82	Russian .83	
	Georgian .81		
	Ukrainian .76		
	German .69		
	English .58		
	American .57		
Eigenvalue	3.07	1.10	
% variance explained	43.86%	15.71	
Ukraine (Ukrainian language schools, Kharkov)	Georgian .73		
	Azeri .70		
	English .69		
	Russian .61		
	Ukrainian .52		
	American .51		
	German .45		
Eigenvalue	2.59		
% variance explained	36.97%		
Ukraine (Russian language schools, Kharkov)	American .77	Georgian .80	
	Ukrainian .68	Azeri .75	
	English .63	German .59	
	Russian .62		
Eigenvalue	1.87	1.63	
% variance explained	26.70%	23.32%	
Georgia (Georgian language schools, Tbilisi)	American .86	Russian .82	Georgian .96
	English .72	Azeri .77	
	German .60	Ukrainian .50	
Eigenvalue	1.85	1.60	1.02
% variance explained	26.36%	22.90%	14.54%
Georgia (Georgians in Russian language schools, Tbilisi)	Ukrainian .79	American .81	
	Azeri .76	Georgian .74	
	German .73	English .60	
		Russian .51	
Eigenvalue	1.90	1.89	
% variance explained	27.08%	27.05%	

Table 5.8   continued

Location of children	Factor 1	Factor 2	Factor 3
Georgia (Armenians in Russian language schools, Tbilisi)	American .84 Russian .76 Armenian .70 English .63 Ukrainian .52	German .81 Azeri .76 Georgian .58	
Eigenvalue	2.56	1.89	
% variance explained	31.95%	23.57%	
Azerbaijan (Azeri language schools, Baku)	English .82 American .77 Ukrainian .64 German .57 Georgian .56	Russian .72 Azeri −.71	
Eigenvalue	2.33	1.40	
% variance explained	33.27%	20.05%	
Azerbaijan (Russian language schools, Baku)	German .77 Georgian .71 Ukrainian .66	American .75 English .67 Azeri .63 Russian .42	
Eigenvalue	1.89	1.71	
% variance explained	27.04%	24.40%	

Notes

Data analysed using principal components analysis with Varimax rotation.

to Spanish people loaded onto the same factor as their attitudes to the four out-groups, revealing that the way these children viewed Spanish people was related to how they viewed other national out-groups rather than to how they viewed Basque people. These children's attitudes to Basque people alone loaded onto the second factor. The southern Spanish and Italian children all showed a simple in-group vs. out-group structure in their attitudes.

Turning to the NIS children, Table 5.8 reveals that both groups of Russian children also exhibited a simple in-group–out-group two-factor structure in their attitudes. The Ukrainian children, however, showed a different structure depending on whether they attended Ukrainian or Russian language schools. The children attending Ukrainian language schools exhibited a one-factor structure, with their attitudes to the in-group loading onto the same factor as their attitudes to all the out-groups. However, those attending Russian language schools showed a two-factor structure; in-group attitudes were related to their attitudes to the more positively evaluated out-groups of American, English and Russian people, with attitudes to the less positively evaluated out-groups of Georgian, Azeri and German people (see Table 5.6) loading onto a second independent factor. The Georgian children attending Georgian language schools show a different kind of factor structure from any other group: attitudes to Western out-groups formed one factor, attitudes to NIS out-groups formed a second factor, and attitudes to the in-group formed a third factor. The Georgian and Armenian children attending the Russian language schools both showed two-factor structures, which appear to reflect perceptions of high vs. low status groups from the particular perspectives of these two groups of children. A similar interpretation can be made of the two-factor structure displayed by the Azeri children attending Russian language schools. Finally, the Azeri children attending Azeri language schools show another novel two-factor structure: attitudes to the in-group loaded negatively onto the same factor as the principal "enemy" out-group, with attitudes to all other groups loading onto a different factor.

The overall conclusion to be drawn from these factor analyses is that any simple generalizations about the relationships that exist between in-group and out-group national and state attitudes in children are not viable. Instead, this relationship varies depending on the particular national and state context, and on the specific situation within that context of the particular group of children involved. Furthermore, although the actual pattern of relationships exhibited by any given group of children may not be predictable in advance without taking into account additional mediating variables, the specific factor structure found can nevertheless usually be interpreted in terms of the prevailing pattern of intergroup relationships within which the child's own national and/or state groups are embedded. Any empirically adequate theory of the development of children's intergroup attitudes must be able to explain this kind of variability both within and across countries in the structure of children's attitudes.

The findings obtained from the affect questions

There were two affect questions, "Do you like or dislike X people?", followed by "Do you like/dislike them a lot or a little?". The findings obtained with these questions are shown in Tables 5.9 and 5.10. The scores here could range from 1 (*dislike a lot*) to 5 (*like a lot*), with 3 being the neutral midpoint of the scale. None of the mean scores from the Western European samples (Table 5.9) was significantly lower than this neutral midpoint (including those measuring the children's affect towards German people). However, within the NIS samples (see Table 5.10), the Russian and Ukrainian children sometimes expressed a dislike of Georgian, Azeri and German people; the Georgian children in Georgian language schools consistently expressed a dislike of Azeri people; and 9- to 15-year-old Azeri children attending Azeri language schools expressed a dislike of Russian people.

Tables 5.9 and 5.10 reveal that the children's feelings towards members of their own in-groups changed with age in different ways in different locations. For example, the Scottish children showed a significant increase in their liking of people from their own in-groups (both British and Scottish) between 6 and 9 years of age. The Italian children living in Vicenza, however, showed a decrease in their liking of Italian people between 6 and 15 years of age. The Georgian children attending Georgian language schools, as well as the Azeri children attending Azeri language schools, instead showed a decrease in liking for their own in-groups only between 12 and 15 years of age. Finally, several groups of children (e.g., the Basque, Russian and Ukrainian children) did not show any changes with age in their liking of people from their own national/state groups.

Feelings towards out-groups also changed with age in different ways in the different samples. In many cases, there were increases in the levels of liking of out-groups with age. However, the specific ages across which this increase took place varied. For example, the Italian children living in Rome showed an increase in their levels of liking of both British and Spanish people between 6 and 9 years of age; the Russian children living in Moscow showed an increase in their levels of liking of Ukrainian people between 9 and 12 years of age; while the Georgian children who attended Russian language schools showed an increase in their levels of liking of German people between 12 and 15 years of age. There were also some cases of decreases in liking with age (e.g., the Georgian children who attended Russian language schools showed a decrease in their levels of liking of Russian people between 9 and 15 years of age). There were also U-shaped developmental curves in affect for some groups (e.g., the liking of German people by the Ukrainian children who attended Ukrainian language schools) as well as inverted U-shaped developmental curves (e.g., the liking of American people by the Russian children living in Moscow). And, finally, there were many cases where no age-related changes occurred in the levels of liking of out-groups (e.g., the levels of liking of British, Spanish, French and German people by the Italian children living in Vicenza). Hence, just as in the case of the trait attributions, a large variety of different developmental patterns was displayed.

The data that appear in Tables 5.9 and 5.10 are recast in Tables 5.11 and 5.12 in terms of the rank order in which each subgroup of children liked the various target groups. The picture that emerges from these two tables is that the children almost always liked their own in-groups more than they liked the various out-groups (although not always to a statistically significant extent); indeed, there was not a single subgroup of children who liked a single out-group *significantly* more than they liked their own in-group. Thus, the pattern here is even more consistent than that obtained with the trait attribution task; compare, for example, the Italian children's profiles shown in Tables 5.5 and 5.11.

Table 5.9

Mean levels of liking expressed towards the target groups by each subgroup of children in the Western European samples

Location of children	Age	British people	Spanish people	Italian people	French people	German people	English people	Scottish people	Catalan people	Basque people
England (London)	6	3.69ᵃ	3.21ᵃ	3.12ᵃ	3.44	2.96	4.54	3.82		
	9	4.34ᵇ	3.53ᵃᵇ	3.61ᵃᵇ	3.53	3.08	4.80	4.10		
	12	4.20ᵇ	3.83ᵇ	3.71ᵇ	3.50	2.93	4.54	4.08		
	15	4.42ᵇ	3.93ᵇ	3.91ᵇ	3.18	3.10	4.65	4.14		
		*	*	*						
Scotland (Dundee)	6	3.43ᵃ	3.37	3.15	3.20ᵃ	3.12	3.39	3.86ᵃ		
	9	4.15ᵇ	3.59	3.29	3.14ᵃ	2.82	4.00	4.82ᵇ		
	12	4.35ᵇ	3.59	3.69	3.81ᵇ	3.22	3.79	4.80ᵇ		
	15	4.14ᵇ	3.76	3.69	3.51ᵃᵇ	2.95	3.58	4.78ᵇ		
		*		(*)	*		(*)	*		
Catalonia (Girona)	6	3.77	3.73ᵃ	3.43ᵃ	3.51ᵃ	3.13			4.66	
	9	3.68	4.09ᵇ	3.55ᵃᵇ	3.41ᵃᵇ	3.24			4.67	
	12	3.89	4.15ᵇ	3.83ᵇ	3.55ᵃ	3.23			4.69	
	15	3.75	3.80ᵃᵇ	3.51ᵃᵇ	3.08ᵇ	3.22			4.75	
			*	*	*					
Basque Country (San Sebastian and Pamplona)	6	3.59	3.66	2.98ᵃ	3.19	3.02				4.46
	9	3.47	3.92	2.98ᵃ	2.93	2.76				4.39
	12	3.64	3.63	3.48ᵃᵇ	3.31	2.93				4.58
	15	3.78	3.59	3.80ᵇ	3.20	3.35				4.79
				*						

Location of children	Age	British people	Spanish people	Italian people	French people	German people	English people	Scottish people	Catalan people	Basque people
Southern Spain (Malaga)	6	3.44	4.65	2.98	3.38	3.28				
	9	3.52	4.90	2.88	3.21	3.09				
	12	3.52	4.82	3.21	3.35	3.11				
	15	3.63	4.90	3.40	3.07	2.94				
			(*)							
Italy (Vicenza)	6	3.48	3.77	4.70^a	3.32	3.18				
	9	3.92	3.48	4.20^{bc}	3.48	2.90				
	12	3.98	3.63	4.23^b	3.73	3.14				
	15	3.67	3.71	3.83^c	3.22	3.36				
				*						
Italy (Rome)	6	2.85a	2.97^a	4.13	3.12^a	2.68				
	9	3.59^b	3.61^b	3.97	3.63^{ab}	2.90				
	12	4.03^b	3.69^b	4.10	3.82^b	3.00				
	15	3.86^b	3.90^b	4.08	3.62^{ab}	3.13				
		*	*		*					

Notes

Where there is a statistically significant effect of age on the levels of liking expressed towards a particular national or state group, an asterisk appears beneath the relevant column of four figures, and the specific location of the significant differences within the column of four figures is shown using superscript letters, with mean scores which do not differ significantly from one another sharing the same superscript letter (where an asterisk appears in parentheses, the age effect could not be located by the post hoc tests). None of the scores in this table is significantly lower than the neutral midpoint of the liking scale (3.00).

Data analysed using ANOVAs, Tukey's HSD post hoc tests and one-sample t-tests.

Table 5.10

Mean levels of liking expressed towards the target groups by each subgroup of children in the NIS samples (see Table 5.9 for an explanation of the use of asterisks and superscripts)

Location of children	Age	Russian people	Ukrainian people	Georgian people	Azeri people	English people	German people	American people	Armenian people
Russia (Smolensk)	6	3.82	3.12	2.85	2.83	3.47^{a}	2.35 #	2.98^{a}	
	9	4.25	3.40	2.87	2.52 #	3.53^{ab}	2.17^{a} #	3.65^{ab}	
	12	4.10	3.47	2.55 #	2.57 #	4.22^{c}	3.07^{b}	3.58^{ab}	
	15	3.87	3.59	2.46 #	2.41 #	4.08^{bc}	3.61^{b}	3.87^{b}	
						*	*	*	
Russia (Moscow)	6	4.63	2.43^{a} #	2.25^{a} #	2.27^{a} #	3.17^{a}	2.28^{a} #	2.80^{a}	
	9	4.85	2.68^{a}	1.50^{b} #	1.58^{b} #	4.10^{b}	2.05^{a} #	4.15^{b}	
	12	4.53	3.77^{b}	3.03^{c}	2.67^{a}	4.38^{b}	3.02^{b}	3.53^{ab}	
	15	4.73	4.20^{b}	2.58^{ac} #	2.72^{a}	4.32^{b}	4.00^{c}	3.27^{a}	
		*	*	*	*	*	*	*	
Ukraine (Ukrainian language schools, Kharkov)	6	4.17	4.42	2.33 #	2.75	3.62^{a}	2.40^{a} #	3.67	
	9	4.08	4.35	2.08 #	2.43 #	3.67^{ab}	1.60^{b} #	3.55	
	12	3.95	4.27	2.50 #	2.65	4.12^{ab}	2.83^{a}	3.88	
	15	4.17	4.50	2.55 #	2.67	4.23^{b}	3.57^{c}	3.77	
						*	*		
Ukraine (Russian language schools, Kharkov)	6	4.37^{a}	4.22	2.75	3.03	3.83	2.45^{a} #	3.22^{a}	
	9	4.07^{ab}	3.93	2.42 #	2.58 #	4.10	1.98^{a} #	3.62^{ab}	
	12	3.67^{b}	4.37	2.77	2.56 #	4.15	2.62^{ab}	3.57^{ab}	
	15	4.23^{a}	4.37	2.72	2.92	3.98	3.20^{b}	3.95^{b}	
		*					*	*	
Georgia (Georgian language schools, Tbilisi)	6	2.81^{a}	3.21^{a}	4.81^{ab}	2.55 #	3.25^{a}	3.63	3.82	
	9	3.42^{b}	3.54^{ab}	4.94^{a}	2.53 #	3.74^{ab}	3.93	4.10	
	12	3.21^{ab}	3.50^{ab}	4.86^{a}	2.49 #	4.06^{b}	3.63	4.09	

Location of children	Age	Russian people	Ukrainian people	Georgian people	Azeri people	English people	German people	American people	Armenian people
	15	3.46^b	3.72^b	4.61^b	2.67 #	3.96^b	3.88	4.06	
		*	*	*		*	*	*	
Georgia (Georgians in Russian language schools, Tbilisi)	6	4.37^a	3.07^a	4.19	2.76	3.59	2.59^a #	3.44^a	4.22
	9	4.23^a	3.05^a	4.59	2.62 #	3.86	2.91^a	3.88^ab	4.56
	12	4.00^ab	3.34^ab	4.58	2.78	3.96	3.03^a	4.04^b	4.41
	15	3.72^b	3.61^b	4.38	3.12	3.98	3.62^b	3.82^ab	4.21
		*	*				*	*	
Georgia (Armenians in Russian language schools, Tbilisi)	6	4.05	3.03	3.37^a	2.73	3.55^a	3.02^ab	3.30^a	
	9	4.31	3.15	3.71^ab	2.79	3.88^ab	2.76^a	3.93^b	
	12	3.91	3.46	3.99^bc	2.91	3.74^ab	3.15^ab	3.99^b	
	15	3.92	3.38	4.38^c	2.74	4.08^b	3.58^b	3.80^b	
				*		*	*	*	
Azerbaijan (Azeri language schools, Baku)	6	2.75	2.92	2.75^a	4.70^a	3.10^a	2.77^a	2.87^a	
	9	2.47 #	2.89	2.90^a	4.79^a	3.37^ab	2.66^a #	3.50^b	
	12	2.38 #	2.95	2.95^ab	4.66^a	3.73^b	2.99^ab	3.77^b	
	15	2.58 #	3.08	3.42^b	4.32^b	3.70^b	3.38^b	3.96^b	
				*	*	*	*	*	
Azerbaijan (Russian language schools, Baku)	6	3.58^a	3.00	2.98^a	4.47^a	3.37	3.00^ab	3.35	
	9	3.08^ab	3.12	3.33^ab	4.63^a	3.83	2.83^a	3.75	
	12	2.85^b	3.21	3.64^b	4.31^ab	3.70	2.75^a	3.57	
	15	2.98^ab	3.30	3.43^ab	3.98^b	3.53	3.48^b	3.70	
		*		*	*		*	*	

Notes

The # indicates that the score is significantly lower than the neutral midpoint of the liking scale (3.00).

Data analysed using ANOVAs, Tukey's HSD post hoc tests and one-sample *t*-tests.

Table 5.11
The target groups ranked in terms of the mean levels of liking expressed towards each target group by each subgroup of children in the Western European samples

Location of children	Age	Target groups
England (London)	6	English[a] Scottish[b] British[bc] French[bcd] Spanish[bcd] Italian[cd] German[d] *
	9	English[a] British[b] Scottish[bc] Italian[cd] Spanish[d] French[d] German[d] *
	12	English[a] British[ab] Scottish[bc] Spanish[bcd] Italian[cd] French[de] German[e] *
	15	English[a] British[ab] Scottish[b] Spanish[b] Italian[b] French[c] German[c] *
Scotland (Dundee)	6	Scottish[a] British[ab] English[ab] Spanish[ab] French[ab] Italian[b] German[b] *
	9	Scottish[a] British[b] English[b] Spanish[bc] Italian[cd] French[cd] German[d] *
	12	Scottish[a] British[b] French[bc] English[bc] Italian[c] Spanish[bc] German[c] *
	15	Scottish[a] British[b] Spanish[b] Italian[b] English[b] French[bc] German[c] *
Catalonia (Girona)	6	Catalan[a] British[b] Spanish[b] French[bc] Italian[bc] German[c] *
	9	Catalan[a] Spanish[b] British[c] Italian[cd] French[cd] German[d] *
	12	Catalan[a] Spanish[b] British[bc] Italian[bc] French[cd] German[d] *
	15	Catalan[a] Spanish[b] British[b] Italian[bc] German[cd] French[d] *
Basque Country (San Sebastian and Pamplona)	6	Basque[a] Spanish[b] British[b] French[b] German[b] Italian[b] *
	9	Basque[a] Spanish[ab] British[bc] Italian[cd] French[cd] German[d] *
	12	Basque[a] British[b] Spanish[bc] Italian[bc] French[bc] German[c] *
	15	Basque[a] Italian[b] British[bc] Spanish[bc] German[bc] French[c] *
Southern Spain (Malaga)	6	Spanish[a] British[b] French[b] German[b] Italian[b] *
	9	Spanish[a] British[b] French[b] German[b] Italian[b] *
	12	Spanish[a] British[b] French[b] Italian[b] German[b] *
	15	Spanish[a] British[b] Italian[b] French[b] German[b] *
Italy (Vicenza)	6	Italian[a] Spanish[b] British[b] French[b] German[b] *
	9	Italian[a] British[ab] Spanish[bc] French[bc] German[c] *
	12	Italian[a] British[ab] French[bc] Spanish[bc] German[c] *
	15	Italian[a] Spanish[ab] British[ab] German[ab] French[b] *
Italy (Rome)	6	Italian[a] French[b] Spanish[b] British[b] German[b] *
	9	Italian[a] French[a] Spanish[a] British[ab] German[b] *
	12	Italian[a] British[a] French[a] Spanish[a] German[b] *
	15	Italian[a] Spanish[a] British[a] French[ab] German[b] *

Notes
An asterisk indicates a statistically significant difference in levels of liking expressed by a particular subgroup of children towards the target groups, and the specific location of the significant differences is shown using superscript letters, with groups which did not receive significantly different levels of liking sharing the same superscript letter.
Data analysed using ANOVAs and Bonferroni-corrected post hoc paired-samples t-tests.

Table 5.12
The target groups ranked in terms of the mean levels of liking expressed towards each target group by each subgroup of children in the NIS samples (see Table 5.11 for an explanation of the use of asterisks and superscripts)

Location of children	Age	Target groups
Russia (Smolensk)	6	Russian[a] English[ab] Ukrainian[abc] American[bc] Georgian[bc] Azeri[bc] German[c] *
	9	Russian[a] American[ab] English[b] Ukrainian[b] Georgian[c] Azeri[c] German[c] *
	12	English[a] Russian[ab] American[bc] Ukrainian[c] German[cd] Azeri[d] Georgian[d] *
	15	English[a] Russian[a] American[a] German[a] Ukrainian[a] Georgian[b] Azeri[b] *
Russia (Moscow)	6	Russian[a] English[b] American[bc] Ukrainian[bc] German[c] Azeri[c] Georgian[c] *
	9	Russian[a] American[b] English[b] Ukrainian[c] German[cd] Azeri[d] Georgian[d] *
	12	Russian[a] English[a] Ukrainian[b] American[bc] Georgian[cd] German[cd] Azeri[d] *
	15	Russian[a] English[ab] Ukrainian[ab] German[bc] American[cd] Azeri[d] Georgian[d] *
Ukraine (Ukrainian language schools, Kharkov)	6	Ukrainian[a] Russian[ab] American[b] English[b] Azeri[c] German[c] Georgian[c] *
	9	Ukrainian[a] Russian[ab] English[b] American[b] Azeri[c] Georgian[cd] German[d] *
	12	Ukrainian[a] English[a] Russian[a] American[a] German[b] Azeri[b] Georgian[b] *
	15	Ukrainian[a] English[ab] Russian[abc] American[bc] German[c] Azeri[d] Georgian[d] *
Ukraine (Russian language schools, Kharkov)	6	Russian[a] Ukrainian[a] English[ab] American[bc] Azeri[cd] Georgian[cd] German[d] *
	9	English[a] Russian[a] Ukrainian[a] American[a] Azeri[b] Georgian[b] German[b] *
	12	Ukrainian[a] English[ab] Russian[bc] American[c] Georgian[d] German[d] Azeri[d] *
	15	Ukrainian[a] Russian[a] English[a] American[a] German[b] Azeri[b] Georgian[b] *
Georgia (Georgian language schools, Tbilisi)	6	Georgian[a] American[b] German[bc] English[cd] Ukrainian[cd] Russian[de] Azeri[e] *
	9	Georgian[a] American[b] German[bc] English[bc] Ukrainian[c] Russian[c] Azeri[d] *
	12	Georgian[a] American[b] English[b] German[bc] Ukrainian[bc] Russian[c] Azeri[d] *
	15	Georgian[a] American[b] English[b] German[b] Ukrainian[b] Russian[b] Azeri[c] *
Georgia (Georgians in Russian language schools, Tbilisi)	6	Russian[a] Georgian[ab] English[bc] American[c] Ukrainian[cd] Azeri[d] German[d] *
	9	Georgian[a] Russian[ab] American[b] English[b] Ukrainian[c] German[c] Azeri[c] *
	12	Georgian[a] American[b] Russian[b] English[b] Ukrainian[c] German[cd] Azeri[d] *
	15	Georgian[a] English[b] American[b] Russian[b] German[bc] Ukrainian[bc] Azeri[c] *
Georgia (Armenians in Russian language schools, Tbilisi)	6	Armenian[a] Russian[ab] English[bc] Georgian[bcd] American[cd] Ukrainian[cd] German[cd] Azeri[d] *
	9	Armenian[a] Russian[ab] American[bc] English[bc] Georgian[cd] Ukrainian[de] Azeri[e] German[e] *
	12	Armenian[a] Georgian[ab] American[ab] Russian[b] English[bc] Ukrainian[bc] German[cd] Azeri[d] *
	15	Georgian[a] Armenian[ab] English[abc] Russian[bc] American[bcd] German[cd] Ukrainian[d] Azeri[e] *

Continued overleaf

Table 5.12 continued

Location of children	Age	Target groups
Azerbaijan (Azeri language schools, Baku)	6	Azeri[a] English[b] Ukrainian[b] American[b] German[b] Russian[b] Georgian[b] *
	9	Azeri[a] American[b] English[b] Georgian[bc] Ukrainian[bc] German[c] Russian[c] *
	12	Azeri[a] American[b] English[b] German[c] Ukrainian[c] Georgian[c] Russian[c] *
	15	Azeri[a] American[ab] English[bc] Georgian[cd] German[cd] Ukrainian[d] Russian[e] *
Azerbaijan (Russian language schools, Baku)	6	Azeri[a] Russian[b] English[bc] American[bcd] Ukrainian[cd] German[cd] Georgian[d] *
	9	Azeri[a] English[b] American[b] Georgian[bc] Ukrainian[c] Russian[c] German[c] *
	12	Azeri[a] English[ab] Georgian[b] American[b] Ukrainian[bc] Russian[c] German[c] *
	15	Azeri[a] American[a] English[a] German[ab] Georgian[ab] Ukrainian[b] Russian[b] *

Notes
Data analysed using ANOVAs and Bonferroni-corrected post hoc paired-samples t-tests.

In addition, in the Western European samples (Table 5.11), German people once again frequently emerged as the least liked out-group (although they were not always liked less than *all* the other out-groups). In the NIS samples (Table 5.12), Russian and Ukrainian children, with the exception of the 15-year-old Russian children, liked Georgian, Azeri and German people the least; Georgian children attending Georgian language schools liked Ukrainian, Russian and Azeri people the least, whereas Georgian and Armenian children attending Russian language schools liked Ukrainian, *German* and Azeri people the least; the Azeri children showed a much less consistent pattern (although, with the exception of the 6-year-olds attending Russian language schools, Russian people were commonly among the least liked groups).

Finally, the children's affect scores can also be factor analysed in order to examine the underlying factor structure within each group of children. The results of these analyses are shown in Tables 5.13 and 5.14. Some of these factor structures are, once again, readily interpretable in terms of the prevailing intergroup relations that characterize the child's own national and state context and the child's own situation within that context; see, for example, the factor structures exhibited by the children living in the Basque Country, southern Spain, Italy (Rome), Russia (both groups), Ukraine (both groups), Georgia (Georgians and Armenians attending Russian language schools), and Azerbaijan (Azeri language schools). However, notice that these factor structures are often different from those that emerged from the factor analyses of the data from the trait attribution task (cf. Tables 5.7 and 5.8); hence, the structure of children's feelings about national and state groups does not always mirror the structure of their trait attributions to those groups. It is also worth noting that some of the other factor structures that emerged

Table 5.13

The results of the factor analyses of the levels of liking of the target groups by each subgroup of children in the Western European samples, together with the factor loadings, eigenvalue and percentage of variance explained for each factor

Location of children	Factor 1	Factor 2	Factor 3
England (London)	English .68 British .67 Scottish .61 Spanish .47	German .77 French .74 Italian .52	
Eigenvalue % variance explained	1.72 24.62%	1.49 21.31%	
Scotland (Dundee)	Scottish .80 British .67	English .71 Spanish .68 German .60	French .84 Italian .64
Eigenvalue % variance explained	1.42 20.34%	1.36 19.39%	1.25 17.91%
Catalonia (Girona)	British .63 German .58 French .55 Italian .53 Spanish .50 Catalan .45		
Eigenvalue % variance explained	1.76 29.37%		
Basque Country (San Sebastian and Pamplona)	German .71 French .69 Italian .67 British .54	Basque −.81 Spanish .60	
Eigenvalue % variance explained	1.92 32.00%	1.19 19.82%	
Southern Spain (Malaga)	German .73 French .71 Italian .66 British .59	Spanish .97	
Eigenvalue % variance explained	1.82 36.38%	1.02 20.42%	
Italy (Vicenza)	British .79 French .65 Spanish .55	Italian .90 German .46	
Eigenvalue % variance explained	1.52 30.39%	1.19 23.72%	
Italy (Rome)	British .75 French .70 Spanish .63 German .53	Italian .97	
Eigenvalue % variance explained	1.73 34.61%	1.02 20.35%	

Notes

Data analysed using principal components analysis with Varimax rotation.

Table 5.14
The results of the factor analyses of the levels of liking of the target groups by each
subgroup of children in the NIS samples, together with the factor loadings, eigenvalue
and percentage of variance explained for each factor

Location of children	Factor 1	Factor 2	Factor 3
Russia (Smolensk)	Georgian .83 Azeri .74 Ukrainian .63	English .77 American .70 German .70	Russian .95
Eigenvalue % variance explained	1.68 24.00%	1.61 22.97%	1.06 15.20%
Russia (Moscow)	Georgian .87 Azeri .87 Ukrainian .57 German .57	English .80 American .78	Russian .98
Eigenvalue % variance explained	2.18 31.17%	1.56 22.28%	1.03 14.75%
Ukraine (Ukrainian language schools, Kharkov)	Georgian .79 Azeri .79 Russian .55 German .44	English .85 American .77 Ukrainian .45	
Eigenvalue % variance explained	1.78 25.37%	1.70 24.28%	
Ukraine (Russian language schools, Kharkov)	Azeri .82 Georgian .77 German .57	English .79 American .62 Ukrainian .48 Russian .43	
Eigenvalue % variance explained	1.76 25.14%	1.58 22.58%	
Georgia (Georgian language schools, Tbilisi)	Ukrainian .71 Azeri .69 English .56 Russian .39	American .83 German .53	Georgian .80 German .58
Eigenvalue % variance explained	1.47 21.00%	1.23 17.51%	1.09 15.63%
Georgia (Georgians in Russian language schools, Tbilisi)	Azeri .78 Russian .58 German .56 Ukrainian .50	American .67 Georgian .63 English .58	
Eigenvalue % variance explained	1.61 23.02%	1.57 22.44%	

Table 5.14   Continued

Location of children	Factor 1	Factor 2	Factor 3
Georgia (Armenians in Russian language schools, Tbilisi)	Azeri .79 Ukrainian .57 Georgian .56 German .53	English .80 American .74	Armenian .81 Russian .52
Eigenvalue	1.62	1.39	1.21
% variance explained	20.18%	17.38%	15.08%
Azerbaijan (Azeri language schools, Baku)	English .77 American .72 Azeri −.52	Georgian .75 Ukrainian .59 German .57 Russian .35	
Eigenvalue	1.49	1.47	
% variance explained	21.22%	21.00%	
Azerbaijan (Russian language schools, Baku)	English .75 American .72 Georgian .58	German .78 Ukrainian .74	Russian .77 Azeri .72
Eigenvalue	1.51	1.45	1.19
% variance explained	21.58%	20.74%	16.95%

Notes
Data analysed using principal components analysis with Varimax rotation.

from the analyses of the children's affect scores are much harder to interpret, for example, those exhibited by the children living in England, Italy (Vicenza) and Azerbaijan (Russian language schools); indeed, in the case of the Georgian children attending Georgian language schools, affect towards German people loaded onto two different factors. However, the important conclusion that emerges quite clearly from Tables 5.13 and 5.14 is that there is considerable cross-national diversity in the factor structures which can underlie children's feelings about national and state groups. Some children (e.g., those living in Catalonia) display a one-factor structure; other children (e.g., those living in southern Spain and in Italy (Rome)) display a simple in-group vs. out-group two-factor structure; others (e.g., those living in the Basque Country and both groups in Ukraine) display other kinds of two-factor structures, which are nevertheless interpretable in terms of the child's own situation within their national and state context; and yet others (e.g., those living in Russia) display more complex but still readily interpretable three-factor structures. Once again, this diversity must be taken into account by any empirically adequate theory of how children's attitudes towards national and state groups develop.

Some broad conclusions from the CHOONGE and NERID projects

The following general picture emerges from the CHOONGE and NERID projects. First, children's trait attributions to national and state groups, including out-groups, tend to be positive overall. In other words, children's trait attributions rarely reveal any out-group denigration. However, children do sometimes exhibit negative feelings towards some out-groups when assessed using a *like–dislike* scale (even though they may not attribute significantly more negative than positive traits to those out-groups). Examination of the specific groups that receive the least positive trait attributions and/or are liked the least supports the view that these are frequently the out-groups with which the child's own country has experienced some kind of conflict or tension, either in the present or in the past. However, there are occasional exceptions to this general rule (as exemplified by the Italian children's attitudes to German people), which are arguably explicable instead in terms of prevailing beliefs about that out-group's activities and actions in the past (rather than in terms of the relations that exist between the out-group and the child's own in-group per se).

The data from these two projects also confirm that a bias towards the in-group is indeed a common phenomenon among children right across this age range, from 6 to 15 years of age. Positive attitudes to the in-group are particularly marked when affect measures are used, and are only slightly less marked when trait attribution measures are used. Importantly, findings concerning in-group bias can vary depending on the specific measure used (e.g., the Italian children's responses on the trait attribution vs. the affect measures; cf. Tables 5.5 and 5.11), and they can also vary depending on the specific national and state context that is involved (e.g., the Italian vs. the Catalan and Basque children's attitudes to their own ingroups as assessed by the trait attribution task; see Table 5.5). This variability needs to be borne in mind, particularly when interpreting previous findings from studies that have only been conducted in a single country, and have only utilized a single measure of children's attitudes.

Arguably the most striking finding to emerge from the CHOONGE and NERID projects is the sheer variability that can occur in the development of children's attitudes and feelings. The data from these two projects clearly show that the age-related changes that occur in children's trait attributions to, and affect for, national and state groups, can vary dramatically. Positive trait attributions, negative trait attributions and levels of liking can sometimes increase, can sometimes decrease, can sometimes both increase and decrease, and can sometimes show no changes at all, as a function of age. Furthermore, the particular pattern shown may vary according to the target group involved, the child's own national and state context, and the child's own situation within that context. This conclusion about the variability that can occur in children's development is further reinforced by the factor structures that were found to underlie the children's attitudes and feelings; these attitudes and feelings sometimes display a one-factor structure, sometimes a two-factor structure (which can be, but is not always, a simple in-group vs. out-group structure), and sometimes a three-factor structure.

The sheer variability and diversity that occurs in children's development in this domain poses severe problems for any developmental theory that posits universal patterns in the development of children's intergroup attitudes. One finding that does emerge from the data, though, both from the factor analyses and from the findings concerning the groups that received the least positive trait attributions and/or are liked least by children, is that the patterning of children's national and state attitudes and feelings does often reflect the set of prevailing intergroup relations within which their own national and/or state groups are embedded; hence the findings concerning "enemy" nations, and the findings concerning relationships such as those between Scottish/English/British, Catalan/Spanish, Basque/Spanish, and Azeri/Russian. We will return to this issue in Chapter 6, when we examine the patterns of children's own subjective identifications with national and state groups, and in Chapter 7, where we consider the type of theory needed to explain children's development in this domain.

THE SOURCES OF CHILDREN'S KNOWLEDGE AND BELIEFS ABOUT THE PEOPLE WHO LIVE IN OTHER COUNTRIES

One issue that we have not yet considered in this chapter is the sources from which children derive their knowledge and beliefs about the people who live in other countries. Lambert and Klineberg (1967) examined this issue by asking the children themselves about the sources of their knowledge (notice that this method does not address the question of whether or not these self-reports are veridical); specifically, they asked each child, after he or she had described a particular out-group and had said whether or not they liked them, the additional question "How do you know about them?". They found that the 6-year-olds said that they had learnt about the various out-groups from their parents, from television and movies, and from direct contact with foreigners. By contrast, the 10- and 14-year-olds tended not to refer to people in their everyday environments, not even their parents. They instead typically referred to impersonal sources, reporting that they had acquired their information primarily from television, movies, books, school coursework, textbooks and magazines and, to a much lesser extent, direct contact with foreigners. Similarly, Barrett and Short (1992) asked the 5- to 10-year-old English children they interviewed about where they thought they had learnt about French, German, Spanish and Italian people from, but using a check-list of possible sources in order to facilitate the children's reports. Television was the most frequently cited source by children of all ages, with parents, holidays and books also being mentioned by these children as their other principal information sources. Byram et al. (1991) also examined the responses produced in their qualitative interviews to identify the sources from which their 10- and 14-year-old English children had derived their knowledge of French, American and German people. Two of the primary sources the children had drawn on to construct their representations of French people were visits to France and the teaching they were receiving in French lessons at school. In the case of American and German people, however, television appeared to be the principal source of the children's representations. Notice that, if school work and school textbooks are a source of children's infor-mation about the people who live in other countries, then the ethnocentric biases in school textbooks and the school curriculum that we examined in Chapter 4 may well be one of the influences driving the contents of children's stereotypes of national and state groups and their positive bias towards their own in-group.

Evidence that television can indeed impact on children's knowledge and beliefs about the people who live in other countries is reported by Himmelweit, Oppenheim, and Vince (1958). They found that 10- to 14-year-old children who had watched television programmes about the people who live in other countries over a period of a year exhibited greater objectivity (i.e., were more factual and less value-laden) in their views of foreign peoples, and their own beliefs matched the way that these groups were being portrayed in television programmes to a greater extent, than children who did not watch such pro-grammes. In addition, Roberts et al. (1974) examined the impact of a specific American series, "The Big Blue Marble", which had been designed to influ-ence children's beliefs about other countries and cultures. It was found that, after just four episodes, 9- to 11-year-olds began to view foreign people as being healthier, happier and more affluent than they had previously been thought to be. The children had also begun to question the previously assumed superiority of Americans.

It is noteworthy that, when the child's own country is either currently, or has historically been, in conflict with another country, then the mass media within the child's own country tend to present negative images of the enemy people (Bar-Tal, 1988, 1993, 1997; Bialer, 1985; English & Halperin, 1987; Hesse & Mack, 1991; Johnson, 1966). For example, during the Cold War era, the American mass media presented negative images of Russians, represent-ing them as primitive, aggressive, cruel and ruthless (Bar-Tal, 1993; English & Halperin, 1987). If television does impact on children's representations in this domain, as it appears to do, then television may well be a significant influence in the acquisition of the negative attitudes towards "enemy" out-groups.

Holloway and Valentine's (2000) study, which we looked at in Chapter 2, provides further support for the view that children acquire information about the people who live in other countries from television. This is the study in which 13-year-old British and New Zealand children were asked to email each other with descriptions of what they thought the other country and its people were like. In Chapter 2, we saw that Holloway and Valentine found frequent references to media images from soap operas and movies in the children's descriptions as the source of their knowledge. This study therefore provides further evidence for the view that children's beliefs about the people who live in other countries are influenced by the representations they view on television.

However, children do not simply absorb information passively from television, from other media sources and texts, or indeed from other people (Durkin, 1985, 2005; Gunter & McAleer, 1997; Salomon, 1983). Instead, children often make active inferences from the information they receive, going beyond the presented information itself and sometimes generating mistaken beliefs in the process. Interestingly, Holloway and Valentine found that the British and New Zealand children in their study frequently held mistaken beliefs about the people who live in the other country, which appeared to have been derived by a process of active inference. For example, most of the British children believed that New Zealanders look like British people but had a better suntan. They seemed to have drawn this inference from their belief that it is always hot and sunny in New Zealand (itself a mistaken belief, which in some cases had been derived from the equation of a country being "in the south" with being hot and sunny, and in other cases from the conflation of Australia and New Zealand). Conversely, some of the New Zealand children described British people as having pale skins, an inference they appeared to have drawn from their belief that Britain has a cold and wet climate. Hence, while children's representations of foreign groups are likely to be influenced by the information they receive from a multiplicity of different sources (including television, movies, magazines, books, the school curriculum, teachers, parents, holidays and direct contact with foreigners), this does not mean that children passively absorb this information from these various sources. Instead, children actively construct their own understandings and beliefs based on the information that is available to them and to which they attend.

CHILDREN'S BELIEFS ABOUT THE FACTORS THAT DETERMINE PEOPLE'S NATIONAL AND STATE GROUP MEMBERSHIPS

One final issue that has received attention from researchers in this field is children's understanding of the factors that determine people's national and state group memberships. The studies conducted into this issue have shown that children frequently emphasize birthplace when they make judgements about people's membership of national and state groups. Carrington and Short (1995, 1996, 2000) have conducted a sequence of interview studies with children that have been very revealing here. In these studies, they asked 8- to 12-year-old children living in England, Scotland and America the question "What makes a person British/American?". Notice that, in the case of the children living in England and Scotland, the state term *British* was used in these studies, rather than the national terms *English* and *Scottish*.

In their responses, the British children said that the crucial criteria were: being born in Britain (with 65% of the children referring to birthplace); speaking English as your first language (32%); living in Britain (18%); and having British parents or grandparents (17%). For example, one child (a white Scottish 9-year-old) said "It's just the way they talk and where they were born", while another child (a white English 10-year-old) said "If they're born in Britain and they were brought up in Britain and they've got relations that are British". In comparison, the American children said that the most important criteria were: birthplace (64%); living in America (31%); and having American citizenship (16%). Very few of the American children referred to the language a person spoke, but references to having formal legal citizenship (i.e., having "papers" or a passport) were higher than they were in Britain. Thus, even though the British children had been cued with the state term rather than with a national term, very few of them displayed a legalistic interpretation of the state category. In all three national contexts, there were very few explicit references to either racialized groups or ethnicity. Thus, place of birth clearly dominated all other factors in the children's reasoning, in both Britain and America.

Carrington and Short also asked the children a second question "Is it possible to stop being British/American and become something else?". When children gave an affirmative answer to this question, the most frequently cited reason, both in Britain and in America, was because people can go and live in another country. For example, one child (a white American 11-year-old) said: "If you move to another country and live there for a long time, you become that [nationality]". However, there were two differences between the British and the American children in their responses to this second question. First, the British children sometimes said that people can change the language they speak and can therefore stop being British for this reason. By contrast, the American children hardly ever referred to people's use of language. Second, when children gave a negative response to this question, references to birthplace as the reason why people cannot change their nationality were far more frequent among the British children. For example, one child (a British Asian 11-year-old) said: "[No,] you've always got the British in you—because you were born in Britain". Nearly a third of the British children referred to birthplace in this way, whereas hardly any of the American children did so. Thus, there were differences in the children's judgements according to the country in which they lived.

Because of the potential problems that can occur with open-ended interviewing, Penny, Barrett, and Lyons (2001) used a different method to examine children's understanding of the determinants of national group membership. They devised a set of simple statements about people (e.g., *this person speaks X, this person lives in X, this person is white, this person is Christian*, etc.), and presented these statements in pairs to English and Scottish 6- to 12-year-old children. The children were asked to make a forced-choice prediction about which person within each pair was more likely to be English (in the case of the English children) or Scottish (in the case of the Scottish children). A consensus occurred in the children's responses, irrespective of the children's age and national group. The order in which the characteristics were used by the children to predict people's national group memberships was: born in X > speaks X > parents are X > lives in X >> is Christian > is white. In other words, the first four criteria clearly dominated over both religion and racialized groups in driving the children's predictions about people's national group memberships. Furthermore, these four primary criteria were themselves ordered systematically in the priority that was accorded to them. Notice that the first four criteria are very similar to those obtained by Carrington and Short in their interview-based studies with British children. But, in addition, this study shows that children as young as 6 years of age already make coherent and systematic predictions about people's national group memberships. In addition, the criteria they use for making their predictions appear to change minimally across the course of middle childhood. The implication seems to be that 6-year-old children have already constructed a naïve theory about the factors that determine national group membership, enabling them to make systematic predictions about the national groups to which people belong.

The studies by Carrington and Short (1995, 1996, 2000) and Penny et al. (2001) therefore suggest that ethnicity and/or race are not considered by children to be important determinants of people's national and state group memberships. That said, the children who were tested in these studies were all either English, Scottish or American. It is possible that different judgements would have been made by children living in other, less ethnically diverse countries. Furthermore, the fact that these British and American children tended not to use either ethnicity or race to make their own judgements does not mean that they are unaware of the salience of ethnicity and race in the judgements that other people might make.

This latter point emerges very clearly from a study by Scourfield and Davies (2003, 2005), who examined Welsh children's accounts of what it means to be Welsh. They conducted both focus groups and semi-structured interviews with ethnic minority and white majority 8- to 11-year-old Welsh children. They found that, in all six schools where the study was conducted, the children construed Welshness in terms of being born in Wales, speaking Welsh, and having Welsh parents. These findings are therefore consistent with those of Carrington and Short (1995, 1996, 2000) and Penny et al. (2001). In addition, however, the white children were clearly aware of both racism and the potential for ethnic minority individuals to feel excluded from the category of Welsh, and these children made explicit attempts to argue for the inclusion of ethnic minority individuals within their notion of Welshness. This occurred particularly in the schools which were virtually "all-white"; in the one school where ethnic diversity was an everyday reality for the children, there was less evidence of the white children having to work so hard in order to justify the ethnic inclusiveness of the Welsh category. Interestingly, however, of the 11 ethnic minority children who participated in the study, only one used the term "Welsh" to describe himself, and that was alongside other alternative identities such as "Muslim". Instead, the ethnic minority children tended to describe themselves as "British", "British Muslim", and/or in terms of their family's country of origin (e.g., "Pakistani"). Hence, while the majority group children strove to be inclusive, the ethnic minority children exhibited a reluctance to claim Welshness for themselves.

SUMMARY

The principal conclusions to be drawn from the body of research which we have been examining in this chapter are as follows.

- As far as children's knowledge and beliefs about the people who belong to different national and state groups are concerned:
  - children as young as 5–6 years of age already hold stereotypes of some national and state groups, and these stereotypes have distinctive contents according to the particular groups they represent
  - initially, at 5 or 6 years of age, children usually express judgements about the characteristics of just a few salient out-groups, attributing distinctive characteristics to the members of those groups, and at this early age, these characteristics primarily concern the typical physical features, clothing, language and behavioural habits of these groups
  - by 10 or 11 years of age, children produce much more detailed descriptions of the distinctive characteristics that are exhibited by the members of a large number of different out-groups, and these characteristics include not only typical physical features, clothing, language and habits, but also psychological and personality traits and sometimes political and religious beliefs as well
  - the amount of individual variation that is acknowledged to exist

within populations around these stereotypes also increases significantly through middle childhood, and by 10–12 years of age children readily concede that most people do not actually conform to these stereotypes

- the contents of children's stereotypes of their own national in-group are not affected by the comparative context in which these stereotypes are elicited
- children appear to derive their knowledge and beliefs about the people who live in other countries from a multiplicity of different sources, including television, movies, magazines, books, school coursework and school textbooks, teachers, parents, visits to other countries, and direct contact with foreigners.

- As far as children's feelings and attitudes towards national and state groups are concerned:
  - children usually exhibit in-group favouritism from 5 or 6 years of age onwards
  - in-group favouritism is most marked when affect measures are used to assess children's attitudes to national and state in-groups and out-groups
  - out-group denigration is not a common phenomenon, and many out-groups are positively liked, just to a lesser degree than the in-group
  - however, out-groups that have been the traditional enemies of the child's own country in the past, or out-groups that are the current enemies of the child's own country, are usually liked less and/or receive less positive trait attributions than other out-groups
  - there is considerable variability in the development of children's attitudes and feelings towards national and state groups, with the age-related changes that occur in children's trait attributions to, and affect for, particular national and state groups varying according the particular target group involved, the child's own national and state context, and the child's specific situation within that context
  - it is notable that, in some groups of children, there are no age-related changes in attitudes to, and feelings towards, national and state groups
  - there is also considerable variability in the factor structures that underlie children's attitudes and feelings towards national and state groups, according to the child's own national and state context, and according to the child's specific situation within that context.

- As far as children's beliefs about the factors that determine people's national and state group memberships are concerned:
  - children as young as 6 years of age are able to make systematic predictions about people's national and state group memberships

- ○ the criteria they use for making these predictions change minimally across the course of middle childhood
- ○ the three most prominent factors driving their judgements are the place where a person is born, the place where a person lives, and the national or state group to which a person's parents or grandparents belong
- ○ in addition, some children use the language that a person speaks, and the legal citizenship of a person, to make their predictions
- ○ in making their judgements about people's national and state group memberships, many children treat race, ethnicity and religion as being irrelevant to these judgements
- ○ however, ethnic minority children can sometimes exclude themselves from a particular national category on the basis of their own ethnicity and/or race.

CHAPTER SIX

The development of children's subjective identifications with their own nation and state

Martyn Barrett, Luciano Arcuri, Mark Bennett, Anna Emilia Berti, Anna Silvia Bombi, Luigi Castelli, Annamaria de Rosa, Arantza del Valle, Rauf Garagozov, Almudena Giménez de la Peña, Thea Kacharava, Giorgi Kipiani, Evanthia Lyons, Valentyna Pavlenko, Santiago Perera, Luixa Reizábal, Tatiana Riazanova, Fabio Sani, Jose Valencia and Ignasi Vila

In the previous chapters, we have seen that many children, from an early age, show a strong emotional attachment to their own country, a pronounced sense of pride in that country, and often display in-group favouritism when making judgements about, and expressing affect towards, national and state groups. These findings imply that children's own country and national and state in-groups occupy a psychologically privileged position in children's judgements, evaluations and feelings. In the present chapter, we turn our attention directly to children's psychological privileging of their own country and national and state in-groups, and to the issue of children's subjective identifications with their own nation and state.

This chapter is divided into three parts. The first part briefly reviews some of the previous studies that have investigated children's national and state self-categorizations. The second part of the chapter then reports the findings on children's self-categorizations and subjective identifications that were obtained in the CHOONGE and NERID projects. As we will see, there is extensive variability in the development of children's national and state identifications. Some of the factors associated with this variability are explored at length in this second part of the chapter. The third part of the chapter then reviews some additional recent studies into the development of children's national and state identifications, which have been conducted using a new scale, the Strength of Identification Scale (SoIS). As we shall see, these studies have confirmed the overall conclusion of the CHOONGE and NERID projects, namely that children living in different national and state contexts often exhibit significantly different patterns of identity development.

PREVIOUS STUDIES INTO CHILDREN'S NATIONAL AND STATE SELF-CATEGORIZATIONS

In thinking about children's subjective identifications with their nation or state, we need to begin by considering the age at which children first start to categorize themselves as members of their own national or state group. Notice that this need not be the same age at which they first acquire a knowledge of the existence of that group, or even the same age at which they first acquire a stereotypical representation of the group. It is quite possible that some children only learn at a later point in their development that they themselves are included within a particular group about which they have already acquired some knowledge and to which they are already ascribing certain traits.

Evidence that this may sometimes occur in young children is reported by Piaget and Weil (1951). As we saw in Chapter 2, they report that the Swiss Genevan children who they interviewed first began to show evidence of knowing the name of the country in which they lived, and the name of their own nationality, from the age of about 5 years. However, between 5 and 10–11 years of age, these children had problems in understanding that they themselves were simultaneously both Genevese and Swiss, exhibiting confusion in their understanding of the fact that they had these multiple group memberships, and sometimes denying that they were Swiss when they had previously affirmed that they were Genevese. Hence, these children's grasp of their own state group membership appeared, at best, to be somewhat fragile up to 10–11 years of age.

However, Jahoda (1963a) investigated this issue more systematically with his sample of 6- to 11-year-old Scottish children. He first asked the children (before either Scotland or Britain had been explicitly mentioned by the interviewer) the open-ended question "What are you?". Ninety per cent of the children responded with their gender, and only 3% described themselves as Scottish in response to this question. He then followed this up with a second open-ended question "What is your country?". Here, 46% of the 6- to 7-year-olds, 69% of the 8- to 9-year-olds, and 85% of the 10- to 11-year-olds responded with either Scotland or Britain. He then asked them the forced-choice *yes–no* questions "Are you Scottish?" and "Are you British?". Sixty-nine per cent of the 6- to 7-year-olds, 81% of the 8- to 9-year-olds, and 100% of the 10- to 11-year-olds responded in the affirmative to at least one of these two questions. So, this study suggests that by 6–7 years of age, the majority of children do categorize themselves as a member of either a national or a state group. Furthermore, 31% of the 6- to 7-year-olds, 56% of the 8- to 9-year-olds, and 90% of the 10- to 11-year-olds responded affirmatively to *both* of these two final questions, indicating that a significant proportion of children younger than 10–11 years also understand the notion of multiple group memberships (contrary to the claims of Piaget and Weil).

In their much larger study conducted in 11 different parts of the world, Lambert and Klineberg (1967) also asked the 6-, 10- and 14-year-old children who they interviewed the question "What are you?" followed by "What else are you?" at the very start of their interviews, to see how the children described themselves, and to ascertain whether they would spontaneously produce the name of their national or state group in response to these questions. Given the diversity of ages and cultures in this study, the children actually produced a surprisingly small number of different self-descriptive themes in their answers. In order of frequency of mention, these were: their gender; the fact that they were persons or human beings, students, or children; and their state, national, regional, religious, or racial backgrounds. State, national, regional, religious and racial backgrounds were not particularly frequent self-descriptors for most of the children, although there was some cross-national variability here. Japanese children used their national and regional background to describe themselves with a relatively high frequency even at 6 years of age; South African Bantu children were the only children who referred to race with any frequency; and Lebanese and Turkish children used religion as a relatively frequent self-descriptor.

Although the children's national and state group memberships were, as a general rule, only infrequently mentioned in response to these open-ended questions, Lambert and Klineberg nevertheless found that all of the children, including the 6-year-olds, held definite views about their own national or state group when they were asked direct questions about it. As we saw in Chapter 5, the children used three kinds of statements to describe their group: factual descriptive statements, evaluative statements, and similarity statements. Lambert and Klineberg comment that the production of the latter kind of statement (i.e., similarity statements such as *they are like us, they dress as we do*, etc.) implies that these particular children are failing to categorize themselves as full members of their own national or state group. Similarity statements were mainly produced by some of the 6-year-olds in some (but not all) countries. In addition, there were two countries (Lebanon and South Africa) where such statements were produced by some of the 10- and 14-year-olds as well; Lambert and Klineberg suggest that this was probably due to the salience of the ethnic, religious and linguistic group differences within the populations of these two countries.

Notice that these early studies tended to rely on open-ended questioning in order to examine children's self-categorizations. However, as we have noted in previous chapters of this book, open-ended questions can underestimate children's knowledge and beliefs. A further limitation of these early studies is that none of them attempted to assess the strength of the children's subjective identifications with their own national and/or state groups. Understanding and acknowledging the objective fact that one is a member of a particular group is a quite different phenomenon from having a strong subjective identification with that group. Thus, it is entirely possible for, say, an American person to acknowledge that they are American, but at the same time to feel that being American is not very important to them and that they are not particularly proud of being American. In other words, having a strong sense of identification with a particular group is a distinct phenomenon from merely knowing that you are, de facto, a member of that group. This is an important point because social-psychological research with adults has repeatedly revealed that the strength of subjective identification with a social group is an important factor that can impact on how individuals think, feel and behave in relationship to the in-group and in relationship to salient comparison out-groups, with there being systematic differences between high and low identifiers (see, for example, Branscombe & Wann, 1994; Grant, 1993; Hinkle & Brown, 1990; Jetten, Spears, & Manstead, 2001; Mummendey, Klink, & Brown, 2001; Perreault & Bourhis, 1998; Schmitt & Branscombe, 2001).

However, the studies by Piaget and Weil (1951), Jahoda (1963a) and Lambert and Klineberg (1967) did not examine the strength of children's subjective identifications with their own national and state groups; instead, they merely examined children's factual knowledge of their membership of these groups. Similarly, and perhaps rather more surprisingly, none of the early studies carried out by Tajfel and his colleagues in the 1960s and early 1970s (Jaspers et al., 1972; Johnson, 1966, 1973; Johnson et al., 1970; Middleton et al., 1970; Tajfel, 1966; Tajfel & Jahoda, 1966; Tajfel et al., 1970, 1972) examined children's strength of identification with their national or state groups either. Indeed, it was not until the CHOONGE and NERID projects were conducted in the 1990s that attempts were made to measure the strength of national and state identification in children.

THE FINDINGS FROM THE *CHOONGE* AND *NERID* PROJECTS

Recall that in the CHOONGE and NERID projects, data were collected from 4211 children aged 6, 9, 12 and 15 years, living in a number of different Western and Eastern European countries (see Table 5.2; see also Chapter 5 for the criteria used to select the children for participation in these two projects, and for a broad description of the methods used in the projects). One of the core aims of these projects was to identify the cross-national constancies and differences that can occur in the development of children's national and state identifications. All of these children were interviewed individually, and the initial section of the interview was devoted to the assessment of their various identifications. At the very start of the interview, and before the children had been asked anything about countries or about national and state groups (i.e., without the children having been cued that the interview was going to be focused specifically on these issues), a task was administered in two parts. The first part of the task was designed to assess the children's own self-categorizations (in order to ascertain whether or not they spontaneously categorized themselves as members of a particular national or state group), while the second part of the task was designed to measure the relative strength of the children's subjective identification with each of the chosen self-categorizations.

The children's self-categorizations

The first part of the task took the following form. The interviewer presented the child with a large set of cards. The following descriptive terms were written (in the local language) on these cards: *6 years old, 9 years old, 12 years old, 15 years old, girl, boy*, the names for inhabitants of the child's city (e.g., *Gironean, Roman*, etc.), a set of national and state identity terms, including all of the terms that might potentially apply to the child (e.g., *English, Scottish* and *British* in the case of the British children, and both *Catalan* and *Spanish* in the case of the Catalan children) as well as a number of distracter terms, and the supranational term *European*. The Western European children received a set of 15 cards in total. In the case of the NIS children, the following terms were additionally included in the set of cards: *Asian, Slav, Caucasian, Christian, Orthodox, Muslim, Believer, Non-believer, citizen of Russia, citizen of Ukraine, citizen of Georgia, citizen of Azerbaijan,* and *resident of NIS*.[17] The NIS children received a set of 29 cards in total. The interviewer spread all of these cards out randomly on the table and said to the child: "Look at these cards. All these words can be used to describe people. Which ones do you think could be used to describe you? You can choose as many as you like". For the younger children, this was followed by: "Shall I help you to read them?" The child was allowed to select as many or as few of the cards as they liked, and if there was any doubt at all about the child's reading ability, the

---

[17] The *citizen of X* descriptors were included because, within the NIS, an explicit distinction is commonly drawn between a person's ethnonational group membership (i.e., *Russian, Ukrainian, Georgian, Azeri*, etc.) and their state citizenship identity (which reflects the country of which the person is a citizen). This is because it is a common occurrence in the NIS for individuals to belong to one ethnonational group but to be a citizen of another country. In most western European countries, a person's state citizenship is normally not marked in everyday language in such an explicit manner.

cards were read out to the child, and the child's choices were subsequently double-checked by the interviewer reading out the chosen cards after the child had made his or her selection. Notice that this method does not require the child to recall his or her own self-categorizations; instead, all the child needs to do is recognize them. Hence, the demands of the task on the child are minimized.

The findings relating to the children's selections of the national and state category terms are shown in Table 6.1. This table shows the percentages of children at each age in each location who chose at least one of the terms that denoted a national or state category in order to describe themselves. Notice that, at 6 years of age, three-quarters or more of the children in 14 of the 16 locations chose at least one of the national or state terms to describe

Table 6.1
The percentages of children in the CHOONGE and NERID projects who spontaneously chose at least one national or state category term as a self-descriptor, broken down by location and age

Location of children	6-year-olds	9-year-olds	12-year-olds	15-year-olds
England (London)	74.6	90.0	93.5	98.3
Scotland (Dundee)	40.8	96.1	90.0	96.7
Catalonia (Girona)	92.2	94.5	98.5	97.5
Basque Country (San Sebastian and Pamplona)	74.6	88.9	93.5	89.7
Southern Spain (Malaga)	88.3	95.0	93.9	98.3
Italy (Vicenza)	98.3	100	96.7	98.3
Italy (Rome)	85.0	84.7	90.0	86.7
Russia (Smolensk)	61.7	93.3	96.7	95.1
Russia (Moscow)	85.0	91.9	93.3	95.0
Ukraine (Ukrainian language schools, Kharkov)	95.0	93.3	95.0	96.7
Ukraine (Russian language schools, Kharkov)	81.7	93.3	91.7	93.3
Georgia (Georgian language schools, Tbilisi)	97.0	100	100	91.7
Georgia (Georgians in Russian language schools, Tbilisi)	96.6	100	100	100
Georgia (Armenians in Russian language schools, Tbilisi)	100	100	100	100
Azerbaijan (Azeri language schools, Baku)	91.7	100	97.3	95.9
Azerbaijan (Russian language schools, Baku)	90.0	93.3	98.4	93.3

themselves, with the children living in Scotland and in Smolensk in Russia forming the two exceptions. Indeed, in 8 of the 16 locations, 90% or more of the 6-year-olds chose a national or state term. And at 9, 12 and 15 years of age, the overwhelming majority of the children in *every* location, including both Scotland and Smolensk, chose at least one of the national or state category terms as a self-descriptor. The precise reason why only a minority of the 6-year-old Scottish children picked either British or Scottish to describe themselves is unclear (and the figure of 40.8% is lower than the figure of 69% that Jahoda obtained with Scottish children of an equivalent age, although Jahoda did use a forced-choice *yes–no* measure that would have yielded a figure of 50% if the children had simply guessed at random). But the important point to emerge from Table 6.1 is that, at the age of 6, the majority of children do usually acknowledge their own membership of one or more national or state groups.

The relative strength of identification with the different self-descriptors

The second part of this task was designed to measure the children's relative strength of identification with each of their chosen self-descriptors. This was done in the following way. After the child had made his or her selection of self-descriptors, the interviewer put away the rejected cards and spread out the cards that had been selected by the child on the table in a random order. The child was then asked: "So all these cards describe you. But if you had to choose only one of these cards because it was the most important for you, which one would you choose?" The chosen card was removed from the set. The child was then asked to choose the next most important card out of those remaining, with the question: "And which one is the next most important to you?" This process was repeated until a rank order of importance had been determined for all of the selected cards. The first-ranked card was assigned a score of 1, the second-ranked card a score of 2, and so on. In the case of those identities that had not been spontaneously selected in the first part of the task, these were assigned the default of the lowest possible rank, which was 7 in the case of the Western European children, and 11 in the case of the NIS children. Thus, a low score represents high relative importance of an identity to a child, while a high score indicates that the identity was less important to (or not chosen by) the child.

The mean scores representing the relative importance the children ascribed to their state, national, gender, age and city identities are shown in Tables 6.2 and 6.3. Table 6.2 also includes the European identity for the Western European children, and Table 6.3 includes the citizenship identities for the NIS children. Notice that, because a larger set of cards was administered to the NIS children than to the Western European children, the scores in

Table 6.2
The mean relative importance of state, national, gender, age, city and European identities to the children in the Western European samples, broken down by age (NB: age identities were not administered in Southern Spain)

Location of children	Identity	6-year-olds	9-year-olds	12-year-olds	15-year-olds	
England (London)	British	6.51^a	5.38^b	4.52^b	4.32^b	*
	English	3.42	3.35	3.34	3.37	
	Gender	2.81^a	1.85^b	2.16^{ab}	2.46^{ab}	*
	Age	2.37^a	2.92^{ab}	3.48^b	3.31^b	*
	City	6.34^a	5.73^{ab}	5.00^{bc}	4.22^c	*
	European	6.83^a	6.72^{ab}	6.24^b	6.36^b	*
Scotland (Dundee)	British	6.53^a	5.63^b	5.37^b	5.48^b	*
	Scottish	5.67^a	3.00^{bc}	3.43^b	2.40^c	*
	Gender	2.37^a	2.22^{ab}	1.72^b	2.20^a	*
	Age	2.00^a	3.12^b	3.10^b	3.43^b	*
	City	3.08	3.20	3.63	3.63	
	European	6.84^a	6.57^{ab}	6.45^b	6.20^b	*
Catalonia (Girona)	Spanish	5.79^a	5.30^{ab}	4.73^b	5.19^{ab}	*
	Catalan	3.17	3.23	2.84	2.73	(*)
	Gender	2.74^a	2.19^b	2.94^a	3.24^a	*
	Age	2.18^a	3.05^b	3.41^b	3.33^b	*
	City	4.14	3.98	3.46	3.40	
	European	6.79^a	5.98^b	5.15^c	5.02^c	*
Basque Country (San Sebastian and Pamplona)	Spanish	6.38^a	5.48^b	5.98^{ab}	5.83^{ab}	*
	Basque	3.44	3.78	2.90	2.69	
	Gender	2.21	2.29	2.42	3.22	(*)
	Age	3.16^a	4.13^b	3.71^{ab}	3.53^{ab}	*
	City	5.87^a	3.89^b	3.76^b	3.79^b	*
	European	6.90^a	6.11^b	5.65^b	6.09^b	*
Southern Spain (Malaga)	Spanish	3.22	2.92	3.00	3.02	
	Gender	2.23^a	3.27^b	2.61^{ab}	2.37^a	*
	City	3.90^a	2.67^b	2.85^{ab}	3.37^{ab}	*
	European	6.12^a	5.35^b	4.21^c	4.43^c	*
Italy (Vicenza)	Italian	2.77	2.60	2.93	2.90	
	Gender	2.33	1.88	2.12	2.17	
	Age	1.97^a	3.23^b	2.88^b	3.05^b	*
	City	4.43^a	3.42^b	3.62^{ab}	4.22^a	*
	European	6.65^a	5.35^b	4.92^{bc}	4.28^c	*

Table 6.2   Continued

Location of children	Identity	6-year-olds	9-year-olds	12-year-olds	15-year-olds	
Italy (Rome)	Italian	3.72	3.12	3.53	3.27	
	Gender	2.38	2.76	2.32	2.78	
	Age	2.25[a]	3.00[b]	3.13[b]	3.10[b]	*
	City	4.50	4.66	3.95	3.58	(*)
	European	6.40[a]	6.14[ab]	5.58[bc]	5.38[c]	*

Notes

Low scores represent high relative importance, and high scores represent low relative importance. Where there is a statistically significant effect of age on the relative importance of a particular identity to a particular subgroup of children, an asterisk appears in the final column, and the specific location of the significant differences within the row of four figures is shown using superscript letters, with mean scores that do not differ significantly from one another sharing the same superscript letters (where an asterisk appears in parentheses, the age effect could not be located by the post hoc tests).

Data analysed using Kruskal–Wallis tests and Bonferroni-corrected post hoc Mann–Whitney tests.

Table 6.3 are higher overall than, and therefore not directly comparable to, those in Table 6.2.

These two tables show that different groups of children exhibited different developmental patterns. One of the patterns displayed involved relatively high importance being attributed to a national or state identity already at the age of 6, with either no changes or only minimal changes in the relative importance of that identity occurring as a function of age. For example, among the western European children, this pattern was displayed by the children living in England in relationship to English identity, Catalonia in relationship to Catalan identity, the Basque Country in relationship to Basque identity, southern Spain in relationship to Spanish identity, and Italy (both groups) in relationship to Italian identity (see Table 6.2). Among the NIS children, this pattern was displayed by the children living in Russia (Moscow) in relationship to Russian identity, Georgia (all three groups) in relationship to Georgian or Armenian identity (as appropriate), and Azerbaijan (Azeri language schools) in relationship to Azeri identity (see Table 6.3). In all of these groups of children, the initial relatively high level of importance attributed to the national or state identity was maintained at all subsequent ages.

A different pattern was exhibited by some of the other groups of children. Here, although a national or state identity category was commonly chosen as a self-descriptor at the age of 6, this identity was not ranked as being especially important at this early age. However, in nearly all of these groups of children, the relative importance attributed to that identity exhibited significant increases with age. Among the western European children, this second developmental pattern was displayed by the children living in England in relationship to British identity, and in Scotland in relationship to both British and Scottish identity (see Table 6.2). Among the NIS children, this

Table 6.3
The mean relative importance of national, citizenship, gender, age and city identities to the children in the NIS samples, broken down by age (see Table 6.2 for an explanation of the use of asterisks and superscripts)

Location of children	Identity	6-year-olds	9-year-olds	12-year-olds	15-year-olds	
Russia (Smolensk)	Russian	6.30[a]	4.58[ab]	4.63[ab]	3.82[b]	*
	Citizen of Russia	9.35[a]	6.82[b]	6.13[b]	4.70[c]	*
	Gender	2.48	2.38	3.02	2.97	
	Age	4.52[ab]	3.97[a]	4.40[ab]	5.08[b]	*
	City	8.10[a]	4.58[b]	4.50[b]	5.46[b]	*
Russia (Moscow)	Russian	4.63	3.48	3.88	3.87	(*)
	Citizen of Russia	9.25[a]	7.56[b]	6.73[bc]	5.20[c]	*
	Gender	3.13	2.87	3.18	3.33	
	Age	3.85[a]	3.53[a]	5.03[b]	5.58[b]	*
	City	4.58	3.97	5.03	4.80	
Ukraine (Ukrainian language schools, Kharkov)	Ukrainian	6.52[a]	3.92[b]	5.18[ab]	5.27[ab]	*
	Citizen of Ukraine	7.90[a]	7.02[ab]	5.38[b]	5.92[b]	*
	Gender	3.57	3.87	2.82	2.92	
	Age	4.35	3.72	3.88	4.27	
	City	5.70	4.98	5.17	5.12	
Ukraine (Russian language schools, Kharkov)	Ukrainian	6.80	6.55	6.77	7.03	
	Citizen of Ukraine	10.58[a]	7.05[b]	5.93[b]	5.77[b]	*
	Gender	2.12	3.08	2.68	2.63	
	Age	4.23	4.65	4.70	5.17	(*)
	City	5.70	4.30	4.13	4.25	
Georgia (Georgian language schools, Tbilisi)	Georgian	3.72	3.44	3.73	3.78	
	Citizen of Georgia	9.64[a]	6.92[b]	5.41[bc]	5.07[c]	*
	Gender	4.49[a]	5.26[ab]	5.86[b]	5.78[b]	*
	Age	4.39[a]	6.31[b]	7.16[c]	7.40[c]	*
	City	4.10[a]	4.67[ab]	5.40[b]	5.44[b]	*
Georgia (Russian language schools, Tbilisi)	Georgian	4.15	3.97	4.72	4.77	
	Citizen of Georgia	8.95[a]	5.98[b]	5.41[b]	5.71[b]	*
	Gender	3.93	4.30	4.74	5.33	
	Age	4.07[a]	5.73[b]	6.50[bc]	7.06[c]	*
	City	3.85[a]	4.09[ab]	5.14[c]	4.97[bc]	*

Table 6.3 Continued

Location of children	Identity	6-year-olds	9-year-olds	12-year-olds	15-year-olds	
Georgia (Armenians in Russian language schools, Tbilisi)	Georgian	9.95	10.60	10.72	10.82	(*)
	Armenian	4.07	3.46	4.06	4.45	
	Citizen of Georgia	9.12^a	6.70^b	5.63^b	5.00^b	*
	Gender	3.78^a	4.57^{ab}	4.91^b	4.24^{ab}	*
	Age	4.22^a	5.81^b	6.59^c	6.21^{bc}	*
	City	4.37	4.11	4.25	4.36	
Azerbaijan (Azeri language schools, Baku)	Azeri	4.72	3.63	4.60	4.45	
	Citizen of Azerbaijan	6.35^a	4.77^{ab}	4.88^{ab}	4.62^b	*
	Gender	4.58	5.06	4.62	4.62	
	Age	5.15	6.26	4.88	5.64	(*)
	City	5.77^{ab}	5.11^a	7.32^b	7.09^b	*
Azerbaijan (Russian language schools, Baku)	Azeri	5.35^a	3.75^b	4.51^{ab}	4.60^{ab}	*
	Citizen of Azerbaijan	7.37^a	7.47^a	6.08^{ab}	5.32^b	*
	Gender	3.87	5.15	3.90	4.37	(*)
	Age	3.72^a	5.23^b	5.74^b	6.08^b	*
	City	6.45	5.67	5.97	6.28	

Notes

Low scores represent high relative importance, and high scores represent low relative importance.

Data analysed using Kruskal-Wallis tests and Bonferroni-corrected post hoc Mann-Whitney tests.

pattern was displayed by the children living in Russia (Smolensk) in relationship to Russian identity, and, to a less marked extent, by the children living in Ukraine (Ukrainian language schools) in relationship to Ukrainian identity, and in Azerbaijan (Russian language schools) in relationship to Azeri identity (see Table 6.3). Notice that all seven groups of western European children exhibited significant increases with age in the relative importance of their European identity (although even at 15 years of age, this identity still remained relatively unimportant to the children living in England, Scotland and the Basque Country). In addition, all nine groups of NIS children exhibited significant increases with age in the relative importance of their citizenship identity. However, the precise ages at which these age-related increases in the relative importance of these various identities took place varied across the different groups of children.

The ages at which these increases occurred also varied depending on the particular identity category involved. For example, the children living in England and in Scotland both exhibited significant increases in the importance of their British identity between 6 and 9 years of age. However, the children living in England did not show any age-related changes in the importance that they attributed to their English identity, while the children living in Scotland exhibited *two* significant increases in the importance of their Scottish identity, the first between 6 and 9 years of age, and the second between 12 and 15 years of age. Thus, in the same group of children, different developmental patterns were exhibited depending on the specific identity that was involved.

Finally, a third distinctive pattern was shown by the children living in Ukraine who attended Russian language schools, in relationship to their Ukrainian identity. These children attributed a relatively low level of importance to their Ukrainian identity at the age of 6, and this relatively low level of importance did not show any subsequent changes with age (see Table 6.3).

The principal conclusion to emerge from Tables 6.2 and 6.3 is that the relative importance attributed to national and state identity exhibits different developmental patterns depending on the specific national and state context within which children live, and depending on the specific identity category involved. The relative importance task is thus very useful for delineating some of the different developmental patterns that can be exhibited by children living in different contexts. However, this task does have certain limitations. These limitations stem primarily from the fact that the task only measures each child's rank ordering of different identities (such as age, gender, city, national and state identities) in terms of their *relative* importance to each other. The task does not measure the *absolute* importance of each individual identity to the child. For this reason, both the CHOONGE and the NERID projects also employed another measure to assess children's strength of national and state identification.

The degree of identification with national and state categories

This second measure assessed the children's degree of national and state identification, and it was administered immediately after the relative importance task. It involved three cards being spread out from left to right on the table in front of the child. These cards had the following words printed on them: *very X, little bit X* and *not at all X* (where *X* was the name of the child's national or state group membership, e.g., *Italian, Russian*, etc.). The child was then asked the question "Which one of these do you think best describes you?". In the case of the children who potentially had multiple group memberships (e.g., Catalan and Spanish in the case of children living in Catalonia), the question was asked separately in relationship to each of these potential group memberships. The children's responses were scored as follows: *very* = 3, *little bit* = 2, *not at all* = 1. The mean scores obtained using this measure are shown in Table 6.4.

Table 6.4
The mean degree of national and state identification, broken down by age

Location of children	Identity	6-year-olds	9-year-olds	12-year-olds	15-year-olds	
England (London)	British	2.00[a]	2.53[b]	2.60[b]	2.55[b]	*
	English	2.70	2.76	2.56	2.53	
Scotland (Dundee)	British	1.46[a]	2.37[b]	2.44[b]	2.14[b]	*
	Scottish	1.71[a]	2.52[b]	2.60[b]	2.69[b]	*
Catalonia (Girona)	Spanish	2.04[ab]	2.28[a]	2.11[a]	1.83[b]	*
	Catalan	2.74	2.67	2.58	2.71	
Basque Country (San Sebastian and Pamplona)	Spanish	2.25[a]	2.21[ab]	1.86[bc]	1.75[c]	*
	Basque	2.74[ab]	2.57[ab]	2.43[a]	2.77[b]	*
Southern Spain (Malaga)	Spanish	2.48[a]	2.57[ab]	2.81[b]	2.73[ab]	*
Italy (Vicenza)	Italian	2.87[a]	2.89[a]	2.67[a]	2.41[b]	*
Italy (Rome)	Italian	2.80	2.71	2.65	2.67	
Russia (Smolensk)	Russian	2.79	2.81	2.76	2.81	
Russia (Moscow)	Russian	2.90	2.87	2.82	2.93	
Ukraine (Ukrainian language schools, Kharkov)	Ukrainian	2.48	2.49	2.43	2.43	
Ukraine (Russian language schools, Kharkov)	Ukrainian	2.50	2.50	2.38	2.32	
Georgia (Georgian language schools, Tbilisi)	Georgian	2.89	2.92	2.96	2.89	
Georgia (Russian language schools, Tbilisi)	Georgian	2.57[a]	2.65[a]	2.45[ab]	2.27[b]	*
Georgia (Armenians in Russian language schools, Tbilisi)	Georgian	1.76[a]	1.56[ab]	1.42[b]	1.52[ab]	*
	Armenian	2.61	2.63	2.49	2.52	
Azerbaijan (Azeri language schools, Baku)	Azeri	2.78	2.93	2.92	2.86	
Azerbaijan (Russian language schools, Baku)	Azeri	2.77[ab]	2.95[a]	2.75[ab]	2.66[b]	*

Notes

Where there is a statistically significant effect of age on the degree of identification in a particular subgroup of children, an asterisk appears in the final column, and the specific location of the significant differences within the row of four figures is shown using superscript letters, with mean scores that do not differ significantly from one another sharing the same superscript letters.

Data analysed using ANOVAs and Tukey's HSD post hoc tests.

This table confirms that many of the groups of children did indeed already identify with their own national or state group to a comparatively high degree (that is, with mean scores higher than 2.50) at the age of 6, and that the degree of identification within these groups did not subsequently change with age. For example, this pattern was exhibited by the children living in England in relationship to English identity, Catalonia in relationship to Catalan identity, Italy (Rome) in relationship to Italian identity, Russia (both groups) in relationship to Russian identity, Georgia (Georgian language schools) in relationship to Georgian identity, Georgia (Armenian children) in relationship to Armenian identity, and Azerbaijan (Azeri language schools) in relationship to Azeri identity. The children living in the Basque Country also identified with being Basque to a high degree at the age of 6, but additionally displayed some fluctuations in their degree of identification with age. In addition, the children living in Ukraine (both groups) identified with the Ukrainian category to a moderate degree at the age of 6, without there being any subsequent age-related changes in their degree of identification.

Other groups of children, however, identified with their national or state group to a lesser degree at the age of 6, and all of these groups displayed age-related changes in their degree of identification. Three of the groups showed increases in identification with age. These were the children living in England in relationship to British identity, Scotland in relationship to both British and Scottish identity, and southern Spain in relationship to Spanish identity. However, six groups of children instead displayed *decreases* in their degree of identification with one of the national or state categories with age. These were the children living in Catalonia and the Basque Country in relationship to the Spanish identity, Italy (Vicenza) in relationship to the Italian identity, Georgia (both Georgian and Armenian children attending Russian language schools) in relationship to the Georgian identity, and Azerbaijan (Russian language schools) in relationship to the Azeri identity.

Notice that, once again, different developmental patterns were sometimes exhibited by the same group of children in relationship to different identities. For example, the children living in England showed a significant increase in their degree of identification with being British between 6 and 9 years of age, but showed no age-related changes in their degree of identification with being English (which was already high at the age of 6).

Thus, this second measure confirms that national and state identification can already be high in some groups of children at the age of 6 (with there being no subsequent changes in the degree of identification as a function of age), but that there are also other groups of children who do exhibit age-related changes in their degree of identification, in some cases increases and in other cases decreases. It also confirms that different developmental patterns may be displayed by the same children in relationship to different identities. The findings from this second measure therefore accord with the principal conclusions derived from the use of the relative importance measure, namely that children can exhibit different developmental patterns in national and state identification depending on the specific national and state context in which they live, and depending on the specific identity involved.

Finally, note that the developmental patterns revealed by the use of this second measure in relationship to any given category do not always coincide with those revealed by the use of the relative importance measure. This is not surprising, given that the relative importance measure yielded information about how important national or state identity is relative to the child's other identities (such as age, city and gender), whereas the degree of identification measure assessed the children's levels of identification on an absolute scale.

The analyses presented so far have shown that the children's national and state identifications can vary depending on their age and the specific national and state context within which they live. However, closer scrutiny of the data from the CHOONGE and NERID projects reveals that there are also variations in children's levels of national and state identification as a function of five further factors: children's geographical location within their country; how the state category is interpreted within children's own local environments; children's ethnicity; children's use of language in the family home; and children's language of schooling. In the following sections, we examine each of these factors in turn.

Differences in children's levels of identification as a function of their geographical location within the country

In two of the countries that participated in the CHOONGE and NERID projects, data were collected from two groups of children who shared the same national identity but who lived in different geographical locations: in Italy, data were collected from children living in Rome and in Vicenza, and in Russia, data were collected from children living in Moscow and in Smolensk. Thus, in these two countries, one of the locations was the capital city, while the other was a provincial city. Consequently, these data allow us to examine whether there are differences in the development of national identification depending on whether the child lives in the capital city or in a provincial city.

To begin with the data collected from the Russian children, analysis of the degree of identification scores revealed that the Moscow children exhibited a significantly higher degree of identification with being Russian than the Smolensk children, at all ages (see Table 6.4). In addition, at 6 and 9 years of age the children living in Moscow attributed greater relative importance to being Russian than the children living in Smolensk; however, at 12 and 15 years of age there were no significant differences between the two groups of children on the relative importance measure (see Table 6.3). Notice that, with increasing age, the children in Smolensk came to attribute greater relative importance to being Russian, whereas there were only marginal changes with age in the relative importance attributed to being Russian by the Moscow children; hence the convergence of the two groups of children by 15 years of age.

It is pertinent to note here that higher levels of both national and state identification among children who live in the capital city have also been found in another, independent study of British children reported by Barrett (2002).[18] The participants in this study were 1208 children aged between 5 and 16 years. These children lived in a number of different locations across Britain, and were of various ethnicities. Locations in which relatively large amounts of data were collected from white English children (i.e., from the ethnic majority group within England) included London, the south-east of England outside London, and the south-west of England. Both relative and absolute measures of British and English identification were used. Analysis of the data from these white English children revealed that the strength of identification among the children who lived in the south-east of England and the children who lived in the south-west of England showed minimal differences: very similar levels of both British and English identification were exhibited by both groups. However, the strength of identification in white English children living within London was found to be significantly higher: both British and English identification were higher among the children who lived in London than among the children who lived outside London.

There are various possible explanations as to why higher levels of national and state identification might be exhibited by children who live in the capital city of a country. First, capital cities tend to have more cosmopolitan and ethnically diverse populations than other locations within the country. Capital cities also tend to be visited by tourists from other countries to a greater extent than other locations. Consequently, children who live in a capital city may encounter members of out-groups more frequently than children who live elsewhere, affording them with a wider range of opportunities for making intergroup comparisons. As a result, national or state identities may be rendered more salient at an earlier age to children who live in a capital city. A second possible explanation is that capital cities are frequently the site of the most important emblems of the state and the nation. Parliament buildings, as well as the official residence of the monarch, president and/or prime minister, are usually situated in the capital city, the most important state ceremonials usually take place within the capital city, and state museums are typically located in the capital city as well. For example, in the case of Britain, the Houses of Parliament, Buckingham Palace and the British Museum are all located in London, and the Changing of the Guards ceremony also takes place

---

[18] The data for this study were collected as part of the British Psychological Society Developmental Section's Centenary Project in 2001.

there. In the case of Russia, both the Kremlin and the Russian Parliament are located in Moscow, as is Red Square, where Russian state ceremonials take place. Hence, a child who lives in the capital city of a country may well have more frequent opportunities to encounter national and state emblems than children who live in other locations within the same country, and these encounters might also serve to enhance the child's sense of national or state identity. Finally, it is also not impossible that when an individual knows that they live in the capital city of a country, this knowledge in itself serves to enhance the sense of either national or state identity in that individual. Hence, there are several possible explanations (which are not mutually exclusive) why children who live in the capital city might exhibit a heightened sense of national and/or state identity.

However, the data that were collected in Italy in the CHOONGE project indicate that the situation is actually more complex than the findings from Russia and Britain imply. Analysis of the Italian data from the relative importance task revealed that the children who lived in Rome consistently ascribed *less* relative importance to being Italian than the children who lived in Vicenza, at all ages (see Table 6.2). This is contrary to the findings obtained in Russia and Britain. And as far as the degree of identification measure is concerned, this instead revealed an interaction between age and location (see Table 6.4). In Vicenza, the degree of identification with being Italian decreased with age, while in Rome the degree of identification did not show any significant changes with age. Thus, while at 6 years of age there was no significant difference between the two groups of Italian children on this second measure, at 15 years of age the children in Vicenza exhibited a significantly lower degree of identification than the children in Rome. Thus, there is a mixed pattern of findings in the case of Italy.

These findings may not be as perplexing as they might at first appear. The city of Vicenza is located in the Italian region of Veneto, not far from Venice. The city of Venice, just like Rome, attracts over 12 million foreign tourists every year. Hence, if opportunities for national intergroup comparisons are an important factor impacting on the salience of children's own national or state identity, living in Vicenza may not differ so much from living in Rome in this respect. A further unusual characteristic of Italy is that emblems of the country are not concentrated in the capital city to the same extent as they often are in other countries. For example, the Tower of Pisa and the Rialto Bridge are located elsewhere (the latter in Venice), and what is arguably the most famous Italian ceremonial event takes place in Siena each year (the Sienese Palio) rather than in Rome. A third factor, which may be just as important as the first two, is that in Vicenza, there is strong local support for the Lega Nord, a separatist political party that declared in 1996 that its aim was the political independence of Northern Italy from the rest of Italy (note that the data for the CHOONGE project were collected in 1995–1996). Thus, it is possible that, in Vicenza, the children's degree of identification with being Italian decreased with age because, by early adolescence, the older children were beginning to appreciate, and perhaps to endorse, the Lega Nord's demands for political separation, with these older children's degree of Italian identification declining as a consequence. Hence, there are a number of possible explanations of the different patterns of identification that were found to occur in the two groups of Italian children compared with the patterns found in the Russian and British children.

Elucidation of these issues clearly requires further research. That said, the evidence that we have already does unambiguously demonstrate that levels of national and state identification in children can vary depending on the child's geographical location within a country. Thus, it is important to be wary about extrapolating from findings obtained from children who live in just one particular location in a country to children who live in other locations within the same country. The evidence indicates that such extrapolations may not be justified.

Differences in children's levels of identification as a function of how the state category is interpreted within their local environments

In the CHOONGE project, data were also collected within both Britain and Spain from different subgroups of children who, de facto, shared the same state category membership (either British or Spanish, respectively) but who differed in terms of how that state category was interpreted within their own local environments. Of course, we need to be extremely careful when making comparisons across these different groups of children within Britain and within Spain, not least because these groups lived in different geographical locations within the two countries. However, the data collected in the CHOONGE project do provide strong prima facie evidence that children's levels of identification with the state category can be affected by the interpretations of that category prevalent in their local environments.

To begin with the case of Britain, data were collected from children living in England and from children living in Scotland. As was noted in Chapter 5, because of the historical dominance of Britain by England both politically and economically, the concept of Britishness has come to acquire strong Anglocentric connotations for many British people. As a result, English adults frequently fail to appreciate the difference between being English and being British and often confuse the two, failing to differentiate between English as a national category and British as a state category (Condor, 1996; Kumar, 2003). By contrast, Scottish adults draw a very clear distinction between being Scottish and being British, commonly viewing Scottish as their national identity and British as their de facto state membership. Scottish people also tend to give higher priority to being Scottish than to being British, and many reject the term "British" as a descriptor for themselves, aspiring to state independence for Scotland instead (McCrone, 2001; Murkens, Jones, & Keating, 2002). Thus, the ways in which the category of "British" is routinely interpreted in Scotland and in England differ, the applicability of this category to people living within Scotland is contested, while ideas of what "the nation" is differ between Scotland and England.

Analysis of the CHOONGE data revealed that, on the degree of identification measure, the children living in England exhibited a significantly higher degree of British identification than the children living in Scotland, at all ages (Table 6.4). And on the relative importance measure, the 12- and 15-year-old children living in England also ascribed significantly higher importance to being British than the 12- and 15-year-old children living in Scotland; however, there were no significant differences between the two groups of children in the relative importance that they ascribed to being British at 6 and 9 years of age (Table 6.2). Thus, the children who lived in England, especially the older children, tended to identify with being British to a greater extent than the children who lived in Scotland. One possible explanation of this finding is, of course, that the children in England lived in London, which is the capital of Britain, whereas the children in Scotland lived in a provincial city instead. However, it seems much more likely that these differential patterns of identification are due to the fact that Britishness itself is interpreted very differently in Scotland and in England.

A parallel situation exists in the case of Spain. Both Catalonia and the Basque Country have distinctive cultural and linguistic heritages, and many adults living in these two regions perceive their own region to be very different from other parts of Spain and are determined to protect their own region against the dominance of Spanish culture and language. Although these two regions are far from homogeneous, many adults living in Catalonia and the Basque Country view Catalan and Basque as their national identities, and Spanish as their de facto state membership; furthermore, many Catalan and Basque people attribute much higher priority to being Catalan and Basque than to being Spanish, and many reject the term "Spanish" as a descriptor for themselves, aspiring to state independence for Catalonia and the Basque Country instead (Balcells, 1995; Guibernau, 2004b; Payne, 1975; Zirakzadeh, 1991). By contrast, in southern Spain, Spanish is an unproblematic category that is routinely viewed as referring to both nation and state, and people living in the south of Spain perceive no incompatibility between being Andalusian (the regional identity) and being Spanish (the national and state identity). In other words, and parallel to the British situation, the ways in which the category of "Spanish" is commonly interpreted within Catalonia and the Basque Country vs. southern Spain differ, the applicability of this category to many of the people who live within Catalonia and the Basque Country is contested, and ideas of what "the nation" is differ between Catalonia and the Basque Country vs. southern Spain.

Analysis of the CHOONGE data revealed that the children in southern Spain ascribed significantly higher relative importance to being Spanish than the children in both the Basque Country and Catalonia at all ages (see Table 6.2). Statistical analysis also revealed that, on the degree of identification measure, the children in southern Spain had a higher degree of identification with being Spanish than the children in both the Basque Country and Catalonia at all ages (see Table 6.4). Thus, identification with Spanishness was consistently lower, on both measures, in the children living in Catalonia and the Basque Country. As in the case of Britain, we need to be cautious here, given the different geographical locations of the three groups of children, and the fact that southern Spain has a high density of foreign tourists, which may enhance local children's sense of their own Spanishness. However, these Spanish findings are consistent with those obtained in Britain in suggesting that levels of state identification in children may well vary depending on how the state category is interpreted within their local environments.

One final feature of the children's development in the Basque Country and Catalonia is worth noting here. On the degree of identification measure (Table 6.4), both groups of children exhibited a significant decline in their levels of identification with Spanishness through the years of early adolescence. From a developmental perspective, this finding is readily interpretable: levels of identification with Spanishness are likely to be increasingly affected by older children's emerging appreciation of the political subordination of their own region to the power of the central Spanish state. In the case of the children living in Scotland, there was a similar but less marked decrease (which was only tendentially significant) in the degree of identification with Britishness during early adolescence.

Hence, while the geographical location explanation of these group differences in the CHOONGE data cannot be entirely ruled out, these patterns are certainly compatible with an alternative explanation, namely that children's levels of identification with their state category are affected by the interpretations of that state category prevalent within their local environments.

Differences in children's levels of identification as a function of their ethnicity

In the NERID project, data were collected not only from majority group children; in Georgia, data were also collected from Armenian ethnic minority children who were living in Tbilisi. Armenians comprise approximately 15% of the population in Tbilisi. The children who were tested in the NERID project all held Georgian citizenship, and attended Russian language schools in Tbilisi. These minority Armenian children could therefore potentially identify with either or both of the Georgian and the Armenian categories, and could potentially adopt either a monocultural, bicultural or hybrid identity. For comparative purposes, the most appropriate group of children with which to compare the Armenian children were the Georgian children who were attending exactly the same Russian language schools (as we shall see later, children's language of education is also related to children's patterns of identification), so this subgroup of Georgian children was used as the comparison group in all of the following analyses.

Analysis of the relative importance ascribed to being Georgian (Table 6.3) revealed an unambiguous picture: while the Georgian children ascribed considerable importance to being Georgian, the Armenian children rejected this category for themselves, frequently not even choosing it in order to describe themselves in the first part of the relative importance task. A similar picture emerged with the degree of identification measure (Table 6.4): at all ages, the Georgian children exhibited a significantly higher degree of identification with the Georgian category than the Armenian children, with large numbers of the Armenian children at all ages selecting the "*not at all Georgian*" option in response to the question that asked them about their degree of identification with the Georgian category (among the Armenian children, 35.0% of the 6-year-olds, 43.1% of the 9-year-olds, 60.3% of the 12-year-olds, and 47.0% of the 15-year-olds chose this response). Thus, there were clear differences in the patterns of identification exhibited by the Armenian children and by the Georgian children who attended the same schools.

However, further analysis revealed that there were also a number of similarities in the identity development of these two groups of children. First, there were no statistically significant differences between the Armenian and Georgian children at any age in the relative importance they ascribed to being a citizen of Georgia, and in both groups of children, the relative importance ascribed to this identity increased significantly between 6 and 9 years of age (see Table 6.3). Second, analysis of the relative importance ascribed to being Armenian by the Armenian children, and the relative importance ascribed to being Georgian by the Georgian children, also revealed that there were no significant differences here between the two groups of children at any age (see Table 6.3). Thus, both groups of children ascribed the same levels of relative importance to their own ethnonational group membership. Finally, the two groups of children did not show any significant differences at 6, 9 and 12 years of age in their degree of identification with their own ethnonational group (see Table 6.4). At 15 years of age, however, the Armenian children did identify to a higher degree with being Armenian than the Georgian children identified with being Georgian. This finding was not unexpected, as it is a common finding in studies with adults that members of minority groups tend to exhibit higher levels of identification with their in-group than members of majority groups (see, for example, Branscombe, Ellemers, Spears, & Doosje, 1999; Ellemers, Doosje, Van Knippenberg, & Wilke, 1992; Ellemers, Kortekaas, & Ouwerkerk, 1999; Simon, Aufderheide, & Kampmeier, 2001). Thus, there were both similarities and differences in the identity development of these two groups of children.

Although no other sets of data were collected from ethnic minority groups within the CHOONGE and NERID projects, data were collected from ethnic minority children in the independent study reported by Barrett (2002). As we have seen already, data were collected in that study from British 5- to 16-year-old children who were living in a variety of different locations across Britain. Within one specific location, namely London, relatively large amounts of data were collected from both ethnic majority and ethnic minority children who were aged between 11 and 16 years old. The ethnic majority children were of white English heritage, while the ethnic minority children were of either African, Indian, Pakistani or Bangladeshi heritage (demographic information collected from these children revealed that they were all either second or third generation). Measures of both British and English identification were taken from all of these children. The data revealed a consistent picture: the white English children ascribed significantly higher importance to being English and to being British, and exhibited a higher degree of identification with both Englishness and Britishness than all four groups of ethnic minority children.

The ethnic minority children's low levels of identification with Englishness are not surprising, and are most likely to be due to the fact that the category of English is frequently regarded by many people within England as an ethnic and/or racial category such that members of visible ethnic minority groups can never be viewed as English, no matter how assimilated they may be in terms of their cultural practices and attitudes (Parekh, 2000; Phoenix, 1995). The low levels of identification with Britishness among the ethnic minority children are much more surprising. This is because the category of British is often held to be the superordinate state category, which de facto includes all ethnic minority individuals who hold British citizenship. However, these ethnic minority children did not identify with being British to the same extent as the white English children. As such, the pattern of identity development that these British minority children displayed was different from that displayed by the ethnic minority Armenian children in Georgia (who did identify with their state citizenship identity to the same extent as the majority group children in Georgia).

The pattern of identification exhibited by the British minority children may be due to several different factors. First, it could be the case that the category of Britishness, because of its historical legacy, still carries colonial and imperial associations. Thus, members of ethnic minority groups may find it difficult to identify with this category because their own groups were precisely those groups that were colonized, subordinated and exploited—and sometimes enslaved and massacred—in the name of the British Empire (Hall, 1999; Kumar, 2003; Parekh, 2000). A second possibility is that, at least for some minority individuals, their religious identity takes priority and precedence over their state or national identity. For example, in the case of individuals who are of Pakistani and Bangladeshi heritage, their sense of belonging to the worldwide Muslim community (the *umma*) may be far more important to them than their membership of a national or a state category. A third possibility is that the category of Britishness, just like the category of Englishness, also carries ethnic and/or racial connotations (Modood et al., 1997; Parekh, 2000; Phoenix, 1995). This might be because the prototypical or stereotypical traits most commonly associated with the category of Britishness are ethnically and/or racially biased, with the consequence that minority individuals feel that they themselves are not so typical of the category as other group members. If people's mental representations of the characteristic features of Britain and Britishness are indeed ethnically and/or racially biased, then this could well be a further reason why members of visible ethnic minority groups find it harder to identify with being British than white English individuals do.

Notice that these various explanations are not mutually exclusive, and it is quite possible that the findings obtained in the British study were a consequence of multiple causal factors. Whatever the reasons for the British findings, however, the findings from both Georgia and Britain are clear and unambiguous: ethnic minority children can exhibit very different patterns of national and state identification from those exhibited by majority group children.

Differences in children's levels of identification as a function of their use of language in the family home

More detailed analysis of the data collected in two of the western European locations in the CHOONGE project, namely Catalonia and the Basque Country, also revealed that children's patterns of identification can be systematically related to the use of language in the family home. In both Catalonia and the Basque Country, in families where parents speak either the Catalan or the Basque language in addition to the Spanish language, those parents often make a conscious decision when their first child is born whether to speak only Catalan or Basque in the family home, only Spanish in the family home, or both languages in the family home. In the CHOONGE project, information was therefore collected about which languages were spoken in the family home in both Catalonia and the Basque Country. The children were then classified according to the linguistic situation that pertained in the

Table 6.5
The mean relative importance (RI) and degree of identification (DI) scores of the
children in Catalonia, broken down by age and by home linguistic situation

Measure	Home linguistic situation	6-year-olds	9-year-olds	12-year-olds	15-year-olds	
RI Spanish	Spanish	4.59[1]	3.93[1]	3.21[1]	2.97[1]	
	Catalan	6.13[a2]	6.13[a2]	5.67[b2]	6.35[a2]	*
	Bilingual	6.00[2]	5.55[2]	5.10[2]	4.87[3]	
		*	*	*	*	
RI Catalan	Spanish	3.59[ab]	4.64[a1]	3.51[b1]	4.47[ab1]	*
	Catalan	3.04[a]	2.56[ab2]	2.22[bc2]	1.85[c2]	*
	Bilingual	3.07	2.45[2]	3.25[1]	2.93[3]	
			*	*	*	
DI Spanish	Spanish	2.44	2.46	2.49[1]	2.38[1]	
	Catalan	1.89[a]	2.12[a]	1.87[a2]	1.54[b2]	*
	Bilingual	2.00	2.37	2.11[2]	2.07[1]	
			(*)	*	*	
DI Catalan	Spanish	2.35[1]	2.20[1]	2.16[1]	2.24[1]	
	Catalan	2.80[2]	2.89[2]	2.91[2]	2.90[2]	
	Bilingual	3.00[a2]	2.95[a2]	2.45[b3]	2.73[ab2]	*
		*	*	*	*	

Notes
Where there is a statistically significant effect of age, an asterisk appears in the final column, and the specific location of the significant differences within the row of four figures is shown using superscript letters. Where there is a statistically significant effect of home linguistic situation, an asterisk appears beneath the column of three figures, with mean scores which do not differ significantly from one another sharing the same superscript numbers. (Where an asterisk appears in parentheses, the significant effect could not be located by the post hoc tests.)
RI data analysed using Kruskal–Wallis tests and Bonferroni-corrected post hoc Mann–Whitney tests, and DI data analysed using ANOVAs and Tukey's HSD post hoc tests.

family home, and the data were examined to ascertain whether children's national and state identifications varied according to their home linguistic situation.

The data from the children who lived in Catalonia are shown in Table 6.5. This table reveals that the children who spoke only the Spanish language in the family home ascribed significantly higher relative importance to the Spanish identity, and exhibited a significantly lower degree of identification with being Catalan, than the other two groups of children at all four ages. And these children who spoke only Spanish in the family home also showed a trend towards ascribing lower relative importance to being Catalan, and a

Table 6.6

The mean relative importance (RI) and degree of identification (DI) scores of the children in the Basque Country, broken down by age and by home linguistic situation (see Table 6.5 for an explanation of the use of asterisks and superscripts)

Measure	Home linguistic situation	6-year-olds	9-year-olds	12-year-olds	15-year-olds	
RI Spanish	Spanish	5.57^1	4.35^1	5.16^1	4.95^1	
	Basque	7.00^2	6.30^2	6.61^2	6.25^2	
	Bilingual	6.31^2	7.00^2	6.47^2	6.33^2	
		*	*	*	*	
RI Basque	Spanish	4.00	5.16^1	3.92^1	3.40^1	
	Basque	3.03^a	2.80^{a2}	2.00^{ab2}	1.75^{b2}	*
	Bilingual	3.46	1.83^2	2.42^2	2.94^1	
			*	*	*	
DI Spanish	Spanish	2.36	2.50	2.36^1	2.17^1	
	Basque	2.00	1.93	1.50^2	1.47^2	
	Bilingual	2.57^a	1.91^{ab}	1.56^{b2}	1.61^{b2}	*
			(*)	*	*	
DI Basque	Spanish	2.53	2.18^1	2.08^1	2.58^1	
	Basque	2.91	2.89^2	2.72^2	2.95^2	
	Bilingual	2.73	3.00^2	2.65^2	2.78^{12}	
			*	*	*	

RI data analysed using Kruskal–Wallis tests and Bonferroni-corrected post hoc Mann–Whitney tests, and DI data analysed using ANOVAs and Tukey's HSD post hoc tests.

trend towards exhibiting a higher degree of identification with being Spanish than the other two groups of children.

The equivalent data from the children who lived in the Basque Country are shown in Table 6.6. These data similarly reveal that the children who spoke only Spanish in the family home ascribed significantly higher relative importance to the Spanish identity than the other two groups of children at all four ages. These children also showed three further trends: towards ascribing lower relative importance to being Basque, towards exhibiting a higher degree of identification with being Spanish, and towards exhibiting a lower degree of identification with being Basque, than the other two groups of children. Thus, the data collected in Catalonia and in the Basque Country are consistent in revealing systematic relationships between language use in the family home and children's patterns of national and state identification.

This variability in children's identifications as a function of their home linguistic situation is almost certainly a consequence of variations in the identifications and practices of the children's parents. It is unlikely that the mere circumstance of speaking a particular language (or pair of languages) at home is itself the causal factor that determines the pattern of national and state identification exhibited by a child. Instead, it is much more likely to be the case that the pattern of language use in the home is determined by the ideological choices and the value systems of the parents in relationship to issues of national and state identity. Sociolinguistic studies have revealed that the use of language by adults in Catalonia and in the Basque Country is related to their national and state identifications: adults who regularly use either Catalan or Basque in their everyday interactions tend to exhibit a strong positive identification with being Catalan or Basque and a weak identification with being Spanish, whereas adults who use the Spanish language instead tend to exhibit a low level of identification with being Catalan or Basque and a strong identification with being Spanish (Azurmendi, Garcia, & Gonzalez, 1998; Elejabarrieta, 1994; Valencia et al. 2003). Such findings are consistent with other studies showing that there is often a close relationship between the use of language and the formation of differentiated identity groups, and that different identity groups often exhibit different linguistic attitudes (Giles, Bourhis, & Taylor, 1977; Sachdev & Bourhis, 1990; Vila, 1996). Within the Catalan and Basque communities, language choice appears to operate as an instrument of intergroup differentiation, with adult speakers using their choice of language as a tactical positioning tool to express their attitudes towards the objective intergroup conflicts (i.e., between Catalans and Spaniards, and between Basques and Spaniards) that exist within the context of the modern Spanish state. Thus, it seems likely that parental national and state identifications, and parental linguistic practices, are the underlying factors that determine both the language(s) spoken by children in the family home and the patterns of national and state identification acquired by those children.

Differences in children's levels of identification as a function of their language of schooling

In addition to these variations in national and state identification as a function of the use of language in the family home, the NERID project revealed that there are also variations in identification as a function of children's language of schooling. In Ukraine, Georgia and Azerbaijan, data were collected not only from children who attended schools that used the Ukrainian, Georgian or Azeri language (respectively) for educational purposes, but also from children who attended schools that used the Russian language for educational purposes. Comparisons of the patterns of identification exhibited by the two groups of children in each of the three countries revealed that, in all three countries, there were variations in the children's identifications as a function of their language of schooling. However, the precise pattern of variation exhibited varied across the three countries.

In Ukraine, the 9-, 12- and 15-year-old children who attended Ukrainian language schools attributed significantly greater relative importance to being Ukrainian than the children who attended Russian language schools (see Table 6.3). At 6 years of age, there was no significant difference between the two groups of children in the importance attributed to the Ukrainian identity, but at this early age, the children who attended Ukrainian language schools did attribute significantly greater relative importance to being a citizen of Ukraine than the children who attended Russian language schools. There were no significant differences in the children's degree of identification with being Ukrainian at any age (Table 6.4).

In Georgia, by contrast, only the 12- and 15-year-old children who attended Georgian language schools attributed significantly greater relative importance to being Georgian than the Georgian children who attended Russian language schools, with there being no significant differences at 6 and 9 years of age (Table 6.3). There were no significant differences in the importance attributed to the citizenship identity by the children who attended the two different kinds of school at any age. However, there were significant differences in the children's degree of identification with being Georgian at all four ages, with the children attending the Georgian language schools consistently exhibiting higher levels of identification on this measure (see Table 6.4).

Finally, in Azerbaijan, there were no significant differences in the relative importance ascribed to being Azeri as a function of the children's language of schooling at any age. However, there were differences in the relative importance ascribed to the citizenship identity at 9, 12 and 15 years of age, with the children attending Azeri language schools ascribing higher importance to this identity than the children attending Russian language schools (see Table 6.3). And on the degree of identification measure, at both 12 and 15 years of age, the children attending Azeri language schools identified with being Azeri to a higher degree than the children attending Russian language schools (Table 6.4).

Although the precise patterns of significant differences therefore varied across the three countries, notice that in every single case where there was a significant difference, this difference was always in the same direction: the children who were receiving their education in the national language exhibited higher levels of national and/or citizenship identification than the children who were receiving their education in the Russian language. There are at least two sources of influences that are likely to be responsible for this pattern.

First, it is likely that this pattern is due, at least in part, to variations in the national identifications and ideologies of the children's parents. In the NIS, parents often choose which type of school their child should attend based on their own ideological values, orientations and aspirations. Because the Russian language is the former imperial language not only in Ukraine, Georgia and Azerbaijan but across the entire NIS, the Russian language operates as an international *lingua franca* across the NIS countries. Thus, one reason why parents often choose a Russian language school for their child is because they wish to prepare their child to operate in this *lingua franca* in his or her future adult life. Another, not unrelated, reason may be because the parents themselves speak Russian as their first-choice language in their everyday lives, either because the parents are culturally russified, or because one of the parents is of Russian descent. Politically, such parents are less likely to support the idea of an independent state outside the Russian Federation, and are more likely to desire closer political and economic relations with Russia in the future. Conversely, the parents of children who attend the national language schools are more likely to support the idea of national and state independence from Russia, and to place far greater value on the distinctive cultural and linguistic heritage of their own nation. Such parents often perceive the past, present and future of their country in a very different way from the more russified parents (and indeed, the political events that took place during the presidential elections in Ukraine in the winter of 2004–5 were a direct reflection of these two very different kinds of aspiration for Ukraine). In other words, children who attend national language vs. Russian language schools typically come from families in which the parents hold very different ideological perspectives. Consequently, these differential parental ideologies may well be the underlying determinant of not only the children's language of schooling but also the children's own differential patterns of national and state identification.

The second set of factors likely to be impacting on the children's identifications are those associated with the school itself. The contents of the school curriculum, as well as the more general ethos of the school, are likely to be critical variables here. As we saw in Chapter 4, the school curriculum, school textbooks and school practices have all been identified as significant influences on the national enculturation of children. There are, of course, significant differences in the language and literature curricula offered by national language vs. Russian language schools. As a consequence, in these two types of schools, children have access to quite different literature-based national narratives for their own personal appropriation and, as a result, the children attending these two different kinds of school may well come to interpret their own national situation very differently (cf. Schiffauer et al., 2004; Tulviste & Wertsch, 1994; Wertsch, 1994, 1998). In addition to these differences in the language and literature curricula, in Georgia, the curriculum in history also differs across the two types of school; furthermore, at the time when the

NERID project was conducted, the Georgian language schools strongly emphasized Georgian history and culture, whereas the Russian language schools still used history textbooks from the Soviet period or textbooks imported from the Russian Federation, which instead emphasized Russian culture and history. However, it is not only the curriculum and textbooks that can vary across the two types of school. School ethos and school practices also vary. Thus, in national language schools, the very fact that the national language is used not only during lessons but also in communications with teachers and in the various social events that take place within the school tends to promote greater respect for the national language, culture and identity. By contrast, within Russian language schools, the national language and culture is far less salient and, indeed, in some of these schools (especially in Georgia), teachers may actively try to avoid all references to ethnonational identities, in order to circumvent the discussion of potentially divisive ethnic issues.

The differences in the patterns of national and state identification found between the children who attended the national language schools and the children who attended the Russian language schools in the NIS were therefore likely to have had multiple causes. Minimally, these causes probably included the differential national ideologies of the children's parents, the differential school curricula and textbooks, and the differential practices of the schools. All of these factors are likely to have been responsible for the differential patterns of identification that were found to occur as a function of the children's language of schooling in the NIS.

The factors related to differences in children's levels of national and state identification: A summary

Thus, the evidence available from the CHOONGE and NERID projects indicates that children's patterns of national and state identification can vary considerably depending on many different factors. There are differences in children's identifications as a function of their age, their country, their geographical location within that country, how the state category is interpreted within their local environments, their ethnicity, their use of language in the family home, and their language of schooling. Notice that the sheer variety of factors related to children's national and state identifications (which is not entirely unexpected) needs to be taken into account by any empirically adequate theoretical framework that is proposed to explain children's development in this domain. In Chapter 7, we will look at the specific type of theory that is needed to explain this range of factors.

Are children's attitudes to different national and state groups related to their strength of national and state identification?

As we have seen in Chapter 5, it is not only children's national and state identifications that can exhibit great variability as a function of the specific context in which they live: children's attitudes towards different national and state groups (both in-groups and out-groups) also show considerable variability according to the specificities of children's context. An interesting issue that therefore arises is whether children's levels of identification are related to their attitudes towards national and state groups. For example, one possibility is that those children who have the strongest identifications are also the children who are the most biased in favour of their own in-groups and who are the most prejudiced against out-groups; by contrast, those children who have much weaker identifications might exhibit far less polarized attitudes towards in-groups and out-groups. The CHOONGE and NERID projects provide a unique opportunity to examine this issue using the data collected from various groups of children living in a number of different national contexts.

As we saw in Chapter 5, the children's attitudes to national and state groups were indexed in the CHOONGE and NERID projects using two measures. One of these was a trait attribution task, which measured the number of positive traits and the number of negative traits that each child ascribed to each of the target groups. By subtracting the number of negative traits from the number of positive traits for each target group, a positivity score for that group can be established. This score represents the child's overall level of positivity towards that particular group. The second measure used in the two projects consisted of a pair of affect questions, "Do you like or dislike X people?" followed by "How much? Do you like/dislike them a lot or a little?". The children's answers to these questions were scored on a 5-point scale, where 1 = *dislike a lot*, 2 = *dislike a little*, 3 = *neither like nor dislike*, 4 = *like a little* and 5 = *like a lot*. Thus, for each of the target groups, there was both an overall trait attribution positivity score and an affect score.

In order to ascertain whether children's attitudes were related to their levels of identification, these two scores were correlated with the relative importance that the children ascribed to their national and/or state identities and with the children's degree of identification with their nation and/or state. The statistically significant correlations found are shown in Tables 6.7 to 6.10. In these tables, the significant correlations are shown for each individual group of children according to their location, broken down by age. In the cases of the children living in England, Scotland, Catalonia and the Basque Country, and in the case of the Armenian children living in Georgia, the correlations were run using both the national and the state identities (i.e., using not only the English, Scottish, Catalan, Basque or Armenian identity, but also the British, Spanish or Georgian identity, as appropriate). In addition, these tables show the significant correlations that emerged when the separate subsamples within each country were collapsed into a single group (i.e., for Britain, Spain, Italy, Russia, Ukraine, Georgia or Azerbaijan as a whole); this has the effect of maximizing the variance within the sample for each individual country (due to the different levels of identification displayed by the different subgroups of children within each country) and of maximizing the size of the sample that is entered into each individual correlation. In these latter correlations, for the children living in Britain, Spain and Georgia, only the British, Spanish or Georgian identity (as appropriate) was entered into the correlations. Finally, it should be noted that, in all four tables, the relative importance (RI) scores were reverse coded prior to running the correlations in order to facilitate interpretation; thus, in these correlations, a high RI score now represents a high (rather than a low) level of identification.

Table 6.7 shows the significant correlations between the trait attribution positivity scores and the various identification scores for the western European samples. In the cases of the children living in England, Scotland, southern Spain and Italy (both locations), only a small handful of significant correlations emerged, around the number that might be expected by chance (or even fewer, in the case of the children living in Italy). However, the children living in Catalonia and in the Basque Country displayed a different pattern. In these two cases, the children's identifications were related to the positivity of their trait attributions to Spanish people and to the positivity of their trait attributions to either Catalan or Basque people (as appropriate). At the age of 6, this relationship was already beginning to emerge in the children's attributions to Catalan/Basque people, and in their attributions to Spanish people in the case of the children living in the Basque Country. At 9 and 12 years of age, a relationship between identification and the positivity of attributions to these two groups was clearly present. At 15 years of age, this relationship was only present in the children's attributions to Spanish people, no longer being present in their attributions to Catalan/Basque people. Notice that, when the data from the children living in all three regions of Spain are analysed together as a whole, there is a strong consistent relationship between the strength of identification with being Spanish and the positivity of trait attributions to Spanish people at all four ages. However, there is no real evidence from Table 6.7 that the Catalan, Basque and southern Spanish children's trait attributions to other out-groups bore any consistent relationship to their levels of identification.

Table 6.8 shows the significant correlations between the western European children's affect scores and the measures of identification. This table shows that, for the children living in Scotland, and for the British children as a

Table 6.7

Correlations between the overall positivity scores of each individual target group and either the relative importance of national or state identity (RI) or the degree of national or state identification (DI), for the Western European samples

Location of children	Age	British people	Spanish people	Italian people	French people	German people	English people	Scottish people	Catalan people	Basque people
England (London)	6	ns	ns	ns	ns	ns	ns	ns		
	9	ns	ns	ns	ns	ns	ns	British RI +		
	12	ns	ns	ns	ns	ns	ns	ns		
	15	English DI +	ns	ns	ns	ns	ns	ns		
Scotland (Dundee)	6	ns	ns	ns	ns	ns	ns	ns		
	9	ns	ns	ns	ns	ns	British DI–	ns		
	12	British DI +	Scottish RI +	ns	ns	ns	Scottish RI–	ns		
	15	ns	ns	ns	ns	ns	ns	ns		
Britain (London and Dundee)	6	British RI + British DI +	ns	ns	ns	British DI–				
	9	ns	ns	ns	ns	ns				
	12	ns	ns	ns	ns	ns				
	15	ns	ns	ns	ns	ns				
Catalonia (Girona)	6	ns	ns	ns	ns	ns			Catalan RI +	
	9	Catalan DI +	Spanish DI +	ns	ns	ns			Catalan RI + Catalan DI +	
	12	Spanish DI–	Spanish RI + Spanish DI + Catalan RI–	Spanish DI– Catalan DI +	ns	Catalan RI + Catalan DI +			Catalan DI +	
	15	ns	Spanish RI + Spanish DI + Catalan RI– Catalan DI–	Catalan DI +	Catalan DI +	ns			ns	

Population	Age						
Basque Country (San Sebastian and Pamplona)	6	ns	Spanish RI+	ns	ns	ns	ns
	9	Spanish DI+	Spanish RI+ Spanish DI+ Basque DI–	Basque RI– Basque DI–	Spanish DI+	Spanish DI+	Basque DI+ Basque RI+ Basque DI+
	12	Spanish DI+	Spanish RI+ Spanish DI+ Basque RI– Basque DI–	ns	ns	Spanish DI+	Spanish DI–
	15	ns	Spanish RI+ Spanish DI+ Basque RI–	ns	ns	ns	ns
Southern Spain (Malaga)	6	ns	Spanish RI+	ns	ns	ns	
	9	ns	ns	ns	Spanish RI+	Spanish RI+	
	12	ns	Spanish DI+	ns	ns	Spanish DI+	
	15	ns	ns	ns	ns	ns	
Spain (Girona, San Sebastian and Malaga)	6	ns	Spanish RI+ Spanish DI+	ns	ns	Spanish RI–	
	9	ns	Spanish RI+ Spanish DI+	ns	Spanish RI+ Spanish DI+	ns	
	12	ns	Spanish RI+ Spanish DI+	ns	ns	ns	
	15	ns	Spanish RI+ Spanish DI+	Spanish RI–	ns	ns	
Italy (Vicenza)	6	ns	ns	ns	ns	ns	
	9	ns	ns	ns	ns	ns	
	12	ns	ns	ns	ns	ns	
	15	ns	ns	ns	ns	ns	

Continued overleaf

Table 6.7 Continued

Location of children	Age	British people	Spanish people	Italian people	French people	German people	English people	Scottish people	Catalan people	Basque people
Italy (Rome)	6	ns	ns	ns	ns	ns				
	9	ns	ns	ns	ns	ns				
	12	ns	ns	ns	ns	ns				
	15	ns	ns	ns	ns	ns				
Italy (Vicenza and Rome)	6	ns	ns	ns	ns	ns				
	9	ns	ns	ns	ns	ns				
	12	ns	ns	ns	ns	ns				
	15	ns	ns	Italian RI +	ns	ns				

Notes

To facilitate interpretation, the relative importance (RI) scores have been reverse coded prior to running the correlations, so that a high RI score in this table represents a high level of national or state identification. ns = no significant correlation. + = positive correlation, − = negative correlation.

Data analysed using Spearman correlation coefficients.

Table 6.8

Correlations between the affect expressed towards each individual target group and either the relative importance of national or state identity (RI) or the degree of national or state identification (DI), for the Western European samples

Location of children	Age	British people	Spanish people	Italian people	French people	German people	English people	Scottish people	Catalan people	Basque people
England (London)	6	British RI +	ns	ns	ns	British RI +	ns	ns		
	9	ns	ns	English RI +	ns	ns	ns	ns		
	12	ns	ns	ns	ns	ns	British DI + English DI +	ns		
	15	ns	ns	ns	ns	ns	ns	ns		
Scotland (Dundee)	6	ns	ns	ns	ns	ns	British DI–	British RI– British DI–		
	9	British RI + British DI +	ns	ns	British DI–	British RI– British DI– Scottish DI–	ns	ns		
	12	Scottish DI +	Scottish DI +	ns	ns	ns	British DI +	ns		
	15	British DI +	ns	British RI +	ns	British RI–	ns	ns		
Britain (London and Dundee)	6	British RI +	ns	ns	ns	British RI +				
	9	British DI +	ns	ns	ns	ns				
	12	ns	ns	ns	ns	ns				
	15	British RI + British DI +	ns	ns	ns	ns				
Catalonia (Girona)	6	Spanish DI +	Spanish RI + Spanish DI +	ns	ns	ns			ns	
	9	Catalan RI +	Spanish RI + Spanish DI +	ns	ns	ns			Spanish DI– Catalan RI + Catalan DI +	

Continued overleaf

Table 6.8 Continued

Location of children	Age	British people	Spanish people	Italian people	French people	German people	English people	Scottish people	Catalan people	Basque people
	12	ns	Spanish RI+ Spanish DI+ Catalan DI−	ns	Catalan RI+	Spanish DI− Catalan DI+			Spanish RI− Catalan RI+ Catalan DI+	
	15	ns	Spanish RI+ Spanish DI+ Catalan RI− Catalan DI−	ns	Catalan DI+	ns			Spanish RI− Spanish DI− Catalan RI+ Catalan DI+	
Basque Country (San Sebastian and Pamplona)	6	ns	Spanish RI+	ns	ns	ns				ns
	9	Spanish DI+ Basque RI− Basque DI−	Spanish RI+ Spanish DI+ Basque RI− Basque DI−	Basque RI− Basque DI−	Spanish DI+	ns				Spanish RI− Spanish DI− Basque RI+ Basque DI+
	12	Spanish DI+ Basque DI−	Spanish RI+ Spanish DI+ Basque RI− Basque DI−	Spanish RI+ Basque RI− Basque DI−	ns	ns				Spanish RI− Spanish DI− Basque RI+ Basque DI+
	15	ns	Spanish RI+ Spanish DI+ Basque RI−	ns	ns	Basque RI−				ns
Southern Spain (Malaga)	6	Spanish RI+	Spanish RI+	ns	ns	ns				
	9	ns	ns	ns	ns	ns				
	12	ns	ns	ns	Spanish DI+	ns				
	15	ns	Spanish DI+	Spanish RI−	ns	ns				
Spain (Girona, San Sebastian and Malaga)	6	ns	Spanish RI+ Spanish DI+	ns	ns	ns				
	9	ns	Spanish RI+ Spanish DI+	ns	Spanish DI+	ns				

	12	ns	ns	Spanish RI + / Spanish DI +	ns	ns	ns
	15	ns	ns	Spanish RI + / Spanish DI +	ns	ns	ns
Italy (Vicenza)	6	ns	ns	ns	Italian DI +	ns	ns
	9	ns	ns	ns	ns	ns	ns
	12	Italian RI−	ns	ns	Italian RI + / Italian DI +	ns	ns
	15	ns	Italian RI−	Italian RI + / Italian DI +	Italian RI + / Italian DI +	ns	ns
Italy (Rome)	6	ns	ns	ns	ns	ns	ns
	9	ns	ns	ns	ns	ns	ns
	12	ns	Italian DI−	ns	ns	Italian DI +	ns
	15	ns	ns	ns	ns	ns	ns
Italy (Vicenza and Rome)	6	ns	ns	ns	Italian DI +	ns	ns
	9	ns	ns	ns	ns	ns	ns
	12	Italian RI−	ns	Italian RI + / Italian DI +	Italian RI + / Italian DI +	ns	ns
	15	ns	ns	ns	Italian DI +	ns	ns

Notes

To facilitate interpretation, the relative importance (RI) scores have been reverse coded prior to running the correlations, so that a high **RI** score in this table represents a high level of national or state identification. ns = no significant correlations. + = positive correlation, − = negative correlation.

Data analysed using Spearman correlation coefficients.

whole, there is some evidence that their liking of British people was related to the strength of their identification with being British. Similarly, for the Italian children living in Vicenza, and for the Italian children as a whole, there is some evidence that their liking of Italian people was related to the strength of their identification with being Italian. However, in both the British and the Italian cases, the evidence is not consistently present at all ages. The evidence is even more patchy for the children living in southern Spain. By contrast, the situation prevailing among the children living in Catalonia and in the Basque Country is very different. In both locations, the children's affect towards Spanish people was consistently linked, at all ages, to their levels of identification with being Spanish, and in the older children to their strength of identification with being Catalan or Basque as well. In addition, the levels of liking of Catalan people among the 9-, 12- and 15-year-olds living in Catalonia were systematically related to the strength of both Spanish and Catalan identification (in the directions which one would anticipate), whilst the levels of liking of Basque people were similarly related to the strength of both Spanish and Basque identification among the 9- and 12-year-old children living in the Basque Country. When the data from the children living in all three regions of Spain were analysed together as a whole, the children's affect towards Spanish people was found to be systematically related to the strength of their Spanish identification at all ages. Once again, notice that affect towards out-groups was not typically related to levels of identification in a systematic way. The only real exception here was the affect towards British and Italian people exhibited by the 9- and 12-year-old children living in the Basque Country.

Before leaving the Western European data, it is worth noting that one possibility why the children living in Catalonia and in the Basque Country displayed these distinctive patterns of correlations might be because there was greater variance within these two samples in their identification scores than there was within the samples living in all the other locations. This possibility was therefore checked. It was found that the variance in the identification scores (on both the relative importance and the degree of identification measures) did *not* differ substantially across the various Western European samples, and in some cases the variance was actually slightly higher elsewhere than in Catalonia and in the Basque Country. Hence, the different patterns of correlations found in Catalonia and in the Basque Country cannot simply be attributed to differences in the amounts of variance that were present in these two subsets of the data.

Moving on to the NIS data, Table 6.9 shows the significant correlations between the trait attribution positivity scores and the identification scores for the NIS children. This table reveals that, in the cases of the children living in Russia and in Ukraine, there were no systematic relationships between the strength of identification and the positivity of the children's trait attribu-

Table 6.9

Correlations between the overall positivity scores of each individual target group and either the relative importance of national identity (RI) or the degree of national identification (DI), for the NIS samples

Location of children	Age	Russian people	Ukrainian people	Georgian people	Azeri people	English people	German people	American people	Armenian people
Russia (Smolensk)	6	Russian RI +	ns	Russian DI–	Russian DI–	ns	Russian DI–	ns	
	9	ns	ns	ns	ns	ns	ns	ns	
	12	ns	ns	ns	ns	ns	ns	ns	
	15	ns	ns	Russian RI +	Russian RI +	Russian RI–	ns	ns	
Russia (Moscow)	6	Russian DI +	Russian DI +	ns	ns	ns	ns	ns	
	9	ns	Russian RI +	ns	ns	ns	Russian DI–	ns	
	12	ns	ns	ns	Russian DI–	ns	ns	ns	
	15	ns	Russian RI +	Russian RI +	Russian RI +	ns	Russian DI +	ns	
Russia (Smolensk and Moscow)	6	Russian RI +	ns	ns	Russian DI–	ns	ns	ns	
	9	ns	Russian RI +	ns	Russian RI +	ns	Russian DI–	ns	
	12	ns	ns	ns	ns	ns	ns	Russian RI +	
	15	ns	ns	Russian RI +	ns	ns	Russian DI +	ns	
Ukraine (Ukrainian language schools, Kharkov)	6	ns	ns	ns	ns	Ukrainian DI +	ns	ns	
	9	ns	ns	ns	ns	ns	ns	ns	
	12	Ukrainian DI–	ns	Ukrainian DI–	ns	ns	Ukrainian DI–	ns	
	15	ns	ns	ns	ns	ns	ns	ns	
Ukraine (Russian language schools, Kharkov)	6	ns	Ukrainian RI +	ns	Ukrainian DI +	ns	ns	ns	
	9	ns	ns	ns	ns	ns	ns	ns	
	12	ns	ns	ns	ns	ns	ns	ns	
	15	ns	ns	ns	ns	ns	ns	ns	

Continued overleaf

Table 6.9 Continued

Location of children	Age	Russian people	Ukrainian people	Georgian people	Azeri people	English people	German people	American people	Armenian people
Ukraine (Ukrainian and Russian language schools, Kharkov)	6	ns	Ukrainian RI +	ns	ns	Ukrainian DI +	ns	ns	ns
	9	Ukrainian RI-	ns	ns	ns	ns	ns	ns	ns
	12	ns	ns	Ukrainian DI-	ns	ns	ns	ns	ns
	15	ns	ns	ns	ns	ns	Ukrainian DI-	ns	ns
Georgia (Georgian language schools, Tbilisi)	6	ns	ns	ns	ns	ns	ns	ns	ns
	9	ns	ns	ns	ns	ns	ns	ns	ns
	12	ns	ns		ns	ns	Georgian RI-	Georgian RI-	ns
	15	ns	ns	ns	ns	ns	ns	ns	ns
Georgia (Russian language schools, Tbilisi)	6	ns	ns	ns	ns	ns	ns	ns	ns
	9	ns	ns	ns	ns	ns	ns	ns	ns
	12	ns	ns	Georgian DI +	ns	ns	ns	ns	ns
	15	Georgian DI +	Georgian DI +	ns	ns	Georgian RI +	ns	ns	ns
Georgia (Armenians in Russian language schools, Tbilisi)	6	ns	Armenian DI-	Armenian DI- / Georgian RI-	ns	ns	Armenian RI +	ns	ns
	9	ns	ns	Georgian RI +	Armenian DI-	ns	ns	Armenian DI-	ns
	12	ns	ns	ns	ns	ns	Armenian DI +	Armenian DI +	Armenian DI +
	15	ns	ns	Georgian DI +	ns	ns	ns	ns	ns
Georgia (all children in Georgian and Russian language schools, Tbilisi)	6	Georgian DI-	ns	Georgian RI + / Georgian DI +	ns	ns	Georgian DI +	Georgian DI +	ns
	9	Georgian RI- / Georgian DI-	ns	Georgian RI +	ns	ns	Georgian RI +	ns	ns
	12	Georgian RI- / Georgian DI-	ns	Georgian RI + / Georgian DI +	ns	ns	ns	ns	ns
	15	ns	ns	ns	ns	ns	ns	ns	ns

	Age							
Azerbaijan (Azeri language schools, Baku)	6	ns	ns	ns	ns	ns	Azeri RI−	ns
	9	ns	ns	ns	ns	ns	ns	ns
	12	Azeri RI−	ns	ns	ns	ns	ns	ns
	15	ns	ns	ns	Azeri DI+	Azeri RI+	Azeri RI+	ns
Azerbaijan (Russian language schools, Baku)	6	ns	ns	ns	Azeri RI+	ns	ns	ns
	9	ns	ns	ns	Azeri RI+	Azeri RI+	ns	Azeri RI+
	12	Azeri RI+	ns	ns	ns	ns	Azeri DI−	ns
	15	Azeri RI+	ns	ns	Azeri DI+	ns	Azeri RI+	ns
Azerbaijan (Azeri and Russian language schools, Baku)	6	Azeri RI−	ns	ns	Azeri RI+	ns	ns	ns
	9	ns	ns	ns	Azeri RI+	Azeri DI−	ns	Azeri RI+
	12	ns	ns	ns	ns	Azeri RI+	ns	ns
	15	Azeri RI+	ns	ns	Azeri DI+	ns	Azeri RI+	ns

Notes

To facilitate interpretation, the relative importance (RI) scores have been been reverse coded prior to running the correlations, so that a high RI score in this table represents a high level of national identification. ns = no significant correlations, + = positive correlation, − = negative correlation.

Data analysed using Spearman correlation coefficients.

Table 6.10

Correlations between the affect expressed towards each individual target group and either the relative importance of national identity (RI) or the degree of national identification (DI), for the NIS samples

Location of children	Age	Russian people	Ukrainian people	Georgian people	Azeri people	English people	German people	American people	Armenian people
Russia (Smolensk)	6	ns	ns	ns	ns	ns	Russian DI–	ns	
	9	ns	ns	ns	ns	ns	ns	ns	
	12	Russian DI +	ns	ns	ns	ns	ns	ns	
	15	ns	ns	ns	ns	ns	ns	ns	
Russia (Moscow)	6	Russian DI +	ns	ns	ns	ns	ns	ns	
	9	ns	Russian DI–	ns	ns	ns	ns	ns	
	12	ns	ns	ns	Russian DI–	ns	ns	Russian RI +	
	15	Russian RI + Russian DI +	ns	ns	ns	Russian RI +	ns	Russian RI +	
Russia (Smolensk and Moscow)	6	Russian RI + Russian DI +	ns	ns	Russian DI–	Russian DI–	ns	ns	
	9	ns	Russian DI–	ns	ns	ns	ns	ns	
	12	ns	ns	ns	Russian DI–	ns	ns	ns	
	15	Russian RI + Russian DI +	Russian RI +	ns	ns	ns	ns	ns	
Ukraine (Ukrainian language schools, Kharkov)	6	ns	ns	ns	ns	ns	ns	ns	
	9	ns	Ukrainian RI +	Ukrainian RI +	Ukrainian RI +	ns	ns	ns	
	12	ns	ns	Ukrainian DI–	Ukrainian DI–	ns	ns	ns	
	15	ns	Ukrainian RI +	ns	ns	ns	ns	ns	

Location	Age								
Ukraine (Russian language schools, Kharkov)	6	ns	Ukrainian RI +	ns	ns	ns	Ukrainian RI +	ns	ns
	9	Ukrainian RI–	ns	Ukrainian RI +	ns	Ukrainian RI +	ns	ns	ns
	12	ns	ns	Ukrainian DI–	ns	Ukrainian DI–	ns	ns	ns
	15	Ukrainian RI–	Ukrainian RI–	Ukrainian RI–	ns	ns	ns	ns	ns
Ukraine (Ukrainian and Russian language schools, Kharkov)	6	ns	Ukrainian RI +	ns	ns	ns	Ukrainian RI +	ns	ns
	9	Ukrainian RI–	Ukrainian RI +	Ukrainian RI +	ns	Ukrainian RI +	ns	ns	ns
	12	ns	Ukrainian RI +	Ukrainian RI–	ns	ns	ns	ns	ns
	15	Ukrainian RI–	Ukrainian RI + / Ukrainian DI +	Ukrainian RI–	ns	ns	ns	ns	ns
Georgia (Georgian language schools, Tbilisi)	6	ns	Georgian DI–	ns	Georgian DI–	ns	ns	Georgian DI–	ns
	9	ns	ns	ns	ns	ns	ns	ns	ns
	12	Georgian RI–	ns	ns	ns	ns	Georgian RI–	ns	Georgian RI–
	15	ns	ns	Georgian RI–	ns	ns	ns	ns	ns
Georgia (Russian language schools, Tbilisi)	6	ns	ns	ns	ns	ns	ns	ns	ns
	9	ns	ns	ns	ns	ns	ns	ns	ns
	12	Georgian DI–	Georgian DI–	Georgian DI +	ns	ns	ns	ns	ns
	15	ns	Georgian DI +	Georgian RI–	Georgian DI +	ns	ns	ns	ns
Georgia (Armenians in Russian language schools, Tbilisi)	6	Georgian RI +	ns	ns	ns	Armenian DI +	ns	ns	Armenian DI–
	9	ns	ns	Armenian RI–	ns	ns	Armenian RI– / Armenian DI– / Georgian RI +	ns	ns
	12	ns	ns	ns	Armenian DI +	ns	ns	ns	Armenian RI +
	15	ns	ns	ns	ns	ns	ns	ns	Armenian RI +

Continued overleaf

Table 6.10 Continued

Location of children	Age	Russian people	Ukrainian people	Georgian people	Azeri people	English people	German people	American people	Armenian people
Georgia (all children in Georgian and Russian language schools, Tbilisi)	6	Georgian DI–	ns	Georgian RI + Georgian DI +	ns	ns	Georgian DI +	ns	
	9	Georgian RI– Georgian DI–		Georgian RI + Georgian DI +	ns	ns	Georgian RI + Georgian DI +	ns	
	12	Georgian RI– Georgian DI–	ns	Georgian RI + Georgian DI +	ns	Georgian DI +	Georgian DI +	ns	
	15	Georgian RI–	Georgian RI + Georgian DI +	Georgian RI + Georgian DI +	ns	ns	ns	Georgian RI + Georgian DI +	
Azerbaijan (Azeri language schools, Baku)	6	ns	ns	ns	ns	ns	ns	ns	
	9	ns	Azeri RI +	ns	ns	ns	ns	ns	
	12	ns	ns	ns	ns	ns	ns	ns	
	15	Azeri DI +	ns	ns	Azeri DI +	ns	ns	ns	
Azerbaijan (Russian language schools, Baku)	6	ns	ns	ns	ns	ns	ns	ns	
	9	ns	ns	ns	Azeri RI +	ns	ns	ns	
	12	ns	ns	Azeri DI–	ns	ns	ns	ns	
	15	ns	ns	ns	ns	ns	ns	ns	
Azerbaijan (Azeri and Russian language schools, Baku)	6	Azeri DI–	ns	ns	Azeri RI +	ns	ns	ns	
	9	ns	ns	ns	Azeri RI +	ns	ns	ns	
	12	ns	ns	Azeri DI–	Azeri DI +	ns	ns	ns	
	15	ns	ns	ns	ns	ns	ns	Azeri RI + Azeri DI–	

Notes

To facilitate interpretation, the relative importance (RI) scores have been reverse coded prior to running the correlations, so that a high RI score in this table represents a high level of national identification. ns = no significant correlations, + = positive correlation, – = negative correlation.

Data analysed using Spearman correlation coefficients.

tions: the few significant correlations that appeared in the analyses of these children's data are only slightly more frequent than one would expect by chance. However, in the case of the Armenian children who lived in Georgia, a greater number of significant correlations did appear, although one of these correlations is actually counter-intuitive (in the 6-year-olds, the positivity of trait attributions to Georgian people was negatively rather than positively correlated with the relative importance of Georgian identification). By contrast, the other two groups of children who lived in Georgia displayed few significant correlations. However, when the three subsets of data collected in Georgia were analysed together, a systematic pattern did appear among the 6-, 9- and 12-year-olds: attributions to Russian people were negatively correlated with the strength of Georgian identification, while attributions to Georgian people were positively correlated with the strength of Georgian identification. In the case of the children who lived in Azerbaijan, those who attended Russian language schools exhibited some evidence at 6, 9 and 15 years of age that the positivity of trait attributions to Azeri people was correlated with the strength of Azeri identification. Although the same relationship was not present in the children who attended Azeri language schools (except at the age of 15), there was evidence of the same relationship when the data from all of the children living in Azerbaijan were analysed together. With the notable exception of the Georgian children's attributions to Russians, there was no other evidence that any of the children's trait attributions to out-groups were systematically related to their strength of identification.

Table 6.10 shows the significant correlations between the NIS children's affect scores and the two measures of identification. Among the children who lived in Russia, there was only partial evidence of a relationship between affect towards Russian people and the strength of Russian identification. The two groups of children living in Ukraine showed even fewer significant correlations between affect towards Ukrainian people and the strength of Ukrainian identification when the data from these two groups were analysed separately. However, when the two subsets of Ukrainian data were analysed together, such a relationship did emerge. When the data from the three groups of children living in Georgia were analysed separately, only the Armenian children showed evidence of a relationship (between the strength of Armenian identification and affect towards Armenian people). However, when the data from all three groups of children living in Georgia were analysed together, some clear relationships did emerge: the strength of Georgian identification was negatively related to affect towards Russian people, and positively related to affect towards Georgian people; and at 6, 9 and 12 years of age, the strength of Georgian identification was also positively related to affect towards German people. Among the children living in Azerbaijan, there were few significant correlations when the data for the two groups were analysed separately. However, when the data from both groups were analysed together, there was evidence that at 6, 9 and 12 years of age, the strength of Azeri identification was positively related to affect towards Azeri people. Notice that, with the exception of the Georgian children's attitudes to Russian and German people, the NIS children's affect towards out-groups was not generally related to their strength of identification.

In summary, there were few relationships between the strength of national or state identification and either trait attributions to, or liking of, national and state out-groups. The main exception to this general finding involved the Georgian children, in particular their attitudes towards Russian people: the stronger their identification with being Georgian, the less positive their trait attributions to Russian people were, and the less they liked Russian people. The younger Georgian children with high levels of Georgian identification also tended to like German people more than children who had weaker levels of identification. These exceptions apart, however, there was very little evidence that the children's identifications were systematically related to their out-group attitudes in either the Western European or the NIS samples.

By contrast, there were many more examples of relationships between the strength of identification and in-group attitudes. The evidence from the children's trait attributions was most clear, and indeed very striking, in the case of the children who lived in Catalonia and in the Basque Country. Additional evidence that the positivity of children's trait attributions to their in-group can sometimes be related to the strength of their identification with that in-group also came from the children who lived in Georgia and in Azerbaijan.

Much more unambiguously, however, the data from the CHOONGE and NERID projects show that children's levels of liking of the people who belong to their own national or state group are often related to their strength of identification with that group. The strongest and most consistent evidence in support of this conclusion came from the children who lived in Spain, Ukraine and Georgia (where, when the data from all subsets of children were examined as a whole, this relationship was present at all four ages); slightly less strong evidence came from the children who lived in Britain, Italy and Azerbaijan (where this relationship was only exhibited at three of the four ages); and the weakest evidence came from the children who lived in Russia (where the same relationship was only shown at two of the four ages).

The perceived status of the national or state group

Because the NERID project was conducted after the CHOONGE project, additional measures not previously used in the CHOONGE project were incorporated into the NERID project. One of these new measures was a set of four items designed to assess the children's perceptions of the status of their own national or state group in the eyes of outsiders; in other words, we tried to assess how the children thought other people, who are not members of their own group, regard that group. This concept is similar to the concept of "public collective self-esteem" (PCSE) developed by Luhtanen and Crocker (1992; Crocker & Luhtanen, 1990), which they define as "one's judgements of how other people evaluate one's social groups" (Luhtanen & Crocker, 1992, p. 305). Luhtanen and Crocker's measure of PCSE consists of four items, which include "In general, others respect the social groups that I am a member of" and "In general, others think that the social groups I am a member of are unworthy". Luhtanen and Crocker's items were judged unsuitable for use with young children, so four alternative items were developed for use in the NERID project. Each of these items involved asking the child to choose one of four response cards using a forced-choice procedure. For example, one of the items consisted of the following set of response cards (where X represents the name of the child's own national group, i.e., Russians, Ukrainians, Georgians, or Azeris, as appropriate):

Most people in the rest of the world think that X are nice people
Some people in the rest of the world think that X are nice people
Only a few people in the rest of the world think that X are nice people
Don't know

These four cards were laid out on the table in front of the child from left to right, and the child was asked: "Here's another set of cards. Let's read these ones together [cards read out to the child]. Which of these cards do you think is right? Would you say that most people in the rest of the world think that X are nice people [pointing to card], or would you say that some people in the rest of the world think that X are nice people [pointing to card], or would you say that only a few people in the rest of the world think that X are nice people [pointing to card]?"

The other three items that were used to measure the perceived status of the in-group were administered using analogous wording, with the following sets of statements forming the four response options:

Only a few people in the rest of the world like X
Some people in the rest of the world like X
Most people in the rest of the world like X
Don't know

Most people in the rest of the world think that X are good at getting things done
Some people in the rest of the world think that X are good at getting things done
Only a few people in the rest of the world think that X are good at getting things done
Don't know

Only a few people in the rest of the world think that X are good people
Some people in the rest of the world think that X are good people
Most people in the rest of the world think that X are good people
Don't know

All four items were coded so that a score of 1 represented a negative image of the child's group, and a score of 3 represented a positive image of that group, with *Don't know* responses being coded as missing values. Separate factor analyses were conducted on the scores that were collected in each of the four countries, and on the scores that were collected from each of the four age groups. These analyses revealed that the four items always loaded onto a single factor in all four countries and at all four ages (eigenvalues ranged from 1.96 to 2.28, the percentage of variance explained ranged from 48.9% to 56.9%, and the item loadings on this single factor ranged from .56 to .78). Reliability analyses further revealed that the four items also scaled reliably in all four countries and at all four ages (Cronbach's alphas ranged from .65 to .75). The scores from the four items were therefore averaged to obtain a mean perceived group status (PGS) score. The mean scores exhibited by each subgroup of children are shown in Table 6.11.

This table shows that, in six out of the nine groups of NIS children, the PGS scores declined with age. In the other three groups, there were no statistically significant changes with age. Precisely why the perceived status of the in-group declined with age in these six groups is unclear. It may be the case that, at a young age, many children, irrespective of the specific country in which they live, have an unrealistically positive image of how they think other people perceive their own group (and the fact that, at the ages of 6 and 9, many of these NIS children did indeed have relatively high scores on this measure would be consistent with this possibility); however, as they enter early adolescence, children may acquire a more realistic understanding of how individuals in other countries view other people's groups. If this is the case, then one might expect this reduction in the perceived status of the in-group during early adolescence to be a general phenomenon that is exhibited by children in many other countries as well. Alternatively, this age-related decline may be a feature that is more specific to children who are growing up within less affluent countries. Further studies are needed to explore these possibilities.

Correlational analyses were carried out to see whether the PGS scores were related to the strength of identification (as assessed using the relative importance measure and the degree of identification measure); that is, whether children who had higher levels of identification with their in-group also had more positive views of how other people regard that group. However, overall, relatively few relationships were found between identification and the PGS scores. Only 8% of the correlations were statistically significant, and these

Table 6.11
The mean perceived group status (PGS) scores of the children in the NIS samples, broken down by age

Location of children	Identity	6-year-olds	9-year-olds	12-year-olds	15-year-olds	
Russia (Smolensk)	Russian	2.23^{ab}	2.36^a	2.28^a	2.01^b	*
Russia (Moscow)	Russian	2.48^a	2.58^a	2.05^b	1.82^b	*
Ukraine (Ukrainian language schools, Kharkov)	Ukrainian	2.35^{ab}	2.42^a	2.40^a	2.18^b	*
Ukraine (Russian language schools, Kharkov)	Ukrainian	2.47	2.49	2.33	2.35	
Georgia (Georgian language schools, Tbilisi)	Georgian	2.54^a	2.55^a	2.53^a	2.26^b	*
Georgia (Russian language schools, Tbilisi)	Georgian	2.17	2.23	2.28	2.08	
Georgia (Armenians in Russian language schools, Tbilisi)	Armenian	2.11	2.09	2.15	2.15	
Azerbaijan (Azeri language schools, Baku)	Azeri	2.41^a	2.43^a	2.28^{ab}	2.16^b	*
Azerbaijan (Russian language schools, Baku)	Azeri	2.55^a	2.42^a	2.32^a	2.07^b	*

Notes

Where there is a statistically significant effect of age on the scores within a particular subgroup of children, an asterisk appears in the final column, and the specific location of the significant differences within the row of four figures is shown using superscript letters, with mean scores which do not differ significantly from one another sharing the same superscript letters.

Data analysed using ANOVAs and Tukey's HSD post hoc tests.

significant correlations were not distributed systematically according to either age or national subgroup.

Correlations were also carried out to examine whether the PGS scores were related to the positivity of the children's trait attributions to the in-group or to the affect the children expressed towards this group. A different picture emerged here. Table 6.12 shows the statistically significant correlations that emerged (age was partialled out from the correlations shown in the table)—83% of the correlations were statistically significant; furthermore, all of these correlations were positive. In other words, with the notable exception of the children living in Georgia who attended Georgian language schools, there was good evidence that those children who held the most positive beliefs about how other people regard their group were also the children who themselves held the most positive attitudes towards that in-group.

Table 6.12

Partial correlations between the perceived status of the national in-group and either the positivity of the children's trait attributions to that in-group or the children's affect towards that in-group (with age partialled out)

Location of children	Target in-group	Positivity of trait attributions to in-group	Affect towards in-group
Russia (Smolensk)	Russian	.24 **	.18 *
Russia (Moscow)	Russian	.23 **	.14 *
Ukraine (Ukrainian language schools, Kharkov)	Ukrainian	.26 **	.23 **
Ukraine (Russian language schools, Kharkov)	Ukrainian	.24 **	.20 *
Georgia (Georgian language schools, Tbilisi)	Georgian	.11 ns	.05 ns
Georgia (Russian language schools, Tbilisi)	Georgian	.40 **	.28 **
Georgia (Armenians in Russian language schools, Tbilisi)	Armenian	.16 *	.09 ns
Azerbaijan (Azeri language schools, Baku)	Azeri	.19 *	.18 *
Azerbaijan (Russian language schools, Baku)	Azeri	.39 **	.28 **

Notes
** = significant at the .001 level, * = significant at the .05 level, ns = not significant.
Data analysed using Pearson partial correlation coefficients.

As with all correlations, the causality underlying this relationship is inherently ambiguous. However, the most straightforward explanation is that children assume that other people view their group in a similar way to themselves. If this is the case, however, it is clear that this is not an invariant characteristic of children's beliefs, as there was one subgroup of NIS children who failed to show this particular relationship (namely the Georgian children who attended the Georgian language schools). Further studies using similar measures on children who are growing up in other state contexts outside the NIS would be useful to establish whether these findings have a more general applicability, or whether they are specific to these particular groups of children and adolescents who grew up in the NIS during the 1990s (i.e., in national and state contexts characterized by considerable social, economic and political change).

THE STRENGTH OF IDENTIFICATION SCALE (SoIS)

As we have seen, in the CHOONGE and NERID projects the strength of national and state identification was assessed using two different measures, the relative importance measure and the degree of identification measure. While these two measures are clearly very useful for differentiating the various patterns of identity development that can occur within different national and state contexts, single item measures can sometimes be psychometrically problematic. For this reason, an initial attempt was also made in the NERID project to develop a new multi-item measure of the strength of national and state identification. Several new items assessing the strength of identification were therefore included in the interview schedule that was administered to the NIS children. The results obtained indicated that either the wordings or the response scales of these items were not optimal, and so after the end of the NERID project further development work took place on the precise wording and response scales of these items.

The Strength of Identification Scale (SoIS) which emerged from this line of work consists of a set of five items. These five items and their response scales are administered either in an interview format with 5- to 11-year-old children (with response options being written on cards and read out to the child), or in a questionnaire format with 11- to 16-year-old children (with rating scales being used instead to capture responses). The five items in the scale are as follows (where X represents the target identity):

1. *Degree of identification*
   Question for 5- to 11-year-olds: "Which one of these do you think best describes you?"
   Response options for 5- to 11-year-olds: *very X, quite X, a little bit X, not at all X*
   Question for 11- to 16-year-olds: "How X do you feel?"
   Response scale for 11- to 16-year-olds: 7-point scale running from *very X* to *not at all X*

2. *Pride*
   Question for all respondents: "How proud are you of being X?"
   Response options for 5- to 11-year-olds: *very proud, quite proud, a little bit proud, not at all proud*
   Response scale for 11- to 16-year-olds: 7-point scale running from *very proud* to *not at all proud*

3. *Importance*
   Question for all respondents: "How important is it to you that you are X?"
   Response options for 5- to 11-year-olds: *very important, quite important, not very important, not important at all*

Response scale for 11- to 16-year-olds: 7-point scale running from *very important* to *very unimportant*, with midpoint labelled *neither important nor unimportant*

4. *Feeling*

Question for all respondents: "How do you feel about being X?"

Response options for 5- to 11-year-olds: *very happy, quite happy, neutral, quite sad, very sad* (administered using a set of five "smiley" faces)

Response scale for 11- to 16-year-olds: 7-point scale running from *very happy* to *very sad*, with midpoint labelled *neither happy nor sad*

5. *Internalization*

Question for all respondents: "How you would feel if someone said something bad about X people?"

Response options for 5- to 11-year-olds: *very happy, quite happy, neutral, quite sad, very sad* (administered using a set of five "smiley" faces)

Response scale for 11- to 16-year-olds: 7-point scale running from *very happy* to *very sad*, with midpoint labelled *neither happy nor sad*.

All five questions are scored with low scores representing a low level of identification, and high scores representing a high level of identification. When 7-point scales are used with 11- to 16-year-olds, the final score is the average score across the five items. When a mixture of 4- and 5-point scales are used with 5- to 11-year-olds, either the item scores are standardized prior to averaging, or the scores on the 4-point scales are rescaled onto a 5-point scale prior to averaging.

The SoIS has now been used in a number of studies with children of different ages and in relationship to a number of different national, state and ethnic identities. These studies are summarized in Table 6.13, which shows that, in all of these studies, the scores produced by the SoIS items always loaded onto a single factor and always scaled reliably. In addition, the test–retest reliability of the SoIS has been assessed in a separate study that took place over an 8-week period of time. A group of 74 English children were used as the participants here. The mean age of these children at the time of first testing was 13.9 years, with their ages ranging from 12.3 to 15.8 years. The questions were asked in relationship to the children's British identity. Cronbach's alpha at the first assessment point was .68, and at the second assessment point it was .74. The correlation between the children's SoIS scores at the two assessment points was .68, indicating acceptable test–retest reliability.

The studies listed in Table 6.13 yielded further evidence concerning the development of national and state identification in children. The study by Penny, Barrett, and Lyons (2001) used the SoIS to measure the strength of English and Scottish identification (as appropriate) in English and Scottish

6- to 12-year-old children. It was found that, before the age of 10, the English children's strength of identification with being English was stronger than the Scottish children's strength of identification with being Scottish; however, at 10–12 years of age, this difference in levels of national identification disappeared. Notice that these findings are consistent with those obtained in the CHOONGE project, where the children living in Scotland also displayed lower levels of national identification than the children living in England at younger ages. In the study by Trimby and Barrett (2005), the SoIS was instead used to measure 6- to 11-year-old Welsh children's strength of identification with being Welsh. Like the Scottish children, these children also exhibited a significant increase in their strength of national identification with age. In addition, the national emblems that the Welsh children associated with Welshness were related to their strength of national identification (see Chapter 4 for details).

Forrest and Barrett (2001) examined a group of 11- to 15-year-old white English children in early adolescence who lived in south-east England (outside London), using the SoIS to measure these children's strength of identification with being English. They found that the children's strength of identification did not vary with age, but that the boys exhibited higher levels of national identification than the girls. This study also revealed that, in contrast to the study by Trimby and Barrett (2005), the historical national emblems that these English children associated with Englishness were *not* related to their strength of national identification (see Chapter 4 for details). Dixon (2002) also used the SoIS with adolescents living in south-east England (again, outside London), but the sample in this study included not only white English children but also ethnic minority children, including white Scottish, white Welsh, white Northern Irish, Caribbean, African, Indian, Bangladeshi and mixed-heritage children. These children's strength of identification with being British was assessed using the SoIS. There were no differences in the children's levels of identification as a function of either age or gender, but the white English, white Scottish, white Welsh and white Northern Irish children displayed significantly higher levels of identification with being British than the visible ethnic minority children. Alexander (2002) also collected data from both ethnic majority and ethnic minority British adolescents; however, the children in this study lived in London. The SoIS was again used to measure the children's strength of identification with being British. It was found that there were no differences in the strength of identification associated with gender, but there was a significant decline in the strength of identification with age. In addition, the majority group individuals had higher levels of identification with being British than the minority group individuals.

Sahlabadi's (2002) study instead focused on Iranian children aged between 11 and 17 years old. Data were collected from Iranian ethnic minority

Table 6.13
Studies conducted using the Strength of Identification Scale (SoIS)

Study	Location of data collection	Children studied	Identity measured	Eigenvalue	Percentage of variance explained	Range of item loadings	Cronbach's alpha
Penny, Barrett, & Lyons (2001)	Oxfordshire, England and Aberdeen, Scotland	75 English and 71 Scottish 6- to 12-year-olds	Either English or Scottish, as appropriate	English: 2.04 Scottish: 2.37	English: 40.8% Scottish: 47.4%	English: .38–.78 Scottish: .41–.78	English: .60 Scottish: .70
Trimby & Barrett (2005)	Cardiff, Wales	109 Welsh 6- to 11-year-olds	Welsh	2.49	49.8%	.51–.87	.74
Forrest & Barrett (2001)	South-east England	437 English 11- to 15-year-olds	English	2.86	57.2%	.58–.86	.81
Dixon (2002)[a]	South-east England	267 British ethnic majority and ethnic minority 10- to 16-year-olds	British	2.33	58.3%	.69–.83	.76
Alexander (2002)[a]	London, England	224 British ethnic majority and ethnic minority 11- to 17-year-olds	British	2.02	50.5%	.53–.84	.66
Sahlabadi (2002)[b]	London, England	55 Iranian ethnic minority 11- to 17-year-olds	Both English and Iranian	English: 2.97 Iranian: 2.75	English: 74.3% Iranian: 68.7%	English: .85–.90 Iranian: .68–.91	English: .88 Iranian: .82

Table 6.13 Continued

Study	Location of data collection	Children studied	Identity measured	Eigenvalue	Percentage of variance explained	Range of item loadings	Cronbach's alpha
Sahlabadi (2002)[b]	Tehran and Esfahan, Iran	78 Iranian ethnic majority 11- to 17-year-olds	Iranian	3.20	80.1%	.81–.95	.91
Manouka (2001)	Athens, Greece	167 Albanian ethnic minority 8- to 13-year-olds	Albanian	2.85	57.0%	.44–.88	.81
Maehr & Barrett (2005)	Berlin, Germany	214 German 12- to 18-year-olds	German	3.30	66.0%	.58–.90	.87

Notes
[a] The "pride" item was not administered in these two studies; the statistics quoted relate to the reduced 4-item version of the scale.
[b] The "internalization" item was not administered in this study; the statistics quoted relate to the reduced 4-item version of the scale.
In all studies, the five items loaded onto a single factor, with eigenvalues, percentage of variance explained and Cronbach's alpha as shown.

children living in London, and from Iranian children living in Tehran (the capital city of Iran) and Esfahan (the second largest city in Iran). The SoIS was used in London to measure the children's strength of identification with being Iranian and their strength of identification with being English, while in Iran it was used only to measure the children's strength of identification with being Iranian. It was found that the children living in Iran identified with being Iranian more strongly than the children living in London (which was contrary to the expectation that identification would be higher when the children were living in a minority context; it may be the case that the special international and religious status of Iran serves to enhance levels of Iranian identification within Iran). In addition, in both locations, the boys identified with being Iranian more strongly than the girls. There were no differences associated with age in the strength of Iranian identification. Among the children living in London, there were no differences with either age or gender in the strength of identification with being English. However, in these children, the strengths of their Iranian and English identifications were negatively correlated with each other; thus, the stronger the children's sense of Iranian identity, the weaker their English identity.

Manouka (2001) also investigated the strength of minority children's ethnic identifications using the SoIS, examining the strength of Albanian identity among a group of 8- to 13-year-old Albanian children who were living in Athens (the capital city of Greece). There were no differences in these children's strength of identification as a function of either age or gender; instead, the scores of both the boys and the girls were relatively high at all ages (i.e., above 4 on the 5-point scale). This finding was consistent with the expectation that ethnic identification would be high because these children were living within a minority context.

Finally, in the study by Maehr and Barrett (2005), the SoIS was used to measure the strength of identification with being German in a group of 12- to 18-year-old German children. This study revealed that there were no differences in the strength of national identification as a function of either the type of school attended (which was related to the children's academic ability) or age, but there was a difference according to the children's gender, with the boys exhibiting a higher level of national identification than the girls. In addition, there were differences in the national emblems that the children associated with Germany as a function of their strength of national identification (see Chapter 4 for details).

The findings of these various studies that have utilized the SoIS provide further support for the overall conclusion of the CHOONGE and NERID projects, namely that different groups of children living in different national and state contexts often exhibit different patterns of identity development. These various studies also demonstrate that the SoIS is indeed a useful and robust measure that can be used to examine the strength of children's national, state and ethnic identifications in a range of different national and state contexts. It is hoped that the availability of both the PGS scale and the SoIS will facilitate the future investigation of some of the unresolved issues in our understanding of how children's subjective identifications with their own nation and state develop.

SUMMARY

The principal conclusions that can be drawn from the research reviewed in this chapter are as follows.

- As far as the development of children's identifications with their own nation and state are concerned:
  - at the age of 6 years, the majority of children do usually acknowledge their own membership of one or more national or state groups
  - however, children's strength of subjective identification with these groups varies considerably at this early age, with some children showing strong identifications at the age of 6 years, whereas other children show much weaker identifications at this early age
  - there is considerable variation in the subsequent development of children's national and state identifications
  - variations in the development of national and state identifications have been found to occur as a function of the specific country in which the children live, children's geographical location within that country, how the state category is interpreted within children's local environments, children's ethnicity, children's use of language in the family home and children's language of schooling
  - the strength of national and state identification in children is not usually related to their attitudes towards out-groups
  - however, the strength of children's identification with a national or state group is frequently related to how much they like that group, and the strength of identification is also sometimes related to the positivity of their trait attributions to that group
  - although evidence on children's perceptions of the status of their own national or state groups has so far only been collected in the NIS, this evidence does suggest that, before adolescence, children often believe that their own group is regarded very positively by people who live in other countries, and that, during early adolescence, this positive view tends to moderate as children acquire what is arguably a more realistic perception of how people living in other countries view their group
  - the perceived status of the national or state group is not related to

children's strength of identification with that group, but it is often related to children's own attitudes to that group.

- As far as the measurement of national, state and ethnic identification in children is concerned:
  - two new scales have been developed in recent years, one for measuring the perceived status of the child's national or state group (the Perceived Group Status Scale, or PGSS), the other for measuring the child's strength of national, state and ethnic identification (the Strength of Identification Scale, or SoIS)
  - studies conducted using these two scales have demonstrated their viability for use with a range of different populations in a range of different contexts
  - these studies have also confirmed the overall finding of the CHOONGE and NERID projects, namely that different groups of children living in different national and state contexts often exhibit different patterns of identity development.

Theoretical accounts of how children's knowledge, beliefs and feelings about nations and states develop

Over the course of the last five chapters, we have reviewed the existing research that has been conducted into children's understanding of, and attitudes to, countries, nations and states and the people who belong to national and state groups. In this final chapter, we consider the theoretical frameworks that might be used in order to explain children's development in this domain.

This chapter is subdivided into three parts. The first part provides a brief summary of some of the key findings that have emerged from the five preceding chapters, which need to be explained by any empirically adequate theoretical framework. In the second part, we review five existing theories that might be used to try and explain children's development in this domain, namely Piagetian stage theory, more recent cognitive-developmental theory, social identity theory, self-categorization theory, and social identity development theory. It will be argued that none of these existing theories is able to explain the full range of phenomena that have been found to characterize children's development in this domain. The third part of this chapter will then provide an outline of a new theoretical framework, namely societal-social-cognitive-motivational theory, which, it will be argued, is able to account for all of the evidence that has emerged across the course of the five preceding chapters. We will begin by summarizing the key findings that need to be explained.

THE KEY FINDINGS REQUIRING EXPLANATION

Variability in children's development

It is apparent from the last five chapters that one of the most pervasive findings that has been obtained in this field is the variability that can occur in children's development in this domain. For example, we saw in Chapter 2 that children's large-scale geographical knowledge of countries exhibits not only cross-national (Axia & Bremner, 1992; Axia et al., 1998; Barrett & Farroni, 1996) but also significant within-country variability. The latter is associated with many different factors, including children's gender (Barrett, 1996; Barrett & Farroni, 1996; Barrett & Whennell, 1998), social class (Barrett et al., 1996; Jahoda, 1963a; Wiegand, 1991a), ethnicity (Wiegand, 1991a), strength of national identification (Barrett & Davey, 2001; Barrett & Whennell, 1998), children's geographical location within their own country (Axia et al., 1998; Barrett et al., 1996), travel experience (Barrett et al., 1996; Rutland, 1998; Wiegand, 1991b), education (Axia et al., 1998) and exposure to information about other countries in the mass media and elsewhere (Holloway & Valentine, 2000; Stillwell & Spencer, 1973).

Similarly, we saw in Chapter 3 that children's understanding of, and attitudes to, the state and government also show considerable variability both across different countries and within individual countries. The cross-national differences appear to be linked to historical-societal factors. For example, adolescents' levels of trust in government, and their perceptions of the responsibilities of government, are related to the recent political history and current economic conditions of the country in which they live (Amadeo et al., 2002; Torney-Purta et al., 2001). Within-country variability in children's knowledge of, and attitudes to, the state is linked to a wide range of different factors, including social class (Amadeo et al., 2002; Hess & Torney, 1967; Torney-Purta et al., 2001), intellectual and academic ability (Hess & Torney, 1967; Moore et al., 1985), levels of attention to the news in the mass media (Amadeo et al., 2002; Moore et al., 1985; Torney-Purta et al., 2001), participation in extra-curricular activities and peer group organizations (Amadeo et al., 2002; Hess & Torney, 1967; Torney-Purta et al., 2001; Verba et al., 1995; Youniss et al., 1997), gender (Amadeo et al., 2002; Moore et al., 1985; Torney-Purta et al., 2001) and a number of educational factors (Amadeo et al., 2002; Emler & Frazer, 1999; Nie et al., 1996; Torney-Purta et al., 2001) including curriculum and textbook content (Berti, 1994; Berti & Andriolo, 2001).

In Chapter 4, we saw that most children, irrespective of the specific country in which they live, tend to display a positive sense of pride in, and to give positive ratings of, their own country (Amadeo et al., 2002; Jaspers et al., 1972; Johnson et al., 1970; Torney-Purta et al., 2001). That said, however, there is significant variability across countries in children's levels of pride (Amadeo et al., 2002; Dennis et al., 1972; Nugent, 1994; Torney-Purta et al., 2001). Moreover, while some children sometimes rate their own country as being better than *all* other countries (Hess & Torney, 1967; Nugent, 1994), other children may rate other countries as being just as good as, if not better than, their own country (Dennis et al., 1972; Middleton et al., 1970; Moore et al., 1985). There are also cross-national differences in the types of issues that make children feel proud about their own country (Dennis et al., 1972). Children's knowledge of, affect for and utilization of national and state emblems similarly exhibit variability both across countries and within countries (Barrett et al., 1997; Cutts Dougherty et al., 1992; cf. also the findings by Jahoda, 1963b; Moore et al., 1985; and Weinstein, 1957); the within-country variability here occurs as a function of children's language group (and probably their ethnic group as well), gender, age and strength of national identification (Forrest and Barrett, 2001; Maehr & Barrett, 2005; Moodie, 1980; Trimby & Barrett, 2005).

Chapter 5 revealed that there is also significant variability in children's knowledge, beliefs and feelings about the people who belong to different national and state groups. For example, some children show no significant changes in their feelings towards out-groups between 6 and 15 years of age; some show linear increases in their levels of liking of out-groups; some show linear decreases; while others show increases followed by decreases, or decreases followed by increases, in their levels of liking of particular national or state out-groups between these same ages (Barrett et al., 1997, 2001; Lambert & Klineberg, 1967). The developmental patterns that children exhibit vary according to the national and state context within which they live, their specific situation within that context and the particular target groups involved. There is also variability in the factor structures that underlie children's national and state attitudes and feelings according to their specific national context, with these attitudes and feelings sometimes displaying a one-factor structure, sometimes a two-factor structure and sometimes a three-factor structure. As far as the in-group is concerned, although children often display a positive bias in their attitudes towards their own national and/ or state group, they do not always provide the most positive descriptions of, or display the most positive feelings towards, their own in-group (Barrett et al., 1997, 2001; Lambert & Klineberg, 1967; Tajfel et al., 1970, 1972). This is consistent with the findings from the studies into children's national and state pride, which have also revealed that children do not always say that their own country is better than all other countries. Moreover, it is not only children's attitudes and feelings towards different national and state groups that vary from country to country. Children's understanding of the factors that determine people's national and state group memberships can vary across countries as well (Carrington & Short, 2000). Thus, children's attitudes, feelings, judgements and reasoning about national and state groups all exhibit significant variability according to the particular country in which they live.

Finally, we saw in Chapter 6 that children's levels of identification with their own nation and state also exhibit considerable variability as a function of many different factors (Barrett et al., 1997, 2001). Thus, in some countries, levels of identification are already high at the age of 6, with there being no subsequent changes in the degree of identification with age, while in other countries children do exhibit age-related changes in their levels of identification; in some cases increases and in other cases decreases. Furthermore, different developmental patterns are sometimes displayed by children in relationship to their identification with their national group and with their state group. Levels of identification also vary according to children's geographical location within their own country, how the state category is interpreted within their local environments, their ethnicity, their use of language in the family home, and their language of schooling. In addition, the relationship between the strength of identification and children's intergroup attitudes varies according to the specific national and state context in which children live.

Thus, one very clear conclusion that emerges from the evidence reviewed in the five preceding chapters is that there are pervasive and substantial levels of variability in the development of children's knowledge, beliefs and feelings about nations and states, and about the people who belong to different national and state groups. As we shall see later on in this chapter, this variability has major implications for several of the theories that have been put forward to explain children's development in this domain.

The role of education

A second conclusion to emerge from the preceding chapters is that school education often plays an important role in the development of children's understanding of, and attitudes to, nations and states. For example, in Chapter 2, we saw that children's geographical knowledge about other countries is enhanced both by formal educational instruction (Axia et al., 1998) and by the informal provision of information about other countries through the display of maps, posters and wall charts on classroom walls (Stillwell & Spencer, 1973).

Similarly, Chapter 3 revealed that children's knowledge of the political institutions of the state is influenced both by the formal educational instruction they receive at school (Berti, 2005; Berti & Andriolo, 2001; Berti & Benesso, 1998; Connell, 1971) and by the contents of the school textbooks they use (Berti, 1994). However, it is not only children's political and civic knowledge that is affected by the school. Children's political attitudes, and their intentions to engage with the political institutions of the state in their future adult lives, are also related to factors such as the political attitudes of their teachers (Hess & Torney, 1967) and their perception that they have an open classroom climate for discussion at school (Amadeo et al., 2002; Torney-Purta et al., 2001).

The studies that were reviewed in Chapter 4 further suggest that the school can be a crucial agent for teaching children about the historical and cultural heritage of their nation and state. First, the school provides children with explicit instruction about the heritage, values, emblems and symbolic imagery of their state and nation, and there is evidence that children's knowledge and utilization of national and state emblems is affected not only by school curricular input (Forrest & Barrett, 2001; Maehr & Barrett, 2005) but also by school practices (cf. Jahoda, 1963b; Moore et al., 1985; Weinstein, 1957). Second, the history textbooks that children use at school typically provide them with an officially approved narrative of the historical origins of their own nation and state that incorporates and prioritizes the core collective values of their own country (Mannitz, 2004b; Schiffauer & Sunier, 2004). Although there are a number of different ways in which children may respond to these historical narratives (Wertsch, 1998), they often internalize these narratives (Wertsch & O'Connor, 1994; Wills, 1994). Third, school practices may be modelled on the collective values on which the nation's civil culture rests, and through their participation in these school practices, children can internalize and appropriate the values, discourse and practices of their own nation's civil culture (Baumann & Sunier, 2004; Mannitz, 2004a, b; Mannitz & Schiffauer, 2004; Sunier, 2004a, b). Fourth, school textbooks are often skewed by ethnocentric biases (Anyon, 1979; Apple, 1993; Preiswerk & Perrot, 1978; Schleicher, 1992) and children do report that these textbooks are a source of their knowledge about foreign peoples (Barrett & Short, 1992; Byram et al., 1991; Lambert & Klineberg, 1967).

Finally, in Chapters 5 and 6 we also saw that children's national and state attitudes, as well as their national and state identifications, vary as a function of their language of schooling (Barrett et al., 2001). The differences that are associated with children's language of schooling are likely to have multiple causes, including the parental ideologies and outlooks that lead parents to select particular schools for their children to attend in the first place. However, the school ethos and the school curriculum almost certainly play important roles in determining and reinforcing children's own attitudes to, and identifications with, nations and states as well. In other words, the evidence is consistent in suggesting that there are indeed links between the development of children's knowledge, beliefs and feelings about nations and states and their schooling.

The role of the mass media

A third conclusion to emerge from the literature reviewed in the last five chapters is that the mass media can also impact on children's knowledge and beliefs about nations and states, and about the people who belong to different national and state groups. For example, in Chapter 2, we saw that television and the movies are particularly prominent sources of children's images of the physical and social geographies of other countries (Holloway & Valentine, 2000), while in Chapter 3 we saw that children's levels of attention to news reports on television and in newspapers are related to their levels of political and civic knowledge about the state (Amadeo et al., 2002; Connell, 1971; Moore et al., 1985; Torney-Purta et al., 2001). In Chapter 4, it was noted that individuals may use information picked up from foreign radio and television broadcasts and from clandestine publications to construct an understanding of the history of their nation (Tulviste & Wertsch, 1994). The mass media also appear to influence the emblems that children use to represent their own nation (Forrest & Barrett, 2001). And in Chapter 5, we saw that the mass media can also influence children's beliefs about the people who live in other countries (Himmelweit et al., 1958; Roberts et al., 1974). Furthermore, when children are asked about the sources from which they have acquired their knowledge of the people who live in other countries, media sources (such as television, the movies, books and magazines) tend to be among the sources most frequently cited by children themselves (Barrett & Short, 1992; Byram et al., 1991; Lambert & Klineberg, 1967). All of this evidence is consistent in showing that the mass media can be an important influence on children's knowledge and beliefs in this domain.

The role of significant others

However, and perhaps rather curiously, relatively little research has been conducted into the role that significant others can play in the development of children's understanding of, and attitudes to, nations and states, and the people who belong to national and state groups The main exception here is the role played by teachers, which has already been noted above. Consequently, any conclusions drawn about the role of parents, in particular, must be tentative at this stage. That said, however, children themselves often cite their parents as one of the sources of their knowledge about the people who live in other countries (Barrett & Short, 1992; Lambert & Klineberg, 1967), although references to parents as a source of knowledge do tend to disappear once children reach adolescence (Lambert & Klineberg, 1967). In addition, conversations with family members and with friends are also sometimes cited by individuals as one of the sources of their information about the history of their nation (Tulviste & Wertsch, 1994).

Other indirect evidence also suggests that parents do indeed play a key role in children's development in this domain. First, we saw in Chapters 5 and 6 that children's attitudes and feelings towards national and state groups, as well as their national and state identifications, are systematically related to the language(s) spoken in the family home (Barrett et al., 1997, 2001). Notice that it is parents who make the decision about which languages are spoken in the home, and this decision itself is often predicated on the parents' own ideological beliefs (Azurmendi et al., 1998; Elejabarrieta, 1994; Valencia et al., 2003; Vila, 1996). Children's attitudes, feelings and identifications also vary according to their language of schooling (Barrett et al., 2001). While some of the variance here almost certainly stems from the different educational curricula and practices adopted in the different schools, it is parents who make the decision about which schools their children should attend. Furthermore, this decision is also often predicated on parents' ideological beliefs. Thus, the differences in children's development that occur as a function of language use in the home and as a function of language of schooling are almost certainly linked, at least in part, to the different value systems and practices prevailing in the family home that are associated with the different ideological perspectives held by children's parents. Hence, despite the lack of direct research into this issue, it does seem highly likely that parents play a key role in their children's development in this domain.

The role of travel to other countries

Relatively little research has also been conducted into how children's travel to other countries, and their personal contact with foreigners, impact on their development. Most of the studies that have examined the effects of travel experience have focused on the effects of travel on children's geographical knowledge. As we saw in Chapter 2, children do appear to derive at least some of their geographical knowledge about other countries from their holidays in those countries (Barrett et al., 1996; Bourchier et al., 1996, 2002; Wiegand, 1991a, b). In addition, as far as children's knowledge of the people who live in other countries is concerned, children sometimes report that they have acquired this knowledge either from direct contact with foreigners or from their holidays in those countries (Barrett & Short, 1992; Byram et al., 1991; Lambert & Klineberg, 1967). However, it is noteworthy that Byram et al. found no effects of either visits to France or contacts with French people on English children's evaluations of, or attitudes to, the French. It would be useful to know whether this finding extrapolates to other children and to other foreign groups, or whether there are particular circumstances under which personal contact does affect children's attitudes to foreigners. The research that has been conducted into the effects of intergroup contact on children's racial and ethnic attitudes (e.g., Aboud, Mendelson, & Purdy,

2003; Khmelkov & Hallinan, 1999; Patchen, 1982; Schofield, 1991, 1995; Stephan, 1978, 1999; Stephan & Rosenfield, 1978; R. Turner, Hewstone, & Voci, in press) suggests that there are likely to be particular circumstances that can moderate children's stereotypes of and attitudes to the people who belong to other national and state groups (such as personal friendships, or collaboration in joint activities with common goals, etc.). There is clearly a need for further research into this issue, to establish under what conditions children's stereotypes and attitudes are or are not influenced by travel to other countries and by personal contact with people from other countries.

The role of domain-general cognitive factors

Similarly, relatively little research has been conducted into the relationship between children's domain-general cognitive competencies and their knowledge of, and beliefs about, nations, states and the people who belong to different national and state groups. Only children's geographical knowledge of countries has been examined to date to ascertain whether their knowledge is linked to such competencies. As we saw in Chapter 2, children's understanding of large-scale geographical territories, in particular young children's understanding of nested geographical hierarchical relationships (such as those that exist between cities, regions and countries), does indeed appear to be related to the development of their capabilities on domain-general class-inclusion and transitivity tasks (Daggs, 1986; Piché, 1977, 1981; Wilberg, 2002). Other authors have argued that the developmental changes that can be observed in children's understanding of the state are also driven by changes to the child's underlying cognitive competencies (Connell, 1971; Moore et al., 1985), and there is evidence to suggest that children's IQ and/or academic ability is related to their level of political understanding (Hess & Torney, 1967; Moore et al., 1985). However, studies employing measures of particular domain-general competencies have not yet been conducted in this area. Furthermore, no studies have yet been conducted to examine whether children's attitudes to national and state groups are linked to their more general cognitive skills. It is noteworthy that children's racial and ethnic biases and prejudices have been found to be linked to a number of such skills (including classification, the perception of similarities between groups, attention to differences within groups, and the ability to understand that different people holding different opinions can both be correct from their own points of view: Bigler & Liben, 1993; Black-Gutman & Hickson, 1996; Clark, Hocevar, & Dembo, 1980; Doyle & Aboud, 1995; Katz, Sohn, & Zalk, 1975). Comparable research is required to establish whether children's biases and prejudices about national and state groups are also related to this same set of general cognitive skills.

Gender differences

One other finding that has repeatedly emerged across the course of the last five chapters is the presence of gender differences. For example, in Chapter 2, we saw that boys tend to have higher levels of large-scale geographical knowledge about countries than girls, particularly in their configurational knowledge, that is, in their knowledge of the spatial relationships that exist between different geographical locations in terms of their direction and distance from each other (Barrett, 1996; Barrett & Farroni, 1996; Barrett et al., 1996; Barrett & Whennell, 1998). Similarly, in Chapter 3, it was seen that boys tend to have more political and civic knowledge about the state than girls (Amadeo et al., 2002; Moore et al., 1985; Torney-Purta et al., 2001). In Chapter 4, we saw that boys also sometimes have higher levels of pride in their own country than girls (Amadeo et al., 2002; Torney-Purta et al., 2001), that boys and girls tend to use different emblems for representing their state or nation (Forrest & Barrett, 2001; Maehr & Barrett, 2005), and that boys sometimes have a greater knowledge of national emblems than girls (Trimby & Barrett, 2005). In Chapter 5, we reviewed one study in which boys were found to hold less positive attitudes to other national/state groups than girls (Byram et al., 1991), while in Chapter 6, we saw that boys sometimes exhibit higher levels of national identification than girls (Forrest & Barrett, 2001; Maehr & Barrett, 2005; Sahlabadi, 2002). Notice that many of these gender differences fall in the same direction, with boys exhibiting higher levels of knowledge than girls, and are sufficiently consistent to suggest that boys and girls may be subject to subtly different patterns of influences in their development.

The relationship between knowledge and affect

In Chapter 1, it was noted that studying children's knowledge, beliefs and feelings about nations, states and the people who belong to different national and state groups provides developmental psychologists with the opportunity to examine the developmental relationship between cognitive and affective functioning in children, and to explore the development of emotionally "hot" cognition. As we have seen in the preceding chapters, the relationship between cognition and affect in this domain is complex.

For example, in Chapter 2, we reviewed the research that has been conducted on children's feelings towards, and geographical knowledge about, other countries. As we saw there, a number of studies have found relationships between knowledge and affect (with children knowing the most about countries they like, and knowing less about countries they dislike), at least in the case of some target countries for particular groups of children (Barrett et al., 1997; Johnson et al., 1970; Stillwell & Spencer, 1973). However, when the covariance of both knowledge and affect with demographic variables and with the extent of children's travel experience is taken into account, these apparent relationships between knowledge and affect disappear (Bourchier et al., 2002). In other words, there does not seem to be any direct relationship between the amount of factual knowledge that children have about other countries and the affect they exhibit towards those countries. However, in the case of the child's own country, a possible relationship has been found. Barrett and Whennell (1998) and Barrett and Davey (2001) found that the strength of English children's identification with their nation (i.e., with being English) and with their state (i.e., with being British) was positively correlated with their levels of factual geographical knowledge of the UK and with their ability to differentiate between typically English and typically non-English landscapes. But, perhaps rather surprisingly, the children's strength of identification was *not* related to their emotional attachment to typically English landscapes (Barrett & Davey, 2001). These findings suggest the complexity of the relationships that exist between children's cognitions and affects in this area. Furthermore, in Chapter 4, we saw that links may also exist between children's strength of national identification and their knowledge and use of national emblems. For example, Trimby and Barrett (2005) found that the number of Welsh national emblems that young Welsh children could generate was correlated with their strength of identification with being Welsh. Trimby and Barrett also found that children with stronger national identifications were more likely to produce certain Welsh national emblems than children with weaker national identifications.

However, as we noted in Chapters 2 and 4, the causality that applies in both cases (that is, to both geographical and emblematic knowledge) is inherently ambiguous. It could be the case that children's acquisition of geographical and emblematic knowledge strengthens children's national identifications; or that a strong sense of national identification motivates the child to acquire geographical and emblematic information about their nation; or that there are other factors involved in the causality here, such as family discourse and practices – it may be that some families attribute greater importance to the nation than others such that children from those families do not only develop a stronger sense of national identification but also acquire more geographical and emblematic knowledge. Further studies are clearly needed in order to disentangle the causality here.

In the case of children's conceptions of, and feelings about, national and state groups, relationships between cognition and affect have once again been found (see Chapter 5). For example, Lambert and Klineberg (1967) discovered that children who like a particular out-group tend to be well informed about that group, and can produce a high number of factual descriptive statements about it (e.g., concerning the people's typical physical appearance, way of life, etc.); in addition, these children tend to use relatively few evaluative terms to describe the group (such as *good, nice,* etc.). However, children who dislike a particular out-group produce very few factual descriptive statements about that group, but instead produce many more (negative) evaluative statements about the group. In other words, Lambert and Klineberg's data suggest that there is a positive correlation between affect for out-groups and knowledge about those groups. But once again, if such a relationship does exist, the causality involved might not be straightforward. And indeed, the data from the CHOONGE and NERID projects suggest that the relationship between cognition and affect here is not direct and unambiguous. In those two studies, most of the 6-year-olds made positively biased trait attributions to at least some out-groups. Interestingly, they sometimes did so even though they had told the interviewer that they did not know anything about those groups. Tajfel (1966) reported a similar phenomenon many years ago: that children are sometimes willing to express an affective or evaluative judgement about an out-group even though they may have very little factual knowledge about that group. However, Tajfel's own studies also found that children actually had more knowledge about disliked countries and out-groups than they had about countries and out-groups towards which they had neutral feelings (Johnson et al., 1970). Notice that if positive affect towards an out-group motivates the child to acquire information about that group, then one might expect negative affect to inhibit the acquisition of such information (perhaps through the child avoiding sources of information about that group). Yet Tajfel's findings suggest that children who feel negatively about a group sometimes acquire *more* information about that group than they do about neutrally regarded groups. The relationship between cognition and affect in relationship to national and state groups is clearly complex and multifaceted, requiring further investigation for proper elucidation.

EXISTING THEORETICAL ACCOUNTS
OF CHILDREN'S DEVELOPMENT

Against this empirical background, we can now survey and evaluate the various theoretical accounts that can be applied to children's development in this domain. There are five principal approaches that we shall explore in this section: Piagetian stage theory (Piaget & Weil, 1951); Aboud's cognitive-developmental theory (Aboud, 1988; Aboud & Amato, 2001; Doyle & Aboud, 1995; Doyle et al., 1988); social identity theory (Tajfel, 1978; Tajfel & Turner, 1986); self-categorization theory (Oakes et al., 1994; J.C. Turner et al., 1987); and social identity development theory (Nesdale, 1999, 2004; Nesdale, Maass, Griffiths, & Durkin, 2003).

Piagetian stage theory

In his seminal paper (Piaget & Weil, 1951), Piaget is relatively reticent concerning his own theoretical perspective, and the paper is largely restricted to a report of the empirical findings he obtained in his study with 4- to 15-year-old Swiss children. In other words, Piaget himself does not explicitly offer a comprehensive or over-arching theoretical explanation of why the development of children's knowledge, beliefs and feelings about countries and about national and state groups might have followed the particular pattern found in his study. However, the empirical findings reported in the paper do lend themselves very readily to a Piagetian explanation, because the children's thinking about countries and the groups of people who live in them appeared to develop through three stages. During the first stage, prior to 7–8 years of age, the children lacked an understanding of both spatial-geographical inclusion relationships (such as that between Geneva and Switzerland) and conceptual inclusion relationships (such as that between being Genevese and Swiss); in the second stage, between 7–8 and 10–11 years of age, the children mastered spatial-geographical inclusion relationships, but still did not understand conceptual inclusion relationships; in the third stage, from 10–11 years of age onwards, the children finally mastered conceptual inclusion relationships as well (see Chapter 2). Piaget and Weil also found that the children's attitudes to, and feelings about, countries and national and state groups followed a similar developmental pattern: idiosyncratic and experientially based preferences were expressed prior to 7–8 years of age; preferences for their home country, based on ideas circulating in their immediate environments, were expressed between 7–8 and 10–11 years of age; and preferences for their home country, based on abstract national and/or state ideals, were expressed from 10–11 years of age onwards. Thus, Piaget and Weil found two major discontinuities in the children's development. The first occurred when the children made the transition from pre-operational to concrete-operational understanding, and the second occurred when the children made the transition to formal-operational understanding.

Consequently, one possible explanation of children's development in this domain is that offered by Piagetian stage theory (Piaget, 1950, 1972; Piaget & Inhelder, 1969). This theory proposes that children's cognitive functioning is domain-general rather than domain-specific; that is to say, at any given point in development, the child's cognitive performance is not task-specific but is relatively homogeneous, being structurally equivalent across a range of different tasks and across a range of different knowledge domains. Transitions from one developmental stage to the next are marked by abrupt but generalized qualitative changes in the child's underlying cognitive structures; as these underlying cognitive structures change, so too does the child's performance on many different tasks across numerous knowledge domains. Thus, the child's thinking in any particular domain is rooted in deeper, domain-general, cognitive structures, and it is the changes that occur to these underlying structures which drive the development of the child's thinking in different domains. These deeper structures themselves change as the child learns from his or her own personal experience in the world, with the driving force behind these changes being the child's need to achieve cognitive equilibrium: as the child tries to explain different phenomena, multiple ways of explaining the same phenomenon are sometimes generated; this internal conflict produces cognitive disequilibrium; this disequilibrium stimulates the child into constructing new, more complex and more abstract ways of reasoning about the phenomenon in question; as these new ways of reasoning are constructed, the internal conflict is resolved and equilibrium is restored (until further cognitive conflicts are encountered). Piaget explicitly argues that successive modes of thinking are integrative and are not interchangeable; each results from the preceding one, and integrates the previous mode of thinking into a superordinate structure, which then prepares the way for the construction of the succeeding structure. Furthermore, the order of succession of stages is postulated to be constant and universal (although the average age at which each particular stage of development occurs may vary according to the individual circumstances of the child). Thus, the process through which children gradually adapt their thinking to the world in which they live is postulated to be universal, with children exhibiting the same developmental sequence irrespective of the specific culture or social context in which they are growing up.

This theory therefore predicts: (1) that children will always exhibit the same stage-based sequence of development irrespective of the specific context or culture in which they live; (2) that children's thinking in any particular knowledge domain will be rooted in deeper underlying domain-general cognitive competencies; and (3) that the development of children's thinking will be driven primarily by endogenous cognitive restructurings, rather than by the exogenous input of information from the environment. However, all three of these predictions are not well supported by the evidence that has now been collected on the development of children's understanding of countries, nations and states.

First, as we saw in Chapter 2, the work of Jahoda (1963a, 1964) showed that the particular sequence of stages identified by Piaget and Weil does not occur in all children, and that this sequence is actually violated by many children (i.e., by those who acquire an understanding of conceptual inclusion relationships before spatial-geographical inclusion relationships). And indeed, at a more general level, Piagetian stage theory would appear to be manifestly unsuitable for explaining the very considerable variability, both across countries and within countries, which we now know characterizes children's development in this domain. Second, concrete evidence that children's thinking in this domain is based on their underlying domain-general cognitive competencies is noticeably absent, despite the theoretical claims made by some researchers to this effect (e.g., Connell, 1971; Moore et al., 1985). Indeed, the only aspect of children's understanding in this domain that has been found to be clearly linked to domain-general cognitive skills so far is children's understanding of nested geographical-spatial inclusion relationships, which has been found to be linked to their competence on domain-general class-inclusion and transitivity tasks (Daggs, 1986; Piché, 1977, 1981; Wilberg, 2002). Third, it is clear that children's development in this domain is highly susceptible to environmental influences, especially influences from education and the mass media (see above). This is directly contrary to Piagetian theory. For all of these reasons, Piagetian theory does not appear to be a very suitable framework for explaining the various phenomena that have now been documented in this field.

Aboud's cognitive-developmental theory

Although Piagetian stage theory itself is unable to explain children's development in this domain, Aboud's more recent adaptation and application of Piagetian theory to the development of children's racial and ethnic prejudice and attitudes (Aboud 1988; Aboud & Amato, 2001; Doyle & Aboud, 1995; Doyle et al., 1988) does offer an alternative cognitive-developmental perspective that can be applied to the development of children's prejudice and attitudes to national and state groups.

In her account of the development of racial and ethnic prejudice, Aboud argues that there is a significant discontinuity in children's development at about 6 years of age. Before the age of 6, she proposes that the egocentricity of the pre-operational child's mode of thinking, and the child's affective processes, tend to dominate the child's responses to other people, with the consequence that in-group favouritism commonly prevails. However, she argues that in-group favouritism peaks at about 6 years, with children of this age exhibiting maximum positive bias in favour of their own racial and ethnic ingroups, and maximum negative prejudice against racial and ethnic outgroups. This polarization in the child's attitudes towards in-groups and outgroups is hypothesized to decline after the age of 6, so that through the course of middle childhood, there are significant decreases in both in-group favouritism and out-group prejudice. In her own studies, Aboud has found that, at the age of 6, children attribute mainly positive characteristics to members of their own in-group, and mainly negative characteristics to members of out-groups. After the age of 6, this polarization in the attribution of traits to in-groups and out-groups decreases, as children gradually come to attribute more negative characteristics to the in-group, and more positive characteristics to out-groups. The net result of this process is a reduction in in-group favouritism, a reduction in out-group prejudice, and an increase in the perceived variability of racial and ethnic groups across the course of middle childhood. Aboud further argues that these changes are driven by the development of the child's domain-general cognitive capabilities, in particular by the acquisition of the ability to perform successfully on conservation tasks, the ability to use multiple classifications, the ability to judge the deeper similarities between superficially different groups, the ability to attend to individual differences within groups, and the ability to understand that different people holding different opinions can both be correct from their own points of view. Aboud argues that these domain-general cognitive capabilities develop between 6 and 11 years of age, and that the developmental changes that occur in the child's racial and ethnic attitudes across this age range are a direct consequence of these underlying domain-general cognitive changes.

As we have noted already, there is evidence available to support the view that children's racial and ethnic biases and prejudices are indeed related to the domain-general cognitive capabilities proposed by Aboud (see, for example, Bigler & Liben, 1993; Black-Gutman & Hickson, 1996; Clark et al., 1980; Doyle & Aboud, 1995; Katz et al., 1975). It would be an interesting extension of this line of research to explore whether children's biases and prejudices in relationship to national and state groups are also related to this same set of cognitive skills. Extrapolating Aboud's cognitive-developmental theory (CDT) to children's national and state attitudes is certainly possible, given that the theory proposes that children's intergroup attitudes are grounded in domain-general cognitive capacities, capacities that should therefore underlie children's attitudes in a number of different domains.

If CDT is extrapolated to the development of children's national and state attitudes in this way, this theory can in fact explain some of the findings that have been obtained in this field. For example, as we saw in Chapter 5, the studies by Barrett and Short (1992) and Barrett et al. (1999, 2003) both found a reduction in in-group favouritism, an increase in positive regard for out-groups, and an increase in the perceived variability of national/state groups through the course of middle childhood. All three developmental trends are consistent with the predictions of CDT. However, as we also saw in Chapter 5, the data from the Lambert and Klineberg (1967) study, as well as the data from the CHOONGE and NERID projects, show that these developmental trends are by no means universal, and that children's attributions of positive and negative characteristics, as well as their expressions of feelings to national and state in-groups and out-groups can actually show a multiplicity of different developmental trends (including linear increases, linear decreases, and both U-shaped and inverted-U-shaped curvilinear trends). In other words, because CDT predicts that the same developmental pattern will be shown in children's intergroup attitudes irrespective of the particular societal and social context in which the child is growing up, CDT is unable to explain the diversity of developmental patterns that are actually exhibited by children.

In addition, CDT cannot explain: the diversity of factor structures underlying children's national and state attitudes that were found in the CHOONGE and NERID projects; why educational input and the mass media should influence children's beliefs about, and attitudes to, other countries and the people who live in those countries (Axia et al., 1998; Barrett & Short, 1992; Byram et al., 1991; Himmelweit et al., 1958; Holloway & Valentine, 2000; Johnson, 1966; Lambert & Klineberg, 1967; Roberts et al., 1974; Stillwell & Spencer, 1973); why children who have visited particular countries sometimes exhibit more positive affect towards these countries than children who have not visited them (Bourchier et al., 2002); or why national and state out-groups that are the traditional enemies of the child's own country are often evaluated significantly less positively than other out-groups (Barrett et al., 1997, 1999, 2001, 2003; Barrett & Short, 1992; Buchanan-Barrow et al., 1999; Jahoda, 1962).

Even more problematically for CDT, there are several findings that run directly counter to the predictions of this theory. First, in-group favouritism at the age of 6 is not, in fact, a universal phenomenon (Lambert & Klineberg, 1967; Tajfel et al., 1970, 1972). Second, children sometimes do not exhibit any changes at all in their national and state attitudes and feelings between 6 and 12 years of age (e.g., the Bantu children studied by Lambert & Klineberg, 1967, and the Basque children studied in the CHOONGE project[19]). Third, attitudes to traditional enemy out-groups sometimes become more (rather than less) negative through the course of middle childhood. For example, in Table 5.3, notice that the Scottish children in the CHOONGE project exhibited an age-related increase (rather than decrease) in the number of negative traits attributed to German people, while the Italian (Vicenza) children exhibited an age-related decrease (rather than increase) in the number of positive traits attributed to German people. These two trends run directly counter to those predicted by CDT. Barrett (2002) also found an increase in negativity towards German people through the course of middle childhood in a separate sample of English children.

In her most recent formulation, Aboud has begun to acknowledge the diversity of the developmental trends that have now been documented in different studies conducted in different cultures and in different historical periods into the development of racial and ethnic prejudice (Aboud & Amato,

---

[19] As Tables 5.3 and 5.9 reveal, the children living in the Basque Country did not show any age-related changes in their attitudes to British, Spanish, French, German and Basque people; only their attitudes to Italian people showed any changes at all between 6 and 12 years of age. For a more extensive discussion of the theoretical implications of the data collected from the children in the Basque Country, see Reizábal et al. (2004).

2001). A number of studies over the years have shown that young ethnic minority children do not always express a clear sense of in-group favouritism (e.g., Asher & Allen, 1969; Bagley & Young, 1998; Katz & Kofkin, 1997; Vaughan, 1964), and that racial attitudes do not always show the predicted reduction in prejudice across middle childhood (e.g., Black-Gutman & Hickson, 1996; Moodie, 1980). Aboud and Amato (2001) suggest that this developmental diversity probably stems either from the presence or absence of ethnic conflict within the society in which the child is growing up, from the majority vs. minority status of the child within that society, and from the influence of socialization agents such as parents and the school curriculum, all of which can alter and modulate the basic developmental pattern that is postulated to stem from the child's underlying cognitive development. However, insofar as these environmental factors are conceded to play a significant role in the development of children's intergroup attitudes, it is clearly necessary for theorizing to move away from an exclusively cognitive-developmental theoretical framework to one that takes into account not only cognitive factors but also exogenous societal and social influences.

Social identity theory

One theory that does explicitly take both societal and social factors into account is social identity theory (SIT). This theory was originally formulated by Tajfel (1978; Tajfel & Turner, 1986). Although Tajfel himself did not formulate the theory in order to explain developmental phenomena, a number of attempts have been made by subsequent researchers to apply this theory to the identity development of children (see Bennett & Sani, 2004, for a recent survey).

SIT is based on the observation that individuals belong to many different social groups (e.g., gender, ethnic, national, state, occupational, social class, etc.) and that these social group memberships may sometimes be internalized as part of an individual's self-concept. SIT postulates that, when this occurs, individuals strive to obtain a sense of positive self-esteem from these social identities. Consequently, in constructing representations of in-groups and out-groups, dimensions of comparison are chosen that produce more favourable representations of in-groups than of out-groups, resulting in in-group favouritism, out-group denigration, or both. The positive distinctiveness that is ascribed to in-groups over out-groups produces positive self-esteem. However, in order for these effects to occur, the individual must have internalized a social group membership as part of his or her self-concept, that is, the individual must subjectively identify with that category. If an individual's subjective identification with a particular group is weak or absent, these effects will not occur. Furthermore, in certain cases (e.g., when one belongs to a group that has a low social status within the society to which one belongs), it may be difficult to achieve positive in-group distinctiveness. Under these circumstances, other strategies (such as changing one's social group membership, or changing the existing social order to improve the status of the in-group) may be used instead to try to achieve a more favourable in-group representation. Thus, SIT posits that the basic human need for positive self-esteem is a fundamental motivation of people's intergroup attitudes. SIT also postulates that there is a cognitive processing bias that affects people's categorical judgements. This bias attenuates within-category differences and accentuates between-category differences. Thus, the knowledge that one belongs to a particular social group produces intra-group homogeneity effects in which the variation among the members of in-groups and out-groups is underestimated, and the differences between members of the in-group and members of out-groups are overestimated. It is this mechanism that results in the stereotyping of in-groups and out-groups.

SIT therefore suggests that phenomena such as in-group favouritism, out-group prejudice and the stereotyping of in-groups and out-groups occur as psychological consequences of identifying with particular social group memberships. Over the years, a number of researchers have drawn several empirical predictions from SIT (see, for example, Bigler, Brown, & Markell, 2001; Bigler, Jones, & Lobliner, 1997; Branscombe & Wann, 1994; Grant, 1992, 1993; Hinkle & Brown, 1990; Kelly, 1988; Mummendey et al., 2001; Nesdale & Flesser, 2001; Perreault & Bourhis, 1998; Powlishta, 1995; Verkuyten, 2001; Yee & Brown, 1992). These predictions include the following: (1) representations of in-groups and out-groups will be based on dimensions of comparison that produce positive in-group distinctiveness and in-group favouritism; (2) the strength of identification with an in-group will correlate either with the positivity of the in-group evaluation, or with the negativity of out-group evaluations, or with the positive distinctiveness that is ascribed to the in-group over out-groups; (3) ingroup favouritism is a consequence of the individual's subjective identification with the in-group. These three predictions can all be tested using the evidence available on children's national and state identifications and their attitudes to national and state in-groups and out-groups.

As far as the first prediction is concerned, although there is evidence from a number of studies that positive in-group distinctiveness and in-group favouritism are indeed widespread phenomena in children's attitudes to national and state groups, these same studies also reveal that these phenomena are *not* universal. For example, as we saw in Chapter 5, Lambert and Klineberg (1967) found that, although most of the children who they interviewed produced positive evaluative statements concerning their own in-group, there were nevertheless some exceptions. For example, the Japanese children tended to say that Japanese people were *poor, intelligent* and *bad*, while the Bantu children tended to avoid the use of evaluative statements altogether, relying on factual and similarity statements to describe their own national in-group instead. Piaget and Weil (1951) also found that, up to the age of about 7 or 8 years, their Swiss children did *not* consistently express in-group favouritism: these young children instead tended to express rather idiosyncratic patterns of likes and dislikes in relationship to national and state groups, and in-group favouritism only emerged from about 7–8 years of age onwards. And Tajfel himself found in his own early studies that although in-group favouritism was exhibited by 6- to 12-year-old English, Dutch, Austrian, Belgian, Italian and Israeli children, it was not exhibited by similarly aged Scottish children, who instead expressed more positive attitudes towards English people (Tajfel et al., 1970, 1972). The CHOONGE and NERID projects revealed similar findings. For example, the data in Tables 5.5 and 5.6 show that, while many of the groups of children who were tested in these two projects did indeed attribute the highest number of positive traits and the lowest number of negative traits to their own national and/or state in-groups, this was not always the case. Similarly, the data shown in Tables 5.11 and 5.12 reveal that the children did not always express significantly higher levels of liking of their own national and/or state in-groups than of all other groups. Thus, the prediction that representations of in-groups and out-groups will be based on dimensions of comparison that produce positive in-group distinctiveness and in-group favouritism is only partially supported by the evidence.[20]

The second prediction made by SIT is that the strength of identification with the in-group should correlate either with the positivity of the in-group evaluation, or with the negativity of out-group evaluations, or with the positive distinctiveness of the in-group over out-groups. Data to test this prediction were collected in the CHOONGE and NERID projects, and were discussed in Chapter 6. As we saw there, relatively few relationships were found between the strength of identification and either trait attributions to, or liking of, national and state *out-groups*. However, partial evidence was found for a relationship between the strength of identification and *in-group* attitudes. In the case of attitudes measured using trait attributions to the in-group, the children who lived in Catalonia and in the Basque Country produced clear evidence of a relationship between their strength of identification and in-group trait attributions. There was also evidence from the children living in all locations that attitudes measured using levels of liking of the people who belong to the in-group are related to the strength of identification with that in-group. Barrett et al. (2004) report further analyses of the data from the CHOONGE project showing that similar conclusions also emerge when the positive distinctiveness of the in-group over the out-group (that is, when

---

[20] A more extensive analysis and discussion of the CHOONGE data in relationship to this specific issue is provided in Barrett et al. (2004).

the discrepancy between in-group and out-group attributions, and the discrepancy between the levels of liking of the in-group and of out-groups) is analysed. In other words, the predicted relationship between the strength of identification and intergroup attitudes is sometimes present but not always, and its presence or absence appears to depend on local factors prevailing within the child's own specific national and state context. Thus, the second prediction made by SIT is, once again, only partially supported by the available evidence.

The third prediction made by SIT is that in-group favouritism is a consequence of the individual's subjective identification with the in-group. This prediction was directly tested by Bennett et al. (1998), using the British data collected in the CHOONGE project. They began by identifying the minority of British children who had failed to identify with being British by responding that they were *"not at all British"* on the degree of identification measure. Focusing on these non-identifying children, Bennett et al. looked to see whether they nevertheless exhibited in-group favouritism. They found that even though these children had failed to identify themselves as being British, they nevertheless assigned more positive traits to British people than to any other national or state group in the trait attribution task, and expressed more positive affect towards British people than towards Italian and German people (although French and Spanish people were liked just as much as British people). In a parallel analysis, it was also found that those children who had failed to identify themselves as being English or Scottish also assigned more positive traits to the English or Scottish group (as appropriate) than to any other national or state group, and expressed more positive affect towards the English or Scottish group (as appropriate) than towards any other national or state group. These findings show that non-identifying children may nevertheless exhibit favouritism towards their own group, even though they do not categorize themselves as being members of that group. From a developmental perspective this finding is important, as it implies that in-group favouritism must, at least in some cases, stem from factors other than subjective identification with the in-group coupled to the motivation for positive self-esteem.

In conclusion, it is clear that the available evidence does not unambiguously support the three predictions of SIT. Instead, there is only partial support for the first two predictions. This outcome suggests that the effects predicted by SIT are moderated or counteracted by other factors or processes over and above those postulated by SIT.

Self-categorization theory

Self-categorization theory (SCT) was developed from SIT in order to account for a number of additional findings that emerged from social-psychological research with adults, especially findings that the presence and degree of both in-group bias and in-group homogeneity (i.e., the perceived variability of the in-group) are affected by the salience of the relevant social categorization in a given setting (Oakes et al., 1994; J.C. Turner et al., 1987). Elaborating on the basic SIT paradigm, SCT postulates that individuals have a multiplicity of personal and social identities that are organized in the form of a category hierarchy. The level in the hierarchy at which the self is categorized at any given moment is hypothesized to depend on: the specific social context in which the individual finds him- or herself; a cognitive process driven by the principle of meta-contrast (whereby categorization occurs at that level in the hierarchy that maximizes between-category differences while minimizing within-category differences in the given context); the fit between the perceiver's normative beliefs about the particular categories that are involved and the actual stimuli contained in the current social situation; and the readiness of the individual to use a particular categorization. When a social identity becomes salient through this mechanism, for example when the social context contains members of both the in-group and a relevant out-group, there is a depersonalization of self-perception (i.e., self-stereotyping occurs), group behaviour appropriate to the social identity is elicited, and in-group homogeneity increases. However, when the social context contains only members of the in-group, self-categorization typically occurs at a lower level in the hierarchy than that of the in-group, and in-group homogeneity decreases. In addition, any other factor that enhances the salience of the social identity for the individual may increase perceptions of in-group homogeneity. For example, when the in-group is a minority group that is perceived as being under threat from a majority out-group, the salience of the in-group category, the strength of subjective identification and in-group homogeneity may be particularly high for those individuals within intergroup situations.

SCT also proposes that the prevailing comparative context will affect stereotype content, including the content of the in-group stereotype. The dimensions used to define the stereotype for a particular social group, as well as the relative prototypicality of the various group members, can change according to the comparative context in which the group is being judged, that is, according to the specific out-groups that are available within any given situation. However, this stereotypical variation will be constrained by what the individual perceiver knows and understands about the particular in-groups and out-groups that are involved, and about the nature of the intergroup relationships.

Thus, SCT suggests that in-group bias, the perceived homogeneity of the in-group and the content of the in-group stereotype can all change as a function of the prevailing comparative context. However, all of these effects will only occur if the individual has internalized the relevant social group membership as part of his or her self-concept. As in the case of SIT, if an individual's subjective identification with a group is weak or absent, these various effects will not occur. Once again, researchers have drawn a number of empirical predictions from these various postulates (e.g., Branscombe et al., 1999; Brown & Wootton-Millward, 1993; Ellemers et al., 1992, 1999; Haslam et al., 1995; Haslam, Turner, Oakes, McGarty, & Hayes, 1992; Hopkins & Cable, 2001; Hopkins et al., 1997; Oakes et al., 1994; Simon, 1992; Simon & Brown, 1987; Simon & Hamilton, 1994). These predictions include the following: (1) in-group stereotype content will change in conjunction with changes in the comparative context, with different dimensions being used to describe the in-group depending on the particular comparison out-groups that are available in the prevailing context; (2) in-group homogeneity will be lower in contexts in which only the in-group is present, and higher in comparative contexts in which relevant out-groups are also present; (3) the strength of identification will correlate with in-group homogeneity; (4) the strength of identification with the in-group may be higher in members of minority groups than in members of majority groups; (5) in-group homogeneity may be higher in members of minority groups than in members of majority groups. These predictions may all be tested using evidence derived from studies into children's national and state identifications and their judgements of national and state groups.

The first two predictions, which concern changes to stereotype content and to in-group homogeneity as a function of the prevailing comparative context, were tested in the study by Barrett et al. (1999). In this study (see Chapter 5 for a detailed description), 5- to 11-year-old English children were asked to attribute traits to English people (i.e., to their own national in-group) in one of three different experimental conditions: the traits were attributed either to just English people on their own (i.e., when only the in-group was present), or while the child was simultaneously attributing traits to either German or American people (i.e., in two different inter-group comparative contexts in which an out-group was also present). The study revealed that, contrary to the first prediction of SCT, the children attributed exactly the same characteristics to English people irrespective of the specific comparative context that prevailed while they were making their trait attributions. In other words, they did not vary their stereotype content according to the prevailing context. In addition, the perceived homogeneity of the English in-group also did not vary according to whether the child's trait attributions were made in a comparative or in a non-comparative context. Thus, neither of the first two predictions was supported by the study.

The third prediction was tested by Barrett et al. (2004), using the data from the CHOONGE project. From the data collected in the trait attribution task, a perceived variability score for each of the target national and state groups was derived. This score was a measure of how variable each group was perceived to be on those descriptive dimensions that the children themselves had used for assigning traits to that group. Recall that two measures of the children's strength of identification with their own national and state groups were also made in the CHOONGE project, using the relative importance measure and the degree of identification measure. Correlations were run between each of these two identification measures and the perceived variability of each individual target group. These correlations revealed that, contrary to the predictions of SCT, the perceived variability of national and state in-groups and out-groups was *not* consistently related to children's strength of identification with their in-groups.

Barrett et al. (2004) also tested the fourth and fifth predictions made by SCT, once again using the CHOONGE data for this purpose. These predictions concern members of minority groups. SCT predicts that the strength of identification with the in-group should be higher in members of minority groups than in members of majority groups. The theory also predicts that the perceived variability of the in-group should be lower among minority individuals. To ascertain whether the strength of identification is stronger in minority individuals, the data collected from the children living in England, Scotland, Catalonia and southern Spain using the relative importance measure and the degree of identification measure were examined. The analyses focused on whether the Scottish children (the minority group) identified with being Scottish more than the English children (the majority group) identified with being English, and whether the Catalan children (the minority group) identified with being Catalan more than the southern Spanish children (the majority group) identified with being Spanish. It was found that the children did *not* display the predicted differences in levels of identification. The perceived variability of the national in-groups was also examined in a parallel manner. This revealed that the 12- and 15-year-old children living in Scotland and England exhibited the pattern predicted by SCT; thus, at these two ages, the minority Scottish children did attribute lower levels of variability to their own in-group than the majority English children. However, the effect was absent at the ages of 6 and 9 years, and the effect was also absent in the Catalan and Spanish children at all four ages. Thus, there was little evidence from the CHOONGE project to support either the fourth or fifth prediction made by SCT.

It ought to be noted here that research conducted with adults has found considerable support for all five predictions (see, for example, Branscombe et al., 1999; Ellemers et al., 1999; Haslam et al., 1992, 1995; Hopkins et al., 1997; Oakes et al., 1994). There is also good evidence that at least some of the effects predicted by SCT do occur in relation to gender identity in 5- to 7-year-old children, who do adjust the contents of their gender stereotypes depending on the specific comparison out-groups that are available within a given context (Sani & Bennett, 2001; Sani et al., 2003; see also Sani & Bennett, 2004). This suggests that there are significant asymmetries in children's development, with phenomena that occur in one identity domain (such as gender identity) not occurring in other identity domains (such as national and state identities) at the same age. Further research is required to determine the point in development at which the various processes and phenomena described by SCT do start to appear in relationship to an individual's national and state identifications. However, it is clear that, at the present time, SCT does not provide an appropriate theoretical framework for explaining the development of children's national and state identities and attitudes.[21]

Social identity development theory

As we noted above, SIT itself was not originally formulated in order to explain developmental phenomena in children. However, in recent years, SIT has been given an explicitly developmental slant by Nesdale (1999, 2004; Nesdale et al., 2003). Like Aboud's CDT, Nesdale's social identity development theory (SIDT) has been primarily formulated in order to explain the development of children's racial and ethnic attitudes. But just like CDT, this theory also lends itself to the explanation of children's attitudes towards national and state groups.

SIDT postulates that racial and ethnic attitudes develop through a sequence of four phases. In the first undifferentiated phase, which occurs before 2–3 years of age, racial and ethnic cues are not yet salient to young children. In the second phase, which starts at about 3 years of age, awareness of racial and ethnic cues begins to emerge, and children gradually become able to identify and distinguish members of different groups (a process that can continue up to 10 or 11 years of age). Nesdale notes that this awareness is most likely to emerge when adults comment on or draw attention to out-group members, especially when this is accompanied by verbal labels naming the social categories to which these out-group members belong. Through this mechanism, young children gradually become aware of those groups that have social significance within their own community. Crucially, at this second phase, self-identification as a member of a particular in-group also occurs. In the third phase, which begins at about 4 years of age as a consequence of self-identification, a particular focus on, and preference for, the in-group emerges. During this third phase, Nesdale argues that out-groups are not actually disliked, or rejected, or conceptualized in negative terms; instead, the in-group is simply preferred over other groups. This preference may be accompanied by an awareness of which groups are more highly regarded, and which are less well regarded by other people, information that is gleaned from the comments that other people make. However, at this third phase, negative

---

[21] For a more extensive analysis of the problems that arise in applying both SIT and SCT to children's development in this domain, see Barrett et al. (2004).

prejudice against out-groups does not appear, and this is one of the principal points that differentiates SIDT from CDT. Finally, in the fourth phase, which begins at around 7 years of age (although Nesdale argues that not all children may enter this final phase), the focus shifts from the in-group to out-groups, and instead of merely preferring the in-group, the child begins to actively dislike out-groups. Hence, between the third and fourth phases there is a shift away from in-group preference towards out-group prejudice. Thus, contrary to Aboud's claim that out-group prejudice increases up to 6 years of age and then decreases, SIDT instead proposes that it is only after 6 years of age that prejudice actually emerges in those children who come to hold prejudiced attitudes (and this does not occur in all children). According to Nesdale, the shift from preference to prejudice involves children shifting their primary focus away from the in-group towards out-groups, and their internalization of the negative attitudes towards those out-groups that prevail within their own social group. The probability of this internalization occurring is hypothesized to increase as a function of several factors: the child's level of identification with the in-group; the extent to which the negative attitudes are shared by the members of the in-group; and the extent to which the members of the in-group feel that their status or well-being is under threat in some way from the out-group concerned.

If we extrapolate SIDT to the development of children's national and state attitudes and prejudice, the theory makes a number of predictions, as follows: (1) shortly after children first acquire an awareness of different national and state groups, they are most likely to focus primarily on their own in-group, rather than on out-groups; (2) at this early point in their development, out-groups should not be disliked or conceptualized in negative terms; instead, the in-group should merely be preferred over out-groups; (3) a shift to negative prejudice against out-groups should only occur, if it occurs at all, from about 7 years of age onwards (or perhaps even later, if national and state groups are less salient than racial and ethnic groups in the child's environment); (4) negative prejudice should only come to be exhibited by children when one or more of the conditions specified by SIDT for the internalization of negative attitudes prevail.

This theory fares much better than CDT in explaining some of the phenomena that characterize the development of children's attitudes towards national and state groups. For example, in Chapter 5, when we discussed the trait attribution data from the CHOONGE and NERID projects, we saw that, at 6 years of age, the Scottish and Azeri children only attributed significantly more positive than negative traits to their own in-group; these young children did not show the same pattern in relationship to any of the targeted out-groups. This finding is consistent with SIDT's postulate that young children focus their attention primarily on the in-group rather than out-groups. Second, we also saw in Chapter 5 that many children do not exhibit any out-group denigration in relationship to national and state groups, but instead express positive affect towards most national and state out-groups, describing them in positive terms, but just less positively than their own in-group (Lambert & Klineberg, 1967; Barrett & Short, 1992; Barrett et al., 1999, 2003). This finding is clearly compatible with SIDT's emphasis on preference rather than prejudice. Third, the fact that out-group denigration, when it does occur, tends to occur in relation to out-groups that have been the traditional enemies of the child's own country in the past, or out-groups with which the child's own country is in conflict at the current time, is also consistent with SIDT's account of the conditions that need to prevail for children to internalize negative attitudes towards a particular out-group. Fourth, SIDT can explain why educational input and the mass media influence children's beliefs about, and attitudes towards, people who live in other countries (Axia et al., 1998; Barrett & Short, 1992; Byram et al., 1991; Himmelweit et al., 1958; Holloway & Valentine, 2000; Lambert & Klineberg, 1967; Roberts et al., 1974; Stillwell & Spencer, 1973): the transmission of information about other national and state groups via education and the mass media is important for helping children to become aware of those out-groups that have social significance in relationship to their own in-group, and to learn about the perceived status of those out-groups from the perspective of their in-group.

However, there are a number of other phenomena that SIDT has difficulty in explaining. First, in the CHOONGE and NERID projects, it was only the Scottish and Azeri children who showed, at 6 years of age, a primary focus on their own in-group; this differentiation between the in-group vs. out-groups was not exhibited by the 6-year-olds living in any of the other locations, all of whom did attribute significantly more positive than negative traits to at least one out-group as well as to their own in-group. Second, SIDT also has difficulty in accounting for the fact that preference for the national or state in-group does not always occur, even at relatively young ages; that is to say, in-group favouritism may be a common phenomenon but, as we have seen, it is by no means a universal phenomenon (Lambert & Klineberg, 1967; Tajfel et al., 1970, 1972). Third, although out-group denigration is a comparatively rare phenomenon, when it does occur, it can already be present at the age of 5 or 6 (Barrett & Short, 1992; Buchanan-Barrow et al., 1999; Jahoda, 1962; Lambert & Klineberg, 1967); indeed, one study conducted in a country under extreme circumstances found out-group denigration to be present at 3 years of age (Povrzanović, 1997). These findings are clearly incompatible with SIDT's postulate that prejudice is only a late-emerging phenomenon. Fourth, while SIDT does propose that children can exhibit different developmental profiles after the age of 7 depending on their social situation, with some children not acquiring out-group prejudice at all, SIDT is not able to explain the sheer diversity and multiplicity of different age-related trends that occur in the development of children's national and state attitudes (recall that the CHOONGE and NERID projects found that these trends included linear increases, linear decreases, both U-shaped and inverted-U shaped curvilinear developmental trends, as well as no changes at all, in the attribution of positive and negative traits to in-groups and out-groups).[22] Fifth, SIDT proposes that children's level of identification with the in-group is one of the predictors of the extent to which they will internalize the negative attitudes towards outgroups that prevail within their own in-group. However, we saw from the CHOONGE and NERID projects that the strength of identification with national and state in-groups only consistently predicts affect towards ingroups; the strength of identification does not usually predict either trait attributions to in-groups or attitudes towards out-groups, whether measured using trait attribution or affect tasks. Thus, SIDT, much like both CDT and SIT, is only able to explain a subset of the phenomena that characterize the development of children's knowledge, beliefs and feelings about nations, states and the people who belong to different national and state groups.

TOWARDS A NEW EXPLANATORY FRAMEWORK: SOCIETAL-SOCIAL-COGNITIVE-MOTIVATIONAL THEORY (SSCMT)

It is clear from the preceding review that none of the existing theories is able to explain the full range of phenomena that characterize children's development in this domain. Neither Piagetian stage theory nor SCT appears to be an appropriate framework for explaining children's development. In addition, CDT places too much emphasis on domain-general cognitive factors, with the result that it underestimates the role played by exogenous societal and social factors. CDT also underestimates the range of developmental diversity that occurs as a function of the specific national and state context within which the child develops. SIT and SIDT are much more sensitive to these societal and social factors. In addition, SIT highlights the importance of motivational factors such as the individual's need for positive self-esteem.

---

[22] Elsewhere, Nesdale and Durkin (1998; see also Nesdale, 2001) draw a distinction between children's explicit and implicit attitudes (cf. Devine, 1989; Fazio, Jackson, Dunton, & Williams, 1995; Greenwald & Banaji, 1995). Importantly, trait attribution tasks and affect questions only assess children's explicit attitudes towards groups. Implicit attitudes have to be assessed using other tasks that are less prone to social desirability concerns and that tap into children's automatic (rather than their consciously mediated) responses to members of social groups. The implicit association test (IAT) is one such task (Greenwald, McGhee, & Schwartz, 1998). It is therefore possible that the developmental diversity documented in the CHOONGE and NERID projects applies only to children's explicit attitudes towards national and state groups, not their implicit attitudes. Until appropriate studies are conducted using implicit rather than explicit measures, it remains an open question whether children's implicit attitudes towards national and state groups exhibit similar developmental diversity.

However, the predictions made by both SIT and SIDT are only partially supported by the empirical evidence.

One notable characteristic of CDT, SIT and SIDT is that they are all primarily aimed at explaining children's intergroup attitudes in relationship to patterns of self-identification as an in-group member. Thus, most of the evidence we have been drawing on in order to evaluate these theories has been taken from the research reviewed in Chapters 5 and 6. However, it is important to bear in mind that children's attitudes to national and state in-groups and out-groups are embedded within a much larger body of knowledge and beliefs that they are in the process of acquiring, including knowledge and beliefs about the physical and social geographies of countries (Chapter 2), knowledge and beliefs about states as political entities (Chapter 3), as well as knowledge and beliefs about nations and states as historical and cultural communities (Chapter 4). It may well be the case that, if we wish to construct a satisfactory theoretical explanation of the development of children's national and state attitudes, these attitudes will need to be viewed within the context of this extensive body of other knowledge and beliefs about countries, nations and states, which children are simultaneously acquiring. A second notable characteristic of CDT, SIT and SIDT is that each theory only includes within its purview a limited subset of the full range of factors that impact on children's development in this domain. It is clear that any empirically adequate theoretical explanation of children's development in this domain will have to incorporate reference to at least four different sets of factors: societal, social, cognitive and motivational.

As far as societal factors are concerned, we have seen that the mass media and the school are two key influences on children's development in this domain. Taking the mass media first, we now have a wide range of evidence that the mass media (especially television and the movies, but also books, magazines, comics and posters) can exert a significant influence on children's knowledge and beliefs in this domain (Amadeo et al., 2002; Barrett & Short, 1992; Byram et al., 1991; Connell, 1971; Forrest & Barrett, 2001; Himmelweit et al., 1958; Holloway & Valentine, 2000; Johnson, 1966; Lambert & Klineberg, 1967; Moore et al., 1985; Roberts et al., 1974; Stillwell & Spencer, 1973; Torney-Purta et al., 2001). As Billig (1995) has shown, the mass media serve to transmit representations of nations to their audiences in an inconspicuous yet pervasive manner that permeates people's everyday lives, and children are no exception here. Notice that, in most countries, the range of media content judged to be appropriate for children at particular ages tends to be circumscribed by the dominant cultural norms and values prevailing within that country. As a consequence, movies are classified and censored so that they can only be viewed by individuals over a particular age, television programmes made for children are often targeted specifically at children within a particular age range, and printed materials are also often aimed at children falling within a particular age range. Thus, the information about countries, nations and states that children receive through the mass media has often been filtered and tailored according to a set of norms and values concerning the type of information that children should be exposed to at particular points in their development, norms and values that therefore constrain and delimit what a child is likely to learn from the mass media at any particular age.

In addition, it is noteworthy that boys and girls differ in their use of the mass media (Durkin, 1985; Gunter & McAleer, 1997). For example, they differ in the television programmes that they choose to watch (with boys watching more sport and action-adventure programmes, and girls watching more soap operas), in their visual attention to characters within television programmes (children tend to pay greater attention to characters who are the same gender as themselves), in their emotional reactions to media content (especially to depictions of violence and gore) and in their recall of television news. Hence, some of the gender differences that occur in children's development in this domain may have their origins in boys' and girls' differential use of the mass media.

The school is also a prominent source of information about the world in which children live, and indeed the school provides children with explicit instruction about the states and nations that make up the contemporary world. Not surprisingly, a large number of studies have shown that the school curriculum, school textbooks and school practices are all significant influences on children's knowledge, beliefs and feelings about countries, nations, states and the people who belong to different national and state groups (Amadeo et al., 2002; Anyon, 1979; Apple, 1993; Axia et al., 1998; Barrett et al., 2001; Barrett & Short, 1992; Baumann & Sunier, 2004; Berti, 2005; Berti & Andriolo, 2001; Berti & Benesso, 1998; Byram et al., 1991; Connell, 1971; Hess & Torney, 1967; Lambert & Klineberg, 1967; Mannitz, 2004a, b; Moore et al., 1985; Preiswerk & Perrot, 1978; Schiffauer & Sunier, 2004; Schleicher, 1992; Sunier, 2004a, b; Torney-Purta et al., 2001; Wills, 1994). Many theorists have argued over the years that states often harness the state-regulated educational system in order to transmit culturally dominant representations of the nation and the state to children (e.g., Gellner, 1983; A.D. Smith, 1991, 1998; Wertsch, 1994, 1998). In the case of children who are exposed to a common educational system, the contents of which are tightly constrained by a prescribed national curriculum (particularly in school subjects such as history, geography, language and literature, and civic education), common representations of the child's own nation and state, as well as common representations of other nations and states, could be acquired by many children within a particular country as a direct consequence of this formal educational input. Again, notice that there are often cultural norms and values concerning the type of information to which children ought to be exposed at school at any given age (which are sometimes formalized in an explicit national or state curriculum). As a result, at least some of the age-related differences in knowledge, beliefs and attitudes that we have been examining in this book could be a product of the prevailing cultural norms and values that have been used to determine the contents of the school curriculum for children of particular ages within particular national and state contexts.

In other words, some of the developmental patterns that have been discussed in previous chapters may be, at least in part, a consequence of cultural norms and values concerning what children should be allowed to view in the mass media, and how children should be educated, at particular ages, rather than being a product of the operation of endogenous cognitive or motivational psychological processes or factors alone. However, in addition to societal institutions such as the mass media and the school, there are several social factors that are also likely to have a significant impact on children's representations and attitudes in this domain.

Crucially, parents are likely to play an especially important role here. As we have seen from the CHOONGE and NERID projects, children's attitudes to national in-groups and out-groups, as well as their patterns of national and state identification, vary systematically according to the language(s) spoken in the family home and according to the child's language of education at school. As has been argued elsewhere in this book, it is unlikely that these effects are a consequence of language use per se. Instead, it is much more plausible that both language use within the home and the language of education are chosen by children's parents either as an ideological or cultural commitment (in the case of Spain, for example) or to obtain the socio-economic advantages that schooling in a politically and economically dominant language may confer on the child (e.g., the Russian language in the cases of Ukraine, Georgia and Azerbaijan). In other words, the child's own sociolinguistic situation is itself likely to be a product of parental positionings and aspirations, which in turn will be, at least in part, a product of parents' own national and state identifications and attitudes. Hence, the varying patterns of national and state identification and attitudes that occur among children as a function of their use of language in the home and school are highly likely to be, in part, a consequence of their parents' attitudes and practices (with the use of language itself merely being a salient marker of those parental attitudes and practices).

Parents probably impact on their children's national and state identifications and attitudes in a number of different ways. First, they presumably do so directly via their own discourse and practices in relationship to nations and states, through which they provide salient models of particular perspectives on, and attitudes towards, states and nations for their children to internalize (possibly through a mechanism of observational learning, as described by social cognitive theory: see Bandura, 1986, 1989). No research has yet been conducted on the relationship that may exist between children's and parents' national and state representations and attitudes, but this is certainly a potentially fertile line of enquiry for future research to pursue.

Second, parents are also likely to influence their children's development indirectly, by selecting or influencing the range of extra-familial settings in which their children are exposed to information or attitudes about nations and states. Most notably, parents choose the schools that their children attend (which, as we have seen, can have important consequences in countries such as Ukraine, Georgia and Azerbaijan). In addition, however, parents may also influence the type of extra-curricular organizations to which their children belong (by either encouraging or prohibiting their children to belong to organizations that may have particular orientations towards the state or nation, such as scouting organizations, army, sea or air cadet organizations, youth clubs with particular political affiliations, etc.). Parents may also impose their own constraints on the movies, television programmes and printed materials that their children are allowed to access at particular ages. In other words, parents might also influence their children's development through the types of settings, social groups and media to which they allow their children access at any given point in their development.

In this context, it is noteworthy that parents often hold beliefs that are culturally specific about the development of children's social behaviours and attitudes (Goodnow & Collins, 1990; Harkness & Super, 1996; Smetana, 1995). These beliefs concern what children are capable of understanding and learning at particular ages, how and when children should be exposed to particular kinds of information during the course of their development, and what the personal and collective goals and outcomes of effective parenting should be. Parents may also hold different beliefs about the development of boys vs. girls. These beliefs commonly lead parents to structure their children's learning environments and their access to particular settings according to the specific age and gender of their children, and to tailor their own interactions, discourse and practices with their children in a way they believe is appropriate for their children's cognitive and social capacities (Rogoff, 1998; Schweder, Goodnow, Hatano, LeVine, Markus, & Miller, 1998). In other words, parents may partially scaffold children's development in this domain, by allowing them access to particular types of information and settings in accordance with their own beliefs about the increasing capacities of their children, as they develop, to appreciate this information and to benefit from these settings.

Parents' beliefs about child development and parenting have been found to vary from culture to culture. They have also been found to vary within the population of any given country. For example, these beliefs tend to be linked to parents' personalities (Sameroff & Fiese, 1992) and to their cognitive outlooks (Pratt, Hunsberger, Pancer, Roth, & Santolupo, 1993). In addition, they may be related to parents' social class and ethnicity. Notice that parental social class and ethnicity will also influence the range of children's personal experiences of other countries and national and state groups in several other ways. For example, family holidays to other countries, the uptake of opportunities to travel to other countries (e.g., via school trips), personal contacts or kinship relations with people living in other countries, family trips to national or state museums and monuments, and the availability within the family home of books, atlases, globes, the Internet and other literacy and visual resources that provide information about states and nations are all likely to vary within any individual country as a function of either the social class or the ethnicity of parents. It is, therefore, perhaps unsurprising to discover that children's knowledge and beliefs about the geographies of countries (Chapter 2), about the political structure and functioning of the state (Chapter 3) and about the people who live in other countries (Chapter 5) vary as a function of social class and ethnicity.

Finally, the geographical location in which the child's family lives is also usually determined by parents' own personal histories, lifestyle decisions and patterns of employment, and this location is likely to affect children's first-hand experience of other countries and of the people who belong to other national and state groups in a number of ways. For example, as was noted in Chapter 6, children who live in the capital city of a country are more likely to have access to national and state museums and monuments and other emblems of the state and nation than children who live elsewhere within the country. These children may also be more likely to encounter members of national and state out-groups in their everyday environments, because capital cities tend to have more ethnically diverse populations, and to be visited by more foreign tourists, than many other cities and locations within the same country. Alternatively, children who live close to the borders of a country may have more opportunities to visit other countries than children who live further from those borders. For example, children living in northern Italy may visit other countries more frequently than children living in southern Italy due to their greater geographical proximity to these countries (and this factor may therefore explain why, for example, northern Italian children have enhanced levels of geographical knowledge when compared to many other children: Axia et al., 1998; Barrett & Farroni, 1996).

In addition to parents, there are likely to be several other extra-familial social factors that influence children's development in this domain. We saw in Chapters 3 and 4 that teachers may well play a pivotal role, not only in the political enculturation of the child (Berti, 1994; Berti & Andriolo, 2001; Connell, 1971; Hess & Torney, 1967; Torney-Purta et al., 2001) but also in transmitting key aspects of the nation's civil culture to the child (Baumann & Sunier, 2004; Mannitz, 2004a, b; Mannitz & Schiffauer, 2004; Sunier, 2004a, b). Just like parents, teachers also hold beliefs about the cognitive and affective capacities of children at particular ages (beliefs that are likely to have been refined and elaborated during the course of their own professional training and practice as teachers), which may well influence their discourse and practices with children in their classes at particular ages (Bruning, Schraw, Norby, & Ronning, 2004; Calderhead, 1996; Kagan, 1992; Nespor, 1987; Pajares, 1992). Thus, teachers might also partially scaffold aspects of children's developing understanding of nations and states through the different ways in which they talk to children of different ages about such matters.

The possible role that the peer group might play in children's development in this domain is yet another issue that still requires investigation. In particular, research needs to be conducted into the extent to which children's representations and attitudes match those of their friends, and the processes through which such convergence, if it is present, takes place. It may be the case that the peer group communicates and reinforces specific attitudes towards particular national or state out-groups. For example, among boys, interactions when playing war games, or discussions about war movies or about international sporting events that have been viewed on television, are two possible sources of peer group influence. Notice that these influences are less likely to occur among girls, as they are less likely to engage in war games and less likely to watch sport and action-adventure programmes on television than boys (Beal, 1994; Gunter & McAleer, 1997; Lever, 1978; Zill, 1986). In other words, peer group influences coupled to media influences may contribute to the gender differences that have been found to occur in this domain. However, no research has yet been conducted into these issues.

So far, we have been focusing on the various societal and social factors that may impact on the development of the child. However, as we noted in Chapter 1, children's knowledge, beliefs and feelings about countries, nations and states are unlikely to be solely a product of exogenous factors. Instead, they are likely to be influenced by endogenous cognitive and motivational factors as well. First, children's uptake of information from all societal and social sources is necessarily affected by intra-individual cognitive factors, including the child's own attentional, retentional and cognitive-representational processes. To this extent, children's representations and attitudes in this domain are inherently dependent on their cognitive capacities and skills, as well as on their own pre-existing cognitive representations, to which any new information needs to be assimilated. Consequently, as children's attentional, retentional and representational capacities and skills change during the course of their development, they will become able to attend to, process and retain types of information about nations and states, which at an earlier age they were simply not capable of processing (for example, information about the large-scale geographies of countries, or information about the apparatus of power that governments use to organize and run states).

Second, these cognitive processes themselves will be influenced by the affective valence and salience of the available information for the individual child, by the child's own perceptual set and motivational state, and by the child's affective preferences. It is likely that a wide range of motivational needs underpins children's psychological functioning in this domain. SIT has drawn attention to self-esteem as a significant motivating factor in the construction of attitudes towards in-groups and out-groups. However, social-psychological research with adults has revealed that there are also many other motivations involved in the construction and maintenance of social identities among adults. These other motivations include the needs for a sense of belonging, distinctiveness, continuity, purpose, meaning, cohesion and self-efficacy (see Baumeister & Leary, 1995; Breakwell, 1986, 1992; Brewer, 1993; Brewer, Manzi, & Shaw, 1993; Brewer & Pickett, 1999; Deaux, 1992, 2000; Hogg & Abrams, 1993; Mlicki & Ellemers, 1996; Vignoles, Chryssochoou, & Breakwell, 2000, 2002; Vignoles, Regalia, Manzi, Golledge, & Scabini, 2006). The motivational underpinning of children's identifications, representations and attitudes in relationship to nations and states still requires proper investigation, in order to establish which of these other motivations might also be involved in the phenomena that characterize children's development in this domain.

It is precisely because children's internalization of information from the environment is necessarily dependent on their attentional, retentional and representational processes (which, in turn, are linked to their motivational and affective processes) that this internalization never consists of the child passively absorbing information from exogenous sources. As we have already noted in Chapter 5, children themselves are active rather than passive processors of information: they actively select the materials in the environment to which they attend depending on their own current level of cognitive development and state of perceptual readiness; they scour the social environment for information that is relevant to their own current motivations, affective preferences and cognitive goals; they sometimes disregard, ignore or resist information that is irrelevant to their own motivational needs and cognitive goals; and they draw their own inferences from the information they find in their social environments, sometimes going significantly beyond the information available to them and sometimes generating mistaken beliefs as a result (see Bandura, 1986, 1989, for a cogent discussion of the reciprocal nature of the relationship between children's cognitive and affective-motivational systems on the one hand, and environmental influences on the other; cf. also Durkin, 1985, 2005; Salomon, 1983). The important point here is that children are active constructors of their own representations, beliefs and attitudes, not passive recipients of information from the environment.

The fundamental argument being made here, therefore, is that societal, social, cognitive and motivational factors *all* play a role in influencing children's knowledge, beliefs and feelings about countries, nations, states and the people who belong to different national and state groups. Furthermore, any theory that neglects to include all of these factors within its purview will not be able to explain the full range of evidence that is now available concerning children's development in this domain. That said, however, the balance between the different factors will almost certainly vary from country to country, and from social group to social group within a country. For example, within the Basque Country and Catalonia, there are particular societal factors (namely those concerning the objective socio-political inter-group relations that exist between the different national groups living within the modern Spanish state) as well as social factors (parents usually hold salient and distinctive attitudes towards those inter-group relations) that are likely to be responsible for the early emerging high levels of national identification among children who live in these two locations. These early high levels of national identification may then be the primary factor driving these children's acquisition of national attitudes. And this could then be the reason why children living within Catalonia and the Basque Country come to display distinctive developmental patterns (in which national and state in-group attitudes, as measured by both trait attribution and affect tasks, are correlated with the children's levels of identification). However, in other national contexts, different factors may be the primary drivers of children's development. For example, in the case of the children who attend national language schools in Ukraine, Georgia and Azerbaijan, parents' ideological commitment to their own nation rather than to the former USSR is likely to be closely associated with family practices and discourse concerning the nation. However, perhaps most crucially in the case of these children, this parental ideological stance is also the factor that leads these parents to send their children to national language schools rather than to Russian language schools. And once their children are attending these schools, it may well be the ethos and the everyday cultural practices of these schools that then become the primary drivers of these children's national and state identifications and attitudes. Or again, in some other countries (perhaps in England and Italy, for example), representations of nations and states on television and in the movies may be the primary drivers of children's national and state identifications and attitudes, rather than either parents or the school. In other words, different factors may be the primary drivers of children's representations and identifications in different national contexts.

One consequence of the view that societal, social, cognitive and motivational factors can all play a role in children's development in this domain is that the developing child needs to be conceptualized as being situated within an ecological niche that itself constantly changes as the child grows older. First, changes to the child's niche occur due to the historical changes that are constantly taking place within any given society. For example, the political and economic circumstances of the child's own state and nation will be continuously changing as the child develops. In addition, in all societies, there are ongoing changes to both the educational system through which children receive their schooling, and to the mass media and the information technologies through which children are able to receive information about other countries and national and state out-groups. Second, the child's niche changes over time as a function of the different discourses, practices and representations to which the child is exposed at different ages by the various agents of enculturation (including both parents and teachers). As a result, some of the developmental patterns that have been observed in this domain may be, at least in part, a product of cultural norms concerning what children should be allowed to view in the mass media, how children should be educated, and how children should be talked to and treated by parents and teachers, at particular ages. Third, the child's niche also changes over time as a function of the child's own cognitive and motivational development. This is because the child's motivational state and cognitive level at any given point in development will determine the types of information that the child will actively seek out in the environment and the types of information that the child is capable of processing and retaining (and is motivated to process and retain). In other words, the agents of enculturation will only exert their effects if the child's cognitive and motivational systems are sufficiently developed for the child to be able to attend to, and to assimilate, their influence. In this sense, then, the child is also a partial determinant of the contents of his or her own "environment of influence". Fourth, as the child expresses knowledge, beliefs or feelings about countries, nations, states and the people who belong to different national and state groups in particular social contexts, other individuals within those contexts, such as parents, teachers or peers, may well respond to these expressions, by reinforcing, supporting, challenging or questioning them, and possibly, in the cases of teachers and parents, by increasing the provision of information about the country, nation, state or group concerned. In this sense, then, there may also be "child effects" on the niche as well. Thus, the argument here is that children's development in this domain takes place through an active, interactive and dynamic process through which the child continually responds to a particular cultural, societal and social niche that itself is constantly changing as that child's cognitive and motivational systems develop. Notice that an implication of this line of reasoning is that the unit of analysis required for understanding the development of the child is not the child per se; nor is it environmental factors per se; instead, the correct unit of analysis is the "child-in-the-environment", with this unit being construed as an integrated and holistic system that is continuously changing over time.

The preceding paragraphs have articulated what can be called a societal-social-cognitive-motivational theory (SSCMT) of children's national enculturation. SSCMT can be summarized diagrammatically as in Figure 7.1. Although this figure includes all of the various factors discussed above, it is important to bear in mind that, within different national and state

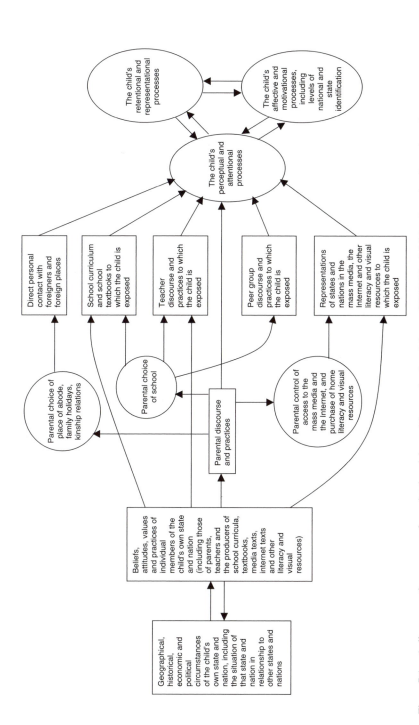

Figure 7.1. A diagrammatic summary of a societal-social-cognitive-motivational theory (SSCMT) of children's national enculturation.

contexts, different constellations of factors are likely to be the primary drivers of the child's development. In other words, the relative weightings that may be assigned to the various arrows in this model may well vary from one national or state context to another.

The starting point of SSCMT is that children's development is always embedded within a particular societal and social context, which itself is always embedded within a much broader set of geographical, historical, economic and political circumstances that characterize the child's own state and nation, including the situation of that state and nation in relationship to other states and nations. These circumstances will partially constrain and influence the beliefs, attitudes, values and practices of the individual members of the child's own state and nation (by providing a framework against which these members position themselves ideologically, politically and socially), although these individuals themselves can also bring about changes to the macro-context of the country via political and social action. It is against this background that the national enculturation of the child takes place. Crucially, parents and teachers, as well as those individuals who are responsible for determining the contents of school curricula, will hold beliefs about child development, about the goals of successful parenting and education and about how to achieve these goals. These individuals will also hold beliefs about, attitudes towards and evaluations of national and state in-groups and out-groups, as will individuals who are responsible for producing representational content for the mass media, for the Internet and for other literacy and visual resources that carry information about countries, nations, states, national groups and state groups (such as books, atlases, globes, photographs/paintings of particular geographical places and peoples, etc.).

Parents are hypothesized to play a particularly prominent role in the national enculturation of the child, not only directly through their own discourse and practices in relationship to states and nations (e.g., by taking stances on political issues, participating in national or state celebrations, visiting national or state museums and monuments, etc.), but also indirectly through their choice of geographical location in which to live, their choice of holiday destinations for the family, their kinship relations with people living in other countries, their choice of school for the child, their control of the child's access to the mass media and the Internet, and their purchase of other literacy and visual resources for the family home. Depending on geographical location, holiday destinations and kinship relations, the child may obtain first-hand personal experience of people who live in other countries and of foreign places. Parents' choice of school will influence the educational curriculum, textbooks, teachers and peer group to which the child is exposed. In addition, parents' control of the child's access to the mass media and the Internet, and their purchase of literacy and visual resources for the family home, will influence the range of representational content to which the child is exposed in the mass media and elsewhere. Notice that many of these parental choices, decisions and actions will be dependent, at least in part, on the parents' socioeconomic situation and levels of affluence.

All of these factors are therefore available as potential sources of information about states and nations for the child: parental discourse and practices; direct personal contact with foreigners and foreign places; the school curriculum and school textbooks; teacher discourse and practices; peer group discourse and practices; and the representational content of the mass media, the Internet and other literacy and visual resources to which the child has access. However, note that these are all only *potential* sources of information for the child. As has been argued above, the information that is actually attended to, processed and assimilated by the child from these various exogenous sources will depend crucially on the child's own perceptual and attentional processes, the child's own retentional and representational processes and the child's own affective and motivational processes (including the child's levels of national and state identification).

SSCMT further postulates that, as the child's cognitive and affective development proceeds, parents and teachers will adjust their own discourse and practices in relationship to the child's perceived level of competence. Moreover, as the child develops, he or she will be exposed to more advanced levels of the school curriculum, to more advanced textbook content, and will progressively have access to a wider range of representational content in the mass media and in other literacy and visual resources. The child's peers will also be developing in their own understandings of, and attitudes to, states and nations at the same time as the child is developing (with each individual child in the peer group similarly developing as a consequence of the various factors and processes shown in Figure 7.1); for this reason, peer group influences will also change over time. Hence, for all of these reasons, the environment of information available to the child will be constantly changing as the child develops. Feedback arrows from the child's perceptual, cognitive and affective systems to the various information sources have been omitted from Figure 7.1 for the sake of clarity. However, the role of such adjustments in environmental information over time in response to the perceived development of the child's perceptual, cognitive and affective systems should not be overlooked.

SSCMT is an integrative model that is comprehensive and parsimonious in the sense that it is able to explain all of the evidence that has been reviewed in this book. For example, it can explain: why children's geographical knowledge of countries varies as a function of their country, social class, ethnicity and geographical location within their own country; why children's beliefs about, and attitudes to, the state vary as a function of their country, social class, academic ability, education, attention to the news in the mass media and participation in peer group organizations; why children's pride in their own country, and their knowledge and utilization of national and state emblems, vary as a function of their country, language group and gender; why children's attitudes, feelings, judgements and reasoning about the people who belong to different national and state groups vary as a function of the national and state context in which they live, their use of language within the family home and their language of schooling; why children's levels of national and state identification vary according to their geographical location within their country, the specific national and state context in which they live, their ethnicity, their use of language in the family home and their language of schooling; why the school curriculum, school textbooks, school practices and the school ethos can all impact on children's understanding of, and attitudes to, countries, nations, states, national groups and state groups; why representational content in the mass media can also impact on children's knowledge of and attitudes to countries, nations, states, national groups and state groups; why children's travel experience is sometimes linked to their knowledge of other countries and of the people who live in other countries; and why boys may sometimes have higher levels of knowledge about the nation and the state, and higher levels of pride and identification, than girls.

In addition, SSCMT has substantial heuristic value, generating numerous empirical predictions for future research to explore. For example, the theory predicts that parents will play a core role in the national enculturation of their children through several different causal routes. It also predicts that children's levels of cognitive and motivational development will partially determine their own "environment of influence", and that children's domain-general cognitive competencies and motivational state will influence their acquisition of knowledge from the various information sources. None of these issues has been examined in any detail to date. Future research will also need to examine the extent to which parents and teachers do indeed tailor their discourse and practices concerning states and nations according to their perceptions of children's levels of cognitive and motivational development. In addition, future studies will have to explore how parents, teachers and peers respond discursively to, and possibly shape, children's expressions of attitudes towards countries, nations, states, national groups and state groups. Finally, SSCMT proposes that different constellations of factors are likely to be influential within different national and state contexts. Once again, future research will need to examine the societal and social conditions under which particular constellations of factors become effective. In this sense, SSCMT serves to generate a significant and substantial research agenda for the future.

CODA

At the beginning of Chapter 1, it was noted that children's understanding of society in general, and their knowledge, beliefs and feelings about nations and national groups in particular, are topics that have been neglected by developmental psychologists in the past. However, as we have seen, this situation is beginning to change, with a number of significant new studies having been conducted by developmental psychologists since the early 1990s. Related research activity in other social science disciplines, including sociology, anthropology, education, geography and political science, is now beginning to grow significantly as well. One of the dangers of disciplinary specialization is that researchers in all of these disciplines will pursue their own specialized research agendas in ignorance of the research conducted in other disciplines. One of the implicit claims underlying this book, which is perhaps worth making explicit at this end point, is that all of these disciplines have a crucial role to play in helping us to understand children's development in this domain. Indeed, their distinctive disciplinary perspectives are essential if we wish to obtain a properly comprehensive understanding of children's development. Throughout this book, we have in fact been drawing on and describing research that has been conducted in all of these various disciplines, for this very reason. The hope is that this book will, in turn, help to catalyse further research on this topic, not only in developmental psychology but in all of these adjacent disciplines as well.

A second claim of this book, but one which has been made much more explicitly throughout the course of the preceding chapters, is that children can develop in very different ways depending on the particular societal and social niches that they occupy. However, within developmental psychology, there has been a tendency for researchers to collect their data within just a single cultural or national context, and for theorizing to then proceed as if the developmental patterns that have been discovered in that context are universal. The research reviewed in this book demonstrates that this research strategy is untenable, at least within the present field: it is clearly incorrect to assume that patterns of development exhibited by children who are growing up in one particular context will necessarily be displayed by children who are growing up in other contexts. Instead, cross-national comparative studies must be conducted in order to establish the range and the limits of the variability that occur in human development.

As we noted at the beginning of this book, the world in which children are now living is undergoing extremely rapid change. Opportunities for buying and consuming goods, cultural media and cultural artefacts that have been produced by people living in other countries, for communicating electronically with people in other countries, for travelling to other countries and for encountering people from other countries within one's own country, have never been as extensive as they are at the present time. Globalization is having an enormous impact on the everyday world of the child, particularly within the more affluent countries. Yet ethnic and national discord, antagonism and conflict show no signs of decline. Politicians and media pundits exhibit no hesitancies in expounding what are sometimes ill-informed and factually incorrect interpretations of these various phenomena and their possible effects. Under such circumstances, developmental psychologists, social psychologists and other social scientists have a significant responsibility to construct an informed scientific understanding of how and why children and adolescents come to hold the national and state loyalties, affiliations and attitudes that they do. It is hoped that this book will contribute to the construction of this understanding.

SUMMARY

The main points to emerge from this chapter are as follows.

- There is a great deal of variability in children's development in this domain, both across different countries and within individual countries:
  - such variability has been found to occur in the development of:
    - children's large-scale geographical knowledge of countries
    - children's understanding of, and attitudes to, the political institutions and processes through which states are governed
    - children's levels of pride in their own country, and the issues that make children feel proud about their own country
    - children's knowledge and utilization of national and state emblems
    - children's knowledge, beliefs and feelings about the people who belong to different national and state groups
    - children's levels of identification with their own nation and state.
- As far as influences on children's development are concerned:
  - the school often plays a major role in the development of children's understanding of, and attitudes to, countries, nations, states, national groups and state groups
  - the school can also be a crucial agent for teaching children about the cultural and historical heritage of their own nation and state
  - the mass media can impact on children's knowledge and beliefs about countries, nations, states, national groups and state groups
  - although the role of parents in children's national enculturation has not yet been studied directly, there is indirect evidence that parents also play a central role in their children's national enculturation
  - children appear to derive at least some of their geographical knowledge about other countries from their holidays in those countries, and to acquire some of their knowledge about the people who live in other countries either from direct contact with foreigners or from holidays abroad
  - however, relatively little research has been conducted into the

relationship between children's domain-general cognitive competencies and their knowledge, beliefs and feelings in this particular developmental domain, with only their large-scale geographical knowledge of countries having been found to be linked to such competencies to date.

- There are also gender differences in children's knowledge, beliefs and feelings about countries, nations and states:
  - boys tend to exhibit higher levels of factual knowledge about countries, nations and states than girls
  - boys also sometimes exhibit higher levels of pride in their own country than girls
  - in addition, boys sometimes exhibit higher levels of national and/or state identification than girls.
- As far as the relationship between cognition and affect in this domain is concerned:
  - there does not seem to be any direct relationship between the amount of factual knowledge that children acquire about other countries and the affect that they exhibit towards those countries
  - in the case of the child's own country, however, the strength of the child's identification with the nation and/or the state is sometimes correlated with the child's levels of factual geographical knowledge of the homeland
  - however, strength of identification with the nation and/or the state is not always related to children's emotional attachment to their homeland
  - there is a sometimes a relationship between children's strength of national and/or state identification and children's knowledge and utilization of national and/or state emblems
  - in the case of children's conceptions of, and feelings about, national and state groups, however, the relationship between cognition and affect is complex and multifaceted, requiring further investigation.
- As far as theoretical frameworks for explaining children's development in this domain are concerned:
  - there are five existing theories that could potentially be applied to explain children's development in this domain:
    - Piagetian stage theory
    - Aboud's cognitive-developmental theory (CDT)
    - social identity theory (SIT)
    - self-categorization theory (SCT)
    - social identity development theory (SIDT)
  - however, neither Piagetian stage theory nor SCT is consistent with the empirical evidence that is now available
  - in addition, CDT, SIT and SIDT are only able to explain a subset of

the full range of phenomena that are now known to characterize children's development in this domain

  ○ any empirically adequate theory must incorporate reference to at least four different sets of factors, namely societal, social, cognitive and motivational factors.

- Societal-social-cognitive-motivational theory (SSCMT) is able to account for all of the findings that have been reviewed in this book:

  ○ SSCMT emphasizes that the child's development is always situated within a particular societal and social niche

  ○ SSCMT emphasizes that all of the following are potential sources of information about countries, nations, states, national groups and state groups for the child:

    - parental discourse and practices
    - direct personal contact with foreigners and foreign places
    - the school curriculum and school textbooks
    - teacher discourse and practices
    - peer group discourse and practices
    - the representational content of the mass media, the Internet and other literacy and visual resources to which the child has access

  ○ SSCMT proposes that the information the child acquires from these various exogenous sources depends on the child's own endogenous cognitive and motivational processes

  ○ SSCMT construes the developing child as being situated within an ecological niche that itself changes constantly as the child grows older, with the child's own cognitive and motivational processes partially determining the available "environment of influence"

  ○ SSCMT is a comprehensive and parsimonious theoretical framework, which can accommodate all of the evidence that has been reviewed in this book

  ○ SSCMT also has considerable heuristic value as it generates a substantial research agenda for the future.

References

Aboud, F. (1988). *Children and prejudice*. Oxford, UK: Blackwell.

Aboud, F., & Amato, M. (2001). Developmental and socialization influences on intergroup bias. In R. Brown & S.L. Gaertner (Eds.), *Blackwell handbook of social psychology: Intergroup processes* (pp. 65–85). Oxford, UK: Blackwell.

Aboud, F.E., Mendelson, M.J., & Purdy, K.T. (2003). Cross-race peer relations and friendship quality. *International Journal of Behavioral Development, 27,* 165–173.

Albornoz, O. (1992). Ethnic challenges in Latin American education. In K. Schleicher & T. Kozma (Eds.), *Ethnocentrism in education* (pp. 173–189). Frankfurt am Main, Germany: Peter Lang.

Alexander, E. (2002). *National and ethnic identity in British adolescents*. Unpublished BSc dissertation, University of Surrey.

Ali, S. (2003). *Mixed-race, post-race: New ethnicities and cultural practices*. Oxford, UK: Berg.

Allen, G.L. (1987). Cognitive influences on the acquisition of route knowledge in children and adults. In P. Ellen & C. Thinus-Blanc (Eds.), *Cognitive processes and spatial orientation in animal and man* (pp. 274–283). Dordrecht, The Netherlands: Martinus Nijhoff.

Amadeo, J., Torney-Purta, J., Lehmann, R., Husfeldt, V., & Nikolova, R. (2002). *Civic knowledge and engagement: An IEA study of upper secondary students in sixteen countries*. Amsterdam: IEA.

Anderson, B. (1983). *Imagined communities: Reflections on the origin and spread of nationalism*. London: Verso.

Anwar, M. (1998). *Between cultures: Continuity and change in the lives of young Asians*. London: Routledge.

297

Anyon, J. (1979). Ideology and United States history textbooks. *Harvard Educational Review, 49,* 361–386.

Apple, M. (1993). *Official knowledge: Democratic education in a conservative age.* London: Routledge.

Armstrong, J. (1982). *Nations before nationalism.* Chapel Hill, NC: University of North Carolina Press.

Asher, S.R., & Allen, V.L. (1969). Racial preference and social comparison processes. *Journal of Social Issues, 25,* 157–166.

Axia, G., & Bremner, J.G. (1992). *Children's understanding of Europe: British and Italian points of view.* Paper presented at the Fifth European Conference on Developmental Psychology, Seville, Spain, September 1992.

Axia, G., Bremner, J.G., Deluca, P., & Andreasen, G. (1998). Children drawing Europe: The effects of nationality, age and teaching. *British Journal of Developmental Psychology, 16,* 423–437.

Aylett, J.F. (1987a). *Russia under Stalin* (2nd ed.). London: Edward Arnold.

Aylett, J.F. (1987b). *Russia in revolution* (2nd ed.). London: Edward Arnold.

Azurmendi, M.J., Garcia, I., & Gonzalez, J.L. (1998). Influencia del uso de las lenguas en contacto con la identidad social en la Comunidad Autónoma Vasca. *Revista de Psicología Social, 13,* 3–10.

Bagley, C., & Young, L. (1998). Evaluation of color and ethnicity in young children in Jamaica, Ghana, England and Canada. *International Journal of Intercultural Relations, 12,* 45–60.

Balcells, A. (1995). *Catalan nationalism: Past and present.* Basingstoke, UK: Palgrave MacMillan.

Bandura, A. (1986). *Social foundations of thought and action.* Englewood Cliffs, NJ: Prentice-Hall.

Bandura, A. (1989). Social cognitive theory. In R. Vasta (Ed.), *Annals of child development, Vol. 6* (pp. 1–60). Greenwich, CT: JAI Press.

Barrett, M. (1996). English children's acquisition of a European identity. In G. Breakwell & E. Lyons (Eds.), *Changing European identities: Social psychological analyses of social change* (pp. 349–369). Oxford, UK: Butterworth-Heinemann.

Barrett, M. (2000). *The development of national identity in childhood and adolescence.* Inaugural lecture presented at the University of Surrey, Guildford, UK, 22 March 2000. [Downloadable from http://www.psy.surrey.ac.uk/staff/MBarrett.htm]

Barrett, M. (2001). The development of national identity: A conceptual analysis and some data from Western European studies. In M. Barrett, T. Riazanova, & M. Volovikova (Eds.), *Development of national, ethnolinguistic and religious identities in children and adolescents* (pp. 16–58). Moscow: Institute of Psychology, Russian Academy of Sciences (IPRAS).

Barrett, M. (2002). *Children's views of Britain and Britishness in 2001.* Keynote address presented to the Annual Conference of the Developmental Psychology Section of the British Psychological Society, University of Sussex, 5–8 September 2002. [Downloadable from http://www.psy.surrey.ac.uk/staff/MBarrett.htm]

Barrett, M. (2005a). Children's understanding of, and feelings about, countries and national groups. In M. Barrett & E. Buchanan-Barrow (Eds.), *Children's understanding of society* (pp. 251–285). Hove, UK: Psychology Press.

Barrett, M. (2005b). National identities in children and young people. In S. Ding &

K. Littleton (Eds.), *Children's personal and social development* (pp. 181–220). Milton Keynes, UK: The Open University/Blackwell Publishing.

Barrett, M., Bennett, M., Vila, I., Valencia, J., Giménez, A., Riazanova, T., Pavlenko, V., Kipiani, G., & Karakozov, R. (2001). *The development of national, ethnolinguistic and religious identity in children and adolescents living in the NIS.* Final Report to the International Association for the Promotion of Cooperation with Scientists from the New Independent States of the Former Soviet Union (INTAS), Open Call 1997 Project No. 1363.

Barrett, M., & Buchanan-Barrow, E. (2005). Emergent themes in the study of children's understanding of society. In M. Barrett & E. Buchanan-Barrow (Eds.), *Children's understanding of society* (pp. 1–16). Hove, UK: Psychology Press.

Barrett, M., & Davey, K. (2001). *English children's sense of national identity and their attachment to national geography.* Unpublished paper, Department of Psychology, University of Surrey. [Downloadable from http://www.psy.surrey.ac.uk/staff/MBarrett.htm]

Barrett, M., Day, J., & Morris, E. (1990). *English children's conceptions of European people: A pilot study.* Paper presented at the Conference on Perception and Cognitive Processes, Trieste, Italy, June 1990.

Barrett, M., & Farroni, T. (1996). English and Italian children's knowledge of European geography. *British Journal of Developmental Psychology, 14,* 257–273.

Barrett, M., Lyons, E., Bennett, M., Vila, I., Giménez, A., Arcuri, L., & de Rosa, A.S. (1997). *Children's beliefs and feelings about their own and other national groups in Europe.* Final Report to the Commission of the European Communities, Directorate-General XII for Science, Research and Development, Human Capital and Mobility (HCM) Programme, Research Network No. CHRX-CT94–0687.

Barrett, M., Lyons, E., & Bourchier, A. (2006). Children's knowledge of countries. In C. Spencer & M. Blades (Eds.), *Children and their environments* (pp. 57–72). Cambridge, UK: Cambridge University Press.

Barrett, M., Lyons, E., & del Valle, A. (2004). The development of national identity and social identity processes: Do social identity theory and self-categorization theory provide useful heuristic frameworks for developmental research? In M. Bennett & F. Sani (Eds.), *The development of the social self* (pp. 159–188). Hove, UK: Psychology Press.

Barrett, M., Lyons, E., Purkhardt, C., & Bourchier, A. (1996). *English children's representations of European geography.* End of Award Report to ESRC, Research Grant No. R000235753. Guildford, UK: University of Surrey.

Barrett, M., & Short, J. (1992). Images of European people in a group of 5–10 year old English school children. *British Journal of Developmental Psychology, 10,* 339–363.

Barrett, M., & Whennell, S. (1998). *The relationship between national identity and geographical knowledge in English children.* Poster presented at XVth Biennial Meeting of ISSBD, Berne, Switzerland. [Downloadable from http://www.psy.surrey.ac.uk/staff/MBarrett.htm]

Barrett, M., Wilson, H., & Lyons, E. (1999). *Self-categorization theory and the development of national identity in English children.* Poster presented at the Biennial Meeting of the Society for Research in Child Development, Albuquerque, New Mexico, USA. [Downloadable from http://www.psy.surrey.ac.uk/staff/MBarrett. htm]

Barrett, M., Wilson, H., & Lyons, E. (2003). The development of national in-group bias: English children's attributions of characteristics to English, American and German people. *British Journal of Developmental Psychology, 21,* 193–220.

Bar-Tal, D. (1988). Delegitimizing relations between Israeli Jews and Palestinians: A social psychological analysis. In J. Hofman (Ed.), *Arab-Jewish relations in Israel: A quest in human understanding* (pp. 217–248). Bristol, IN: Wyndham Hall Press.

Bar-Tal, D. (1993). American convictions about conflictive USA-USSR relations: A case of group beliefs. In S. Worchel & J. Simpson (Eds.), *Conflict between people and peoples* (pp. 193–213). Chicago, IL: Nelson Hall.

Bar-Tal, D. (1997). Formation and change of ethnic and national stereotypes: An integrative model. *International Journal of Intercultural Relations, 21,* 491–523.

Baumann, G. (2004). Introduction: Nation-state, schools and civil enculturation. In W. Schiffauer, G. Baumann, R. Kastoryano, & S. Vertovec (Eds.) (2004), *Civil enculturation: Nation-state, school and ethnic difference in the Netherlands, Britain, Germany and France* (pp. 1–18). New York: Berghahn Books.

Baumann, G., & Sunier, T. (2004). The school as a place in its social space. In W. Schiffauer, G. Baumann, R. Kastoryano, & S. Vertovec (Eds.), *Civil enculturation: Nation-state, school and ethnic difference in the Netherlands, Britain, Germany and France* (pp. 21–32). New York: Berghahn Books.

Baumeister, R.F., & Leary, M.R. (1995). The need to belong: Desire for interpersonal attachments as a fundamental human motivation. *Psychological Bulletin, 117,* 497–529.

Beal, C.R. (1994). *Boys and girls: The development of gender roles.* New York: McGraw-Hill.

Beck, I.L., & McKeown, M.G. (1994). Outcomes of history instruction: Paste-up accounts. In M. Carretero & J.F. Voss (Eds.), *Cognitive and instructional processes in history and the social sciences* (pp. 237–256). Hillsdale, NJ: Lawrence Erlbaum Associates Inc.

Beck, I.L., McKeown, M.G., & Gromoll, E.W. (1989). Learning from social studies texts. *Cognition and Instruction, 6,* 99–158.

Beck, I.L., McKeown, M.G., Sinatra, G.M., & Loxterman, J.A. (1991). Revising social studies text from a text-processing perspective: Evidence of improved comprehensibility. *Reading Research Quarterly, 26,* 251–276.

Bennett, M., Barrett, M., Karakozov, R., Kipiani, G., Lyons, E., Pavlenko, V., & Riazanova, T. (2004). Young children's evaluations of the ingroup and of outgroups: A multi-national study. *Social Development, 13,* 124–141.

Bennett, M., Lyons, E., Sani, F., & Barrett, M. (1998). Children's subjective identification with the group and ingroup favoritism. *Developmental Psychology, 34,* 902–909.

Bennett, M., & Sani, F. (Eds.) (2004). *The development of the social self.* Hove, UK: Psychology Press.

Berkes, N. (1964). *The development of secularism in Turkey.* Montreal: McGill University Press.

Bernal, M.E., & Knight, G.P. (Eds.) (1993). *Ethnic identity: Formation and transmission among Hispanics and other minorities.* Albany, NY: State University of New York Press.

Bernal, M.E., Knight, G.P., Garza, C.A., Ocampo, K.A., & Cota, M.K. (1990). The development of ethnic identity in Mexican American children. *Hispanic Journal of Behavioral Sciences, 12*, 3–24.

Berti, A.E. (1994). Children's understanding of the concept of the state. In M. Carretero & J.F. Voss (Eds.), *Cognitive and instructional processes in history and the social sciences* (pp. 49–75). Hillsdale, NJ: Lawrence Erlbaum Associates Inc.

Berti, A.E. (2005). Children's understanding of politics. In M. Barrett & E. Buchanan-Barrow (Eds.), *Children's understanding of society* (pp. 69–103). Hove, UK: Psychology Press.

Berti, A.E., & Andriolo, A. (2001). Third graders' understanding of core political concepts (law, nation-state, government) before and after teaching. *Genetic, Social and General Psychology Monographs, 127*, 346–377.

Berti, A.E., & Benesso, C. (1998). The concept of nation-state in Italian elementary school children: Spontaneous concepts and effects of teaching. *Genetic, Social and General Psychology Monographs, 124*, 185–209.

Berti, A.E., & Ugolini, E. (1998). Developing knowledge of the judicial system: A domain-specific approach. *The Journal of Genetic Psychology, 159*, 221–236.

Berti, A.E., & Vanni, E. (2000). Italian children's understanding of war: A domain-specific approach. *Social Development, 9*, 478–496.

Bettis, N.C. (1974). *An assessment of the geographic knowledge and understanding of fifth-grade students in Michigan.* Unpublished doctoral dissertation, Michigan State University.

Bialer, S. (1985). The psychology of US-Soviet relations. *Political Psychology, 6*, 263–273.

Bigler, R.S., Brown, C.S., & Markell, M. (2001). When groups are not created equal: Effects of group status on the formation of intergroup attitudes in children. *Child Development, 72*, 1151–1162.

Bigler, R.S., Jones, L.C., & Lobliner, D.B. (1997). Social categorization and the formation of intergroup attitudes in children. *Child Development, 68*, 530–543.

Bigler, R.S., & Liben, L. (1993). A cognitive-developmental approach to racial stereotyping and reconstructive memory in Euro-American children. *Child Development, 64*, 1507–1519.

Billig, M. (1995). *Banal nationalism.* London: Sage.

Black-Gutman, D., & Hickson, F. (1996). The relationship between racial attitudes and social-cognitive development in children: An Australian study. *Developmental Psychology, 32*, 448–456.

Bloom, L. (1998). Language acquisition in its developmental context. In D. Kuhn & R.S. Siegler (Eds.), *Handbook of child psychology, Vol. 2: Cognition, perception and language* (5th ed., pp. 309–370). New York: Wiley.

Boswell, D., & Evans, J. (1999). *Representing the nation: A reader. Histories, heritage and museums.* London: Routledge.

Bourchier, A., Barrett, M., & Lyons, E. (2002). The predictors of children's geographical knowledge of other countries. *Journal of Environmental Psychology, 22*, 79–94.

Bourchier, A., Barrett, M., Lyons, E., & Purkhardt, C. (1996). *English children's representations of European geography.* Paper presented at the Annual Conference of the Developmental Section of the British Psychological Society, Oxford, September 1996.

Bourdieu, P. (1990). *The logic of practice*. Cambridge: Polity Press.

Branscombe, N.R., Ellemers, N., Spears, R., & Doosje, B. (1999). The context and content of social identity threat. In N. Ellemers, R. Spears, & B. Doosje (Eds.), *Social identity* (pp. 35–58). Oxford: Blackwell.

Branscombe, N.R., & Wann, D.L. (1991). The positive social and self-concept consequences of sports team identification. *Journal of Sport and Social Issues, 15*, 115–127.

Branscombe, N.R., & Wann, D.L. (1994). Collective self-esteem consequences of outgroup derogation when a valued social identity is on trial. *European Journal of Social Psychology, 24*, 641–657.

Brass, P.R. (1991). *Ethnicity and nationalism: Theory and comparison*. London: Sage.

Breakwell, G.M. (1986). *Coping with threatened identities*. London: Methuen.

Breakwell, G.M. (1992). Processes of self-evaluation: Efficacy and estrangement. In G.M. Breakwell (Ed.), *Social psychology of identity and the self concept* (pp. 35–55). London: Academic Press.

Breuilly, J. (1993). *Nationalism and the state* (2nd ed.). Chicago, IL: University of Chicago Press.

Brewer, M.B. (1993). The role of distinctiveness in social identity and group behaviour. In M.A. Hogg & D. Abrams (Eds.), *Group motivation: Social psychological perspectives* (pp. 1–16). New York: Harvester Wheatsheaf.

Brewer, M.B., Manzi, J.M., & Shaw, J.S. (1993). In-group identification as a function of depersonalization, distinctiveness and status. *Psychological Science, 4*, 88–92.

Brewer, M.B., & Pickett, C.L. (1999). Distinctiveness motives as a source of the social self. In T.R. Tyler, R.M. Kramer, & O.P. John (Eds.), *The psychology of the social self* (pp. 71–87). Mahwah, NJ: Lawrence Erlbaum Associates Inc.

Brown, R., & Wootton-Millward, L. (1993). Perceptions of group homogeneity during group formation and change. *Social Cognition, 11*, 126–149.

Bruning, R.H., Schraw, G.J., Norby, M.M., & Ronning, R.R. (2004). *Cognitive psychology and instruction* (4th ed.). Upper Saddle River, NJ: Prentice Hall.

Bryant, C.G.A. (2003). These Englands, or where does devolution leave the English? *Nations and Nationalism, 9*, 393–412.

Bryant, P., & Bradley, L. (1985). *Children's reading problems: Psychology and education*. Oxford: Basil Blackwell.

Buchanan-Barrow, E., Bayraktar, R., Papadopoulou, A., Short, J., Lyons, E., & Barrett, M. (1999). *Children's representations of foreigners*. Poster presented at the 9th European Conference on Developmental Psychology, Spetses, Greece, September, 1999.

Burke, P., & Reitzes, D. (1991). An identity theory approach to commitment. *Social Psychology Quarterly, 54*, 239–251.

Bussey, K., & Bandura, A. (1999). Social cognitive theory of gender development and differentiation. *Psychological Review, 106*, 676–713.

Bynner, J., & Ashford, S. (1994). Politics and participation: Some antecedents of young people's attitudes to the political system and political activity. *European Journal of Social Psychology, 24*, 223–236.

Byram, M., Esarte-Sarries, V., & Taylor, S. (1991). *Cultural studies and language learning: A research report*. Clevedon, UK: Multilingual Matters.

Calderhead, J. (1996). Teachers: Beliefs and knowledge. In D. Berliner & R. Calfee (Eds.), *Handbook of educational psychology* (pp. 709–725). New York: Macmillan.

Carey, S. (1985). *Conceptual change in childhood*. Cambridge, MA: MIT Press.

Carr, R. (Ed.) (2001). *Spain: A history*. Oxford, UK: Oxford University Press.

Carrington, B., & Short, G. (1995). What makes a person British? Children's conceptions of their national culture and identity. *Educational Studies, 21*, 217–238.

Carrington, B., & Short, G. (1996). Who counts; who cares? Scottish children's notions of national identity. *Educational Studies, 22*, 203–224.

Carrington, B., & Short, G. (2000). Citizenship and nationhood: The constructions of British and American children. In M. Leicester, C. Modgil, & S. Modgil (Eds.), *Politics, education and citizenship* (pp. 183–193). London: Falmer Press.

Case, R. (1985). *Intellectual development: Birth to adulthood*. Orlando, FL: Academic Press.

Castelli, L., Cadinu, M., & Barrett, M. (2002). Lo sviluppo degli atteggiamenti nazionali in soggetti in età scolare. *Rassegna di Psicologia, 19*, 49–65.

Ceci, S.J., & Bruck, M. (1998). Children's testimony: Applied and basic issues. In I.E. Sigel & K.A. Renninger (Eds.), *Handbook of child psychology, Vol. 4: Child psychology in practice* (5th ed., pp. 713–774). New York: Wiley.

Ceci, S.J., Markle, F.A., & Chae, Y.J. (2005). Children's understanding of the law and legal processes. In M. Barrett & E. Buchanan-Barrow (Eds.), *Children's understanding of society* (pp. 105–134). Hove, UK: Psychology Press.

Chaffee, S.H., Ward, L.S., & Tipton, L.P. (1970). Mass communication and political socialization. *Journalism Quarterly, 47*, 447–459.

Chitnis, S. (1992). Ethnocentrism in the Indian education. In K. Schleicher & T. Kozma (Eds.), *Ethnocentrism in education* (pp. 139–151). Frankfurt am Main, Germany: Peter Lang.

Clark, A., Hocevar, D., & Dembo, M.H. (1980). The role of cognitive development in children's explanations and preferences for skin colour. *Developmental Psychology, 16*, 332–339.

Condor, S. (1996). Unimagined community? Some social psychological issues concerning English national identity. In G.M. Breakwell & E. Lyons (Eds.), *Changing European identities: Social psychological analyses of social change* (pp. 41–68). Oxford, UK: Butterworth Heinemann.

Connell, R.W. (1971). *The child's construction of politics*. Carlton, Australia: Melbourne University Press.

Connor, J.M., Schackman, M., & Serbin, K.A. (1978). Sex-related differences in response to practice on a visual-spatial test and generalization to a related test. *Child Development, 49*, 24–29.

Connor, J.M., & Serbin, K.A. (1977). Behaviourally based masculine and feminine activity preference scales for preschoolers: Correlates with other classroom behaviors and cognitive tests. *Child Development, 48*, 1411–1416.

Connor, W. (1978). A nation is a nation, is a state, is an ethnic group, is a . . . *Ethnic and Racial Studies, 1*, 378–400.

Connor, W. (1994). *Ethno-nationalism: The quest for understanding*. Princeton, NJ: Princeton University Press.

Connor, W. (2004). The timelessness of nations. *Nations and Nationalism, 10*, 35–47.

Coulby, D. (1995). Ethnocentricity, postmodernity and European curricular systems. *European Journal of Teacher Education, 18*, 143–153.

Cox, M.V. (1992). *Children's drawings*. Harmondsworth, UK: Penguin.

Crawford, K. (2000). Research the ideological and political role of the history textbook: Issues and methods. *International Journal of Historical Learning, Teaching and Research, 1*, 1–8.

Crocker, J., & Luhtanen, R. (1990). Collective self-esteem and ingroup bias. *Journal of Personality and Social Psychology, 58*, 60–67.

Culpin, C. (1986). *Making history: World history from 1914 to the present day* (2nd ed.). London: Collins Educational.

Cutts Dougherty, K., Eisenhart, M., & Webley, P. (1992). The role of social representations and national identities in the development of territorial knowledge: A study of political socialization in Argentina and England. *American Educational Research Journal, 29*, 809–835.

Daggs, D.G. (1986). *Pyramid of place: Children's understanding of geographic hierarchy*. Unpublished MS thesis, Pennsylvania State University, Pennsylvania.

Deaux, K. (1992). Personalizing identity and socializing self. In G.M. Breakwell (Ed.), *Social psychology of identity and the self concept* (pp. 9–33). London: Academic Press.

Deaux, K. (2000). Models, meanings and motivations. In D. Capozza & R.J. Brown (Eds.), *Social identity processes: Trends in theory and research* (pp. 1–14). London: Sage.

Dennis, J., Lindberg, L., & McCrone, D. (1972). Support for nation and government among English children. *British Journal of Political Science, 1*, 25–48.

Dennis, J., Lindberg, L., McCrone, D., & Stiefbold, R. (1968). Political socialization to democratic orientations in four Western systems. *Comparative Political Studies, 1*, 71–101.

Department of Education and Science. (1991). *Geography in the National Curriculum*. London: HMSO.

de Rosa, A.S., & Bombi, A.S. (1999). Se sentir heureux d'être Italiens? La construction de l'identité nationale et supranationale dans les représentations sociales de son propre pays ou du pays d'autrui chez des enfants et chez des adolescents. In M.L. Rouquette & C. Garnier (Eds.), *La genèse des représentations sociales* (pp. 136–170). Montreal, Canada: Editions Nouvelles.

Devine, P.G. (1989). Stereotypes and prejudice: Their automatic and controlled components. *Journal of Personality and Social Psychology, 56*, 5–18.

Devine-Wright, P., & Lyons, E. (1997). Remembering pasts and representing places: The construction of national identities in Ireland. *Journal of Environmental Psychology, 17*, 33–45.

Dixon, A. (2002). *Social identity theory and the development of national identity in British adolescents*. Unpublished BSc dissertation, University of Surrey.

Douglass, D. (1969). *Spatial preference: A multivariate taxonomic and factor analytic approach*. Unpublished MS thesis, Penn State University, University Park, PA.

Downs, R.M., Liben, L.S,. & Daggs, D.G. (1988). On education and geographers: The role of cognitive developmental theory in geographic education. *Annals of the Association of American Geographers, 78*, 680–700.

Doyle, A. (2002). Ethnocentrism and history textbooks: Representation of the Irish Famine 1845–49 in history textbooks in English secondary schools. *Intercultural Education, 13*, 315–330.

Doyle, A.B., & Aboud, F.E. (1995). A longitudinal study of white children's racial prejudice as a social-cognitive development. *Merrill-Palmer Quarterly, 41*, 209–228.

Doyle, A.B., Beaudet, J., & Aboud, F.E. (1988). Developmental patterns in the flexibility of children's ethnic attitudes. *Journal of Cross-Cultural Psychology, 19*, 3–18.

Durkin, K. (1985). *Television, sex roles and children.* Milton Keynes, UK: Open University Press.

Durkin, K. (2005). Children's understanding of gender roles in society. In M. Barrett & E. Buchanan-Barrow (Eds.), *Children's understanding of society* (pp. 135–167). Hove, UK: Psychology Press.

Easton, D., & Dennis, J. (1965). The child's image of government. *The Annals of the American Academy of Political and Social Science, 361*, 40–57.

Easton, D., & Dennis, J. (1969). *Children in the political system.* New York: McGraw-Hill.

Easton, D., & Hess, R.D. (1961). Youth and the political system. In S.M. Lipset & L. Lowenthal (Eds.), *Culture and social character: The work of David Riesman reviewed* (pp. 336–351). Glencoe, IL: Free Press.

Easton, D., & Hess, R.D. (1962). The child's political world. *Midwest Journal of Political Science, 6*, 229–46.

Eckes, T., & Trautner, H.M. (Eds.) (2000). *The developmental social psychology of gender.* Mahwah, NJ: Lawrence Erlbaum Associates Inc.

Elejabarrieta, F. (1994). Social positioning: A way to link social identity and social representations. *Social Science Information, 33*, 241–253.

Ellemers, N., Doosje, B.J., Van Knippenberg, A., & Wilke, H. (1992). Status protection in high status minorities. *European Journal of Social Psychology, 22*, 123–140.

Ellemers, N., Kortekaas, P., & Ouwerkerk, J. (1999). Self-categorization, commitment to the group and social self-esteem as related but distinct aspects of social identity. *European Journal of Social Psychology, 29*, 371–389.

Emler, N., & Frazer, E. (1999). Politics: The education effect. *Oxford Review of Education, 25*, 251–274.

English, R., & Halperin, J.J. (1987). *The other side: How Soviets and Americans perceive each other.* New Brunswick, NJ: Transaction Books.

Fazio, R.H., Jackson, J.R., Dunton, B.C., & Williams, C.J. (1995). Variability in automatic activation as an unobtrusive measure of racial attitudes: A bona fide pipeline? *Journal of Personality and Social Psychology, 69*, 1013–1027.

Fiske, S., Lau, R., & Smith, R. (1990). On the varieties and utilities of political expertise. *Social Cognition, 8*, 31–48.

Flanagan, C.A., & Tucker, C.J. (1999). Adolescents' explanations for political issues: Concordance with their views of self and society. *Developmental Psychology, 35*, 1198–1209.

Flavell, J.H., Miller, P.H., & Miller, S.A. (2002). *Cognitive development* (4th ed.). Englewood Cliffs, NJ: Prentice-Hall.

Forrest, L., & Barrett, M. (2001). *English adolescents' sense of national identity, identity motivations and national historical icons.* Unpublished paper, Department of Psychology, University of Surrey. [Downloadable from http://www.psy.surrey.ac.uk/staff/MBarrett.htm]

Freeman, N.H. (1980). *Strategies of representation in young children: Analysis of spatial skills and drawing processes.* London: Academic Press.

Fryman, J.F., & Wallace, J. (1985). Distorted cognitive maps: College students' misperceptions of nation size. *Perceptual and Motor Skills, 60,* 419–423.

Gecas, V. (1991). The self-concept as a basis for a theory of motivation. In J. Howard & P. Callero (Eds.), *The self-society dynamic: Cognition, emotion and action* (pp. 171–187). Cambridge, UK: Cambridge University Press.

Gellner, E. (1964). *Thought and change.* London: Weidenfeld & Nicolson.

Gellner, E. (1983). *Nations and nationalism.* Oxford, UK: Blackwell.

Gelman, R., & Gallistel, C.R. (1978). *The child's understanding of number.* Cambridge, MA: Harvard University Press.

Ghuman, P.A.S. (1999). *Asian adolescents in the West.* Leicester, UK: BPS Books.

Ghuman, P.A.S. (2003). *Double loyalties: South Asian adolescents in the West.* Cardiff, UK: University of Wales Press.

Giddens, A. (1985). *The nation-state and violence.* Cambridge, UK: Polity Press.

Giles, H., Bourhis, R.Y., & Taylor, D.M. (1977). Towards a theory of language in ethnic group relations. In H. Giles (Ed.), *Language, ethnicity and inter-group relations* (pp. 146–170). London: Academic Press.

Giménez, A., Belmonte, L., Garcia-Claros, E., Suarez, E., & Barrett, M. (1997). *Acquisition of geographical knowledge.* Poster presented at the 7th European Conference for Research on Learning and Instruction, Athens, Greece, August 1997.

Giménez, A., Canto, J.M., Fernández, P., & Barrett, M. (1999). La identificacion social como regulador del estereotipo lo que piensan los ninos Andaluces. *Boletin de Psicologia, 64,* 81–99.

Giménez, A., Canto, J.M., Fernández, P., & Barrett, M. (2003). Stereotype development in Andalusian children. *The Spanish Journal of Psychology, 6,* 28–34.

Golledge, R.G., Smith, T.R., Pellegrino, J.W., Doherty, S., & Marshall, S.P. (1985). A conceptual model and empirical analysis of children's acquisition of spatial knowledge. *Journal of Environmental Psychology, 5,* 125–152.

Goodnow, J.J., & Collins, A.W. (1990). *Development according to parents: The nature, sources and consequences of parents' ideas.* Hillsdale, NJ: Lawrence Erlbaum Associates Inc.

Gould, P.R. (1973). The black boxes of Jönköping: Spatial information and preference. In R.M. Downs & D. Stea (Eds.), *Image and environment: Cognitive mapping and spatial behaviour* (pp. 235–245). Chicago, IL: Aldine.

Gould, P., & White, R. (1986). *Mental maps* (2nd ed.). Boston, MA: Allen & Unwin.

Grant, P.R. (1992). Ethnocentrism between groups of unequal power in response to perceived threat to valued resources and to social identity. *Canadian Journal of Behavioural Science, 24,* 348–370.

Grant, P.R. (1993). Reactions to intergroup similarity: Examination of the similarity-differentiation and similarity-attraction hypothesis. *Canadian Journal of Behavioural Science, 25,* 28–44.

Greenstein, F.I. (1960). The benevolent leader. *American Political Science Review, 54,* 934–943.

Greenstein, F.I. (1961). More on children's images of the President. *Public Opinion Quarterly, 25*, 648–654.

Greenstein, F.I. (1965). *Children and politics*. New Haven, CT: Yale University Press.

Greenwald, A.G., & Banaji, M.R. (1995). Implicit social cognition: Attitudes, self-esteem, and stereotypes. *Psychological Review, 102*, 4–27.

Greenwald, A.G., McGhee, D.E., & Schwartz, J.K.L. (1998). Measuring individual differences in implicit cognition: The implicit association test. *Journal of Personality and Social Psychology, 74*, 1464–1480.

Grosvenor, I. (1999). "There's no place like home": Education and the making of national identity. *History of Education, 28*, 235–250.

Guibernau, M. (1999). *Nations without states*. Cambridge, UK: Polity Press.

Guibernau, M. (2004a). Anthony D. Smith on nations and national identity: A critical assessment. *Nations and Nationalism, 10*, 125–141.

Guibernau, M. (2004b). *Catalan nationalism: Francoism, transition and democracy*. London: Routledge.

Gunter, B., & McAleer, J. (1997). *Children and television* (2nd ed.). London: Routledge.

Hahn, C. (1998). *Becoming political: Comparative perspectives on citizenship education*. Albany, NY: State University of New York Press.

Hall, S. (1999). Un-settling "the heritage": Re-imagining the post-nation. Keynote address presented to the conference on *Whose Heritage?: The Impact of Cultural Diversity on Britain's Living Heritage*, The Arts Council of England, Manchester, November 1999.

Harkness, S., & Super, C.M. (Eds.) (1996). *Parents' cultural belief systems*. New York: Guilford Press.

Harris, L.J. (1981). Sex-related variations in spatial skill. In L. Liben, A.H. Patterson, & N. Newcombe (Eds.), *Spatial representation and behaviour across the life span* (pp. 83–125). New York: Academic Press.

Harris, P.L. (1989). *Children and emotion: The development of psychological understanding*. Oxford, UK: Basil Blackwell.

Haslam, S.A., Oakes, P.J., Turner, J.C., & McGarty, C. (1995). Social categorization and group homogeneity: Changes in the perceived applicability of stereotype content as a function of comparative context and trait favourableness. *British Journal of Social Psychology, 34*, 139–160.

Haslam, S.A., Turner, J.C., Oakes, P.J., McGarty, C., & Hayes, B.K. (1992). Context-dependent variation in social stereotyping 1: The effects of intergroup relations as mediated by social change and frame of reference. *European Journal of Social Psychology, 22*, 3–20.

Haste, H., & Torney-Purta, J. (Eds.) (1992). *The development of political understanding: A new perspective*. San Francisco, CA: Jossey-Bass.

Hatano, G., & Takahashi, K. (2005). The development of societal cognition: A commentary. In M. Barrett & E. Buchanan-Barrow (Eds.), *Children's understanding of society* (pp. 287–303). Hove, UK: Psychology Press.

Helwig, C.C., & Prencipe, A. (1999). Children's judgments of flags and flag-burning. *Child Development, 70*, 132–143.

Hengst, H. (1997). Negotiating "us" and "them": Children's constructions of collective identity. *Childhood, 4*, 43–62.

Hess, R.D. (1963). The socialization of attitudes toward political authority: Some cross-national comparisons. *International Social Science Journal, 25,* 542–559.

Hess, R.D., & Easton, D. (1960). The child's changing image of the President. *Public Opinion Quarterly, 24,* 632–644.

Hess, R.D., & Easton, D. (1962). The role of the elementary school in political socialization. *School Review, 70,* 253–265.

Hess, R.D., & Torney, J.V. (1967). *The development of political attitudes in children.* Chicago, IL: Aldine.

Hesse, P., & Mack, J.E. (1991). The world is a dangerous place: Images of the enemy on children's television. In R.W. Rieber (Ed.), *The psychology of war and peace: The image of the enemy* (pp. 131–151). New York: Plenum Press.

Himmelweit, H.T., Oppenheim, A.N., & Vince, P. (1958). *Television and the child: An empirical study of the effect of television on the young.* Oxford, UK: Oxford University Press.

Hinkle, S., & Brown, R. (1990). Intergroup comparisons and social identity: Some links and lacunae. In D. Abrams & M.A. Hogg (Eds.), *Social Identity Theory: Constructive and critical advances* (pp. 48–70). Hemel Hempstead, UK: Harvester Wheatsheaf.

Hobsbawm, E. (1983). Introduction: Inventing traditions. In E. Hobsbawm & T. Ranger (Eds.), *The invention of tradition* (pp. 1–14). Cambridge, UK: Cambridge University Press.

Hobsbawm, E. (1990). *Nations and nationalism since 1780.* Cambridge, UK: Cambridge University Press.

Hogg, M.A., & Abrams, D. (1993). Towards a single-process uncertainty-reduction model of social motivation in groups. In M.A. Hogg & D. Abrams (Eds.), *Group motivation: Social psychological perspectives* (pp. 173–190). New York: Harvester Wheatsheaf.

Holloway, S.L., & Valentine, G. (2000). Corked hats and Coronation Street: British and New Zealand children's imaginative geographies of the other. *Childhood, 7,* 335–357.

Hopkins, N., & Cable, I. (2001). Group variability judgements: Investigating the context-dependence of steretoypicality and dispersal judgements. *British Journal of Social Psychology, 40,* 455–470.

Hopkins, N., Regan, M., & Abell, J. (1997). On the context-dependence of national stereotypes: Some Scottish data. *British Journal of Social Psychology, 36,* 553–563.

Horowitz, D. (1985). *Ethnic groups in conflict.* Berkeley, CA: University of California Press.

Horowitz, E.L. (1940). Some aspects of the development of patriotism in children. *Sociometry, 3,* 329–341.

Howard, S., & Gill, J. (2001). "It's like we're a normal way and everyone else is different": Australian children's constructions of citizenship and national identity. *Educational Studies, 27,* 87–103.

Hutchinson, J. (1994). *Modern nationalism.* London: Fontana.

Hutnik, N. (1986). Patterns of ethnic minority identification and modes of social adaptation. *Ethnic and Racial Studies, 9,* 150–167.

Hutnik, N. (1991). *Ethnic minority identity in Britain: A social psychological perspective.* Oxford, UK: Clarendon Press.

Hutnik, N., & Barrett, M. (2003). *Ethnic minority identity: Twenty years on.* Poster presented at the 11th European Conference on Developmental Psychology, Milan, Italy, August 2003. [Downloadable from http://www.psy.surrey.ac.uk/staff/ MBarrett.htm]

Ignatieff, M. (1993). *Blood and belonging: Journeys into the new nationalism.* London: Chatto & Windus.

Inagaki, K., & Hatano, G. (2002). *Young children's naïve thinking about the biological world.* New York: Psychology Press.

Ishumi, A.G.M. (1992). Colonial forces and ethnic resistance in African education. In K. Schleicher & T. Kozma (Eds.), *Ethnocentrism in education* (pp. 121–138). Frankfurt am Main, Germany: Peter Lang.

Jacobson, J. (1997). Perceptions of Britishness. *Nations and Nationalism, 3,* 181–199.

Jahoda, G. (1962). Development of Scottish children's ideas and attitudes about other countries. *Journal of Social Psychology, 58,* 91–108.

Jahoda, G. (1963a). The development of children's ideas about country and national-ity, Part I: The conceptual framework. *British Journal of Educational Psychology, 33,* 47–60.

Jahoda, G. (1963b). The development of children's ideas about country and national-ity, Part II: National symbols and themes. *British Journal of Educational Psych-ology, 33,* 143–153.

Jahoda, G. (1964). Children's concepts of nationality: A critical study of Piaget's stages. *Child Development, 35,* 1081–1092.

Jahoda, G., & Woerdenbagch, A. (1982). Awareness of supra-national groupings among Dutch and Scottish children and adolescents. *European Journal of Political Research, 10,* 305–312.

Jaspers, J.M.F., Van de Geer, J.P., Tajfel, H., & Johnson, N. (1972). On the develop-ment of national attitudes in children. *European Journal of Social Psychology, 2,* 347–369.

Jenkins, B., & Copsey, N. (1996). Nation, nationalism and national identity in France. In B. Jenkins & S.A. Sofos (Eds.), *National identity in contemporary Europe* (pp. 101–124). London: Routledge.

Jennings, M.K., & Niemi, R.G. (1968). The transmission of political values from parent to child. *American Political Science Review, 62,* 169–184.

Jetten, J., Spears, R., & Manstead, A.S.R. (1997). Distinctiveness threat and proto-typicality: Combined effects on intergroup discrimination and collective self-esteem. *European Journal of Social Psychology, 27,* 635–657.

Jetten, J., Spears, R., & Manstead, A.S.R. (2001). Similarity as a source of differen-tiation: The role of group identification. *European Journal of Social Psychology, 31,* 621–640.

Johnson, N. (1966). What do children learn from war comics? *New Society, 8,* 7–12.

Johnson, N. (1973). Development of English children's concept of Germany. *Journal of Social Psychology, 90,* 259–267.

Johnson, N., Middleton, M., & Tajfel, H. (1970). The relationship between children's preferences for and knowledge about other nations. *British Journal of Social and Clinical Psychology, 9,* 232–240.

Kagan, D.M. (1992). Implications of research on teacher belief. *Educational Psycho-logist, 27,* 65–90.

Kail, R. (1990). *The development of memory in childhood* (3rd ed.). San Francisco: Freeman.

Kallis, A. (1999). Coping with the uncomfortable past: A comparative analysis of the teaching of World War II and the role of historical education in the construction of a "European" identity. In A. Ross (Ed.), *Young citizens in Europe. Proceedings of the First Conference of the CICE* (pp. 281–289). London: CICE.

Karakozov, R., & Kadirova, R. (2001). Socio-cultural and cognitive factors in Azeri children and adolescents' identity formation. In M. Barrett, T. Riazanova, & M. Volovikova (Eds.), *Development of national, ethnolinguistic and religious identities in children and adolescents* (pp. 59–83). Moscow: Institute of Psychology, Russian Academy of Sciences (IPRAS).

Katz, P.A., & Kofkin, J.A. (1997). Race, gender and young children. In S.S. Luthar, J.A. Burack, D. Cicchetti, & J. Weisz (Eds.), *Developmental psychopathology: Perspectives on adjustment, risk and disorder* (pp. 51–74). New York: Cambridge University Press.

Katz, P.A., Sohn, M., & Zalk, S.R. (1975). Perceptual concomitants of racial attitudes in urban grade-school children. *Developmental Psychology, 11,* 135–144.

Keating, M. (2002). *Plurinational democracy: Stateless nations in a post-sovereignty era.* Oxford, UK: Oxford University Press.

Kedourie, E. (1960). *Nationalism.* London: Hutchinson.

Kelly, C. (1988). Intergroup differentiation in a political context. *British Journal of Social Psychology, 27,* 321–327.

Khmelkov, V.T., & Hallinan, M.T. (1999). Organizational effects of race relations in schools. *Journal of Social Issues, 55,* 627–645.

Kipiani, G. (2001). Ethnic identification in the structure of personal identifications and sociocultural conditions of development. In M. Barrett, T. Riazanova, & M. Volovikova (Eds.), *Development of national, ethnolinguistic and religious identities in children and adolescents* (pp. 84–104). Moscow: Institute of Psychology, Russian Academy of Sciences (IPRAS).

Klahr, D., & MacWhinney, B. (1998). Information processing. In D. Kuhn & R.S. Siegler (Eds.), *Handbook of child psychology, Vol. 2: Cognition, perception and language* (5th ed., pp. 631–678). New York: Wiley.

Knischewski, G. (1996). Post-war national identity in Germany. In B. Jenkins & S.A. Sofos (Eds.), *Nation and identity in contemporary Europe* (pp. 125–151). London: Routledge.

Kozma, T. (1992). Education without indoctrination? In K. Schleicher & T. Kozma (Eds.), *Ethnocentrism in education* (pp. 227–264). Frankfurt am Main, Germany: Peter Lang.

Krosnick, J.A., & Milburn, M.A. (1990). Psychological determinants of political opinionation. *Social Cognition, 8,* 49–72.

Kumar, K. (2003). *The making of English national identity.* Cambridge, UK: Cambridge University Press.

Kushner, D. (1977). *The rise of Turkish nationalism, 1876–1908.* London: Frank Cass.

Kwang, J. (1985). Changing political culture and changing curriculum: An analysis of language textbooks in the People's Republic of China. *Comparative Education Review, 21,* 197–207.

Laeng, M. (Ed.) (1985). *I nuovi programmi della scuola elementare* (3rd ed.). Rome: Giunti & Lisciani.

Lamb, M.E., & Brown, D.A. (2006). Conversational apprentices: Helping children become competent informants about their own experiences. *British Journal of Developmental Psychology*, *24*, 215–234.

Lamb, M.E., Sternberg, K.J., Orbach, Y., Hershkowitz, I., & Epslin, P.W. (1999). Forensic interviews of children. In A. Memon & R. Bull (Eds.), *Handbook of the psychology of interviewing* (pp. 253–277). Chichester, UK: Wiley.

Lambert, W.E., & Klineberg, O. (1967). *Children's views of foreign peoples: A cross-national study*. New York: Appleton-Century-Crofts.

Lever, J. (1978). Sex differences in the complexity of children's play and games. *American Sociological Review*, *43*, 471–483.

Linnenbrink, L., & Anderman, E.M. (1995). *Motivation and news-seeking behaviour*. Paper presented at the Annual Meeting of the American Educational Research Association, San Francisco, CA.

Lisovskaya, E., & Karpov, V. (1999). New ideologies in postcommunist Russian textbooks. *Comparative Education Review*, *43*, 522–541.

Loewen, J.W. (1996). *Lies my teacher told me: Everything your American history textbook got wrong*. New York: Simon & Schuster.

Luecke-Aleksa, D., Anderson, D.R., Collins, P.A., & Schmitt, K.L. (1995). Gender constancy and television viewing. *Developmental Psychology*, *31*, 773–780.

Luhtanen, R., & Crocker, J. (1992). A collective self-esteem scale: Self-evaluation of one's social identity. *Personality and Social Psychology Bulletin*, *18*, 302–318.

Lunn, K. (1996). Reconsidering "Britishness": The construction and significance of national identity in 20th-century Britain. In B. Jenkins & S.A. Sofos (Eds.), *National identity in contemporary Europe* (pp. 83–100). London: Routledge.

Lyons, E. (1996). Coping with social change: Processes of social memory in the reconstruction of identities. In G.M. Breakwell & E. Lyons (Eds.), *Changing European identities: Social psychological analyses of social change* (pp. 31–39). Oxford, UK: Butterworth Heinemann.

MacInnes, J., & McCrone, D. (Eds.) (2001). Stateless nations in the 21st century: Scotland, Catalonia and Quebec. *Scottish Affairs, Special Issue*, Edinburgh 2001.

Maehr, S., & Barrett, M. (2005). *German pupils' sense of national identity and knowledge of national symbols*. Unpublished paper, Department of Psychology, University of Surrey. [Downloadable from http://www.psy.surrey.ac.uk/staff/MBarrett.htm]

Mannitz, S. (2004a). Pupils' negotiations of cultural difference: Identity management and discursive assimilation. In W. Schiffauer, G. Baumann, R. Kastoryano, & S. Vertovec (Eds.), *Civil enculturation: Nation-state, school and ethnic difference in the Netherlands, Britain, Germany and France* (pp. 242–303). New York: Berghahn Books.

Mannitz, S. (2004b). Limitations, convergence and cross-overs. In W. Schiffauer, G. Baumann, R. Kastoryano, & S. Vertovec (Eds.), *Civil enculturation: Nation-state, school and ethnic difference in the Netherlands, Britain, Germany and France* (pp. 307–333). New York: Berghahn Books.

Mannitz, S., & Schiffauer, W. (2004). Taxonomies of cultural difference: Constructions of otherness. In W. Schiffauer, G. Baumann, R. Kastoryano, & S. Vertovec (Eds.), *Civil enculturation: Nation-state, school and ethnic difference in the Netherlands, Britain, Germany and France* (pp. 60–87). New York: Berghahn Books.

Manouka, A. (2001). *Self-concept and ethnic identity of Albanian children who have emigrated in Greece.* Unpublished MSc dissertation, University of Surrey.

Matthews, M.H. (1984). Environmental cognition of young children: Images of journey to school and home area. *Transactions of the Institute of British Geographers,* New Series, *9,* 89–106.

Matthews, M.H. (1987). Sex differences in spatial competence: The ability of young children to map "primed" unfamiliar environments. *Educational Psychology, 7,* 77–90.

Matthews, M.H. (1992). *Making sense of place: Children's understanding of large-scale environments.* Hemel Hempstead, UK: Harvester Wheatsheaf.

Maw, J. (1991a). Understanding ethnocentrism in the history classroom. In H. Fry, J. Maw, & H. Simons (Eds.), *Dealing with difference: Handling ethnocentrism in history classrooms* (pp. 6–22). London: Institute of Education.

Maw, J. (1991b). Ethnocentrism, history textbooks and teaching strategies: Presenting the USSR. *Research Papers in Education, 6,* 153–169.

McCrone, D. (2001). *Understanding Scotland: The sociology of a nation* (2nd ed.). London: Routledge.

McGee, C. (1982). Children's perceptions of symbols on maps and aerial photographs. *Geographical Education, 4,* 51–59.

Merkl, P. (1992). A new German identity? In G. Smith, W.E. Paterson, & S. Padgett (Eds.), *Developments in German politics* (pp. 327–348). London: Palgrave Macmillan.

Meyer, J., Tyack, D., Nagel, J., & Gordon, A. (1979). Public education as nation-building in America: Enrollments and bureaucratization in the American states, 1870–1930. *American Journal of Sociology, 85,* 591–613.

Middleton, M., Tajfel, H., & Johnson, N. (1970). Cognitive and affective aspects of children's national attitudes. *British Journal of Social and Clinical Psychology, 9,* 122–134.

Mlicki, P.P., & Ellemers, N. (1996). Being different or being better? National stereotypes and identifications of Polish and Dutch students. *European Journal of Social Psychology, 26,* 97–114.

Modood, T., Berthoud, R., Lakey, J., Nazroo, J., Smith, P., Virdee, S., & Beishon, S. (1997). *Ethnic minorities in Britain: Diversity and disadvantage.* London: Policy Studies Institute.

Moodie, M.A. (1980). The development of national identity in white South African schoolchildren. *Journal of Social Psychology, 111,* 169–180.

Moore, S.W., Lare, J., & Wagner, K.A. (1985). *The child's political world: A longitudinal perspective.* New York: Praeger.

Moss, N., & Blades, M. (1994). *Travel doesn't broaden the mind.* Poster presented at the Annual Conference of the Developmental Section of the British Psychological Society, Portsmouth, September 1994.

Mummendey, A., Klink, A., & Brown, R. (2001). Nationalism and patriotism: National identification and out-group rejection. *British Journal of Social Psychology, 40,* 159–172.

Murkens, J.E., Jones, P., & Keating, M. (2002). *Scottish independence: A practical guide*. Uhrichsville, OH: Barbour Books.

Nesdale, D. (1999). Social identity and ethnic prejudice in children. In P. Martin & W. Noble (Eds.), *Psychology and society* (pp. 92–110). Brisbane, Australia: Australian Academic Press.

Nesdale, D. (2001). The development of prejudice in children. In M. Augoustinos & K.J. Reynolds (Eds.), *Understanding prejudice, racism, and social conflict* (pp. 57–72). London: Sage.

Nesdale, D. (2004). Social identity processes and children's ethnic prejudice. In M. Bennett & F. Sani (Eds.), *The development of the social self* (pp. 219–245). Hove, UK: Psychology Press.

Nesdale, D., & Durkin, K. (1998). Stereotypes and attitudes: Implicit and explicit processes. In K. Kirsner, C. Speelman, M. Mayberry, A. O'Brien-Malone, M. Anderson, & C. MacLeod (Eds.), *Implicit and explicit mental processes* (pp. 219–232). Mahwah, NJ: Lawrence Erlbaum Associates Inc.

Nesdale, D., & Flesser, D. (2001). Social identity and the development of children's group attitudes. *Child Development, 72,* 506–517.

Nesdale, D., Maass, A., Griffiths, J., & Durkin, K. (2003). Effects of ingroup and outgroup ethnicity on children's attitudes towards members of the ingroup and outgroup. *British Journal of Developmental Psychology, 21,* 177–192.

Nespor, J. (1987). The role of beliefs in the practice of teaching. *Journal of Curriculum Studies, 19,* 317–328.

Nie, N.H., Junn, J., & Stehlik-Barry, K. (1996). *Education and democratic citizenship in America*. Chicago, IL: University of Chicago Press.

Niemi, R.G. (1974). *The politics of future citizens*. San Francisco, CA: Jossey-Bass.

Niemi, R.G., & Jennings, M.K. (1991). Issues and inheritance in the formation of party identification. *American Journal of Political Science, 35,* 970–988.

Niemi, R., & Junn, J. (1998). *Civic education: What makes students learn?* New Haven, CT: Yale University Press.

Niemi, R.G., & Kent, J.M. (1974). *The political character of adolescence: The influence of families and schools*. Princeton, NJ: Princeton University Press.

Nieto, S. (1996). *Affirming diversity: The sociopolitical context of multicultural education*. White Plains, NY: Longman.

Nugent, J.K. (1994). The development of children's relationships with their country. *Children's Environments, 11,* 281–291.

Oakes, P.J., Haslam, S.A., & Turner, J.C. (1994). *Stereotyping and social reality*. Oxford, UK: Blackwell.

O'Callaghan, B. (1987). *A history of the twentieth century*. Harlow, UK: Longman.

Otto, L.B. (1975). Extracurricular activities in the educational attainment process. *Rural Sociology, 40,* 162–176.

Pajares, M.F. (1992). Teachers' beliefs and educational research: Cleaning up a messy construct. *Review of Educational Research, 62,* 307–332.

Parekh, B. (2000). *The future of multi-ethnic Britain: The Parekh report*. London: The Runnymede Trust/Profile Books.

Patchen, M. (1982). *Black-white contact in schools: Its social and academic effects*. West Lafayette, IN: Purdue University Press.

Pavlenko, V., Kryazh, I., Ivanova, O., & Barrett, M. (2001). Age characteristics of social identifications and ethno-national beliefs in Ukraine. In M. Barrett, T. Riazanova, & M. Volovikova (Eds.), *Development of national, ethnolinguistic and religious identities in children and adolescents* (pp. 105–131). Moscow: Institute of Psychology, Russian Academy of Sciences (IPRAS).

Payne, S.G. (1975). *Basque nationalism.* Reno, NV: University of Nevada Press.

Penny, R., Barrett, M., & Lyons, E. (2001). *Children's naïve theories of nationality: A study of Scottish and English children's national inclusion criteria.* Poster presented at the 10th European Conference on Developmental Psychology, Uppsala University, Uppsala, Sweden, August 2001.

Perner, J. (1991). *Understanding the representational mind.* Cambridge, MA: MIT Press.

Perreault, S., & Bourhis, R.Y. (1998). Social identification, interdependence and discrimination. *Group Processes and Intergroup Relations, 1,* 49–66.

Phinney, J. (1990). Ethnic identity in adolescents and adults: Review of research. *Psychological Bulletin, 108,* 499–514.

Phinney, J., & Devich-Navarro, M. (1997). Variations in bicultural identification among African American and Mexican American adolescents. *Journal of Research on Adolescence, 7,* 3–32.

Phoenix, A. (1995). The national identities of young Londoners. *Gulliver, 37,* 86–110.

Piaget, J. (1928). *Judgment and reasoning in the child.* London: Routledge & Kegan Paul.

Piaget, J. (1950). *The psychology of intelligence.* London: Routledge & Kegan Paul.

Piaget, J. (1972). *The principles of genetic epistemology.* London: Routledge & Kegan Paul.

Piaget, J., & Inhelder, B. (1969). *The psychology of the child.* London: Routledge & Kegan Paul.

Piaget, J., & Weil, A.M. (1951). The development in children of the idea of the homeland and of relations to other countries. *International Social Science Journal, 3,* 561–578.

Piché, D. (1977). *The geographical understanding of children aged 5 to 8 years.* Unpublished doctoral thesis, University of London, London.

Piché, D. (1981). The spontaneous geography of the urban child. In D.T. Herbert & R.J. Johnston (Eds.), *Geography and the urban environment: Progress in research and applications, Vol. IV* (pp. 229–256). Chichester, UK: John Wiley.

Pimlott, T. (1985). *The Russian revolution.* London: Macmillan Education.

Portes, A., & Rumbaut, R.G. (2001). *Legacies: The story of the immigrant second generation.* Berkeley, CA: University of California Press.

Povrzanović, M. (1997). Children, war and nation: Croatia 1991–4. *Childhood: A Global Journal of Child Research, 4,* 81–102.

Powlishta, K.K. (1995). Intergroup processes in childhood: Social categorization and sex role development. *Developmental Psychology, 31,* 781–788.

Pratt, M.W., Hunsberger, B., Pancer, S.M., Roth, D., & Santolupo, S. (1993). Thinking about parenting: Reasoning about developmental issues across the lifespan. *Developmental Psychology, 29,* 585–595.

Preiswerk, R., & Perrot, D. (1978). *Ethnocentrism and history: Africa, Asia and Indian America in western textbooks.* New York: Nok.

Puri, J. (2004). *Encountering nationalism.* Oxford, UK: Blackwell Publishing.

Reber, A.S. (1985). *The Penguin dictionary of psychology*. Harmondsworth, UK: Penguin.

Reizábal, L., Valencia, J., & Barrett, M. (2004). National identifications and attitudes to national ingroups and outgroups amongst children living in the Basque Country. *Infant and Child Development, 13*, 1–20.

Rhum, M. (1997). Enculturation. In T. Barfield (Ed.), *The dictionary of anthropology* (p. 149). Oxford, UK: Blackwell.

Riazanova, T., Sergienko, E., Grenkova-Dikevitch, L., Gorodetschnaia, N., & Barrett, M. (2001). Cognitive aspects of ethno-national identity development in Russian children and adolescents. In M. Barrett, T. Riazanova, & M. Volovikova (Eds.), *Development of national, ethnolinguistic and religious identities in children and adolescents* (pp. 164–196). Moscow: Institute of Psychology, Russian Academy of Sciences (IPRAS).

Roberts, D.F., Herold, C., Hornby, K., King, S., Sterne, D., Whitely, S., & Silverman, T. (1974). *Earth's a Big Blue Marble: A report of the impact of a children's television series on children's opinions*. Unpublished paper, Stanford University, CA.

Rogoff, B. (1998). Cognition as a collaborative process. In D. Kuhn & R.S. Siegler (Eds.), *Handbook of child psychology, Vol. 2: Cognition, perception and language* (5th ed., pp. 679–744). New York: Wiley.

Rosenberg, S., & Gara, M.A. (1985). The multiplicity of personal identity. *Review of Personality and Social Psychology, 6*, 87–113.

Rossteutscher, S. (1997). Between normality and particularity—national identity in West Germany: An inquiry into patterns of individual identity constructions. *Nations and Nationalism, 3*, 607–630.

Ruble, D.N., & Martin, C.L. (1998). Gender development. In W. Damon & N. Eisenberg (Eds.), *Handbook of child psychology, Vol. 3: Social, emotional and personality development* (5th ed., pp. 933–1016). New York: Wiley.

Rutland, A. (1998). English children's geo-political knowledge of Europe. *British Journal of Developmental Psychology, 16*, 439–445.

Rutland, A. (1999). The development of national prejudice, in-group favouritism and self stereotypes in British children. *British Journal of Social Psychology, 38*, 55–70.

Saarinen, T.F. (1973). Student views of the world. In R.M. Downs & D. Stea (Eds.), *Image and environment: Cognitive mapping and spatial behaviour* (pp. 148–161). Chicago, IL: Aldine.

Sachdev, I., & Bourhis, R.Y. (1990). Language and social identification. In D. Abrams & M.A. Hogg (Eds.), *Social Identity Theory: Constructive and critical advances* (pp. 211–229). Hemel Hempstead, UK: Harvester Wheatsheaf.

Sahlabadi, M. (2002). *The strength of national identity, identity motivations and beliefs about war of Iranian adolescents raised in England and Iran*. Unpublished BSc dissertation, University of Surrey.

Salomon, G. (1983). Television watching and mental effort: A social psychological view. In J. Bryant & D.R. Anderson (Eds.), *Children's understanding of television* (pp. 181–198). San Diego, CA: Academic Press.

Sameroff, A.J., & Fiese, B.H. (1992). Family representations of development. In I.E. Sigel, A.V. McGillicuddy-De Lisi, & J.J. Goodnow (Eds.), *Parental belief systems: The psychological consequences for children* (2nd ed.). Hillsdale, NJ: Lawrence Erlbaum Associates Inc.

Sani, F., & Bennett, M. (2001). Contextual variability in young children's gender ingroup stereotype. *Social Development, 10,* 221–229.

Sani, F., & Bennett, M. (2004). Developmental aspects of social identity. In M. Bennett & F. Sani (Eds.), *The development of the social self* (pp. 77–100). Hove, UK: Psychology Press.

Sani, F., Bennett, M., Mullally, S., & McPherson, J. (2003). On the assumption of fixity in children's stereotypes: A reappraisal. *British Journal of Developmental Psychology, 21,* 113–124.

Schaffer, H.R. (1996). *Social development.* Oxford, UK: Blackwell Publishers.

Schama, S. (1987). *The embarrassment of riches: An interpretation of Dutch culture in the golden age.* London: William Collins.

Schiffauer, W., Baumann, G., Kastoryano, R., & Vertovec, S. (Eds.) (2004). *Civil enculturation: Nation-state, school and ethnic difference in the Netherlands, Britain, Germany and France.* New York: Berghahn Books.

Schiffauer, W., & Sunier, T. (2004). Representing the nation in history textbooks. In W. Schiffauer, G. Baumann, R. Kastoryano, & S. Vertovec (Eds.), *Civil enculturation: Nation-state, school and ethnic difference in the Netherlands, Britain, Germany and France* (pp. 33–57). New York: Berghahn Books.

Schleicher, K. (1992). Ethnicity and ethnocentrism—a problem to the global community? In K. Schleicher & T. Kozma (Eds.), *Ethnocentrism in education* (pp. 1–15). Frankfurt am Main, Germany: Peter Lang.

Schmitt, M.T., & Branscombe, N.R. (2001). The good, the bad, and the manly: Threats to one's prototypicality and evaluations of fellow in-group members. *Journal of Experimental Social Psychology, 37,* 510–517.

Schneider, W., & Bjorklund, D.F. (1998). Memory. In D. Kuhn & R.S. Siegler (Eds.), *Handbook of child psychology, Vol. 2: Cognition, perception and language* (5th ed., pp. 467–521). New York: Wiley.

Schofield, J.W. (1991). School desegregation and intergroup relations: A review of the research. In G. Grant (Ed.), *Review of research in education, Vol. 17* (pp. 335–409). Washington, DC: American Educational Research Association.

Schofield, J.W. (1995). Review of research on school desegregation's impact on elementary and secondary school students. In J.A. Banks & C.A. McGee (Eds.), *Handbook of research on multicultural education* (pp. 597–616). New York: Macmillan.

Schweder, R.A., Goodnow, J., Hatano, G., LeVine, R.A., Markus, H., & Miller, P. (1998). The cultural psychology of development: One mind, many mentalities. In R.M. Lerner (Ed.), *Handbook of child psychology, Vol. 1: Theoretical models of human development* (5th ed., pp. 864–937). New York: Wiley.

Scourfield, J., & Davies, A. (2003). National and ethnic identities in children: Reflections on social processes and disciplinary tensions. *Cardiff School of Social Sciences Working Paper* No. 37. Cardiff, UK: Cardiff University.

Scourfield, J., & Davies, A. (2005). Children's accounts of Wales as racialized and inclusive. *Ethnicities, 5,* 83–107.

Shukla, S. (1992). Ethnic facts and national sentiments in South Asian education. In K. Schleicher & T. Kozma (Eds.), *Ethnocentrism in education* (pp. 153–171). Frankfurt am Main, Germany: Peter Lang.

Siegal, M., & Peterson, C. (Eds.) (1999). *Children's understanding of biology and health.* Cambridge, UK: Cambridge University Press.

Silova, I. (1996). De-sovietization of Latvian textbooks made visible. *European Journal of International Studies*, *7*, 35–45.

Simon, B. (1992). The perception of ingroup and outgroup homogeneity: Reintroducing the intergroup context. *European Review of Social Psychology*, *3*, 1–30.

Simon, B., Aufderheide, B., & Kampmeier, C. (2001). The social psychology of minority-majority relations. In R. Brown & S.L. Gaertner (Eds.), *Blackwell handbook of social psychology: Intergroup processes* (pp. 303–323). Oxford, UK: Blackwell.

Simon, B., & Brown, R.J. (1987). Perceived intragroup homogeneity in minority-majority contexts. *Journal of Personality and Social Psychology*, *53*, 703–711.

Simon, B., & Hamilton, D.L. (1994). Self-stereotyping and social context: The effects of relative in-group size and in-group status. *Journal of Personality and Social Psychology*, *66*, 699–711.

Smetana, J. (Ed.) (1995). *Beliefs about parenting: Origins and developmental implications*. San Francisco, CA: Jossey-Bass.

Smith, A.D. (1991). *National identity*. Harmondsworth, UK: Penguin.

Smith, A.D. (1998). *Nationalism and modernism*. London: Routledge.

Smith, A.D. (2001). *Nationalism*. Cambridge, UK: Polity Press.

Smith, A.D. (2003). *Chosen peoples: Sacred sources of national identity*. Oxford, UK: Oxford University Press.

Smith, A.D. (2004). History and national destiny: Responses and clarifications. *Nations and Nationalism*, *10*, 195–209.

Smith, C. (1994). The war as a textbook case. *World Press Review*, *41*, 19–27.

Snellgrove, L.E. (1981). *The modern world since 1870* (2nd ed.). Harlow, UK: Longman.

Spelke, E.S. (1991). Physical knowledge in infancy: Reflections on Piaget's theory. In S. Carey & R. Gelman (Eds.), *The epigenesis of mind: Essays on biology and cognition* (pp. 133–169). Hillsdale, NJ: Lawrence Erlbaum Associates Inc.

Stephan, W.G. (1978). School desegregation: An evaluation of predictions made in Brown vs. Board of Education. *Psychological Bulletin*, *85*, 217–238.

Stephan, W.G. (1999). *Reducing prejudice and stereotyping in schools*. New York: Teachers University Press.

Stephan, W.G., & Rosenfield, D. (1978). Effects of desegregation on racial attitudes. *Journal of Personality and Social Psychology*, *36*, 795–804.

Stillwell, R., & Spencer, C. (1973). Children's early preferences for other nations and their subsequent acquisition of knowledge about those nations. *European Journal of Social Psychology*, *3*, 345–349.

Stryker, S. (1987). Identity theory: Developments and extensions. In K. Yardley & T. Honess (Eds.), *Self and identity: Psychosocial perspectives* (pp. 83–103). New York: Wiley.

Stryker, S., & Serpe, R. (1982). Commitment, identity salience and role behavior: Theory and research example. In W. Ickes & E.S. Knowles (Eds.), *Personality, roles and social behavior* (pp. 199–218). New York: Springer Verlag.

Sunier, T. (2004a). National language and mother tongue. In W. Schiffauer, G. Baumann, R. Kastoryano, & S. Vertovec (Eds.) (2004). *Civil enculturation: Nation-state, school and ethnic difference in the Netherlands, Britain, Germany and France* (pp. 147–163). New York: Berghahn Books.

Sunier, T. (2004b). Argumentative strategies. In W. Schiffauer, G. Baumann,

R. Kastoryano, & S. Vertovec (Eds.), *Civil enculturation: Nation-state, school and ethnic difference in the Netherlands, Britain, Germany and France* (pp. 210–241). New York: Berghahn Books.

Szabolcsi, M. (1992). The ethnic factor in Central European education. In K. Schleicher & T. Kozma (Eds.), *Ethnocentrism in education* (pp. 103–120). Frankfurt am Main, Germany: Peter Lang.

Tajfel, H. (1966). Children and foreigners. *New Society, 7*, 9–11.

Tajfel, H. (1978). *Differentiation between social groups: Studies in the social psychology of intergroup relations.* London: Academic Press.

Tajfel, H. (1981). *Human groups and social categories.* Cambridge: Cambridge University Press.

Tajfel, H., & Jahoda, G. (1966). Development in children of concepts and attitudes about their own and other nations: A cross-national study. *Proceedings of the XVIIIth International Congress in Psychology*, Moscow, Symposium 36, 17–33.

Tajfel, H., Jahoda, G., Nemeth, C., Campbell, J., & Johnson, N. (1970). The development of children's preference for their own country: A cross-national study. *International Journal of Psychology, 5*, 245–253.

Tajfel, H., Jahoda, G., Nemeth, C., Rim, Y., & Johnson, N. (1972). The devaluation by children of their own national and ethnic group: Two case studies. *British Journal of Social and Clinical Psychology, 11*, 235–243.

Tajfel, H., & Turner, J.C. (1986). The social identity theory of intergroup behaviour. In S. Worchel & W.G. Austin (Eds.), *Psychology of intergroup relations* (2nd ed., pp. 7–24). Chicago, IL: Nelson-Hall.

Tanaka, S. (1994). History—consuming pasts. *Journal of Narrative and Life History, 4*, 257–275.

Tilly, C. (1990). *Coercion, capital and European states, AD 990–1990.* Oxford, UK: Blackwell.

Tomasello, M. (1992). *First verbs: A case study of early grammatical development.* Cambridge, UK: Cambridge University Press.

Torney, J., Oppenheim, A.N., & Farner, R.F. (1975). *Civic education in ten countries: An empirical study.* New York: John Wiley.

Torney-Purta, J. (2002). The school's role in developing civic engagement: A study of adolescents in twenty-eight countries. *Applied Developmental Science, 6*, 203–212.

Torney-Purta, J., Lehmann, R., Oswald, H., & Schulz, W. (2001). *Citizenship and education in twenty-eight countries: Civic knowledge and engagement at age fourteen.* Amsterdam: IEA.

Torney-Purta, J., Schwille, J., & Amadeo, J. (Eds.) (1999). *Civic education across countries: Twenty-four national case studies from the IEA Civic Education Project.* Amsterdam: IEA.

Trew, K., & Benson, D.E. (1996). Dimensions of social identity in Northern Ireland. In G. Breakwell & E. Lyons (Eds.), *Changing European identities: Social psychological analyses of social change* (pp. 123–143). Oxford, UK: Butterworth-Heinemann.

Trimby, H., & Barrett, M. (2005). *The development of Welsh children's sense of national identity.* Unpublished paper, Department of Psychology, University of Surrey. [Downloadable from http://www.psy.surrey.ac.uk/staff/MBarrett.htm]

Tulviste, P., & Wertsch, J.V. (1994). Official and unofficial histories: The case of Estonia. *Journal of Narrative and Life History, 4*, 311–329.

Turner, J.C., Hogg, M.A., Oakes, P.J., Reicher, S.D., & Wetherell, M.S. (1987). *Rediscovering the social group: A self-categorization theory*. Oxford, UK: Blackwell.

Turner, R., Hewstone, M., & Voci, A. (in press). The impact of direct and extended cross-group friendship: Affective mediators and explicit and implicit attitudes. *British Journal of Social Psychology*.

Valencia, J., Elejabarrieta, F., Perera, S., Reizabal, L., Barrett, M., Vila, I., Gil de Montes, L., Ortiz, G., & M. Larrañaga (2003). Conflictual national identities and linguistic strategies as positioning tools in children and adolescents. In M. Lavallée, S. Vincent, C. Ouellet, & C. Garnier (Eds.), *Les représentations socials: Constructions nouvelles* (pp. 17–38). Montréal, Canada: Université du Québec à Montréal. [Electronic monograph available from http://www.unites.uqam.ca/geirso/livre_repres_sociales/index_livre.php]

Van Ginkel, R. (2004). Re-creating Dutchness: Cultural colonisation in post-war Holland. *Nations and Nationalism, 10*, 421–438.

Vaughan, G.M. (1964). The development of ethnic attitudes in New Zealand school children. *Genetic Psychology Monographs, 70*, 135–175.

Verba, S., Schlozman, K.L., & Brady, H.E. (1995). *Voice and equality: Civic volunteerism in American politics*. Cambridge, MA: Harvard University Press.

Verkuyten, M. (2001). National identification and intergroup evaluation in Dutch children. *British Journal of Developmental Psychology, 19*, 559–571.

Vignoles, V.L., Chryssochoou, X., & Breakwell, G.M. (2000). The distinctiveness principle: Identity and the bounds of cultural relativity. *Personality and Social Psychology Review, 4*, 337–354.

Vignoles, V.L., Chryssochoou, X., & Breakwell, G.M. (2002). Evaluating models of identity motivation: Self-esteem is not the whole story. *Self and Identity, 1*, 201–218.

Vignoles, V.L., Regalia, C., Manzi, C., Golledge, J., & Scabini, E. (2006). Beyond self-esteem: Influence of multiple motives on identity construction. *Journal of Personality and Social Psychology, 90*, 308–333.

Vila, I. (1996). Perspectives de futur de la immersió lingüística". *Veus Alternatives, 8*, 30–35.

Vila, I., del Valle, A., Perera, S., Monreal, P., & Barrett, M. (1998). Autocategorizacion, identidad nacional y contexto linguistico. *Estudios de Psicologia, 60*, 3–14.

Volovikova, M., & Kuznetzova, O. (2001). Representations about Europe and Europeans of children and adolescents who live in Moscow region and in Stanitsa Veshenskaya (on the Don river). In M. Barrett, T. Riazanova, & M. Volovikova (Eds.), *Development of national, ethnolinguistic and religious identities in children and adolescents* (pp. 145–163). Moscow: Institute of Psychology, Russian Academy of Sciences (IPRAS).

Volovikova, M., Riazanova, T., & & Grenkova-Dikevitch, L. (2001). The specificities of religious identification in contemporary Russia: An analysis of answers given by children from Smolensk. In M. Barrett, T. Riazanova, & M. Volovikova (Eds.), *Development of national, ethnolinguistic and religious identities in children and adolescents* (pp. 132–144). Moscow: Institute of Psychology, Russian Academy of Sciences (IPRAS).

Waugh, D., & Bushell, T. (1992). *Key geography: Connections*. Cheltenham, UK: Stanley Thornes.

Weber, E. (1979). *Peasants into Frenchmen: The modernisation of rural France, 1870–1914*. London: Chatto & Windus.

Weinstein, E.A. (1957). Development of the concept of flag and the sense of national identity. *Child Development, 28*, 167–174.

Weissberg, R. (1974). *Political learning, political choice, and democratic citizenship*. Engelwood Cliffs, NJ: Prentice-Hall.

Wellman, H.M., & Gelman, S.A. (1998). Knowledge acquisition in foundational domains. In D. Kuhn & R.S. Siegler (Eds.), *Handbook of child psychology, Vol. 2: Cognition, perception and language* (5th ed., pp. 523–573). New York: Wiley.

Wertsch, J.V. (1994). Introduction: Historical representation. *Journal of Narrative and Life History, 4*, 247–255.

Wertsch, J.V. (1998). *Mind as action*. New York: Oxford University Press.

Wertsch, J.V., & O'Connor, K. (1994). Multivoicedness in historical representation: American college students' accounts of the origins of the United States. *Journal of Narrative and Life History, 4*, 295–309.

Wiegand, P. (1991a). The "known world" of primary school children. *Geography, 76*, 143–149.

Wiegand, P. (1991b). Does travel broaden the mind? *Education, 3*, 54–58.

Wiegand, P. (1995). Young children's freehand sketch maps of the world. *International Research in Geographical and Environmental Education, 4*, 19–28.

Wilberg, S. (2002). Preschoolers' cognitive representations of their homeland. *British Journal of Developmental Psychology, 20*, 157–169.

Wills, J.S. (1994). Popular culture, curriculum, and historical representation: The situation of Native Americans in American history and the perpetuation of stereotypes. *Journal of Narrative and Life History, 4*, 277–294.

Wilson, H., Barrett, M., & Lyons, E. (1995). *English children's beliefs and feelings about national groups in Europe: A pilot study*. Paper presented at the Second European Workshop on Children's Beliefs and Feelings about their Own and Other National Groups in Europe, University of Girona, Spain, July 1995.

Winter, C. (1997). Ethnocentric bias in geography textbooks: A framework for reconstruction. In D. Tilbury & M Williams (Eds.), *Teaching and learning geography* (pp. 180–188). London: Routledge.

Yee, M.D., & Brown, R.J. (1992). Self-evaluations and intergroup attitudes in children aged three to nine. *Child Development, 63*, 619–629.

Yoshino, K. (2001). Japan's nationalism in a marketplace perspective. In M. Guibernau & J. Hutchinson (Eds.), *Understanding nationalism* (pp. 142–163). Cambridge, UK: Polity Press.

Young, C. (2001). Nationalism and ethnic conflict in Africa. In M. Guibernau & J. Hutchinson (Eds.), *Understanding nationalism* (pp. 164–181). Cambridge, UK: Polity Press.

Youniss, J., McLellan, J.A., & Yates, M. (1997). What we know about engendering civic identity. *American Behavioral Scientist, 40*, 620–631.

Zill, N. (1986). *Happy, healthy, and insecure: A portrait of middle childhood in the United States*. New York: Cambridge University Press.

Zirakzadeh, C.E. (1991). *A rebellious people: Basques, protests, and politics*. Reno, NV: University of Nevada Press.

Author Index

Subject Index